THE BRITISH MARKET HALL

THE BRITISH MARKET HALL
A Social and Architectural History

James Schmiechen
and
Kenneth Carls

Yale University Press
New Haven and London

Published with assistance from
the Annie Burr Lewis Fund.

Designed by Kenneth Carls and set in Trump Medieval type.

Printed in the United States of America
by Edwards Brothers, Ann Arbor, Michigan.

A catalogue record for this book is available from the British Library.

The paper in this book meets the guidelines
for permanence and durability of the Committee on
Production Guidelines for Book Longevity of
the Council on Library Resources.

10 9 8 7 6 5 4 3 2 1

Library of Congress Cataloging-in-Publication Data

Schmiechen, James.
The British market hall: a social and architectural history /
James Schmiechen and Kenneth Carls.
p. cm.
Includes bibliographical references and index.
ISBN 0-300-06064-5 (alk. paper)
1. Markets—England—History. 2. Food supply—England—
History. 3. Commercial buildings—England—History. 4.
Public spaces—England—History. 5. city and town life—
England—History.
I. Carls, Kenneth. II. Title.
HF5474.G7S36 1999
381'.456413'00942—dc21

98-25841
CIP

CONTENTS

ACKNOWLEDGMENTS

This was an unusual book in the making. It began as an intellectual adventure sparked by a Victorian Society Fellowship that James Schmiechen received for study in London in 1980. Here Lizbeth Cohen and Robert Thorne and others discussed the relations between space, architecture, and social history with him. These conversations continued over a number of years with Ken Carls, and came to center on Schmiechen's intention to write a book on Victorian building types. However, the pervasiveness of a most interesting (and neglected) building type, the market hall, led to a joint research enterprise with Carls and, ultimately, to this volume. In several thousand miles of crisscrossing Britain over a period of five years we discovered hundreds of market structures, some hidden away and almost forgotten in local history archives, but many as alive and well as the day they were first opened. Subsequently, we spent many hours studying market sites and contemplating the Victorian world at its best and its worst: in the formation of urban space.

Schmiechen is grateful for a Fulbright appointment to Scotland which led to a long-standing love affair with Glasgow, its people, and its extraordinary collection of nineteenth-century architecture. This and subsequent appointments at Strathclyde University, Glasgow, gave him the opportunity to carry on research in market architecture.

It is with great gratitude that we thank the many dozens of librarians in England, Wales, and Scotland who searched for materials, guided us through their archives, and provided us with the sort of insights into local history that only local librarians can provide. This book, and particularly its Gazetteer, would not exist without their help. To list every person would be impossible, but we would like to single out the librarians at the Mitchell Library, Glasgow, the University of Glasgow Library, and Central Michigan University Library for their years of assistance.

A number of people have read portions of the manuscript along the way and pointed out errors, given advice, and provided encouragement. In particular, we thank Donald Olsen, Walter Arnstein, Hamish Fraser, Robert Thorne, and the members of the history faculty research seminar at Central Michigan University. Bill Kemperman provided several fine drawings and Doyle Moore many of the photographs. Catherine Dunkle undertook the task of organizing the illustrations.

We owe a particular word of gratitude to our editor at Yale University Press, Susan Laity, for helping us not only avoid numerous errors but tell a better story. The Central Michigan University Research Board provided support for the purchase of photographs. Jane Somera and Cinda Pippenger of the University of Illinois Library were particularly helpful in providing access to materials for photographic reproduction. We also acknowledge the assistance of Annette Davis, Elaine Dawson, Mark Gillfoyle, Jim Lucky, Susan Pyecroft, and Derek Day (in Michigan), Ken Powls (of Howden), Marion Ogden (of Wokingham), Nigel Pugh (of Aberdare), Margaret Hastie and Jean Fraser (in Glasgow), and John Rule (of Derby).

Portions of Chapter 4 derive from "The Victorians, the Historians, and the Idea of Modernism," *American Historical Review* 93 (April 1988), and portions of Chapters 5 and 6 from lectures given at Strathclyde University in Glasgow, and the Victoria and Albert Museum, London, in 1992.

FOOD, MARKETS, AND HISTORY

AFTER A CENTURY OF DEBATE, HISTORIANS OF THE AGE OF INDUSTRIALIZATION continue to disagree about when and how the people who lived during the first 150 years of industrialization and urbanization experienced improvement in their standard of living. Changes in housing, health, and sanitation have been the subject of much controversy. But diet—both what we eat and how we get it—one of the basic indicators of the quality of life, has received less attention than might be expected, considering its importance. In particular, we know little about how people of the late-eighteenth- and nineteenth-century industrial towns obtained their food.

An examination of conditions in just about any town in the mid- to late nineteenth century enables us to fill in some of the gaps. When the Lancashire town of Southport opened its colossal new "market hall" in 1879 (see fig. 5.39), for example, it had become so commonplace for the townspeople to buy their food in an enormous and grandly decorated public building, rather than on the street or in an open-air market, that the town newspaper casually pronounced that the new market hall showed "at a glance that the building is a large hall to be dedicated to the purpose of a market."[1] In matter-of-factly proclaiming that a simple glance would enable an observer to identify a "market hall," that is, a particular species of building, the writer fails to note that only fifty years earlier, a "market hall" would have been completely foreign to the urban dweller—and most people would have found it inconceivable that they could purchase the majority of their food and household goods somewhere other than in the open air.

This book is about how and why that building type, the market hall, evolved. It is about food, architecture, and the transformation of public space. It is about an urban revolution in which the buying and selling of comestibles and other commodities was transferred from dirty and windswept streets and "marketplaces" into an enclosed and "modern" building that boasted a number of amenities and, in many instances, considerable architectural panache.

The extraordinary growth in urban population that took place after about 1750 taxed the existing food-distribution system beyond its capacity. Local governments sought to increase the food supply by inventing a new public market system, and as a result, urban dwellers learned to be consumers in the modern sense—that is, they mastered the rituals by which buying and selling became the central feature of modern life. Additionally, with the transformation of the local public market, culture became commercialized. Here, working people found cheap fish, potatoes, and imported meat, toys, prints, and bicycles; here was an affordable lesson in consumerism. In short, for many people, the public market hall paved the way for the modern chain store (or multiple shop, as it was called in Britain), the department store, the "supermarket," and, eventually, the shopping mall.

Historians have shown how urbanites were affected by changes in the supply and price of food. Food riots, change in mortality rates, and marriage and fertility patterns were all variously tied to the food supply. Yet little has been written about how local governments and ruling elites responded to urban food needs, how food was distributed within the town, and how the character of the market affected the food supply. Beyond studies of individual markets in the context of their local history and the debate over the importance and timing of the retail-shop revolution, the geography and politics of the urban food supply have not been explored.[2] Even less has been written about the market hall as a building type.[3]

Part of this omission is understandable. Other than the struggle over the price of grain (set by the Corn Laws), and unlike such issues as sanitation, factory conditions, and poor-law reform, issues related to food did not lead to the creation of national pressure groups or constitute a part of the "administrative revolution" of the Victorian regulatory state; hence, few central government records exist that can help the historian reconstruct a national food picture. As a result, it has been easy to conclude that in a laissez faire age there was virtually no government food policy. The fact is that instead of being dealt with on a national level at Westminster, the issue of the supply and distribution of food was left to be battled out by town citizens.[4]

And battles there were. Many issues surrounded the regulation of local food supplies, but the most important centered on the rearrangement and reformation of the actual market space—the ancient marketplace. Whereas medieval and early modern urban food policy centered on how to create a more equitable distribution of the existing food supply (for example, by way of price regulation and restrictions on selling to middlemen), by the late eighteenth century, local policy centered on the principle that the best way to increase the food supply was to provide better market facilities. Often these reforms had to be preceded by a transfer in the ownership of the market from the manorial lord to the modern corporation or improvement commissioners. The underlying economic argument of this book is that in undertaking market reform, local government bodies made a notable contribution to the urban diet. Local market improvement in facilities and management (including efficiency in distribution and storage) meant an overall increase in the amount of food reaching the consumer and a probable change in food-consumption patterns. Indeed, a study of the nineteenth-century public market may well support a more optimistic interpretation than we might have expected of the general standard of living of the period.

Social and moral reformers believed that social behavior could be better controlled if public buying and selling moved off the streets and into a single building. Indeed, the rearrangement of the public marketplace is a good example of how architects, working for local government, sought to redefine human interaction in public spaces.

Until its late-twentieth-century resurgence in popularity, Victorian architecture was condemned as focusing exclusively on useless decoration; Victorian architects were dismissed as men who were uninterested in social issues and, worse, paid little attention to function or the honest use of materials. But after studying hundreds of new market buildings in terms of their origins, how they functioned, how they were planned and designed, and how they influenced popular taste, we have come to the conclusion that the Victorian revolution in architecture and public space was an appropriate and positive social move. The market hall, we claim, should be viewed alongside the railway station, the hotel, and the seaside holiday pier as one of the most remarkable accomplishments of Victorian architecture.

This book is also about how and why buildings of a particular type, the market hall, came to be abandoned, forgotten, and in many instances demolished. As the first large-scale, environmentally controlled general-merchandise retail space, the market hall paved the way for the department store, the supermarket, and the shopping mall—all of which made the old market halls look shabby and obsolete. Yet the market hall introduced glass roofs, the multiple shop-front façade, several shops under one roof, and large-scale ventilation, heating, and lighting, as well as many modern display and pricing practices. Equally important, the market hall was often the centerpiece of urban renewal. Because market halls needed larger sites than were generally available, their construction usually led to the demolition of existing buildings and the reconfiguration of streets, changes that kept the public market at the heart of the town's commercial life.

In reality, many market halls fell out of fashion not because they were no longer functional (they were), but because they didn't fit into the current thinking about public space by professional planners, architects, and government officials—a thinking that centered on massive, unitary town rebuilding schemes and that showed an aversion to architectural historicism. Equally significant, much of the neglect of market buildings is the result of twentieth-century misunderstanding of Victorian society, in particular, the belief that the Victorians used architecture largely to promote a set of rigid (and exploitative) moral and social codes. In reality, the primary aim of the Victorians may have been to impose order on the world. We hope to show that the architecture of the market buildings was a part of this search for order.

We shall direct our examination of the market halls to their social and cultural context. In particular, we consider the architecture of the public market in the framework of the Victorian tenet that architecture should be a reflection of social and moral beliefs; the market as a public building thus made a statement of what was regarded as cultural truth. Indeed, for many nineteenth-century towns the market hall was the principal building and, like the cathedral of old, its decoration offered a lesson in civic and moral virtue. In this regard, then,

INTRO.1. BILLINGSGATE FISH MARKET, LONDON, 1852

Although the market hall as a new building type first appeared in provincial towns like Leeds and Liverpool, London's Billingsgate wholesale fish market, built in 1850, inspired architects and town officials elsewhere to consider large-scale retail market projects, including the addition of a central market tower to announce the market's presence. London had no corresponding market halls for retail purchases.

the public market was part of a Victorian or "bourgeois" revolution in values and was held up as the principal agent in the moral and social elevation of the masses and the general remaking of society.

Finally, a word must be said about why we exclude London from our study. Aside from a few failed private experiments (the splendid Columbia Market Hall in Bethnal Green, built 1869, is the best example. see fig. 5.54), London had no public retail markets to match its great public wholesale markets: Smithfield (meat), Covent Garden (vegetables), and Billingsgate (fish). True, Charles Fowler's innovative designs for the Covent Garden and Hungerford markets in London in the early 1830s could not have failed to draw national attention to the modernization of market facilities. And the new Billingsgate wholesale market of two decades later was equally impressive (fig. Intro.1). But although some food was sold directly to consumers in these markets, they were in fact wholesale markets, set up to sell to subcontractors or large retail firms. They did little or nothing to move London's retail trade off the streets. Even today London's public retail markets are essentially street markets. The fact that London is such an anomaly in the history of the public market may explain why scholars have not taken up the study of the "modern" public market. Henry Mayhew's mid-nineteenth-century description of London costermongers is legendary, and the open-air street marketing of Dickens's London has become (wrongly) the popular image of British urban public marketing in the nineteenth century. Unlike markets in provincial towns, London's open-air street markets were so underregulated that they were open on Sundays. Indeed, few contrasts between the great metropolis and the provincial towns are as striking as the fact that for the poorer parts of London, Sunday was market day, and Londoners bought their goods in the street, whereas for most provincial towns the public market was held within a modern market hall that was closed on Sundays.[5]

As we shall see, it was in the provinces—particularly growing cities like Liverpool and Leeds—where the revolution in public marketing occurred. It is our good fortune that today, more than a century after the market hall building boom peaked, the trend toward destruction has lessened. Many old market halls have been restored, new market halls have been built, and once again the market hall has assumed its prominent position as a component of the British townscape and an important part of consumer life.

PART ONE

URBAN SPACE AND THE REINVENTION OF THE PUBLIC MARKET

CHAPTER ONE

❧

THE TRADITIONAL MARKET

FROM MEDIEVAL TIMES WELL INTO THE NINETEENTH CENTURY, THE MOST IM-
portant economic and social center of urban life and a dominant feature of the townscape was
the public market. Like the medieval town with which it had common beginnings, the public (or manorial) market space was subject to the vagaries of fortune. Famine, agricultural and
commercial changes, and fluctuations in population all left their imprints on the town's public
spaces. Nevertheless, the physical layout and architectural form of the market, those things
we identify as the traditional market typology, remained in the mid-eighteenth century much
as they had been several hundred years earlier. Specifically, in most British towns, the buying and selling of consumer goods took place in the open air, centered in particular streets or
often in a designated "marketplace," on certain days of the week (frequency depended on the
size of the town and its relation to the regional economy). A large number of towns were known
as market towns; their markets specialized in one or more of the region's agricultural products (corn, malt, fruit, butter, livestock), and they served outlying towns and villages as well
as supplying local needs. Most markets existed under rights granted by royal charter or statute, and they held a virtual monopoly on the marketing for a particular area. Fourteenth-century common law, for example, held that markets must be seven miles apart from one another. Little distinction was made between wholesale and retail trading. In addition, although
in earlier times some buying and selling had taken place in churches or on church property,
by late medieval and early modern times fairs and markets had been banned from church land.

1.1. MARKET CROSS,
MIDDLETON, 1791

The marketplace, designated by the town officials or the manorial lord, now occupied a square or quadrangle or portion of the street in the town center.[1]

By the eighteenth century, the typical market consisted of a ramshackle collection of stalls (or stances). At its center was the market cross, a silent reminder that the marketplace had historically been the center for peace and the rule of law. The cross itself might be as boldly classical as the Middleton cross, with its fine cupola, cornice, and arcade (fig. 1.1), or as simple and traditional as the single stone shaft surrounded by steps of the Haddington cross (fig. 1.2). Close by were the whipping post, stocks, and pillory for the punishment of dishonest traders as well as other offenders.

Stockport's market, typical of this entire period, still looked much as it had in 1680: it had occupied the same site for four centuries, and, along with the parish church, it formed the center of the town (fig. 1.3). Within the marketplace were the butchers' shambles, where animals were slaughtered and meat was sold; a market house (where the town scales were kept and where a few vendors kept sheltered stalls) with an open, arcaded ground floor and a gabled and timbered upper story; a water conduit; and the market cross. Access to the market was by way of four streets, which linked the town to the surrounding villages. Opposite the market house was a public meal-and-cheese house, where farmers brought grain and cheese to sell. At the center of the market were a pillory, a ducking stool, and a whipping post.

Throughout Britain, market space was subject to the vagaries of urban growth. Between 1766 and 1835 Stockport's population grew from about 2,000 to nearly 45,000; by the end of this period, the seemingly well-ordered marketing system no longer met the town's needs.

1.2. BUTTER CROSS, HADDINGTON, N.D.

1.3. TOWN PLAN, STOCKPORT, 1680

Visible are the butchers' shambles (15) in the center of the marketplace, the market cross (14), where butter and eggs were sold, and a market house (12).

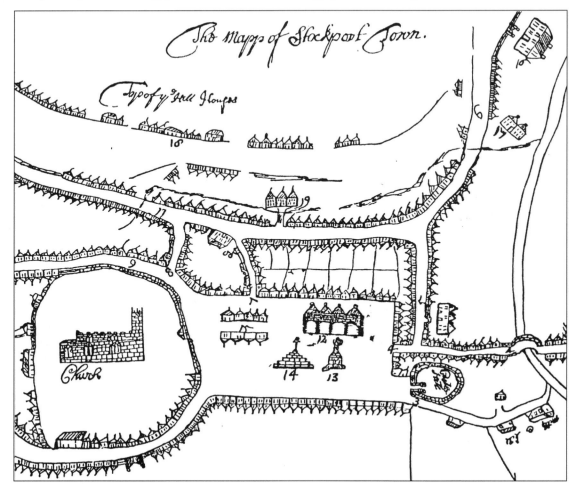

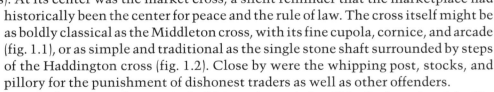

The mapp of Stockport Towne.

1.4. MARKET PLACE, YEOVIL, CA. 1830

This was also true of the old medieval market square of Abergavenny, which virtually disappeared because the walled town had nowhere to grow; hence, the marketplace was invaded by new streets and buildings. In Plymouth the old medieval market expanded so far around St. Andrew's Church that the walls of the church were hidden by the market stalls.[2]

In larger towns the market gradually split into specialty markets, which often spread out up and down nearby streets, and which were the only places at which specific goods could legally be sold. Even the market cross was often designated the site for the sale of a particular good; individual crosses acquired names like Butter Cross, Cheese Cross, or Fish Cross in consequence. Merchants were rarely allowed to sell outside the market, although exceptions were made for the special fairs that were held periodically. In Abergavenny in 1794, for example, officials declared that "all Corn and other Grain, Meal, Flour, Butchers Meat, Fish, Poultry, Butter, Cheese, Vegetables, and all other matters of things usually exposed to sale in the late Market-house, or in the public streets and places within the said town . . . shall be exposed to sale, and sold within such New Market-place, and not elsewhere, under the penalties mentioned in the said Act."[3]

The butchers' market (or shambles), like the fish market, presented special difficulties. Smells needed to be contained, sunlight had to deflected so that the meat did not spoil, and both stall and street needed to be so situated that they could be washed and drained. To the chagrin of nearby residents, in towns that had no slaughterhouse the shambles was frequently used for slaughtering animals as well as for selling the meat, creating additional problems of noise. Other traders were assigned particular spots, such as "fish stones" for setting out fish or the "corn pitch" for corn and oats. As in many towns, the streets of Salisbury, with names like Oatmeal Row, Ox Row, Oatmeal Corner, Fish Row, and Poultry Cross, tell us not only what people ate but where the town's food was distributed.

In addition to open-air market spaces, it became increasingly common for market towns to provide some kind of covered space—although it appears that as late as 1831 only a fraction of towns had a market house. The market cross itself was occasionally built as a roofed area, "for poore market folkes to stande dry when rayne cummith," as the Malmesbury officials put it. Often a wooden stall with a cloth or wooden roof stood at the market cross or near the tollbooth (where market tolls were collected) or town gate and served as a place where farm women sold eggs, butter, and poultry. In addition, some sort of covering was frequently erected for the users of the meat shambles. Newcastle-upon-Tyne's Old Flesh Market had crude wooden stalls with cloth roofs to protect the meat as well as the butchers from the sun and rain (see fig. 4.1). The parishioners of Hemel Hempstead built a "women's market house" on land belonging to the vicar, while Yeovil's shambles and market house of about 1700 were freestanding shedlike buildings located in the town center; by 1830, when the town could boast some "modern" shop fronts, these buildings seemed oddly placed and behind the times (fig. 1.4). By the late eighteenth century, some market folk in towns like Berwick-upon-Tweed

1.5. TOWN HALL AND MARKET PIAZZA, BERWICK-UPON-TWEED, 1761

The Town Hall occupied the upper stories and the market the ground floor. This view shows the side and rear of the arcaded market.

1.6. MARKET HOUSE,
MARKET HARBOROUGH,
1614

were able to do some of their selling under arcaded walkways or piazzas, often consisting of rows of arches with classical columns of stone (fig. 1.5).[4]

Most sizable towns had, near or at the center of the market, a market house or, as it was called in many Scottish towns, a tollbooth (or tron), built specifically for the collection of municipal or manorial tolls, for the weighing and measuring of goods, and, often, for the storage of grain. Sometimes the market house served as the market keeper's residence as well. Edinburgh had a tron for weighing goods in its market until 1663, when it was replaced by the Tron Church. The typical market house had an open arcade on the lower level, which served as a shelter for highly perishable goods (eggs, butter, and poultry) or, more commonly, for such administrative functions as weighing goods and collecting tolls. The upper floor served as the town hall or a guildhall or, in some cases, the town jail.

Even though by the seventeenth and early eighteenth centuries the style of the buildings was changing—the timber-framed vernacular structures were being replaced by classical stone structures—the form of the market house remained basically the same. In the town of Market Harborough, the town market of 1614 was conducted beneath a timber-posted grammar school, whose sign still proclaims that it was built "to keepe the market people drye in tyme of foule wether" (fig. 1.6), and at Whitby almost two hundred years later, market people were provided with a classical stone market house (fig. 1.7) for the same purpose. Shrewsbury's elegant Old Market Hall (1596, fig. 1.8) is an early example of the drift toward a more formal classical style. Bridgnorth's market house (fig. 1.9) embodies the stylistic transition from vernacular to classical in that its market, erected in 1650, was only partially new: the lower level was a modern structure of stone arches, while the upper level was a timber-frame barn.

1.7. MARKET HOUSE,
WHITBY, 1788

1.8. OLD MARKET HALL,
SHREWSBURY, 1596

Less common was the single-story roofed pavilion, as in the market houses of Hesket Newmarket and Coventry (fig. 1.10). But the form and function of all these market houses remained virtually unchanged from the late middle ages to the mid-eighteenth century. Note the difference in period but similarity in form, for example, between Witney's Elizabethan Butter Cross, with its open market space below and four gabled chambers above, and the nearby Town Hall of a century later, supported on arches and well-proportioned stone pillars but containing similar components: market below, a town chamber, and surrounding area for an open market (fig. 1.11).

These covered spaces notwithstanding, the dominant visual feature of the traditional market was, as the view of the market at Kingston-upon-Hull suggests (fig. 1.12), its open, cluttered, and rather unplanned appearance. Shrewsbury's elegant, late sixteenth-century market house was not extraordinary, but far more common was the unsightly old fish shambles at Barnstaple (fig. 1.13).

Centralization

Another characteristic of the traditional market was the continual tension between centralization and decentralization of market activity. While on the one hand, the market was subject to decentralizing pressure as commercial and demographic growth pushed marketing activity outward from the town center, on the other hand, the market was being forced by law and tradition to remain in its centralized physical space. Markets were regulated on the principle of the Roman maxim "ubi est multitude, ibi esse rector" (where there is a crowd, someone should be responsible for its control); the need for governance over market activities, including toll collection, drew these activities toward the market center. This centralization was an important characteristic of the early modern market. The town or manorial lord's responsibility for enforcing a multitude of regulations concerning the supply and price of food, the collection of tolls, and the weighing of goods according to official town scales

helped contain the market space.

For most towns, particularly those with considerable market activity, the regulation of the market was undertaken with vigor and an underlying mistrust of market sellers. As the inscription on Truro's Old Market House suggests (fig. 1.14), market officials stressed honesty in weight and measure in the most consequential language. In Leeds the "infamous traffic" in unwholesome meat had become so entrenched that in 1841 the meat inspector's wage was raised to keep him from taking a bribe. In Glasgow the town magistrates and council enacted a set of bylaws that prohibited, among other things, having dogs in the market, selling "bull beef," selling meat that was "blown, forked, unsound, or unwholesome," the unhealthful slaughtering of cattle, and "covering the legs or joints of lamb and veal with tallow" to add to its weight. Fraud in Glasgow's meat market was so bad that consumers petitioned the council for a daily inspection. In Coventry the town officials ordered all the market activity to be contained in a central marketplace to prevent illegal trading, including food hoarding. In other towns, attempts at centralization and control

1.9. TOWN HALL AND MARKET, BRIDGNORTH, 1652

1.10. OLD MARKET HOUSE, COVENTRY, CA. 1835

1.11. TOWN HALL AND
BUTTER CROSS, WITNEY,
1920
The Town Hall, on the left,
has the market beneath. The
older Butter Market is in the
center.

1.12. MARKET DAY,
KINGSTON-UPON-HULL, CA.
1810

were less successful. Manchester's marketplace, complete with market cross, stocks and pillory, and a jumble of market stalls, appears to have been a sort of Hogarthian scene of benign disorder (see fig. 2.1).[5]

More food and easier access to food supplies for many parts of Britain in the late seventeenth century resulted in an increase in market activity and a consequent increase in market-town tensions; but it was in the second half of the eighteenth century that the centralizing push of regulation and the decentralizing pull of growth turned the marketplace into a battleground. Population explosion and industrial encroachment led to what Sidney and Beatrice Webb called the "devastating torrent of public nuisances," namely overcrowding, lack of sanitation, and pollution. As demand increased for more and more market pitches, stalls, and carts, many markets became so crowded it was almost impossible to conduct business (fig. 1.15). The Scottish town of Perth is typical. Before the mid-eighteenth century, Perth

1.13. FISH SHAMBLES, BARNSTAPLE, CA. 1837

had little cart and carriage traffic, but with the introduction of carts for urban use in the first half of the eighteenth century, the town experienced so much street congestion that it was forced to remove its market cross and city gates.[6]

By the late eighteenth century, cloth, books, kitchen wares, and other household goods were no longer sold at the traditional fairs; rather, along with food, they were offered at the weekly town market. More important, significant improvements in agriculture, regional transportation, and international trade resulted in a number of new products being brought into the marketplace. This led to the further congestion of most urban markets, while still others, as regional trade centers, suffered even more. Meanwhile, improvements in wages, particularly in the early nineteenth century, pulled more and more consumers into the market.

The Market as a Public Nuisance

Picturesque as it may be to the twentieth-century eye, the traditional market was never without its problems, for by its very openness, it encouraged lower-class lawlessness, particularly with regard to food. Paradoxically, although in the eighteenth century an increase in the food supply kept people (barely) alive who in earlier times would have died, these people never had enough food, so that a growing underclass of poor people was constantly at a level of near-starvation. In addition to being the locus for the business of buying and selling, therefore, the market increasingly became the center of fraud in pricing and weighing, crime (theft, murder, and so on), food adulteration, fighting, and even food riots. In towns like Dundee, which in 1835 had a population of 50,000 but only six policemen, it was believed that town officials were "incapable of preserving the peace of the town." Thus, by its mere existence, the market was the stage for the community's often daily battles over food, particularly in times of shortage. The market at Radstock in 1827 was described as the kind of market "where if a man purchases a piece of meat he cannot put it out of his hand but it was immediately stolen," and Derby's chroniclers tell of a man who in 1701 robbed a girl of her groceries and as a punishment was flogged round the marketplace tied to the back of a cart.[7]

Stealing food and haggling over prices could easily turn into a mob activity, which could, as town officials knew too well, lead to a full-scale riot. Food riots were frequent during the agricultural crises of the last decades of the eighteenth century and the first decades of the nineteenth, the early 1830s, and the "hungry forties." One way towns traditionally dealt with the problem of high prices was to allow consumers to regulate prices by means of riots—in fact, the lower classes regarded riots as their rightful response to high prices and food shortage. Thus, the ruling classes of preindustrial Britain accepted marketplace disturbances as

1.14. INSCRIPTION ON THE MARKET HOUSE, TRURO, 1615

an almost legitimate, if unfortunate, way to meet the economic crises that were often brought on by food hoarding by local or out-of-town market speculators. The food riot was, in short, endemic to the so-called moral economy of licensed disorder; in many cases it was tolerated by officials and others who hoped that the "mob [might] be the cat's paw . . . to a reduction of prices." Indeed, municipal magistrates often agreed with the general public that stoning

1.15. MARKETPLACE,
SWANSEA, 1799

1.16. BULL BAITING IN THE
OLD MARKETPLACE,
WOKINGHAM,
SEVENTEENTH CENTURY

market stallholders was a justified way to check dishonest practices. Conditions were particularly bad in 1766, when a widely read journal, the *Annual Register,* recorded many of the riots, including this one in Newbury: "We hear from Newbury, that on Thursday last a great number of poor people assembled in the market-place during the time of the market, on account of the rise of wheat, when they ripped open the sacks, and scattered all the corn about, took butter, meat, cheese, and bacon, out of the shops, and they put it into the streets; and so intimidated the bakers, that they immediately sell their bread 2d in the peck loaf, and promised next week to lower it still more."[8]

Looking the other way was not always seen as the best or most desirable municipal policy, however; and as the French Revolution proved to the ruling classes, the uncontrolled mob and the food riot could lead to the destruction of a society. As long as the town was not able to guarantee a regular and cheap supply of goods, the marketplace, as a public space, was apt to become a political battlefield.

To make market confusion and congestion even worse, most working-class entertainment took place in the same spaces in which most marketing occurred. Many towns, like Manchester, Birmingham, Hull, Boston, and Stamford, had a bull-ring in the marketplace. In Taunton one of the shamble keeper's duties was to provide a collar and rope for the bull. Bull baitings, with their savage bulls and dogs and lower-class audiences, were indicative of the unsavory activities connected to the market. Cock fighting and bull baiting went on in the Newcastle-upon-Tyne market until 1768 and were popular pastimes in Barnsley, Wokingham (fig. 1.16), and Petworth into the early nineteenth century. Bull baiting was described in Penzance, in 1814, with considerable disdain for the "savage" and "brutal" spectators it attracted to the streets.[9]

Edinburgh, the most crowded city in Europe in the eighteenth century, offers a good example of how traditional markets had became a public nuisance and a source of fear. Its markets were appalling. With the exception of a covered wooden market dating to 1601—and despite proposals going back as far as 1752 to remove the markets from the streets—all of the town's buying and selling took place in the streets until well past 1800 (fig. 1.17).[10] Every conceivable kind of merchandise could be bought in the High Street. Fruit and vegetable sellers were packed around the old Tron Church; a fish market was held in a nearby alley or close; stretched along the High Street were the herb market and the egg and poultry market; and a series of connected closes that reached down to the bottom of the steep hill held the open butchers' market, the refuse of which was swept into the North Loch.

This sort of street marketing made the congestion of cities like Edinburgh intolerable. In addition, the traditional street market was open to wind and rain, which turned the ground into mud and made its users ill; this in turn kept the market in a generally unsanitary state. Unless the marketplace had designated stalls, food was displayed in a number of disparate ways, as in the Welsh town of Haverfordwest, where meat was hung on hooks affixed to the churchyard walls. The butchers' shambles was condemned as a malodorous eyesore, and the connection between open-air marketing and street congestion was a subject of near-universal urban concern. It is not an exaggeration to say that by the early nineteenth century, problems arising out of street marketing, particularly on Saturdays, were on a scale beyond anything that had gone before. A common market-day occurrence in many towns was a loose animal, usually a cow that had escaped the hands of the local trader or butcher, running wild through the streets.

Complaints about animals, particularly pigs and cows, in the streets were common. These animals, as it was told in Dundee (where the horse market and butchers' shambles were in the "narrowest" street), "seldom failed to stick their horns into the first unguarded inhabitant that came in their way, resulting in trembling scenes for parents, guardians, and rela-

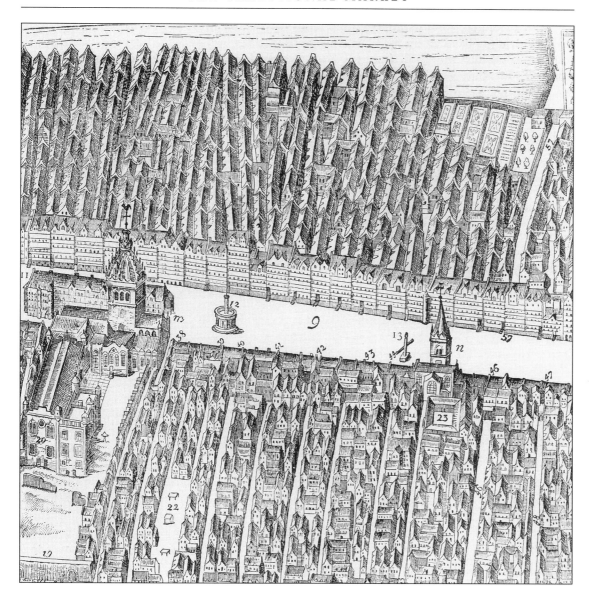

tions . . . and a rich harvest for surgeon, undertaker, and grave digger." Although the "verie loathsome practice" of slaying and bleeding cattle in the street at Glasgow's Trongate came to an end with municipal prohibitions in the late seventeenth century, cattle sales in the streets continued in Glasgow until the 1790s; and it was not until the 1840s and the establishment of an outlying slaughterhouse that cattle were no longer driven through the streets. Indeed, the sale of cattle in the streets continued in some towns well into the eighteenth century, when St. Helier officials heard complaints of careering pigs in the market, while the noise and congestion from the market made it difficult to do business at the nearby Royal Court. As late as 1866 it was noted that streets in particular parts of Glasgow contained more pigs than houses, and as late as 1888, well-bred women in Salisbury would not go into the streets on market days because of the large number of animals being driven through the streets.[11]

1.17. PLAN OF EDINBURGH FROM ST. GILES KIRK TO THE TRON KIRK

Several of the town's principal markets were relocated to remove congestion from the High Street. The Meal Market (19), Fish Market (22), and Butchers' Market (23) were all moved to designated quarters. Nevertheless, much of the town's marketing activity continued to take place in the High Street between the Tollbooth (11) and the Tron (13). See figure 2.4 for Fleshmarket Close, where the butchers' markets were located.

Pedestrians complained so strongly about the wheelbarrows on Birmingham streets that in 1791 an act of Parliament prohibited wheelbarrows on any of Birmingham's footpaths. In Manchester, where the run of carriages, trading carts, and wagons on market days was so great that it was dangerous to walk on certain streets, the market streets were widened in 1821 to keep pedestrians from being crushed. As late as 1872 the *Glasgow Herald* reported the year's toll of accidents by cart and carriage as ninety-three, twenty-two of which were fatalities. Town officials in Bury described its streets and marketplace as "greatly obstructed and dangerous" and the market stalls as "troublesome."[12] It was not uncommon for local merchants to ask town officials to put an end to street marketing because the raucousness of the market caused them to lose trade.

The Market and Bourgeois Sensibilities

Not all opposition to the traditional market system arose from a desire to protect life and limb. Opposition also stemmed from the newly developed bourgeois social sensibilities, some of which reflected new, "enlightened" attitudes toward work, gender, public space, and crime, but which also showed a less lofty desire to make shopping respectable for wives and daughters in the growing number of families that regarded themselves as a part of respectable society. Streets had traditionally been places for trade, sport, and discussion. The bourgeois desire for respectability (along with a more general concern for safety) led to an effort to use the streets only for traffic and to rid them of the insubordinate poor, the "unrespectable" working classes, and the criminal classes, who had long enjoyed a freedom of the streets that was unique in Europe at the time. Although lower-class domination of the streets had been lamented since the days of Henry Fielding and William Hogarth, with the French Revolution it became perceived as a threat to order, one that the middle and upper classes could no longer allow.

1.18. "Auld Hawkie,"
mid-nineteenth century

"Minde your own business" was the engraved message in the old Bridgwater marketplace. But in reality, eighteenth-century and early nineteenth-century urban life revolved around the open-air market as an extension of the street; the buying and selling of goods not only impeded but was itself interrupted by other activities. In addition to an economic locus, the market served as the town's principal public meeting place, both formal and informal. Public announcements were made—marriage banns, for example—but voices were raised for other purposes as well. London's fish market was called "the college of bad language." Recall that public punishments, in the form of stocks, pillory, and whipping post, were also features of the market. In Aberdeen the public hangman was paid a fee of one fish from each seller's basket on market days. The Oswestry Borough Council record for 8 May 1794 describes the sort of punishment being executed just when the market was its busiest: "Ordered that Mary Windsor (convicted of felony) wife of Philip Windsor be imprisoned in the Common Goal of the said town until the hour of four o'clock on Saturday next, and that she be then publickly whipped in the open marketplace at The Cross by the Beadle of the said Town, who shall give her twelve lashes on her bare back and then be discharged."[13]

Indeed, the marketplace was the scene of some of the community's most uncivilized behavior, as illustrated by the sale of his wife by a man in the Bodmin market in 1818: "A man named Walter, of the parish of Lanivet, led forward his wife, by a halter, which was fastened round her waist and publicly offered her for sale. A person called Sobey, who has lately been discharged from the 28th regiment, bid sixpence for her, as was immediately declared the purchaser. He led off his bargain in triumph, amidst the shouts of the crowd; and to the great apparent satisfaction of her late owner."[14]

Energetic bookmakers interfered with the marketgoers in Newcastle, and Edinburgh town officials had to act on complaints of brawlers and riotous apprentices in the street market, as well as charges that butchers' wives "quarreled, scolded, and swore in the open market" and that a number of people squabbled over the quality of the market goods. In the market at Market Drayton, one Thomas Poole "drewe blood upon Thomas Short upon the market day"; and in Oswestry's open market, youngsters used spiked sticks to steal fruit from the baskets of unwary market sellers. Brawls occurred among sellers over the demarcation of market spaces—before the improvements in the layout of the Manchester markets, officials had to deal with quarrelers, mostly women, who used language "unfit for Christians let alone a female." Indeed, market squabbling became an established part of urban folklore. In Devizes, for example, market officials posted the cautionary tale of a woman who had dropped dead in the market after wishing that she should do so if she was lying about whether she had paid for a sack of grain—while concealing the money in her hand.[15]

The respectable town dwellers also objected to the fact that the traditional market attracted all sorts of street characters, such as Glasgow's "Auld Hawkie," a crippled street

1.19. THOMAS ROWLANDSON, *MARKET DAY*, CA. 1800

hawker and ballad singer (fig. 1.18). Although such people were often venerated (particularly in Glasgow, which was famous for its colorful street people), and artists like Thomas Rowlandson found the markets a rich source of vivid and often humorous human activity (fig. 1.19), the middle classes usually urged that beggars, cripples, "misfits," and the poor be removed from public view. The French social commentator Alexis de Tocqueville noted that Salisbury's marketplace was full of prostitutes, and "on market days there were frequent brawls"; elsewhere, Kirkby Lonsdale's market cross was known as the assembly place of the town "roughs" who hurled abuse at passersby; Gloucester's streets were reported to be "infested with apple women"; and the Scarborough market was attacked for its "unfortunate Billingsgate character." "Wherever a street market existed," it was said of Scarborough, "it tended to keep down the standard of public taste. The too often filthy and unsightly appearance of the stands themselves, and the idle, the rude, and the dissipated loungers that collect in a market street, all tend to produce an uncivilized state of society . . . [that is] repulsive to persons of taste and refinement." Street stalls, it was argued in Manchester, were not simply a hindrance to traffic but brought together "a class of persons of indifferent character and generally lowered the tone of the immediate neighborhood."[16]

Particularly offensive to the new public sensibilities was the age-old custom of street peddling or hawking. This practice of selling from a cart (or simply a basket) was used for all sorts of goods by sellers who either occupied a regular corner or market spot or who trod regular routes, often going from house to house in residential districts. To those who set social policy and formed social opinion, the hawker (or costermonger, who traditionally sold from a cart) was "a nuisance to quiet families"; such people had "the effect of vulgarising" the shopping encounters of the decent workingman's wife.[17]

The sale of old clothing was viewed with equal concern. Most of the urban lower classes relied on used clothing, usually bought in the public market or off the street, for a significant portion of their wardrobe. Towns generally had a particular gathering place, such as Newcastle's Milk Market in the Sandgate (fig. 1.20), where the sellers of old clothing would spread their goods on the ground. But by the late eighteenth century this important urban commercial activity was attacked for lowering the tone of the marketplace and the streets where it took place; in addition, it was seen as endemic to the problems of theft and the spread of disease, and a substitute for respectable employment because it encouraged the working classes to pawn their possessions. The controversy over the sale of old clothing was an issue of some note in local politics. In Glasgow the superintendent of police expressed what was a commonly held view—that the open-air used-clothing market should be closed down because it was a haven for thieves and "semi-destitute people from the sister isle, in the endeavour to eke out a miserable existence in dealing in rags, when energies might be more usefully employed."[18]

Indeed, by the early nineteenth century, the market had assumed much of the social function of the old fairs—many of which had been closed down because they were regarded as centers of wickedness and immorality. (The village of Keith, Scotland, for example, was said to have "attracted great crowds of vagabonds and thieves.") Open-air markets, argued one Dundee newspaper, "possess all the features of a country fair, and are resorted to by rough and perilous characters of both sexes. The huckstering and the jostling that prevail, and the rude and offensive language that assails the ears on all hands, prevent the more respectable portion of the inhabitants from frequenting those places." "It is not right," said one critic of Oldham's open market, "that the market be turned into a beer garden [as] young men and women come [into the marketplace] in hundreds [using] foul language . . . and . . . rushing and pushing each other." On Saturday night in Dundee, it was claimed, "some of our streets and closes are the scenes of debauchery and wickedness and frequently of outrage and riot," while in London it was generally acknowledged that Saturday-night shopping rendered many streets impassable.[19]

Traditional open-air marketing practices were also regarded as promoting bad habits and low morals, such as heavy drinking, poaching, and the avoidance of the market toll. The absence of enclosed accommodations, particularly in bad weather, encouraged the movement of trade into public houses and thus encouraged drinking, as at Swindon, where the sale of corn in public houses led it to be known as the "gin and water" market. In fact, removing the temptation of the public house was seen as one of the virtues of municipal market reform. Equally offensive to many, the open marketplace was the scene of selling practices that if not illegal were socially questionable. The "higgler" who picked up bargains—poached rabbits, stolen fruit—with no questions asked would then resell them in the market, move out, and not return until the exploit was forgotten. More common were the crimes of forestalling (hoarding food for speculation) and regrating and engrossing (selling outside the market), along with the illicit weighing of goods. These were of perennial concern to the town officials. Added to this was the problem of bakers selling bread above the bread assize, the price set by municipal authorities. By the eighteenth century, the unenclosed and poorly regulated urban marketplace had come to be viewed by "respectable" residents as a place of disorder and chaos and a magnet for the worst elements of society. The underlying problem was that the marketplace was the unintended victim of unprecedented urban corruption, new forms of transportation, and increases in the amount and variety of foods and comestibles entering the town.[20]

2.1. OLD MARKETPLACE,
MANCHESTER, CA. 1810

Here the chaos resulting
from mixing buying and
selling with other activities
of the street is apparent.
Although Manchester's
marketplace had covered
stalls on two sides, the
interference of carriage, cart,
and pedestrian traffic turned
it into an urban battlefield.

CHAPTER TWO

❦

INVENTING THE MARKET HALL

FISH FOR SALE SPOILING ON A WINDSWEPT BEACH, SECONDHAND CLOTHING
lying on the soggy ground, meat and vegetables rotting under the sun or in the rain—all these
were, for hundreds of years, unwelcome conditions of market life. "I had to crawl underneath
the van to get out of the rain," complained a market seller in Brighton. Fish spoiled in the
outdoor market at Loughborough; sellers in Bacup had to set up shop under what they called
the "barbarism" of wooden stalls and tents; Manchester's marketgoers competed with all sorts
of street activity (fig. 2.1) and market users in Scarborough contended with a dirty market
exposed to winter storms. "It is rather too much to expect," stated a critic of the unenclosed
Bolton market, to come to the market and "stand there with wet clothes on."[1]

     Beginning in the late eighteenth century, problems like these were no longer accepted as
unalterable. The change in attitude came about in part because urban growth had exacerbated
the problem to a point where a solution simply had to be found (Hull's population, for example,
grew from about 29,000 in 1801 to close to 200,000 by 1861), and in part because people began to view public and private space as separate. The emerging "enlightened" view of urban
life held that the street and the open marketplace, which had long been the turf of the lower
classes and site of their independence in action and culture, should be reshaped according to
"rational" and "educated" middle-class models of respectability, social order, and civic virtue. Central to this view was an old notion, newly resurrected, that the proper arrangement
of the townscape could correct human behavior and thus create a better (and safer) society.
Public spaces thus came to be viewed as spheres of anonymity and "respectability" that needed
to be clearly separated from social activities. The street was now to serve as the arena for the
elevation of men and women of all social orders, a space within which all could interact in
good health and by formal rules of public order. It was for precisely these reasons that towns
and private citizens alike began to report, research, and survey what was being done about
the streets. Police protection, street paving and lighting, sidewalk (or "footpath") improvements, and the elimination of street congestion from such activities as hawking goods in open-
air markets became the aim in every town. The reformation of the street into a circumscribed
environment and the isolation of public markets were early victories for middle-class control in the struggle for urban spatial hegemony. In short, control of location became a characteristic of the capitalist city.[2]

The Decentralized or "Scattered" Market

From late medieval times until well into the eighteenth century, the public retail market had
its own rather anarchistic way of dealing with the problems of crowdedness and disorder: it
simply invaded the surrounding streets with stall and cart, scattering market activity throughout the town. Plymouth was a typical example. Here the butchers' shambles invaded a nearby
churchyard, and the streets were filled with market stalls. In Southampton the vegetable
sellers moved out of the marketplace and took control of the High Street. And despite peri-

odic attempts by the town council to contain the market in Coventry, it overflowed into surrounding streets and public spaces.[3]

In many reform-minded towns, particularly rapidly growing ones, this age-old pressure to scatter or decentralize the market was rationalized. In late eighteenth-century Glasgow, for example, the old market, whose center lay at the market cross where the town's four main streets intersected, was broken up into a number of new specialty markets located in surrounding streets or on specific sites. Between 1756 and 1810 the old milk, butter, and egg market was moved to the steps and square in front of St. Andrew's Church (to the annoyance of the nearby residents); an array of specialty retail markets, including grain, vegetables, and meat,

2.2. LONDON ROAD MARKET, MANCHESTER, 1824

2.3 VICTORIA STREET MARKET, MANCHESTER, 1854

These were two of a number of markets established to draw market activity away from the town's traditional marketing center at the Market Place, which, with its Old Shambles nearby, had become intolerably congested. But by 1846 it was clear that this decentralization process was not meeting the town's needs, and the markets were recentralized into a vast new market that was built at Shudehill.

was established near the old cross in Candleriggs and King streets; and the old clothing market and a bird-and-dog market were established elsewhere. The new Candleriggs market was a large enclosed space, open to the sky but separated from the street. Beginning in 1766 and extending over half a century, crowded Manchester with its "perpetual throngs" and innumerable stalls in Market Street diversified the market center to a dozen new specialty markets. By 1846, when the Corporation of Manchester purchased the markets from the Lord of the Manor, Manchester, like Glasgow in earlier years, had become a city of scattered markets: two vegetable markets, four butchers' markets (one solely for pork), a fish market (with its own handsome stone building), and a dozen other markets spread throughout the city (figs. 2.2 and 2.3). Between 1822 and 1829, Leeds decentralized its markets by creating three new general markets (one of them covered) and a new meat shambles; Liverpool had a system of giant markets located in three residential districts of the city; and beginning about 1806, Newcastle's narrow and crowded Sandhill market was broken up and the butchers', general, and fish markets were moved to new locations.[4]

Although the decentralization of Edinburgh's markets had begun in 1477, when James III

2.4. FLESHMARKET CLOSE, EDINBURGH, CA. 1845

By the early nineteenth century the butchers' market had been removed to a series of courts called Fleshmarket Close off the High Street.

designated areas for particular marketplaces away from the crowded High Street, the effort continued with only mixed success well into the nineteenth century (see fig. 1.17), when marketing activity had to be drawn away from the High Street once again—this time to the area under the North Bridge and along a crowded and narrow residential street called Fleshmarket Close, which became the home of three butchers' markets (fig. 2.4). Edinburgh's market problem was particularly difficult because the town's growth was largely "intensive" rather than "extensive," that is, it took place within the confines of the old town. In other towns, decentralization of the public market followed urban (and suburban) growth. Generally, "extensive" urban growth did not occur until after mid-century.

Removing the Market from the Street

Decentralizing the market often became the problem rather than the solution because it generated more selling in the streets. By 1800 it had become increasingly apparent that one of the chief causes of crowding in the early industrial town was the enormous amount of buying and selling that took place in the streets peripheral to the traditional marketplace. It was also clear that when town officials tried to spread the market around town, they simply transferred the problem from one crowded space to another crowded space—or from one street to another. Unless they could provide an entirely new market area, the problem would not go away.

To be sure, the old open-air marketplace had a variety of problems as well, but nothing was as overwhelming as the congestion, noise, and unacceptable behavior that accompanied

2.5. STREET MARKETING IN LUTON, 1925

The clash of street selling and street traffic continued well into the twentieth century. This photograph was taken in 1925 to mark the final day of the old street market. The street, with its tramway tracks running alongside the market, suggests how such markets operated in places that were both convenient and dangerous. The Luton market was relocated in a nearby market hall.

street buying and selling. Henry Mayhew's well-known account of street marketing in London in the mid-nineteenth century was probably an accurate picture of conditions that had become commonplace in dozens of towns much earlier. Street selling, with its attendant evils, had long been obnoxious to respectable town dwellers and town officials—"a very rough affair," as it was called in Loughborough. As towns grew, matters became worse. Larger towns meant more coaches (and, later, railways and trams) rumbling into the marketplace to deposit and collect their passengers; more carts of coal, iron, and lime; more market-bound animals running through the streets (fig. 2.5). The growth of towns too often came without a corresponding growth in market services. Doncaster, for example, had increased from a population of about 2,000 in 1750 to one of 10,000 in 1851, but its Butter Cross market could still accommodate only twenty-five to thirty saleswomen and their baskets, while five times that number were forced to stand outside, unprotected from the weather and blocking the streets. In Aberystwyth, tourists arriving at the railway station were greeted by hawkers touting their goods; and Birmingham in the late eighteenth century was typical of many of Britain's rapidly growing towns on market days: "Here a brawl, the consequence of the sloppings from a trundled mop flying in the face of some passerby. . . . Burly butchers and wily horse dealers wrangling with country folks round the droves of pigs and sheep and horses in New Street . . . and fights and runaway cattle in the beast market. . . . Groups of idle men and women and mischievous boys crowding round the Welsh Cross, hooting and yelling and pelting the unfortunate offender in the pillory with mud, bad eggs, and offensive garden stuff, or men and lads with fighting dogs at the corner."[5]

The commerce that took place amid such scenes had long cast buyer and seller into a vulgar, even criminal environment that was viewed as neither progressive nor edifying. Not the least offensive aspects of this unruly street culture were the uninhibited dancing, the singing of obscene or "low" songs, the noise of the organ grinders, and the presence of shooting galleries. In one town, a stage for mountebanks so swelled the confusion of the marketplace that it had to be removed by town officials, and as late as 1817 in at least one Scottish town, women convicted of offenses were still flogged through the streets. A late seventeenth-

Barnstaple Markets.

WHEREAS

GREAT Danger and Inconvenience are experienced by the Inhabitants and others resorting to this Market, by reason of the Panniers being suffered to be placed on both sides of High Street, and in an irregular manner. To prevent therefore the recurrence of so dangerous a Practice, and to accommodate all Persons resorting to the Market, It is hereby ordered, that from and after this Day, the Panniers be pitched in a single Row, at the distance of Six Feet from the Houses, on the WEST SIDE of High Street only, commencing from Maiden Street, and extending towards North Gate, leaving a Space of Six Feet between every Ten Pair of Panniers: And that all Stalls and Standings, of any other description, be placed at the end of the Panniers towards North Gate; And that no Person do pitch or place any Pannier, Stall, or Standing, in any other part of the said Street, on pain of being proceeded against according to Law.

The above arrangement to continue in force till the 29th Day of September next, from and after which Day, the Panniers, Stalls, and Standings to be placed in the same order on the EAST SIDE of High Street.

(Signed) *Wm. Chappell Pawle,*
Mayor and Clerk of the Market.

Barnstaple, July 7th, 1815.

SYLE, Printer and Bookbinder, Barnstaple.

2.6. PUBLIC NOTICE CONCERNING BARNSTAPLE MARKETS, 1815

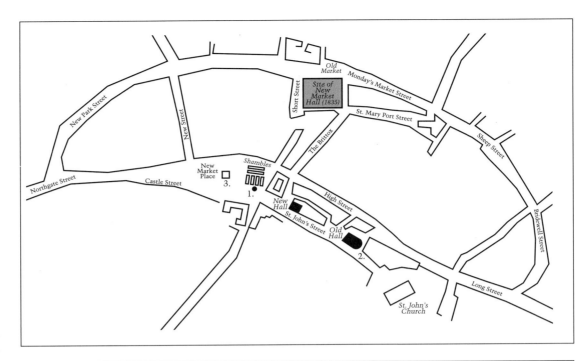

2.7. PLAN OF DEVIZES (DRAWN FROM DORE'S PLAN OF 1759)

In Devizes, marketing was decentralized, some of it allocated to open spaces and some to enclosed or semi-enclosed spaces, but all scattered throughout the center of the town. Aside from the new Market Place, which held the measuring house, the cross (1), and the butchers' shambles (which took the form of a set of uncovered stalls), sellers found themselves relegated to distant locations. Grain was sold in the old Market, the Cheese Market shifted back and forth from the Old Hall to the "Cheese Hall" (the New Hall), butter was probably sold at the Butter Cross (site unknown), fish was sold on St. John's Street (2), poultry in Wine Street, and vegetables and fruits in stands south of the White Swan Hotel. By 1803 most of this activity had been moved to a new market house, called the Measuring House (3), and then to a new Market Hall in 1835.

2.8. PLAN OF THURSO BY SIR JOHN SINCLAIR, MID-EIGHTEENTH CENTURY

One of more than a hundred planned towns and villages in Scotland, Thurso boasts a seemingly ideal layout: the town square—called Macdonald Square—is separated from marketing activities, which are nonetheless centralized and enclosed near the town port. Only the corn market is located some distance from the rest of the markets. It was not unusual for entrance to the larger market to be limited to one entryway, but it is curious that here the lane leading to that entrance is so narrow.

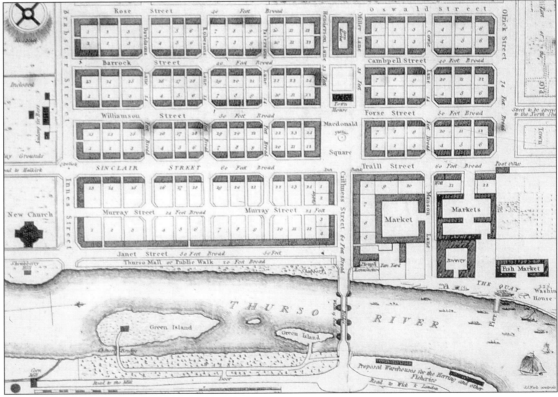

century doggerel verse about the old Guildhall of South Molton, center of the town's marketing life, offers a somewhat jaded view:

> If our Guildhall should happen to fall
> On the rogues and knaves who there resort—
> If it should fall and kill them all,
> I think 'twould be very good sport.[6]

Town and market authorities throughout the country sought schemes that would allow more rational traffic and marketing. Barnstaple converted certain streets to one-way cart traffic and limited vendors from the country to operating out of their market baskets, or panniers, lined up in single file on one side of the street (fig. 2.6). Another solution was to pull down buildings to enlarge the existing marketplace or to pave and arrange the market into separate divisions for the various kinds of goods on sale. But many urban dwellers and town officials wished to remove buying and selling from the streets altogether. Glasgow's overflowing market and the consequent street congestion caused many to ask whether the town ought to allow country vendors of plants, fruits, and vegetables in the town streets. Here and elsewhere they were swayed in part by the complaints of the "legal" vendors, who paid rent or market tolls, that street hawkers (who did not and thus contributed nothing to the town's coffers) offered unfair competition.

At some point in the nineteenth century, most British towns—some only after considerable public debate—placed either complete or partial bans on street selling. Some relied on ancient market charters to argue that street selling fell outside the confines of the legal marketplace; in others, the clauses relating to markets and fairs that were incorporated into the Public Health Act of 1847 gave local authorities power to prohibit street hawking. Thus, by the 1850s, with the exception of London, where street selling remained rampant, separate spheres for street traffic and public marketing had become the norm. Of the ten municipal boroughs in West Riding, Yorkshire, that had control of their markets (Batley, Bradford, Doncaster, Halifax, Harrogate, Huddersfield, Leeds, Rotherham, Pontefract, and Dewsbury), all but one (Batley) outlawed market sales in the streets and took steps to draw marketing into one building. Glasgow and Birmingham began restricting street selling in the 1750s and 1760s, through limiting stall-building, issuing a "hawking" license, and establishing mandatory off-street market facilities.[7]

Street vending was never fully phased out. In some towns, particularly the heavily suburbanite towns of the southeast of England, it prevailed because it benefited the well-to-do urban dwellers, while in London most poor people obtained their food from street vendors. In towns like Torquay, it proved impossible to eliminate street hawking altogether or to prevent its resurgence. Sunderland could not fully ban street selling from the town, nor could Halifax, where officials succeeded only in reducing the number of street hawkers from 214 to 177. In Cockermouth, in Cumberland, town officials were unable to stop butchers from selling their meat door to door on Saturday nights. In Aberystwyth in 1900, after thirty years of heated debate over street trading, poultry and eggs could still be bought only on street corners.[8]

All in all, however, the trend was in the opposite direction. By 1886, two-thirds of Britain's principal municipal boroughs had, in theory at least, prohibited marketing on the street, except for the occasional designated location, and about half of all towns appear to have actually removed buying and selling from the traditional marketplace, replacing it with some form of enclosed space. Overall, the proportion of the nation's food purchased off the streets declined dramatically.[9]

Nevertheless, the prohibition on street selling and the decentralization of urban commerce didn't work. Neither solved market problems nor met the preference of British shoppers for a central market. Holding the market in different parts of the town proved to be inconvenient and unpopular with buyer and seller alike. Country vendors shied away from decentralized markets, arguing that a central market ensured them a large mass of customers. Devizes maintained markets that were scattered throughout the town center until 1793 (fig. 2.7). By the 1880s, Hull had become something of an anomaly in that it maintained a decentralized marketing system. One market served Hull's East Riding agriculturalists, another those from Lincolnshire, and still another everything else—despite the fact that all three markets sold the same types of goods. Hull's market sellers disliked this three-market system because, in their view, it made it impossible to draw the desired large crowd to any single market. Bringing farm goods to Hull was less profitable than going to a large central market elsewhere. Throughout the first half of the nineteenth century, some towns continued to try for market decentralization. Birmingham experimented with a few scattered markets, largely for outlying neighborhoods, but they all failed. Liverpool eventually shut down its markets in residential districts and used one of them, St. Martin's market hall, for the sale of old clothing. The old scattered markets of Hereford were, as users complained, "too detached from one another." "Our markets have hitherto been divided," it was observed in Winchester, "one thing being sold at one place and another at the other."[10]

The Enclosed, Centralized Market and the Birth of the Market Hall

A way had to be found to create a central market while maintaining order in the town's streets. The solution, as taken up in Winchester, was "to bring every species of commodity under

2.9. ENCLOSED MARKET, ST. HELIER, 1804

An excellent example of an early-nineteenth-century "enclosed" (and partially roofed) public market, complete with classically inspired entrance gates on the left, this market revolutionized the town's market life by removing the market from its traditional location in the streets.

one roof." Such recentralization made sense for a number of reasons beyond mere convenience: in particular, the imposition of custom dues, the collection of tolls, and the enforcement of market bylaws became easier and potentially more effective. There was also a widely held belief among consumers that only a large central market inspired the sort of cutthroat pricing expected in a public market. Indeed, the fashion among "enlightened" town planners of the late eighteenth and early nineteenth centuries was to lay out the town with a main square divorced from buying and selling but markets that were enclosed at a logically central point. Thus did Sir John Sinclair plan Thurso (fig. 2.8).

The most important step in recentralizing the market and separating it from the street was its relocation into a new "enclosed" (but not necessarily fully covered) central market space. St. Helier's new market of 1803, with its elegant entrance consisting of three classical columned gateways in an iron fence, made a clear statement that the market had been centralized and cut off from the street (fig. 2.9). Enclosure was also instituted by 1776 in Bristol (fig. 2.10) and on a large scale in Halifax beginning in 1790, in Plymouth in 1804-07, in Glasgow in 1817, and in Manchester after the city had purchased the markets from private owners in 1846. The new, centralized Plymouth market, which replaced the market held in the streets around and under the Guildhall, was a three-acre, open-air, general market for vegetables, butter, fish, poultry, meat, pots, and other merchandise. Its most unusual feature was that its walled-in space had access only by three entrances. The open-air market was contained within this space, though there were also three market buildings—classical pavilions with grand granite Doric columns that were reserved for the sale of fish, vegetables, and meat (fig. 2.11).

Glasgow was one of the first of the large towns to segregate much of its marketing into a single enclosed walled space, known as the Bazaar, that was completely removed from the streets. Here the farmer's carts could be arranged as stands, and all the town's market vendors (except the butchers, who were given a separate space nearby) could be accommodated. The new Bazaar included a wide range of separate shops in the interior, some of which formed a fashionable covered arcade, and was at that time one of the largest single retail markets in Britain. Over the next half-century, in a rather jumbled manner, this market was added to, rearranged, partially rebuilt, and eventually fully roofed (fig. 2.12).[11]

These central, enclosed marketplaces were revolutionary, for they freed the market from the nonmarketing activities of the traditional marketplace. Public access was usually limited to a number of carefully selected points for pedestrians and one for carts, thus giving the town officials greater control over who and what passed through the market. The weights and measures were housed in the market, as, typically, were the grain storage units; and there one could often find a corn exchange space set aside for the weekly grain sales (usually by sample). Some enclosed markets had separate roofed spaces for shops and stalls, and often the market was divided into specialty areas, as was the case at Ipswich (fig. 2.13). Here entrance was by way of a single lane which ran between two markets lined with covered loggias. Neath's new market of 1837 consisted of covered space in the center and around the in-

2.10. St. James's Market, Bristol, ca. 1776
This enclosed market was an outgrowth of the ancient fair held on the grounds of St. James's Church.

2.11. NEW ENCLOSED
PANNIER MARKET,
PLYMOUTH, 1807

Although the market appears to be somewhat crowded and disorderly, it is a fully walled space with limited cart traffic that was built specifically for marketing. It covered three acres, cost £10,000, and was erected on an open field to replace a congested street market that had grown so much that the walls of St. Andrew's Church (seen in the distance) were hidden by market stalls. The new market included a number of covered, classically inspired sheds within. Fish and vegetables were sold in the sheds in the foreground, and a meat shambles can be seen beyond. By 1873 this market was being called "inconvenient" and a new market hall replaced it in 1889.

terior circumference, with space in between for open-air marketing. Often, as in Stamford's elegantly classical market (see fig. 5.15), some of the stalls were covered. It was not unusual for the entire market to be eventually roofed over. Tewkesbury's 1789 market house was of similar classical form but must have been one of the earliest to be fully covered (fig. 2.14).

Not all towns favored the enclosed, covered central market. A late nineteenth-century survey found that of 605 retail and wholesale markets in England, some 231 (including cattle and corn markets) were still held entirely in the open air. Well into the twentieth century, the open-air market remained the norm for many towns. Although most of these were small towns, there were some notable exceptions. Nottingham relied on open-air marketing in its famous market square until 1928, and large open-air markets were held in Norwich, Great Yarmouth, Northampton, and Barnsley. York's ancient shambles and open market were considered by some to be the finest in England. In Derby and elsewhere the debate over open and closed markets was resolved by having both; and at Wolverhampton it was argued that the covered market would not succeed as long as an open market was available. Indeed, in 1887 the royal commissioners on markets and tolls found that a majority of the nation's markets included some open-air venues.[12]

When a town created a centralized, enclosed marketplace, it opened the way for considerable spatial and architectural experimentation. What often began as walled shelters evolved into a new architectural building type, the market hall, and with it the prospect of a new architectural language (discussed in chapter 4). The natural progression of the public market was from the traditional, open-air marketplace to a combination of marketplace and street market, to an enclosed market site, to a roofed market hall. Each step in this process further aided in the separation of marketing from the street, thereby pushing towns ever closer toward solving the age-old problems endemic to it. In response to these problems the market hall logically emerged as an architectural form, one that was destined to become an influential social and economic force in British daily life.

Market halls were almost exclusively provincial; they developed outside of London in the market towns and regional capitals and manufacturing cities. One of the most remarkable features of their evolution is that the earliest halls were among the largest. Few build-

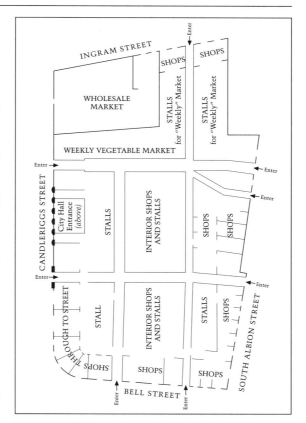

2.12. FLOOR PLAN, BAZAAR MARKET, GLASGOW, 1817-1914

Unlike most market halls, which were designed and built within a brief period of time, the Glasgow market evolved over more than half a century of building, adding on, and rebuilding on the site of a former bowling ground near the town center. The original partially roofed Bazaar Market was formed on the Candleriggs side of the plot in 1817 and by 1834 had spread to the South Albion side of the plot. Eventually, the entire market was roofed over. The section on the right with a wide alley through it was the Weekly or Vegetable Market, that on the left the Bazaar Market, originally a collection of nineteen separately roofed shops, but rebuilt and remodeled. On this plan, it contains thirty-two street-front shops and two alleys that run the length of the market. On the level above and between the Vegetable Market and the Bazaar was the City Hall, a large public assembly hall, whose entrance can be seen at the lower center of the plan. Further extensions were made in 1866 and 1888.

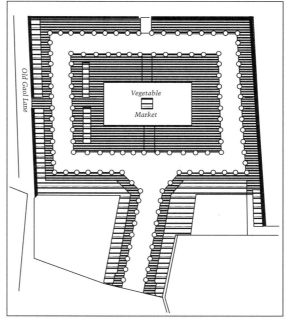

2.13. PLAN OF THE PROVISION MARKET, IPSWICH, 1810

The principal entrance to this market was by way of a lane encircled by rings of colonnaded corridors for pedestrians and small shops. The inner ring served as the vegetable market. This tightly designed space replaced an earlier street market that had become so endangered by cart traffic that on market days the town bailiffs had to place posts and rails across the streets at the marketplace entrances.

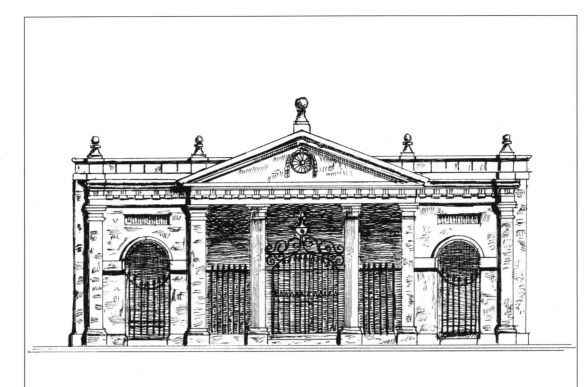

2.14. MARKET HOUSE, TEWKESBURY, 1789

An early single-purpose and apparently fully roofed market house, Tewkesbury's market was privately financed by twenty individuals. Although it was said in 1830 that the shareholders "have had no cause to regret their speculation," the market later fell into disuse when marketers moved to an area closer to the railroad station.

2.15. ST. JOHN'S MARKET HALL, LIVERPOOL, 1822

The first and one of the largest of the new market halls, St. John's Market was arranged in shopping "avenues" which corresponded to groupings of food. The view here is toward Avenue 5, containing the vegetable section on one side and fish on the other. This market, which was gaslit, ushered in the modern concept of a covered and environmentally controlled space for shopping, one that also allowed evening shopping for the convenience of the working classes.

2.16. St. John's Market Hall, Liverpool, 1882

Half a century after its construction, the same market appears to have thrived. Although new lighting has been installed, and the presentation and organization of the foods have become more systematized, the customer is still served by a clerk who stands in front of his or her goods.

2.17. St. John's Market Hall, Liverpool, ca. 1922

The character of the market changed between the two world wars. Now, separately roofed and lighted "lock-up" stalls allowed the seller to work behind an individual counter, as in a traditional shop. For a diagram of the earlier floor plan see figure 5.22.

ings in Britain compared in size to the new market halls at Newcastle in 1835 and Aberdeen in 1842. In response to the overwhelming need placed upon them by their burgeoning populations, Liverpool in 1822 and Birmingham a few years later built massive covered markets.

Liverpool's St. John's Market, a building nearly two acres in size that contained a clerestory to provide maximum interior light in the day and gas fixtures to give illumination at night, set in motion a veritable social, economic, and architectural revolution (figs. 2.15, 2.16, and 2.17).

The market hall was an original but not surprising invention that by the second half of the nineteenth century had become arguably the most important public building in the British townscape and one that continued to evolve well into the twentieth century. It stands as an outstanding example of nineteenth-century municipal social policy and urban planning, and in it lay the embryo of the modern environmentally controlled retail spaces: the department store, the supermarket, and the shopping mall.

OWNERSHIP, TOLLS, AND MARKET REFORM

THE SELF-CONTAINED MARKET HALL WOULD NOT HAVE MATERIALIZED IF not for a widespread shift in market ownership from private to public hands. Municipal control of the town market was crucial for the retail revolution that the modern market hall came to represent. Most English and Welsh markets were owned and operated by individuals, usually a local or nearby manorial lord, by town governments or, later, by a body of improvement commissioners or a trust. Such ownership was ordinarily a "prescriptive right," that is, granted by custom and tradition (often confirmed by statute), or through ancient charters that had been granted by the crown. In medieval and early modern times, as market trading grew in importance, the crown assumed the right to permit or deny fairs and markets, and thus the number of royal charters grew. Between the eleventh and the fourteenth centuries, around two thousand market charters had been granted to individuals or parties in trading centers, which became known as market towns. Although most market charters were granted after the Norman Conquest of 1066, very often the market itself antedated the charter. Both charter and prescriptive rights stipulated the geographic boundaries within which all of the town's trading could take place and usually fixed the day of the week, the place, and often the times of day that market officials could proclaim the opening and the closing of the market. These charters ordinarily gave their holders the right to provide market structures (such as stalls or a market house), regulate the market, and collect tolls. The charter often restricted or prohibited altogether any relocation of the market. Serving literally to impose trading monopolies, the charter proscribed anyone, town officials and private interests alike, from establishing "opposition markets." Furthermore, common law stipulated that markets be at least seven miles apart. Some new settlements, therefore, were enjoined from having any market at all.[1]

Occasionally, with the market rights came an added proscription limiting the scope of business undertaken by local shopkeepers in private premises or even that of the ancient fairs. Custom and law held that if one party was entitled to hold a market and a second party set up an opposing fair or market nearby, it was a violation of the first party's rights. In Manchester a large new marketplace created to serve the growing Pool Fold district was closed down after its promoters lost a long legal battle with Lord Mosley, owner of the town market rights.[2]

The Benefits of Market Monopoly

The town market was a symbol of town freedom, particularly for those lucky enough to hold their market independent of private (usually manorial) ownership. The benefits of market ownership were considerable: first, market tolls and the rent from stalls were healthy sources of revenue, and second, ownership provided an opportunity to enforce public order and to supervise the town's food supply. As a result, market owners were protective of their rights and privileges. They objected to the erection of new markets which were in violation of existing franchises, and to the establishment of new markets in towns, an infringement of trading monopolies. In part, these objections resulted from fears of a dwindling food supply. Newcastle, for example, opposed the establishment of markets in the nearby towns of Tynemouth and North and South Shields because, it claimed, they infringed upon Newcastle's rights to the area's food supply, including fish. Much of the history of local markets centers around attempts by market officials to curtail what were considered illegal practices: toll collection by competing markets, forestalling (the unpopular and illegal practice of selling goods before they reached the marketplace), bakers and brewers selling at prices that exceeded the assize, butchers and fishmongers selling meat and fish past their prime, and tanners selling improperly tanned leather. In the main, those who challenged the established market monopoly were treated unsympathetically by the courts. It was not unusual, for example, for butchers in private shops to be restrained from going into competition with the local market, or at least from selling meat on public market days; and well into the nineteenth century, many towns mandated that meat and dairy products could be sold only at the town market. Macclesfield's town monopoly on the sale of meat and fish prevented the establishment of retail meat and fish shops in that town until the 1840s, when the market monopoly was broken "and shops were created all over the town." At Chard, six butchers paid the market owner three shillings a week for the privilege of selling in their own shops outside the public market.[3]

Market Ownership and Reform

In the period from 1700 to 1846, only ninety-three royal charters were granted for new markets, a reflection of the fact that the ultimate authority for public markets had shifted from the crown to Parliament. Increasingly, it was Parliament which granted hundreds of nineteenth-century market holders (generally towns) permission to expand, rebuild, or even sell their markets. As this happened, the town market became defined more as a public good for the benefit of the community than as a franchise held by elites. More and more frequently, Parliament, as the grantor of the market rights, expected these markets to exhibit proper regulation and adequate accommodation for all.[4]

Although the switch in control of market rights may have encouraged a new sense of public accountability, the pace, character, and origin of market reform was almost always connected to the nature of local ownership. Scottish markets had tended to be under municipal control from the start and were generally better managed. Because English and Welsh towns either did not hold market rights or were constrained by charter and law on their management of those they did, their freedom from manorial control went only so far. Even simple changes in a market's facilities were often next to impossible; most towns, for example, had to go so far as to seek special parliamentary permission to make such minor changes as altering the day and opening hours of the market, removing a building or widening a street to increase the size of the marketplace, or even installing street lamps. Towns that did not own their market charters were in worse shape; they had no power to make market reforms. Furthermore, until the late eighteenth century, many town leaders had only a limited interest in the common good, because town management tended to reside in self-selecting and sometimes corrupt elites. Such was the case in the Nottinghamshire town of East Redford, where the town bailiff regularly spent a large portion of the market profits on an annual dinner for himself and other town officials. Too often the nominal government of the town functioned as a private, not a public, institution.[5]

Until about 1800 most markets belonged to the local manorial family. A currently held historical view is that overall these aristocratic landowners had limited influence on urban land use.[6] But urban markets owned by aristocrats suggest otherwise: by the late eighteenth century, markets owned by manorial lords were generally badly managed, inconvenient for the town inhabitants, and the subject of much complaint. Often, manorial owners blocked market reforms and drained the market's revenue, leaving it in a constant state of disrepair. More serious, perhaps, the monopolistic rights of the manorial lord acted in many cases to discourage the growth of the town's food supply.

Most manorial owners subordinated the interests of the public to their own profits from the market. Ancient records called the Hundred Rolls reveal the extent to which manorial lords guarded their market rights and privileges and the way they sought royal support in protecting their franchise against new markets or infringement on their rights to tolls and to set prices. In their operation of the marketplace, market improvements tended to be piecemeal and inexpensive at best. Ironically, private or manorial market owners often had more legal flexibility than their municipal counterparts in correcting the evils of the traditional marketplace, but these same private owners, unfortunately, were generally the least interested in reform. The Mosley family, which operated Manchester's market, fell into this category, while the Duke of Norfolk, who held the Sheffield market, and the Earl of Derby, owner of the Bury market, are exceptions; these private owners maintained relatively well-managed markets. The Mosleys aggravated town residents by holding the markets on the most frequented thoroughfares in the center of town, by shifting markets from place to place, and by refusing to maintain the markets adequately. In Wakefield it was reported that the market owner was purposely mismanaging the market in order to force the town authorities to purchase it because it had become a nuisance.[7]

Historians generally view the mayors and town councils of the eighteenth- and early nineteenth-century towns as almost uniformly corrupt, ineffective, and neglectful of the needs of the townspeople—particularly when it came to public services. In reality, especially with regard to the public market, this view is misleading. The anarchic state of so many particular markets had less to do with local corruption or mismanagement than with the fact that many local authorities had little power to effect reforms. Even when towns owned their markets, it was often legally impossible for them to borrow funds to make improvements, to be able to finance the legal fees involved in petitioning Parliament, or even to use market tolls for the purpose. Winchester's market committee had to solicit the Lords of the Treasury at Westminster for permission to raise a mere £194 in order to repair its old market, and even then they feared that their trivial request might not be approved. The municipality of Carlisle planned a new market in 1849 but was forced to abandon the proposition in the face of the parliamentary costs.[8]

During the nineteenth century market ownership underwent a monumental shift from private to public. Indeed, the process of public acquisition and ownership of private market rights was so widespread that by the third quarter of the century, local governments had acquired a significant influence over the sale and distribution of the urban food supply. In 1888, of the 769 known town markets in England and Wales, 274 were still in manorial hands, but nearly half (352) were controlled outright by local government or improvement commissioners (table 3.1). Municipal control was even more common in large towns. A survey in 1887 of more than two hundred of the nation's largest towns found that only twenty of their town markets still had manorial owners, nine were owned by market companies or groups of trustees, and the remaining two hundred were owned by municipal governments.

There are some regional variations in these generalizations. In the south and the southwest of England, it was most common for the town rather than the local lord to hold the market charter. Of the ten towns with municipal borough status in Cornwall, for example, all but two held the town's market rights through ancient charter. Of these two, the borough of Bodmin purchased the town markets in 1815 and Launceton

Table 3.1 Market Owners in England and Wales in 1888 (Excluding London)	
Owner	Number of Markets
Local authorities	313
Trading companies	64
Private persons	274
Commissioners	39
Unclear	22
No owner	57
Total	769

Source: Royal Commission on Markets and Tolls, vol. 11, "Final Report," 18.

did the same in 1840, both through private acts of Parliament. Bodmin immediately built a new enclosed marketplace, and Launceton built two new market houses (at a cost of £8,000), one of which eventually became the town hall. In the north of England, however, towns did not usually own their market rights by charter. In West Riding, Yorkshire, for example, only the towns of Leeds, Doncaster, and Pontefract held their markets by charter, while the other dozen municipal boroughs had to undergo the costly and difficult process of acquiring their markets from the manorial lord. More than half of the parliamentary acts which gave specific towns the power to purchase their markets were for towns in the midlands and north of England.[9]

Market Commissioners and Parliamentary Legislation

Between the age of manorial ownership (at the end of the eighteenth century) and that of municipal ownership (the end of the nineteenth century) a third type of market ownership flourished, ownership by public commissions or, as they were variously called, "market trusts," "police commissions," or "improvement commissions." Their heyday was the early nineteenth century, and they demonstrate the same sort of reliance on self-regulation which marked much of nineteenth-century life. In 1888 thirty-nine of these were still in existence. Sometimes merchants who held the market rights would establish and run these commissions in order to protect their trade interests, but for the most part the commissions consisted of public-spirited citizens who were interested in enacting the kind of market reform town governments were unable or unwilling to. Ashton-under-Lyne had neither a market nor a private or public market owner; when the town's ratepayers demanded a marketplace, therefore, the commissioners of police obtained the necessary parliamentary permission (an act of 1828) to construct a market square and a market hall. In the colliery town of Houghton-Le-Spring, where the population had outstripped the food supply, the approach was even simpler. "Far-seeing and enterprising men" of the town stepped in and, without bothering with an act of Parliament, raised £2,600 through subscriptions to create a limited-liability company, which, in turn, built a new combination market and town hall.

Indeed, market commissions and trusts were sometimes the only means by which towns could wrest the market from its manorial owners. Before 1835 most towns did not have the legal power to purchase market rights, so reform-minded citizens and reform-minded town officials were forced to form quasi-private parochial commissions to purchase and operate the market as a trust on behalf of the town, sometimes taking the form of a market company. Glasgow's Bazaar was owned by a market trust, but it was managed by a committee of the town council. Some private, for-profit market companies were created to carry out market improvements, although the royal commissioners of 1888 found that public markets which were held by private stock companies were often badly managed and lacking in sanitary facilities. Tewkesbury's market house was erected by a market company to whom the corporation awarded toll rights for ninety-nine years, and in Salisbury and Aberdeen, marketing was recentralized in a new market hall financed and operated by a private company that had been established by reform-minded citizens.[10]

In a real sense, these improvement bodies harkened back to the days when guild and town council shared control of the town. From about 1750 many of the commissions were formed by way of private or "local" parliamentary bills. Somewhat similar to the local Poor Law Boards of Guardians, which were, in effect, surrogate municipal corporations, the commissions sought to provide such urban services as street lighting, paving, construction of town halls and markets, and, often, the management of markets as well. This system of control perpetuated the many-layered nature of civic administration endemic to most British towns and makes it difficult for us to make a clear distinction between the interests and the actions of individuals as private citizens, or as members of improvement commissions or trusts, as shareholders in a private company, or as public officials. In Crymmych, Wales, the subscribers to the new Crymmych Market Hall Company, which erected a combination market and public assembly hall, were three farmers, an auctioneer, a local squire, and two Crymmych shopkeepers; but in Leeds the Improvement Commission was made up of the borough magistrates and nineteen members elected by the vestry; and in Glasgow the Market Trust comprised members of the town council.

The starting point for much nineteenth-century market reform was locally initiated parliamentary action. From 1800 to 1883, market interests (town government, improvement commissioners, or the like) in 206 British towns initiated more than three hundred local acts of Parliament for the purpose of reforming a particular market. These reforms might entail building or financing a new market, rebuilding an old one, enlarging or otherwise altering a market, purchasing or leasing a market from a private owner, or improving the regulation of the market. More than half of these local acts of Parliament, which either supplemented, amended, or replaced the towns' ancient market charter, gave towns new regulatory and borrowing powers. No less than three hundred local improvement commissions were set up as extralegal bodies whose overview of the public welfare continued well into the latter part of the century, when central (that is, national) legislation (through Local Government acts, Food and Drug acts, and Public Health acts) facilitated local government purchase and regulation of markets. About one in four English markets passed from private to public ownership during this period—and most of these transfers were costly. Darlington, for example, paid the Bishop of Durham £7,854 for the town's markets, Newport paid the Duke of Beaufort £16,500, and Oldham put up £10,652 for the acquisition of Oldham's markets. By 1900 few of the large markets were in private hands.[11]

This legislation also allowed market reformers to carry out important urban spatial rearrangements. More than a quarter of the local improvement acts made it possible for a town to remove its market from the marketplace, street, or market house, and erect a new marketplace or building. In Bognor Regis, for example, an 1822 act of Parliament created a "Board of Commissioners for the Improvement of the Town of Bognor." This body was given authority, among other things, to establish a new market, improve and repair roads, remove obstructing carts and carriages from the roadways, prevent nuisances on the footpath, and provide a pound for straying cattle. In Aberdeen a magnificent (and costly) new market hall was built in 1840-42 as part of an urban redevelopment and reconstruction scheme that was carried out without encouragement of the town council by a group of citizens who had formed themselves into a town improvement company by an act of Parliament in 1838. About the same time another act allowed the town of Cardiff to remove its market from the marketplace, and in Maidstone a corporation committee to investigate the state of the borough's markets led to an 1825 act which gave the town permission to borrow £14,000 to build a new market, remove the old market, and place administrative authority in the hands of a new markets committee. In Taunton an act of Parliament gave twenty-five trustees (two-thirds from the town and one-third being "gentlemen in the neighborhood") the right to purchase and operate the market—and to apply market profits to educating, clothing, and apprenticing children of the poor.[12]

The Municipal Reform Act of 1835 dramatically changed the direction of market reform. By opening the way for granting borough or "corporation" status to some 179 English and Welsh towns, this act, in effect, shifted control of the markets directly to local governments. The 1835 act was "permissive" legislation: it allowed towns to acquire a charter of incorporation, which in turn gave them new powers over the public markets. In so doing it allowed (but did not require) the improvement commissioners to transfer their powers to the new "corporations," as municipal governments were called. Although the 1835 act included only one new compulsory service (every incorporated town had to have a borough police force), it did mandate wider citizen participation in government and greater local initiative and control. As was said of Warrington, towns could now do something about their "fossilized appearance."[13]

A series of Public Health acts (1848, 1875) had somewhat the same effect. These gave local governments expanded powers in many areas, including the public market. About the same time, through the Markets and Fairs Clauses Act (1847), towns acquired greater independent powers to purchase, regulate, and operate their markets. Most important, perhaps, were the Local Government acts (1858, 1875), which enabled many towns to purchase market rights more easily. All in all, these acts expanded the scope of municipal authority to "an appropriate level of civic response," as it was stated in the town of Darwen. The Local Government Act of 1858 and the Public Health Act of 1875, for instance, were particularly important in giving local authorities (local board of health, town council, or improvement commission-

ers) new powers—including the power to construct a market, purchase a market, and make market bylaws. They were even granted the right of compulsory land purchase for market purposes. But the act gave no right of compulsory purchase of the market itself. The 1847 Markets and Fairs Clauses Act (later revised and extended) reiterated the ancient right of the market owner to prohibit sales of certain articles outside the market or shops, made it the duty of the local authorities to provide proper weighing scales and facilities for commodities sold in the market, delineated the mode in which tolls could be collected, and so on.[14]

Most of this new legislation for markets was permissive rather than mandatory. As a result, the pace and character of market reform varied from town to town, for it was dependent upon the interests and resolve of local authorities. When Halifax achieved incorporation status in 1848, for example, it allowed the town to build a new market and purchase the market rights from the trustees, who had earlier purchased the market itself for the town from its manorial owner. Accrington, not yet an incorporated borough in 1868, built a new market in 1869 under the leadership of Samuel Dugdale, chairman of the Board of Health (fig. 3.1), through the authority granted it by the Board of Health and Local Government acts. Darlington had done the same several years earlier. It was the Markets and Fairs Clauses Act of 1847 which made it possible for citizens of Clevedon to petition the local board of health to get rid of street peddlers. In Huddersfield, where the Ramsden family had held the manorial charter since the time of Charles II, the anger of market sellers over poor conditions and that of the town citizens over the high cost of food forced the town in 1876 to purchase the market rights from Sir John Ramsden for the sum of £38,800—an amount which many considered extortionate on Sir John's part. Soon after this, the town constructed an enormous retail and wholesale market building at the cost of £31,000. Birmingham was an unincorporated town and hence did not have the legal status necessary to purchase the town's markets from their manorial owner. Nevertheless, because the markets were intolerably dirty and crowded, a local parliamentary act in 1769 gave an improvement group, the Birmingham Street Commissioners, the power to purchase the markets from the lord of the manor and to qualify (later) for the expanded market powers granted by the Public Health and Markets and Fairs Clauses acts. The commissioners, who passed ownership on to the town in 1854, carried on extensive market reforms, including removing stalls from the streets, clearing out the Bull Ring for a centralized general market, and erecting a vast market hall, which was opened in 1835.[15]

Not all towns fared as well. Grantham, in Lincolnshire, with its "tumble down" marketplace and dilapidated Butter Hall as the only covered market facility, received parliamentary permission to purchase its markets from its manorial owner in 1879, but the town council and the lord could not come to an agreement; as a last resort, the market trustees in 1887 leased out the market house. In Rochdale, in Lancashire, the town council used a parliamentary market reform act to improve the market by purchasing it from Lord Byron in 1823, but then did nothing until a private company took over and built a market hall in 1844. This private ownership was to the chagrin of marketgoers, who claimed that the new market hall offered only poor-quality goods and accommodations that were not up to the standards promised in the reform act.[16]

Market Ownership in Scotland

Only the largest Scottish towns follow the English pattern of construction of a "modern" central market hall to replace open-air marketing, and of these, two towns (Aberdeen and Dundee) acquired their market halls through private or market trust ownership, and two others (Glasgow and Edinburgh) eventually abandoned their once-thriving public retail markets because of their highly developed system of retail shops. Outside of Scotland's industrial Glasgow-Edinburgh belt and Aberdeen, most Scottish towns experienced a slower pace of commercialization. It appears that this is why the demands for market reform were fewer. It is also probable that open-air markets remained the norm in Scotland because they were traditionally better managed. As we have seen, in Scotland most municipalities or burghs had no manorial controls and thus could hold markets and fairs independent of the rights of the crown or a manorial or ecclesiastical landlord. In Glasgow, for example, the bishop's royal grant to hold markets had by the eighteenth century been absorbed by the town merchants. In some burghs, in fact, merchants held trade rights that extended to foreign trade.[17]

Generally then, most Scottish towns found it legally easier to undertake market management and regulation, even though Scotland lagged behind England and Wales in terms of national legislation. If Scottish towns met impediments in market reorganization they were due either to lack of funds or to the fact that (at least until 1846) the merchant elites (the burgesses or guild members) were able to exclude outsiders (such as country butchers)—and even some townsfolk—from carrying on trade within the town. Burgh trade rights often covered territory beyond the town and blocked the development of markets in distant hamlets and villages that did not have burgh status. Further, in addition to owning land within the town itself, many Scottish burghs owned grazing and tillage land (called common-good land) outside the town, along with the right to sell or collect rents from these lands. By these holdings the burgh was, in theory at least, able to raise funds to spend on public services; and it was through the common-good concept that many local governments took on an explicitly authoritative and protective role in "promoting the general advantage of the community," including the public market. Nevertheless, by the nineteenth century, many Scottish towns lacked sources of common-good funding while facing an increasing number of infrastructure demands. Dundee, with a population of more than 45,000 in 1831, was limited by law to spending a maximum of £4,000 for public services—paving, lighting, police, street cleaning, and markets. This was less than a quarter of what was called for. Not surprisingly, Dundee's sole market structure was a meal market (which also served as the town police office), and its marketplace was merely a number of stalls in a meadow. Dundee had to wait until 1881 for a modern market hall.[18]

In spite of the many developments favoring market reform, regardless of the market (English, Welsh, or Scottish), initiating reform was often a slow and costly process. For most of the period under consideration, markets held under a charter or by private owners could not be interfered with, even by a legislative procedure like a Public Health act. Chichester's Common Council decided in 1802 to centralize its markets by building a market house, but it took four years for the architect to be hired, and the new building did not open its doors for trading until January 1808. Carlisle had sought a new market in 1846 but abandoned its plans because the expense of pushing through a private act was too great. And in Harrogate a board of improvement commissioners, which had received statutory powers under an improvement act in 1841 to renovate the town markets, had to postpone building a market hall for thirty years because of popular fears of increased rates (that is, taxes).[19]

Tolls and Stallage

Whereas a market toll is the tax levied on products (or sometimes containers or transport devices from which products are sold) brought into the market for sale, stallage is a rental payment for the use of a portion of the market—commonly, a stall. From ancient days well into the early nineteenth century, a toll by weight, piece, or volume was commonly imposed on certain goods sold in the town. It was collected at the town gate, a bridge, or a tollbooth, or in the marketplace itself. Some markets had the right to charge both toll and stallage, as Manchester did until 1883.[20]

If the town charter was the historic symbol of town freedom, market tolls were often the historic reminder of oppression and corruption, and nearly every town has a story about toll collection to add to its folklore. Coventry's early nineteenth-century market, for example, was the scene of a wintertime altercation between the town's ruthless toll collector and a poor boy who stood shoeless in the marketplace with a bunch of holly for sale. When the boy could not pay the twopenny (2d) toll, the collector confiscated the holly, thereby becoming a symbol of cruel rigidity. The marketplace of the town of Stockport was the scene of demonstration of contempt by a disgruntled farmer, who showed his opposition to a new toll on saddlehorses by entering the market riding, in saddle, his cow (fig. 3.2). But it was the dissimilarities in tolls from town to town which probably generated the most criticism. In Birmingham in 1888, the toll on a whole carcass of meat was 1 shilling, 4 pence (1s4d), but in Chester it was double that. In Liverpool the toll on two carts of carrots was 3s, whereas in Manchester the same two carts would be charged 4s; likewise, for potatoes the charges would be 1s in Liverpool and 2s in Manchester. Stall fees in Stockport in 1875 were 1s9d per week, while in Halifax twenty years later the rental for shops varied between 5s and 8s per week.[21]

In the early nineteenth century, the citizens, or "freemen," in some towns paid smaller market rents than outsiders—as at Banbury, where stallholders who were town residents paid only half the rent charged to strangers. In Glasgow the town's burgesses were not liable to

3.2. "The Cheshire Farmers Policy or Pitt Outwitted" Stockport 1784

Farmer Thatcher rides his cow into the marketplace to protest a new toll on saddlehorses. Most local governments did their utmost to attract local farmers to the town market, but in this case, the government at Westminster, by taxing transportation, discouraged one link between farmers and the market.

pay a "ladle" (toll) on grain. Some towns charged market tolls more than once on the same goods as they passed from wholesaler to a succession of retailers in the same market. An observer in Manchester's market, for instance, noted that a toll of 4s was paid four times on the same rhubarb, making a total of 16s, whereas in Liverpool the vendor would have paid only 1s6d because the Liverpool market prohibited reselling within the market. In some towns the market tolls were sold or "let," sometimes by auction, to the highest bidder, in return for the toll collector's paying the rates and rents on the market and, in some instances, managing the market (fig. 3.3).[22]

It is doubtful, however, that excessive tolls were more than an isolated problem at any time in the nineteenth century. The most widespread abuse of tolls appears to have been collections on days that were not authorized by charter. Such would have been the case when a town extended its market days from, say, two days a week to five days a week and then collected tolls on the additional days. At Bridgwater, the daily market was authorized for only three days a week, but the market was actually open five, thus making the tolls on two of the days illegal. The market investigators of 1887-88 found that the amount of toll relative to price was very "meager," and although in some cases the tolls were proportionally higher on articles consumed by the poor, no compelling reason was put forth to eliminate market tolls and rents.[23]

In the nineteenth century, market tolls were increasingly regarded as a tax on daily sustenance and a restraint of local trade. As a result many tolls were abandoned altogether or simply converted into stall rental fees. From its creation in 1817, the Saturday market of Glasgow's enclosed Bazaar was free, while its daily market stalls let for £6-15 a year. To be sure, as soon as one market eliminated its tolls, others were under pressure to do likewise. It was said in the 1880s that Lancaster's continued toll charges led to a decline in its market because nearby towns, including Preston and Kendal, had earlier eliminated their toll charges. Lancaster's market authorities were persuaded to do likewise and create a "free market." Liverpool replaced its traditional tolls (called "ingates" and "outgates") with a new toll called "toll and stallage," which was in essence a rental fee based on surface space used in the market. Similarly, Bridgwater's market seems to have been fairly typical in its charges in that the "toll" was actually a mix of rental fees and volume charges (on baskets), rather than a charge on each item sold (tables 3.2 and 3.3).[24]

Table 3.2 Toll Charges, Bridgwater Market Hall, 1887	
Butcher's stall, per week, by size	8s-2s6d
Poultry market, table, per day	8d
Packing butter table	2d
Basket of eggs or butter	2d
Basket of live poultry	3d
Vegetables, standing room, market days	6d
Vegetables, standing room, other days	4d
Vegetables, single basket	2d
Fruit, standing room, market days	6d
Fruit, standing room, other days	4d
Fruit, single basket	2d
Fish, stall, per week	2s6d
Fish, stall, market day	10d
Fish, stall, other days	8d

Source: Royal Commission on Markets and Tolls, vol. 3, "Bridgwater."

Table 3.3 Toll and Stallage Charges, Liverpool Market, 1872	
By boxes (8 superficial feet)	2d
By baskets (8 superficial feet)	2d
By barrels (4 superficial feet)	2d
By carts (108 superficial feet)	1s6d
By sacks and bags (6 superficial feet)	2d
By small sieves (40 superficial feet)	1s0d
By large sieves (60 superficial feet)	1s8d
By skips or round hampers (12 superficial feet)	4d
By small crates (18 superficial feet)	6d
By large crates (24 superficial feet)	9d
By small hampers (3 superficial feet)	2d
By large hampers (4 superficial feet)	3d
By hogsheads (12 superficial feet)	6d
By tierces (9 superficial feet)	4d
By wagons (200 superficial feet)	2s6d
By carts of potatoes (80 superficial feet)	1s0d
By produce articles/things on ground (per superficial foot)	1/2d

Source: Liverpool Market's Committee Minutes, "Report on Manchester Markets," Report One, 25 March 1872, 173.

Because it is impossible to determine the volume of goods sold by particular vendors in the Bridgwater market, it is difficult to say whether Bridgwater's toll charges encouraged or discouraged trade—although it appears that the tolls listed in table 3.2 were slight compared to probable sales income. Bridgwater's market revenues at this time were averaging £800 per annum, some of which went to market upkeep and expenditure, and the rest to the borough fund. In Chard the toll on fruit was 1d per basket; on "manufactured goods," 1s6d per cart; on a vegetable cart, 6d; a covered cart was 9d. Liverpool's tolls were also assessed according to volume—largely in the form of charges per container, irrespective of actual product, although the charges appear to be higher than those at Chard.

Did market tolls and rents result in an increase in the cost of food? Liverpool's charges represented a minute portion of a basket of groceries for a working-class family. Although it was frequently asserted that unfair tolls led to unreasonable food prices, a parliamentary investigation found that tolls were so low that economies of scale and the competitive nature of the market more than compensated for the charges. On balance, food was still cheaper in the market than in the shops. At the same time, there is little dispute that many municipal corporations, some of which operated the largest and most progressive markets, made more profits on their markets than their capital outlay warranted. One government official complained that thirty-two of the country's largest markets were making excessive profits.[25]

Only a few cases can be found wherein market revenue was less than the amount needed for market construction. Generally, profits had become lavish by 1900. Indeed, in 1881, Huddersfield's market revenues were five times the amount spent on the market, and well into the twentieth century, towns boasted that the "handsome profits" brought in by the market would help reduce local taxes, or rates. Revenue from the Carlisle market in 1887 was twice that of market expenditure, and the profits went to reduction of rates; in Bolton the situation was similar: income was more than double market expenditure, and the market hall regularly paid £1,000 a year for the reduction of rates. In Reading in the late 1880s, market revenue was three times that of market expenditures, and a portion of the balance was applied to the rates. The Local Government Board estimated in 1887 that the sum of town council (and other urban authority) revenue from the market was £383,700; of this, £150,000 was actually spent for market purposes (administration, maintenance, and the like, but not new construction), making the profit on markets more than double the expenditure. A survey of forty major markets, all in the hands of local authorities, shows that revenue was nearly triple expenditure; the rate of return on capital investment was, on average, 5.72 percent.[26]

Nevertheless, in fairness to market authorities, it should be noted that most towns were prevented by law from banking market profits in escrow accounts for future improvements—hence, market profits had to be spent within the normal fiscal cycle of the town government. As a result, large capital expenditures, such as a new market, were only possible when the town borrowed money. The public market thus suffered from two public misconceptions: that it charged excessive tolls and that it cost too much to keep up. Further, "private" market companies appear to have made even greater profits. Cannock's Market Hall Company had first-year revenues of £227 and expenditures of £60, which allowed for a 10 percent return to investors and a reserve of £45—all in all, a healthy venture at a time when interest on loans for construction would have been about 3 percent.[27]

TRURO FAIRS AND MARKETS

To be LET, for ONE YEAR, from the First day of March next, the TOLLS and DUES arising from THE FAIRS AND MARKETS, *Of the Corporation of the Borough of Truro.*

Together with the SHOPS, STALLS, STANDINGS, and all other the Appurtenances thereto belonging, (save and except the Dues arising from Shows, Show-carts, and Caravans, which the council will keep under their own control).

The taker to pay for the supply of Gas to the market, together with all rates, taxes, and outgoings, to pay one month's rent in advance, and to find security for the due payment of the remainder by monthly instalments.

For the above purpose, Tenders in writing will be received by N. F. BASSETT, Esq., Mayor of the said Borough, on or before the hour of Noon, on FRIDAY, the 23rd day of February instant.

All further particulars may be known, and a form of the Lease seen, on application at the Office of Mr. GEO. NICOLLS SIMMONS, Town Clerk.

Truro, February 7th, 1844

3.3. NOTICE OF MARKET TOLLS TO BE SUBCONTRACTED BY THE TOWN GOVERNMENT TRURO MARKET 1844

PART TWO

THE ARCHITECTURE AND DESIGN OF THE PUBLIC MARKET

❧

GREAT EXPECTATIONS: MORAL ARCHITECTURE
AND SOCIAL PURPOSE

MARKET REFORM IN THE LATE EIGHTEENTH AND EARLY NINETEENTH CENTURIES was part of a revolution in both architectural form and the arrangement of public space. Unlike the twentieth-century shopping mall, the public market hall was planned as a feature of everyday urban life which went beyond commerce into the realm of human behavior and social values. If buying and selling were to be conducted in a respectable, orderly fashion, then people needed to be educated in the appropriate virtues; it was believed that the proper spatial arrangement and visual language of the market environment would serve as instructors in such moral lessons. For the Victorians, beauty, truth, and civic virtue were one. Architecture, which had always conveyed visual messages about the use of space, was now put to work identifying the acts of buying and selling as separate from the life and culture of the street. As a result, the street became a more private environment, and the public activity of marketing became more focused. For centuries the traditional open-air marketplace, with its occasional market house and its customary plethora of dirty wooden stalls, had stood only as the locus for commerce; it had not aspired to a higher purpose. In the rustic market scenes at Newcastle-upon-Tyne and Wokingham (figs. 4.1, 4.2) one can observe the straightforwardness of the old market, where market activity had no visual accoutrements but the street, the elements of nature, and the activities of the surrounding town; here the market was but one element of the streetscape—an extension of the street itself—as thoroughfare, meeting

4.1. THE OLD FLESH MARKET, NEWCASTLE, CA. 1800

This scene reminds us that at the beginning of the nineteenth century the traditional market was an integral part of the street—subject to street traffic, other town activities, and the vagaries of the weather.

place, and playground. Wokingham's market is typically "vernacular" in that it makes no pretense to a particular architectural style and is of old-fashioned construction and local materials. By 1837, however, Penzance's new, tall imposing granite Ionic market house (fig. 4.3) was presenting marketing as something both separate from the street and noble in its connection to civic responsibility. The new market building was designed to direct its users' attention away from the vulgarity of the streets and the uninspired and often depressingly ugly uniformity of the town. The aim of the architect of Hereford's Butter Market (fig. 4.4) was typical: he strove not to make the new market fit into the existing townscape but to make it stand out, to show that here in mundane Hereford was a place for lofty activities. Until that time, Hereford's marketing and other street activity had mingled in the open-air sixteenth-century market house located in the town square. With its distinctive 80-foot clock tower, the new market hall acted as an advertisement for the activities of the market as noble and well-ordered, worthy of an environment that is separate from those of the street. The public market had joined the church and the town hall as an idealized institution.

Accordingly, the dominant architectural rule in designing the façade of a market building was that the building should carry out this ideal. In spite of the frenetic atmosphere inside most market halls—quite similar to that of the old open-air markets—the visual message of the exterior was decidedly different. "We do not mean to say we can get the picturesque effects of the old markets of Shrewsbury, Salisbury, Peterborough, Leominster, Hereford, and other old towns," advised the *Building News* in 1878, "but we can do something to make them somewhat different from huge railway sheds and Crystal Palaces." Thus, the nineteenth-century forms that would later be venerated by the twentieth-century modernists—the utilitarian factory, the Crystal Palace, and other vernacular traditions in architecture—were not considered elevated enough for public buildings in the nineteenth century. Devonport's Italianate tower (fig. 4.5) was much more to the "modernist" taste of the nineteenth century than the so-called modernism that we now identify with the 1851 Crystal Palace. In a century in which rapid change and wide-scale emigration from the countryside left many city

4.2. MARKETPLACE AND GUILDHALL, WOKINGHAM, CA. 1800

The stocks and jail can be seen below the Guildhall. The girl in the cart holds a basket of chickens. Is she an early arrival for the 8 o'clock market?

4.3. Market House,
Penzance, 1837

4.4. Butter Market,
Hereford, 1860

dwellers with a feeling of rootlessness, utilitarian design was the problem, not the solution. Even Joseph Paxton, one of the creators of the Crystal Palace, believed that architectural ornamentation was not only essential but linked to improvement in moral character. Indeed, Leeds officials pulled down Paxton's enormous utilitarian glass-and-iron market hall partly because they desired a building of "a more picturesque design."[1]

Market Architecture and Aesthetic Theory

Until around the 1980s, because of its focus on historical style and decoration, Victorian architecture was widely regarded as ostentatious, ugly, and antithetical to function. The monumental but elegant stone Doric screen and portico which formed the exterior façade of George Dymond's Market Hall at Exeter (see fig. 5.30) has been dismissed as "deeply conservative" because the exterior design is unrelated to the marketing function of the space within; similarly, Alexander Clifton-Taylor complained of Ludlow's Market Hall (fig. 4.6) that "there is nothing that could be said in favour of its fiery brick or useless Elizabethan detail." But the Victorians saw architectural decoration as a way to dissociate life and work from the conditions—the grime, smoke, fumes, and gloom—that much industrial urban building conveyed and promoted. The people of the city, it was claimed, were being "shocked and choked" by "rude" and "crude" buildings. In short, the nineteenth-century city and city life needed beautification, and nearly every town "guide" promoted it. As late as 1907 one observer of the industrial town of Middlesbrough lamented that "there is no picture-gallery: indeed, there is not a picture anywhere that the ordinary public can go to see." Considering the centrality of the public market to both the geography and the life of the town, it is not surprising that one of the functions of the market hall was to be an "ornament to the town." Nor is it surprising that some towns, like Ludlow and Bradford, may have built market halls that were more elaborate and expensive than necessary for mere marketing. The truth of the matter was that many towns in the industrial north and midlands consisted of little but vast stretches of cheap housing standing alongside lines of factories surmounted by smokestacks. As a result, along with the railway station, the church, the town hall, and even the corner pub, the

4.5. MARKET HALL TOWER, DEVONPORT, 1854

4.6. Market and Town Hall, Ludlow, 1883
The hall was nicknamed "Ludlow's bad luck" because of its "obtrusively prominent" style, but a more sympathetic evaluation would take into consideration the fact that its florid design was intended to elevate buying and selling to a moral and behavioral level above that of the street market it replaced.

market hall came to be one of the few visual delights of a town and a way of promoting a new sort of connectedness to place and society among city dwellers dismayed by the increasingly impersonal nature of urban life. This was the case in the textile town of Huddersfield, where the imposing clock tower, turreted façade, and the great entry gate of the market hall of 1880 acted as a refreshing antidote to what was regarded to be the "dull form" of the town (fig 4.7).[2]

Market reformers were well aware that the rapid growth of towns had raised many questions about population control; furthermore, during the first half of the nineteenth century many middle- and upper-class families believed that the poor and working classes were their natural enemies, with whom they might have to fight for their property. During the 1820s and 1830s rioting and popular disturbances were rife in towns and agricultural villages throughout England; the Chartist years of 1837 through the 1840s brought "unusual turbulence," as Britain faced bread riots, violent strikes, worker demonstrations, and the threat of working-class revolution—all at the time when police protection was almost nonexistent. In this atmosphere, architecture became a commonly understood language of municipal reform and civic virtue, a visual link between prevailing social-economic and political thought and the physical environment. The function of architecture, argued George Godwin, the editor of *The Builder* magazine, was to build "social bridges" that would break down class barriers and create a common culture and a common set of behavioral norms. Godwin was reflecting popular thought. The market hall as an architectural language went beyond merely providing escape from the ugliness of industrialization. The links between architecture, social order, and social improvement were considered almost divinely ordered by generations of men and women after the industrial and political revolutions that began in the late eighteenth century. Perhaps more than any of the new building types of the nineteenth century, the market hall was the manifestation of a popular new aesthetic theory of "associational" or "social" functionalism that linked social ideals to architecture. Taking a didactic view of public space, the Victorians declared that aesthetic form must follow social function. This theory rested further on the notion that architecture—through the design of better housing, better schools, and the like—should be a primary agent of social reform and moral improvement. The organization of space, the invention of interior and exterior ornamentation, and the erection of special structures for specific functions would lessen the threat of social upheaval, reduce the antagonism between classes, and improve the physical well-being of all.[3]

The key to this social and spatial functionalism was the aesthetic principle of "association." This was based on the Enlightenment idea that architecture, art, and design are agents that excite and stimulate our minds because of the associations we make between the object viewed and the values the object represents in our memory. Applied design, whether of building, chair, or flower vase, serves as a chain of connection for the internalization of a universally accepted social code. In short, architecture is a visible language. As the Scottish writer on architecture John Loudon stated, "The mere circumstance of familiarizing the mind with orderly arrangements, regular features, [and] symmetry . . . either in building, in furniture, or in gardens, must have an influence on conduct. Order is the fundamental principle of all morals: for what is immorality but a disturbance of the order of civilized society?" Or, as an observer of Bolton's new market hall, which he considered the town's finest architectural ornament, claimed, the level of "architectural displays" that adorn the town can be regarded as "an index of the intellectual and sound status of their inhabitants."[4]

This idea of treating architecture as a language or mirror that draws on the past to create a new form was considered forward-looking and "modern." One component of this "modernism" was embellishment: of ornamentation, texts, and sculpture, all of which made reference to certain values and ideas, many rooted in history. Designers of buildings, interior spaces, and objects were encouraged to search the past for an analogue to the present in order to counteract the "element of decay" in society. One of Glasgow's leading architects, Charles Wilson, argued that "modern architecture" must take its lessons from the Italians, who, by "covering their buildings with commemorative work of sculpture and painting taught the Italian [the] truths of his religion and the greatness of his country." "Nothing," noted an observer of market design, "can be truer than the assertion that human beings inevitably become assimilated to their material surroundings." Thus while market reform often meant

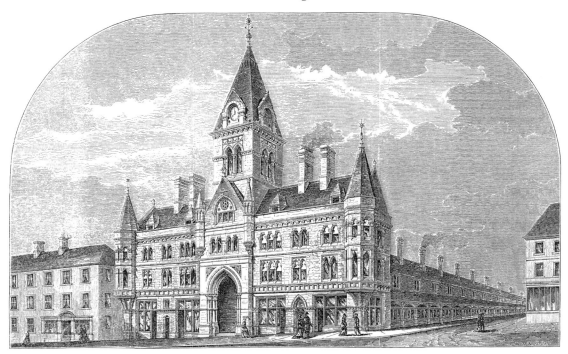

4.7. MARKET HALL, HUDDERSFIELD, 1880

The architect, Edward Hughes, served in the office of Sir George Gilbert Scott (the most prolific of the mid-nineteenth-century Gothic revivalists) for twelve years. Built in what was called "domestic Gothic" style, this hall was designed to counteract the utilitarian nature of the town's visual landscape. The building was of stone, with a green slate roof, ornamented capitals holding up corner turrets, finely carved finials, and a carved string course around the lower portion. The first covered market in Huddersfield's history, it was regarded as "in every respect substantial and good" by the *Huddersfield Weekly News* (3 Apr. 1880).

pulling down ancient (and very often vernacular) buildings and perhaps even destroying the ancient marketplace, great efforts were made to connect the new market building with local, national, and even ancient history, literature, and art. Many markets sought to sell themselves proponents of a modern intellectual viewpoint by carrying the ancient symbols that were the latest fashion in the Victorian world. Exterior sculpture was particularly well-suited to the expression of these views and—typical of the Victorians—to the glorification of work. A popular subject was Ceres, the Roman goddess of cereals and the harvest, who was often placed above the doors of the market hall. On the front of Manchester's fish market were figures that illustrated various aspects of the fishermen's and fish merchants' trades. The pediment over the principal entrance of the new market hall at Burton-on-Trent contained a sculptured panel showing King John granting an abbot a charter

4.8. MARKET HALL, SOUTHPORT, 1881

Stallholders in masquerade costumes at the opening of the new market hall.

to hold a market at Burton, thus giving the new market and its users ties with a romantic past, a degree of respectability and validation, and an unspoken lesson in social and class deference. In Southport, "an exceedingly picturesque and animating" opening day of the new market hall was marked by appearance of the stallholders attired in "old English" costumes— the very kind of activity which similarly encouraged the preservation of class deference" (fig. 4.8). In Gloucester the motto over the new market, "The earth is the Lord's, and the fullness thereof," was thought to be "highly appropriate," and the beautiful but intimidating interior of Bethnal Green's Columbia Market featured the Ten Commandments inscribed on the walls. The inscription on the exterior façade of the Trowbridge Market Hall was even more to the point: "A false Balance is Abomination to the Lord." In Blackburn the connection between the market's past and present was marked with a poem, "The Rise of Blackburn Market," which suggested in the manner of heroic poetry that the idea for a new covered market had begun in the deep past:

> First let me sing the latent plan,
>   How to supply the wants of man,
> Some few there were, a native clan,
>   Who with prophetic strains began,
> Long since, with logic deep and sound,
>   To argue forth to all around—
> That there need be upon the ground
>   A neatly Covered Market

Thus the new, orderly, civilized marketplace became the perfect testing ground for a visual language which would liberate the people from the sordidness of street life. This use of architecture to link past virtue with present social goals explains why Victorian market hall design was expected to go beyond mere utilitarian form—it had to supply "something to elevate its citizens," as was said of the Carlisle market hall. Like Scarborough's market hall, the building was to be "a great educational process," of more importance to the working classes than the Mechanics' Institutes. In Bolton the opening of the new market was seen as an agent in the "moral regulation" of the borough. Indeed, many middle-class people were dubious about the morals of working men and women, a category that encompassed everything from religious duty to social behavior and even consumption habits. Buying from the street costermonger, despite the low price of the goods, was seen as an unwanted exposure to bad language and habits as well as to the wrong sort of people (particularly the Irish). Some middle-class families feared that the absence of public markets would drive the "less fortunate" to the cooperative stores, where, it was presumed, they could pick up revolutionary political ideas. People had to be taught what they ought to desire. Working-class people were viewed as vulnerable to indulgence and luxurious living on payday—"buying dear and rare articles at the Market for a Sunday's dinner"—and thus likely to be impoverished the rest of the week. As an ironmaster put it in 1835: "The great evil with colliers is, they overstimulate themselves by their irregular habits of living: after having received their wages, which is once a fortnight, they live on the fat of the land for the next three or four days, and during the remainder are obliged to starve themselves. With many it's either a feast or a fast."[5]

Like a classroom, the market hall could educate the populace in the new rules of accepted public manners, promote more prudent and acceptable habits of consumption, and protect both buyer and seller from the most offensive kind of lower-class street culture and people, including the town "roughs," who often made the old market their home. These young men and women were described as pouring into the Oldham market "by the hundreds," using foul language, throwing stones, and "rushing and pushing." The market hall could also protect consumers from some of the "temptations" of the traditional market, such as the necessity of conducting business in public houses because of inadequate market facilities. Typically, for example, "crying of fish" or other articles for sales was banned; in the new Dundee market hall, no rude language was allowed, no persons under the influence of drink permitted to enter, and no shouting by sellers tolerated. Likewise, the market hall in Reading was thought to be a means of controlling "these fish people who seem to be allowed to do anything they like." Middle-class Victorians believed that "by strict adherence to these rules, order and decorum can be easily maintained, and the quiet and respectable members of the community can visit the market without the risk of having their feelings shocked by vulgar and profane language." Better facilities would bring an end to the bad language and quarreling of the women in Manchester's market. Buying and selling had been elevated from an activity of the streets to an institution comparable to those of religion and government.[6]

Indeed, the designing and redesigning of markets was frequently associated with the protection of women. One cynical observer of the unreformed open-air market in Manchester criticized the town's male elite who, from their lounge chairs in the magnificent Exchange building, would watch their wives "patiently trudging, or rather struggling through the mud" of the old market, and standing under dripping stalls and umbrellas "entangled in the inextricable confusion which has for a century or more distinguished this busy scene." With a proper market building, town councillors no longer need listen to complaints that respectable females had to wash themselves after shopping in the public market. The day had come when respectable women could shop in the market without being subject to crude and vulgar street people and the dangers of street traffic. The female farm vendors would benefit as well as the urban housewives. During the winter months, before the erection of Barnstaple's vast market hall, some 350 farm women traveled five or six miles to the town each Friday to sell their eggs, butter, poultry, fruit, and vegetables in the wind- and rain-swept streets. They had no shelter but cloak and umbrella, under which they served a waiting army of some 1,200 townswomen "whose weaker frames and constitutions [had to] be protected" from such a "barbarous, unbecoming, and perilous exposure." The new market hall might be aimed at helping the one, but the other would also find shelter.[7]

The Market as an Agent of Class Unity and Civic Virtue

The market hall, as both architectural and social marvel, was also viewed as an agent for the promotion of class unity—a way of harmonizing the classes or, perhaps more accurately, of lifting the lower classes to the cultural and behavioral level of the middle class. Hence the market was often spoken of as a factor in helping the town become a "happy family." The market hall was projected as a place where people of all classes could come together and thus, as an antidote to the general nineteenth-century urban tendency toward class segregation. It was believed that the "greatness and glory" of the ruling classes "rested upon the happiness of those beneath them" and that market reform was a way for town government to protect the poor "against the fraud and deceit which otherwise be so effectively practiced upon them." The Leeds markets committee expressed the same sentiment when it noted the need for "protecting the inhabitants of this borough, as especially the working classes, from fraud and deficient weight."[8]

4.9. LAYING THE FOUNDATION STONE FOR THE MARKET HALL, HARROGATE, 28 FEBRUARY 1874

The chairman of the Harrogate Improvement Commissioners, John Barber, is in the center; the architect, Arthur Hiscoe, at front left.

More important, the quality of the public market was often considered a visual proof of the town's "honourable reputation." The public market was a measure of the town's progressiveness, independence, and economic self-sufficiency, a test of the town's responsiveness to the needs of its citizens. In this sense the reformed market was seen as being the demonstration of the "improving" civic spirit of a rich and increasingly powerful urban middle class. This spirit is captured in the faces of the townsmen laying the foundation stone for the new market hall at Harrogate in 1874 (fig. 4.9). As elsewhere, the Harrogate market warranted great public fanfare. Indeed, working-class people everywhere saw the market hall as a boon and did not hesitate to translate their pleasure into political payoff: the mayor who built the market hall could consider it a political asset.[9]

Indeed, the condition of the market was an important issue in local elections. In this sense, market reform was tied to the steady drift toward "municipalization," a process that improved

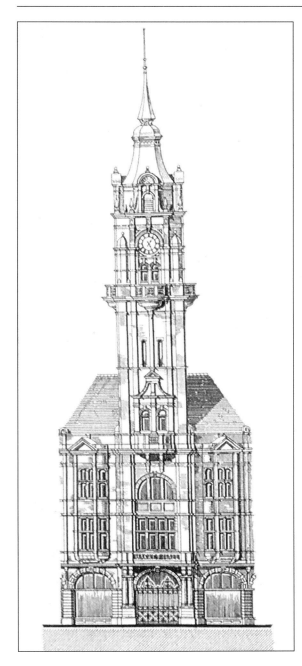

life in many nineteenth-century towns. It was based on the idea, perhaps best worked out in Birmingham and Glasgow, that it was the duty of the town government or corporation not only to provide adequate public services, such as water, sanitation facilities, public transport, and parks, but also to raise the living standards of the lower classes by providing for slum clearance and publicly financed low-cost housing, public baths, and public markets. Municipal services became a measure of a town's progressiveness. The corporation, many believed, should be the benevolent parent whose duty it was to provide a market hall for his children. One of Durham's citizens observed of that town that "when a stranger . . . passes through its narrow streets and looks up its dirty lanes—when he enquires what has been done for the good of the mass of the people . . . where is the market-place? . . . and when he sees this wretched corner wherein the people are crowded together without shelter—without space—without accommodation of any sort, he turns away in pity and disgust."[10]

This emphasis on civic reform and civic virtue increased after about 1835, as more and more towns achieved borough status—which made local reform initiatives more achievable. Certainly, the spirit of improvement was contagious. "To have a town like Warrington without a covered market was worthy of barbarous times" commented its mayor. "Warrington was behind the age, and in that and other respects had begun to assume a fossilized appearance in the midst of other towns of Lancashire." This connection was made over and over again in nineteenth-century Britain. In Manchester it

4.10. MARKET HALL, GOOLE, 1894
Tower and principal entrance of the winner in the design competition.

was said that "of all the public places in Manchester there are none so disgracefully inconsistent with its population and importance as the Market Place." Darwen's citizens were told that their new market would stop the ridiculous practice of importing food that could be grown locally, and Blackburn boasted that it had a market hall "unequalled by any market house in Lancashire" and one which "confers a brilliant era in the progress of the public spirit of the inhabitants of Blackburn." "Almost every town of any pretensions has its market and arcade" reported the *Dundee Advertiser* in 1872—a notion, no doubt, in the minds of Darwen officials when they substituted a plan for a new town hall with that of a new market hall. One Launceton citizen lamented that "some of us wish to remove the [old] market house [because] we think in such an age as this, when towns are making such improvements, it is time that such as that should be removed altogether." And as the chairman of the Salisbury market company put it in 1859: "Look, for instance, at what has been going forward throughout this county.

You see at Chippenham, at Devizes, at Swindon, at Warminster, that great market conveniences have been afforded, and was it for Salisbury, the capital of the Southern Division of the County, to hold back?" That Barnstaple, which prided itself on being the "Metropolis of North Devon," should not have a covered market was considered by its reformers a contradiction that would be difficult to explain—particularly since covered markets had long been conspicuous in most other towns in the north of Devon.[11]

Hence the market hall became a way to measure one town against another, and towns like Goole competed with one another in building grander, larger, and more elegant market halls than the last (fig. 4.10). Worcester's new 233-foot-long market hall was "almost a copy of the Crystal Palace," with a glass roof supported by hollow cast-iron pillars which conveyed the rainwater from the roof to the drains and which "vied with any other of its size in the kingdom—for elegance of design and accommodation." When Trowbridge citizens complained that the town was not keeping up with neighboring Frome, the lord of the manor erected a new market hall, and at Accrington it was believed that the town's new market hall ("a work of art to look upon") proved that the town deserved to be elevated to a parliamentary borough. In Carlisle it was urged that the town have buildings "suitable to the dignity and the position of Carlisle among the cities of England"; and in Truro the new market hall was offered as proof that Truro was entitled to become the new ecclesiastical seat of Cornwall.[12]

The Celebration of Virtue

Few public celebrations could match that of the opening of the town's new market hall—and this celebration was very much in keeping with the building's architectural language: both set the proper moral tone for the users of the market and placed it within a new landscape of civic virtue. The opening of Middleton's new market was marked by a commemorative jug bearing an illustration of the market, together with the date and an inscription which read "While the Rich are deliciously fed / May the Poor of this Town ne'er want bread" (fig. 4.11). Darwen's town council persuaded the tradesmen and mill owners to grant a one-day holiday for the workers on the opening day of the new market hall. In Darwen and elsewhere, market openings were marked by huge public spectacles: the town would be decked out with flags and streamers, a great procession of dignitaries, merchants, and schoolchildren would parade to the new hall, and long speeches would celebrate the town's dedication to progressive reform. Free entertainment of some sort was usually provided—a band concert or even acrobatic display inside the new building, huge public dinners for prominent townsmen and construction workers, and often an evening of further concerts and fireworks. The opening of the market hall at Batley was celebrated with four bands in performance. Like the building itself, the opening ceremonies were planned to have a culturally uplifting and edifying impact on the populace, as well as to remind them that the new market was a symbol of the wisdom and paternal care of their governors. The Halifax Borough Market Hall was opened in 1896 by the Duke and Duchess of York, thereby not only adding glamour to the occasion but initiating the market with a heavy dose of class consciousness. What better way to celebrate the end of the vulgar cries of the fisherwomen than with respectable conversation and uplifting music? The opening of the Derby market hall centered on a grand production of Handel's *Messiah* in the hall itself, performed by a band, a chorus of six hundred, and "a powerful and effective organ" (fig. 4.12). The inauguration of the new market hall at Aberystwyth in 1870 included "one of those choral gatherings peculiar to Wales," at which between three and four thousand persons were present. Accrington's gigantic new market hall had opened in the previous year with the town mills being stopped at noon, after which came a street procession containing two bands and 6,000 school children, followed by two concerts and a free dinner for 1,300 of the town's elderly population. An evening "grand concert" featured seven "artistes" performing such pieces as "Maid of Athens," "The Death of Nelson," and "Ye Banks

4.11. COMMEMORATIVE
JUG, OPENING OF
MIDDLETON MARKET,
1791
The market was built for the
town by Lord Suffield.

and Braes o' Bonny Doon": "A platform had been erected at the back part of the interior, and
in front were placed the reserved seats, whilst at the sides were the first seats. Both these and
the gallery were filled by a large and respectable audience. The interior was in a great measure painted, and the decorations, especially above the gallery, presented an Egyptian appearance, that was very pleasing to the beholder. Gaslights were formed into devices, such as Prince
of Wales' feathers . . . and placed in various parts of the building; and these together with the
gas jets, finely illuminated the hall."[13]

   Some of this tradition of performing edifying music in the market hall continued as the
hall was opened to its ordinary business of buying and selling. Saturday-night shoppers in
Torquay's market hall in 1902 were accompanied by the music of the town's Italian Band;

4.12. BROADSIDE
ANNOUNCING THE
OPENING OF THE DERBY
MARKET HALL, MAY 1866
In a manner somewhat
reminiscent of the opening
of the Crystal Palace in
London's Hyde Park fifteen
years earlier, this performance of Handel's *Messiah*
launched a new age of
marketing in Derby on both
a democratic and an elevated
moral note. The entire town
population was encouraged
to attend, and special trains
were arranged to bring
observers, at half fare, from
Birmingham, Sheffield, and
elsewhere.

and in the Halifax market hall, crowds as large as 5,000 were drawn to the Wednesday-evening band concerts—all while the market was open for business.[14]

Most opening celebrations included long speeches of self-congratulation mixed with moral homilies, often as part of the "public" ceremony but equally frequent as a part of an elaborate male-only dinner that took place in the market hall that evening. In attendance would be the mayor and the town officials, the town clergy, members of Parliament, local gentry, and military officials. Occasionally, women were allowed to observe from a nearby gallery. The dinners featured seemingly endless toasting, mixed with extemporaneous and often highly didactic speeches describing the moral and physical benefits to be accrued from the new market—speeches which would be repeated verbatim in the local press. The enthusiastic audience of this spectacle was entertained not only by a number of popular singers but also by a public reading of the market rules. Not all celebrations marking the opening of a new market were so respectable. The opening of the new hall at Torquay was accompanied by a dinner for 1,200 men which erupted in such drinking and toasting that the Grand Duchess Marie of Russia, one of the observers allowed to watch from a specially constructed gallery, was so overcome with amusement that she had to receive medical attention.[15]

As an economic institution, then, the public market hall acquired what was in the nineteenth century a strikingly modern non-economic function—a language of personal morality and civic virtue. As will be seen in the next chapter, this was applied with great enthusiasm to the planning and design of the building itself.

❧

MARKET HALL ARCHITECTURE:
TYPOLOGY AND DESIGN

SOON AFTER THE 1851 ERECTION OF THE GREAT CRYSTAL PALACE EXHIBITION
hall in Hyde Park (fig. 5.1), a nervous writer to *The Builder* warned of the dangers of following the Crystal Palace example: "Londoners! Look after your open spaces and squares, and
do not readily allow them to be covered." In

retrospect, considering the nineteenth-century disposition to fill all available urban
space with buildings, this worry about the
impact of urban redevelopment on the
town's open spaces was fully warranted. In
two important ways, however, the oracle
misdirected his admonition: first, it was not
London but the provincial cities and towns
which would most strenuously embrace the
iron-and-glass concept of enclosed public
space; and, second, the process of covering
public outdoor market space was well under
way by the time the Crystal Palace was both
enrapturing and appalling the British public. Market halls were the earliest of the public structures created in the new industrial-

5.1. THE CRYSTAL PALACE,
LONDON, 1851

urban world of railway stations, hotels, and office blocks, and their designers experimented
with glass and iron long before the Crystal Palace was conceived.[1]

Rethinking the Traditional Market House-Town Hall, 1750-1820

For many British towns in the late eighteenth and early nineteenth century, social disorder
and economic growth necessitated a reorganization of urban space. Often the first step toward such spatial reorganization was the modernization of the traditional mixed-use market house-town hall. Like the half-timbered market house at Wymondham (fig. 5.2), built
around 1550, these structures often appeared to be as old as the town itself and, in fact, played
a dual role in municipal life. As a market house, the building addressed the problems of street

disorder and food distribution; as a town
hall, it embodied public order and civic
pride. But the market space was generally
not used for marketing as such but rather for
administrative functions like weighing
goods, collecting tolls, and settling accounts, and it could accommodate only a
few sellers at a time. Much space was given
over to such civic activities as court, school,
and jail. Specific areas for the performance
of these tasks were always defined; but

5.2. MARKET CROSS,
WYMONDHAM, CA. 1550

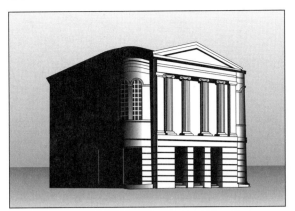

5.3. MARKET HOUSE-
TOWN HALL,
LUTTERWORTH, 1836

5.4. MARKET HOUSE-
TOWN HALL, YEOVIL,
1849

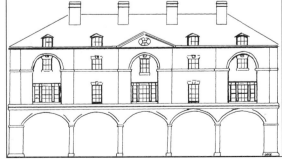

5.5. MARKET HOUSE,
IRONBRIDGE, CA. 1790

spaces might serve one function at one time of the day or week and another at others.

In the eighteenth century the requirements of civic administration and marketing became more complex, and activities that could once have been managed in a single space were increasingly split into two larger, distinctly separate spaces. The market portion of the building was used more often for buying and selling in addition to administration, even though the enlarged building retained its basic traditional form: a two-story structure, with the town meeting rooms (including a courtroom perhaps, and a civic hall or assembly rooms) above, and the market space (often an arcaded open space) below. But with the town offices above, the market portion of the building usually remained dark and limited in size, and generally one or more sides were exposed to the weather. Only a few of the mixed-use structures were large enough to accommodate the entire market, and those exceptions were designed primarily as markets with town offices of a sort as subordinate appendages. More often, the mixed-use market house-town hall functioned more as town hall than market.

Hundreds of these reborn mixed-use structures were built between 1750 and 1850. They generally made a distinct emotional appeal because of their picturesque architectural language, such as the solid and imposing ashlar face of the market house-town hall at Lutterworth in 1836 (fig. 5.3), the one at Yeovil in 1849 (fig. 5.4), and the one at Ashbourne in 1851. Structures like these, with their urban classical manner, stood in strong contrast to their shabby vernacular predecessors of wood and brick. In some cases, marketing lost out to other uses. Petworth's dignified but plain stone market house of 1793 originally had open lower arches for the space allotted to marketing, but these were soon closed and the space used as a subscription reading room and working-men's institute. Ironbridge converted its open arched space to shops (fig. 5.5), while at Horsham the lower arches of the market house were boarded up so that the building could accommodate the county assize courts.[2]

The Enclosed Market, Precursor to the Market Hall

By 1820, the overwhelming trend was toward fully enclosing the market in a walled and sometimes roofed structure. The origins of the enclosed-market concept lay in a complex amalgam of social imperative and architectural precedent. Responding to pressing contemporary requirements for market reform, architects and civic authorities abandoned the mixed-use market house-town hall structure and sought inspiration from the past, looking to such spatial concepts as the classical agora and temple, the renaissance piazza, the middle-eastern bazaar (which fascinated the British in the early years of the nineteenth century), and the late eighteenth-century French glass-covered arcade. Early nineteenth-century contemporary examples based on these concepts can best be viewed as three types: the circular market, the agora market, and the arcade market.

THE CIRCULAR MARKET. The first modern enclosed-market type was a roofed circular or octagonal structure. At first open-sided, this form evolved out of the old market cross, which over time had become a functional covered marketing space, having outgrown its earlier role of legal and moral stanchion. In 1756 Doncaster built open-sided and roofed butter cross

5.6. BUTTER MARKET AND
SHAMBLES, DONCASTER,
1756

5.7. FISH MARKET,
NEWCASTLE, 1829

The Fish Market, designed
by John Dobson, is the half-
circle and open colonnade
appendage to the Guild Hall.

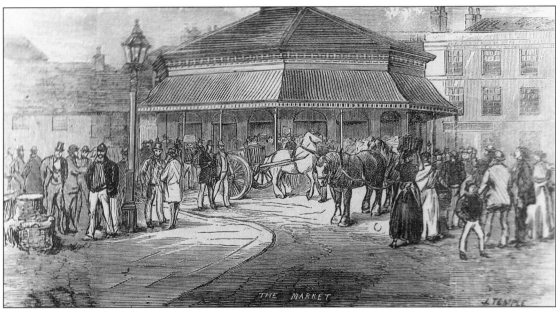

5.8. FISH MARKET,
HASTINGS, 1870

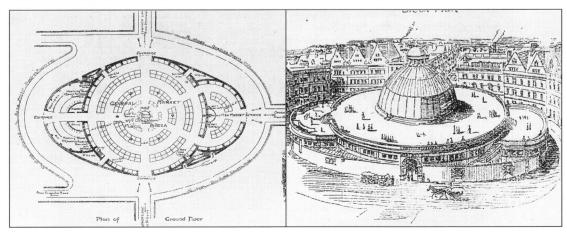

5.9. PROPOSAL FOR
LEATHER LANE MARKET,
HOLBORN, LONDON, 1893

and shambles markets in the Roman Doric manner (topped off with a very proper lantern), intended for use by farm women selling dairy products (fig. 5.6). Here the civic planners of Doncaster breathed modern life into archaic architectural forms. Godalming built something similar in 1814, as did Chagford in 1862; architect John Dobson's ingenuous use of a circular range of Doric columns for the Newcastle fish market in 1823 (fig. 5.7) looked quite different from Hastings's fish market (fig. 5.8) of half a century later, but in reality the two structures share the same form. These circular or multisided markets were usually low in height, relatively small, and built to fit into a former open-market site. The Swindon market, in the Gothic style, was considerably larger. With its hexagonal, 40-feet-in-diameter roof, thirty-two interior shops, and central fountain, it attracted considerable attention, as did several idealistic late nineteenth-century schemes which posited circular markets (in one case with roof gardens) as a means to improve the slum neighborhoods in London's East End (fig. 5.9). In practical terms, however, circular markets were valued mostly as historical messengers, offering proof that the town and its people valued their classical or Gothic heritage. The circular form was simply not expandable enough to be functional, and those buildings large enough to meet the demands of burgeoning urban populations were ill-suited for most market sites. An exception was the elegant modern circular market constructed at Bridgwater in 1830 (fig. 5.10). But even there the large circular Ionic portico of Bath stone, with its dome and lantern, did not constitute the entire market space but rather served largely as an entrance to the main market, enclosed in a large rectangular hall set behind. This market entrance provided a symbolic link to the past.

THE AGORA OR LOGGIA MARKET TYPE. Equally common, particularly in the early nineteenth century, was the agora market type, which would not have appeared out of place in the ancient world or in Renaissance Italy as an enclosed piazza, and which gave a historical, even mythic, meaning to the rapidly changing city. Copied from the open agora of the ancient Greeks, with its "peristylium" or multisided colonnade or loggia, and not unlike the forums found in most late republic Roman towns, these temples of commerce used the central courtyard as a general market and the loggia for permanent stalls or even shops. Such classically inspired civic architecture was accomplished, somewhat awkwardly, at Dewsbury in 1826 (fig. 5.11), where a "modern" version of the temple-cum-cross was placed atop a series of enclosed market stalls. In some cases the courtyard was partially or wholly covered.

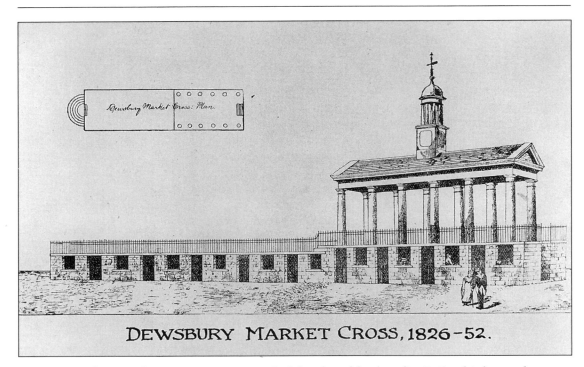

Dewsbury Market Cross: Plan

DEWSBURY MARKET CROSS, 1826-52.

5.11. MARKET CROSS,
DEWSBURY, 1826

Doncaster's long and narrow Roman temple-like shambles (see fig. 5.6), which stood next to its octagonal butter market, is a good expression of the form. Built in 1756, the colonnaded building was originally open-sided, but demands for an enclosed space led to the openings being filled in with brick in 1780. Worcester's new market of 1804 had an arched stone entrance, with Tuscan pillars supporting a paneled entabulature on each side under which were smaller entrances—all leading to an open market interior. This same piazza concept was also carried out with considerable rustic charm at Dartmouth in 1828 (fig. 5.12); here a market house is situated in the middle of an open court, surrounded by a colonnaded and covered

5.12. MARKET HALL,
DARTMOUTH, 1828

A view of the covered loggia
from the interior court.

5.13. ROTUNDA MARKET,
TORQUAY, 1820

loggia. In Torquay the circular and agora types meld in its famous Rotunda Market of 1820 (fig. 5.13), a partially covered colonnaded market with an open courtyard for marketing that presented a rustic and picturesque scene. A portion of this structure stands today.

The markets at Stamford, Ipswich, Tewkesbury (see fig. 2.14), and Chichester are more sophisticated examples of the type, in that the agora is larger, more enclosed, and returns to the ancient covered temple for its organization and exterior form. A colonnaded portico provided entrance to a partially roofed enclosure, and the portico was often flanked by two wings. The celebrated architect John Nash built two such markets, one at Abergavenny (1796, rebuilt in 1826) and another at Chichester (1808). The Chichester market still stands as a simple and dignified façade nearly 50 feet in width, featuring six Doric columns which support a classical entabulature (fig. 5.14). A balustrade ran above the entabulature and linked

5.14. MARKET HALL,
CHICHESTER, 1808

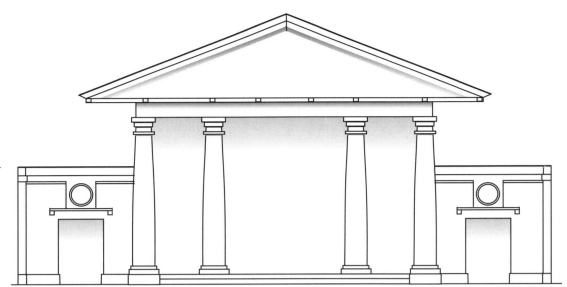

5.15. STAMFORD MARKET ENTRANCE PORTICO, 1808

the portico to the pair of slightly projecting wings. Advanced for its time, the building was divided into three sections: an open market space, closed shops, and a fish market. The shops, with wood-paneled interiors and brick floors, could be locked. The wings, the fronts of which had niches to hold water fountains, extended backward for the entire 95-foot length of the market and accommodated shops of whitewashed brick. Purbeck stone floors extended over the fish market, under which was sunk an enormous drainage tank. The rear of the market was open, and an archway on one side provided entry from a side street. The market was partially roofed with slate (an upper story was added later) and was secured by iron gates in front.[3]

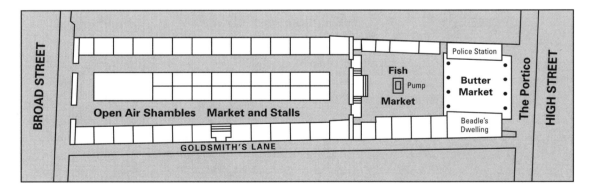

5.16. STAMFORD MARKET, 1808

In this age obsessed with classicism, an exceptionally fine modern translation of classical civic architecture was the Stamford portico market and shambles completed in 1808 (figs. 5.15, 5.16), by W. D. Legg. An even much more ambitious market than Chichester's, the Stamford market was fronted by an ashlar portico supported by four Tuscan columns. A wide overhanging pediment provided protection to a 41-foot-by-28-foot open propyleum with adjacent side wings. Doorways from the side wings led to the police station on one side and the watchman's dwelling on the other. Within the propyleum, which was supplied with additional light from windows above the side wings, was the butter market. Walking straight into the market, one first passed through the fish market, with a stone-paved floor and water pump, and then stepped down into a long open-air market which stretched the remainder of the block to Broad Street; this space served primarily as a meat shambles and held fifty-three stalls in four rows. With the exception of a small side entrance from Goldsmith's Lane, the Stamford market is a long and fairly wide passageway or avenue linking two streets, akin to an arcade.

The most impressive of the agora-type market buildings was the one built at Ipswich in 1810 (fig. 5.17 and fig. 2.13) by architects William Brown and B. B. Catt. Occupying nearly an acre of ground in the town center, the market consisted of two concentric quadrangles: the larger was lined with a loggia and surrounded the smaller, which served as the vegetable market, creating a market within a market. A large classical obelisk serving as the market fountain was situated within the smaller. The market extended out to the street by way of a broad entry lane, also lined with a loggia for shops. This lane ran in a ring between the large and small quadrangles.

Of considerable influence in the design of early and mid-nineteenth-century retail markets were the designs of Charles Fowler for two London wholesale markets, Covent Garden (1830) and Hungerford (1835), the first of which was a large porticoed structure not unlike the Stamford market of two decades earlier but with a cast-iron addition in the rear. The meat-and-fish market added later had a remarkable open-sided cast-iron roof with a clerestory. Although it may be an exaggeration to regard Fowler's work as a "new school" of market architecture, his highly publicized London works popularized the forms used in earlier markets in Stamford and Ipswich.[4]

Although the identification of commercial and public market interests with classical (particularly Grecian) taste diminished as the century progressed, it did not entirely disappear. In fact, the forms themselves became larger, as in Winchester's "Doric Temple" market (1857), whose two lateral colonnades opened into a partially glass-roofed, partially open market. The large (18,000 square feet) quadrangular Wolverhampton market of 1853 (fig. 5.18), with an iron and glass roof that surrounded the building's open inner courtyard, held 104 shops facing onto the central open-air market and presented a more modern translation of the ancient agora. Although market shoppers were not completely protected from the elements,

5.17. PROVISION MARKET,
IPSWICH, 1810

5.18. Market Hall,
Wolverhampton, 1853

5.19. Fruit and Flower
Arcade, Exchange
Market, Bristol, 1908

they were confined to an exclusively pedestrian space with a specific function. The culmination of the semi-enclosed piazza, Wolverhampton's market (and later Bridgwater's) was eventually roofed over, transforming it into a new type—the market hall.

THE ARCADED MARKET TYPE. The last enclosed-market type was the long skylit passageway, or arcade. This allowed customers to shop unhampered by traffic or inclement weather and provided a pedestrian passage between the streets. Not unlike the fashionable shopping arcades which sprang up in eighteenth-century Paris, Glasgow, and London, this market type took its historical cue as well from the late medieval covered walkway, or loggia, such as Chester's "rows."

The first modern arcaded public market was built by Samuel Glascodine at Bristol in 1745 (fig. 5.19). This was an arcaded market avenue, with an impressive Palladian entrance and

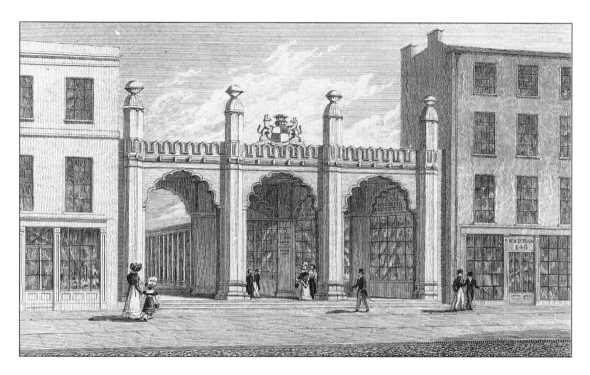

5.20. BAZAAR MARKET, CHELTENHAM, 1823

Venetian windows, that echoed its neighbor, the Bristol Exchange, with which it shared a common wall. Described at the time as the most beautiful and commodious marketplace in England, it served first as Bristol's meat market and subsequently as a flower market. By the 1830s, however, its rows of wooden butchers' stalls, wooden roof, and the tall glazed windows running along one side were viewed as "rustic," which helps explain why the market was reconstructed and extended in 1849 into a three-avenue arcaded market with a new roof of iron, glass, wood, and slate.[5]

Other municipalities followed Glascodine's lead, and the public market arcade, at times only partially covered, became popular. The market built at Cheltenham in 1823 (fig. 5.20) reinterprets this form in what was described as the Gothic style. The main attraction of the arcade was that it provided both a space for market activity and a link between busy city thoroughfares; but in the long run, the arcade proved to be much too simple a conversion of open street to enclosed market, and, like the early circular form, it could not be expanded to provide the massive spaces required to meet the general marketing needs of burgeoning urban populations.

5.21. St. John's Market, Liverpool, 1822

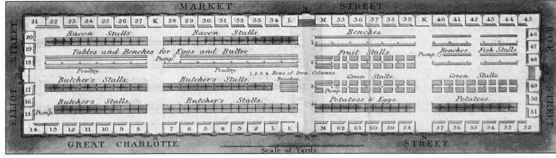

5.22. Plan of St. John's Market, Liverpool, 1822

The Large Early Market Halls

When in 1820 John Foster, city architect of Liverpool, presented his plans for a huge new market hall to be called St. John's (figs. 5.21, 5.22), he was proposing to create something unheard-of in terms of function and scale. Bold and inventive, the concept for St. John's was rooted in the single-use, semi-enclosed, and partially roofed markets which had thrived since the late eighteenth century. Hence, though highly innovative and massive in scale, Foster's market hearkened back to more than fifty years of market planning and building history and structures that included the Bristol arcade market (1745), Stamford's piazza market (1808), and the Ipswich market (1810).

Liverpool's St. John's Market, completed in 1822, was not only one of the largest buildings of its time, it was an inventive and revolutionary approach to public retail marketing: a fully enclosed, roofed market hall. This "stupendous building" consisted of a simple parallelogram nearly two acres in size, built of brick, with 136 stone-trimmed classical arched window bays, and supported by 116 interior cast-iron pillars. It had a five-division (span) wooden roof, two divisions of which were raised above the others to form a windowed clerestory that illuminated and ventilated the market below. The interior of light-painted brick was divided into five shopping avenues; the center avenue was 21 feet wide. Each avenue was lined with stalls. The outside avenues had sixty-two shops, carefully organized into depart-

5.23. GRAINGER MARKET
HALL, NEWCASTLE-UPON-
TYNE, 1835

View of one of the butchers'
market arcades from the
Grainger Street entrance to a
fountain in the vegetable
market.

5.24. GRAINGER MARKET
HALL, NEWCASTLE-UPON-
TYNE, 1835

A view of the butchers'
market avenue.

ments, facing inward along the perimeter walls. Although by later standards St. John's Market was regarded as low and dark, to the evening visitors in its early days its 549-foot front-to-rear vista of columns illuminated with successive rows of brilliant gas lamps formed an impressive perspective and a picture of grandeur.[6]

Variations on the Liverpool invention—the giant parallelogram with cast-iron columns and a wooden or wood-and-iron roof with added clerestory—were executed repeatedly in large- and medium-sized towns throughout Britain in the 1830s and 1840s: at Brighton (1830), Bridgwater (1830), Birmingham (1835), Newcastle (1835), Aberdeen (1842), Birkenhead (1845),

5.25. PLAN OF GRAINGER
MARKET HALL,
NEWCASTLE-UPON-TYNE,
1835

Blackburn (1848), and Doncaster (1849), to name a few. One of the most impressive of the early market hall giants was Newcastle's Grainger Market of 1835 (figs. 5.23, 5.24, 5.25), by John Dobson, an architect best known for his innovative design of Newcastle's Central Railway Station. To the glee of the townsfolk, who boasted that the meat and vegetables at Liverpool's St. John's Market were "black with passion" and "jaundiced with jealousy," the Newcastle structure was Britain's—perhaps Europe's—largest market hall. While Dobson's masterpiece has great local significance because it revolutionized the social and economic world of Newcastle, its architectural contribution is no less noteworthy. The market consisted of two adjacent parallelograms—a butcher's

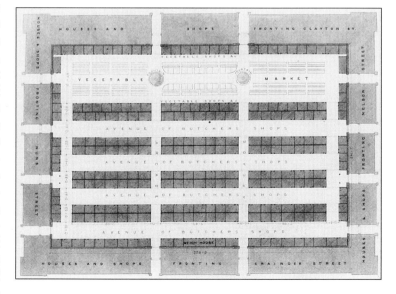

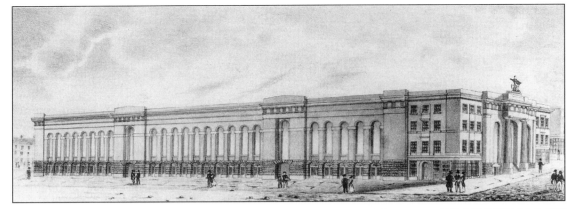

5.26. Market Hall, Birmingham, 1835

5.27. New Market Hall, Brighton, 1830

5.28. Market Hall, Aberdeen, 1842

For a later view, see figure 9.7.

hall and a vegetable hall—that together made up a 410-foot-by-312-foot space, with a wooden roof and clerestory that were higher than those of St. John's and had in addition fifty skylights. The vegetable hall had the nave-and-aisle construction popularized by the Crystal Palace a decade later, which became a common feature of market buildings thenceforth. Equally impressive, the butchers' market consisted of five wide arcaded aisles, each with shops on both sides and interior walls banked with clerestory windows. Two great fountains were installed in the vegetable market at the intersections of the axes connecting the four entrances. From these points, one had a grand view through a series of interior Roman arches to the butchers' hall beyond. All in all, the Newcastle market is one of the largest and most original nineteenth-century classical-revival monuments to commerce.[7]

Another early large hall was Birmingham's "Bull Ring" Market Hall of 1835 (fig. 5.26), which was constructed as a broad covered avenue (365 feet by 108 feet) between two main

5.29. MARKET HALL, BIRKENHEAD, CA. 1900
View of a side aisle.

thoroughfares—the old Bull Ring marketplace (which it replaced) and Worcester Street. Massive Doric columns flanked the new hall's principal entrances on opposing ends, as well as its side entrances to basement shops. The marketing space was organized into three avenues (one of which was for manufactured goods) along which were arranged the market's six hundred stalls. A 60-foot-high wooden roof with skylights was supported by painted cast-iron pillars. The space was lighted by twenty-five enormous windows along the sides, some of which were eventually fitted up with blinds to regulate the incoming sunlight.

Two equally impressive statements of modern marketing were Brighton's market hall of 1830 (fig. 5.27), a nave-and-aisle hall in the shape of an extended **T**, with an interior colonnade and clerestory, and the hall Archibald Simpson designed for Aberdeen in 1842 (fig. 5.28). The Aberdeen market was of extraordinary height and was one of the first market halls with

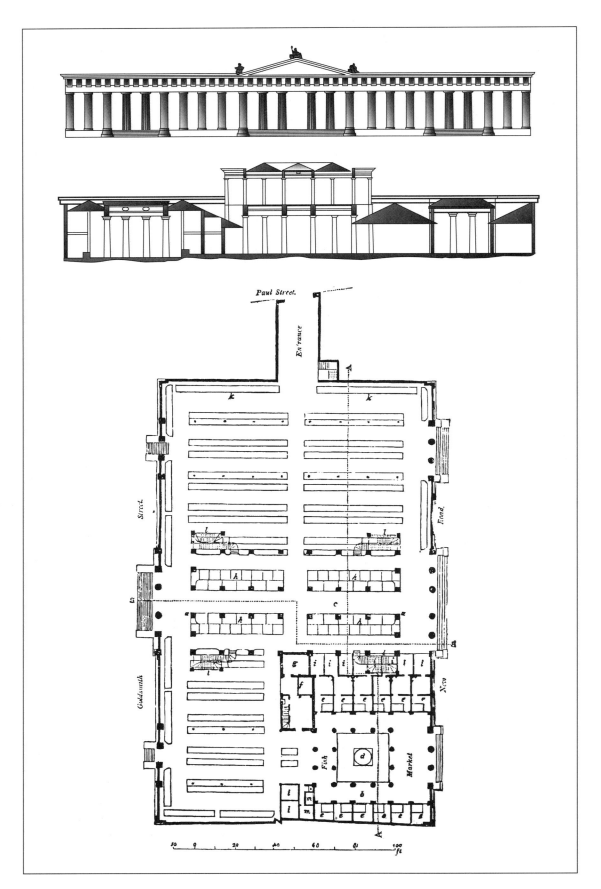

5.30. Façade, Roof Structure, and Plan of Higher Market Hall, Exeter, 1838

The principal entrances are in the center (on both sides) and open into a wide marble colonnaded vegetable aisle, while the fish market has a separate entrance—an effort to segregate fish sales from those of other products. Key to area shown: *d*, fountain basin; *e*, fish shops; *f*, marketman's house; *g*, office; *h*, fruit and vegetable stalls; *i*, fruit and vegetable shops; *k*, potato bins; *l*, stairs to gallery; *m*, urinals. Behind the historicist façade was an innovative roof concept. The roof cross section shows how the roof sections were arranged with spaces between them to admit light.

a mezzanine gallery. In terms of construction, the most innovative early market hall was the Birkenhead Market Hall of 1845 (fig. 5.29), built by the engineers Fox and Henderson of the well-known Birmingham Iron Works. The Birkenhead hall featured a triple nave rather than the customary nave-and-aisle plan. Fox and Henderson broke from tradition with their expansive glass-and-wrought-iron roof, which was supported by a system of cast-iron girders and 115 cast-iron pillars. These gave the Birkenhead hall the distinction of being the largest cast-iron supported building in the world, rivaling any of the age's great railway stations. A popular tourist attraction during its construction, acclaimed as "one of the most graceful and perfect structures of the kind in the kingdom," the Birkenhead hall introduced much of Britain to the advantages of massive expanses of glass and iron and was a prototype for Fox and Henderson's best-known project, the Crystal Palace. Equally important, Fox and Henderson's work at Birkenhead must alter the traditional perception that it was the gardener from Chatsworth, Joseph Paxton, who was the principal influence in the design of the Crystal Palace (see Chapter 6).[8]

While these great new halls seem to have taken their cue from the parallelogram pioneered in Liverpool, George Dymond's Higher Market at Exeter of 1838 (fig. 5.30), with construction supervised by Charles Fowler, looks more directly to the semi-enclosed agora form of Stamford and elsewhere. Considered "the most magnificent example" of a Grecian temple used for a public market, the 140-foot-by-230-foot Exeter Higher Market has two open sides and all the simplicity and majestic beauty of the Doric style. But this most "classical" of the giant market halls was undoubtedly the most modern and convenient public marketing facility of its time in England. Its central pedimented entrance, crowned with a figure of Britannia, and two lateral acroteria with figures of Peace and Plenty, opens onto an interior avenue of granite pilasters running to another colonnaded entrance opposite. This avenue contained the ground-floor fruit and vegetable market and featured an upper horticultural gallery that was reached by an iron staircase and lit by skylights and large side windows. To the left of the central entrance a separate fish market was enclosed by a four-sided Doric colonnade; a decorative and functional water fountain rose from the center; the fish stalls were fitted out with white marble slabs and water taps. Beyond the fish market were the general markets. Supported by both granite and cast-iron columns—which also acted as drains for the roof—the roof covering the structure was a complex arrangement of wood and skylights: some sections were solid while others were glass, and yet others were open to the outside for ventilation and additional light. Various sections of the roof stood at varying heights. With its colored stucco interior walls, stone floors, cast-iron ornamental railings, and rows of columns, the market presented a stunning contrast to the street market it replaced.[9]

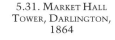

5.31. MARKET HALL TOWER, DARLINGTON, 1864

The Market Tower and the Arcaded Passageway

The first tower incorporated into the market hall façade appeared at Blackburn at mid-century and was added to give the market further visual authority in an increasingly complex urban landscape. The precedent for this was the prominent position the town market held as a visual reference point, where the market cross announced the town

ARCADE ENTRANCE

center. The market was the destination of a large segment of the population, both local and neighboring; hence, its tower functioned as an important urban marker. Some towers had majestic dignity and extraordinary height: Darlington's 1864 tower had clock faces 7 feet in diameter (fig. 5.31); Coventry tower of 1867 (fig. 5.32), was 15 by 15 feet at the base and 135 feet high. Some served a particular market purpose in the market: Blackburn's tower of 1848 was the residence of the market keeper; others housed the water tank in case of fire.

Another major addition to the basic parallelogram of the early market halls was a separate arcade that served as an entrance to the market, in particular, to provide access to landlocked spaces or to connect markets or, as in Bristol (the first arcaded public market), as a market in itself. Glasgow's Bazaar Market of 1817 was one such. The later markets at Pontypool (1893) and Carlisle used the arcade to move customers and sellers into spaces with limited street frontage (see fig. 6.5), thus allowing the town to add a huge retail space to the town center without disturbing the existing streetscape. The entrance arcade as a link between streets reached its zenith with Leeming and Leeming's Halifax market in 1896 (fig. 5.33). With twenty-five shops stretching a block and a half to connect the new market hall with one of the town's principal streets, the Halifax Albany Arcade remains as much a visual delight and functional space today as it was in 1896 when the market hall first opened. Indeed, the shopping arcade of the Halifax market is similar to late twentieth-century shopping malls with their enclosed pedestrian streets of shops.

Dozens of the parallelogram archetype were erected between the late 1840s and the 1890s, with seemingly endless variations in the plan and architectural style of the façades. Some interiors were long and narrow: Barnstaple's Pannier Market of 1855 (see fig. 7.1) measured 68 feet by 320 feet and Huddersfield's hall of 1880 was 71 feet by 231 feet—excluding the arcade of butchers' shops added to the outside. The large market hall (218 feet by 300 feet) built at Bolton from 1853 to 1856 (figs. 5.34, 5.35) was an innovative variation on the parallelogram archetype in that its two naves crossed: a broad nave (50 feet wide and 54

feet tall) with side aisles was intersected by
a shorter nave of equal width and height.
This created a central dramatic focus for an
elaborate fountain. The Bolton Market Hall
remained for many years one of Britain's
largest, and set a precedent for later markets.
The Kirkgate Market at Bradford (1872),
with its two octagonal glass-domed central
pavilions, 50 feet in diameter and 60 feet in
height, expanded upon the idea of a dominant central hall (fig. 5.36). The halls at
Leeds (fig. 5.37) and Halifax with their im-

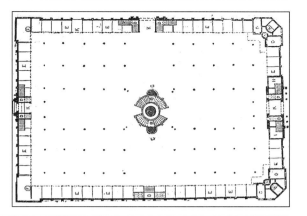

5.34. PLAN OF MARKET
HALL, BOLTON, 1853-56

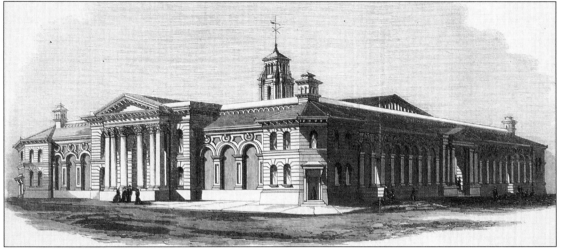

5.35. MARKET HALL,
BOLTON, 1853-56

5.36. KIRKGATE MARKET
HALL, BRADFORD, 1872

The shopper entered into
this octagonal pavilion,
which provided access to six
avenues of stalls and shops.
The interior was of glass and
ornamental ironwork pain-
ted in green, gold, and
bronze. The shop interiors
were white glazed brick, and
the entire market was lit by
"gaseliers" or gaslights,
made by the Midland Architectural Metal Company.

5.37. KIRKGATE MARKET HALL, LEEDS, 1904

View of the central octagonal glass dome and roof sections.

5.38. KIRKGATE MARKET HALL, LEEDS, CA. 1904

View of the central octagonal section with the market clock under the glass dome.

posing octagonal glass domes and curved glass roofs by Leeming and Leeming carry the concept of the glass market pavilion to its conclusion. Although their Leeds Kirkgate Market of 1904 (fig. 5.38) was smaller than the market at Halifax and did not have a transept, its glazed central octagonal dome and curved glass nave roof finish the design work begun by Fox and Henderson in 1845. The Leeds hall remains today not only one of the finest examples of market

hall architecture but also a reminder of the market hall's pioneering glass-roof design for commercial purposes.[10]

Medium-Sized Market Halls

If the large towns invented a new market building type which was revolutionary in size and visual form, smaller towns were not far behind in adapting the type to their own need. In the 1850s smaller municipalities— Torquay (1853), Scarborough (1854), Sheffield (1856)—constructed drab, modest market buildings with conventional (often wood) peaked roofs, clerestory lighting, and rather plain semiclassical and sometimes noble-looking façades. Radstock's market (1897) was unusual for its absence of a stylish architectural façade. The trend, as in larger towns, was toward the parallelogram plan, with avenues, glass-and-iron roofs, and external towers; but rarely did these smaller-scale markets incorporate the central axis or octagonal dome. This was the case, for example, in Stalybridge in 1868 and in Louth in 1866: their markets were modest but functional, and they had considerable visual interest. Even today Louth's restored market hall and tower testify to the Victorians' renewed interest in the aesthetic value of brickwork.

5.40. ARTISTS' RENDERING
of MARKET HALL,
BURNLEY, 1870
The tower was never added.

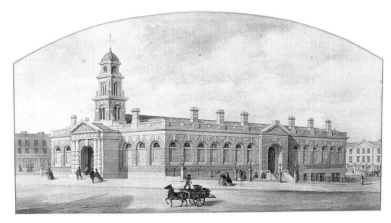

Southport's market of 1879 (fig. 5.39) was notably posh. A town which had grown rapidly between 1850 and 1880, Southport was anxious to proclaim itself worthy of national political and economic attention. It therefore built this, its third public market, in the grand Italian

5.41. MARKET HALL,
HARROGATE, 1874

style—although modest in size, it had a great deal of ornamentation and a large glass octagonal dome—which was viewed by some outsiders as a model, but for which the town paid a
very fancy price. Burnley's 1870 hall (fig. 5.40) had much the same classical exterior as those
of Bolton and Wolverhampton, but it lacked the central transept; the plan instead showed
the more common three-span roof over a central nave with side aisles. Galleries were added
later. Harrogate's market hall (1874) illustrates how the parallelogram continued to broaden,
here with three wide naves of equal size (fig. 5.41), while the 1867 market at Ashton-under-
Lyne of 1867, originally designed as a nave and three aisles, was widened by additions in 1881
and 1937. The stately hall at Gloucester (1856) had one broad, long avenue and a side aisle

5.42. FLOOR PLAN OF
MARKET HALL, SWANSEA,
1889
The hall was not completed
until 1897.

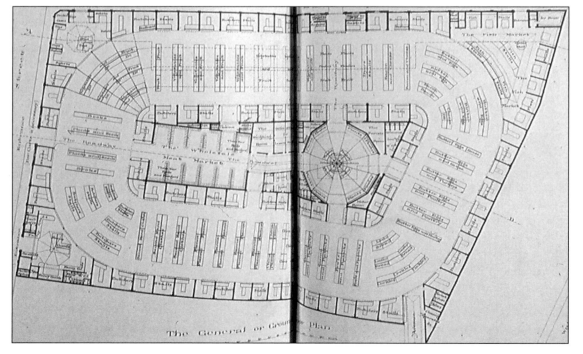

that ran along for a portion of its length, giving the market an **L** shape.[11]

The most radical variation on the parallelogram plan was to the market hall built in Swansea in 1897 (fig. 5.42), where a wide single nave with shops on either side was extended into an oblong nearly a mile in circumference, enclosing a large general market, a grand central domed flower market, and a wholesale market. This was a brilliant alternative to the multiple-aisle plan used at Newcastle and elsewhere.

Architectural Style

While the market hall was wildly inventive as a functional building type, its exterior architectural format, or style, was not pathbreaking. The British market hall architects used neither London's Crystal Palace nor Paris's Halles Centrales as their exterior models. Although the market hall *interior* was a predecessor of sorts to the Crystal Palace, the building's popularity led to only a few market halls borrowing its utilitarian glass-frame form for their exteriors; among them were Leeds's second Kirkgate market hall of 1857, constructed almost entirely of glass and iron (fig. 5.43); Stockport's market of 1861, derided as a glass umbrella on stilts (see fig. 6.1); and the enormous Manchester Shudehill Market (see fig. 6.21), fronted

5.43. KIRKGATE MARKET HALL, LEEDS, 1857

and covered over with glass and iron beginning in 1854; similarly, Manchester's Camphill markets (1877), the Huddersfield wholesale market (1888), and Bradford's James Street Market of 1905 (fig. 5.44) all had impressive glass-and-iron exteriors.

For most markets, however, the language of the exterior was different from that of the interior. The exterior did not speak of the honesty of its materials and the modernity of glass and iron; rather, it conveyed the powerful message that the business of buying and selling could aspire to a plane above the ugly, the utilitarian, and the profane. In this regard, the mammoth parallelogram-shaped hall posed a particularly difficult architectural design problem: its proportions—the inordinate length for its height—and the fact that it was generally exposed to public view on all sides created a leviathan-sized page onto which to inscribe this message. Although the market hall could be a building of considerable height, it was at first usually a single story (at least until the advent of the multistory shop-front façade in the 1870s), so its façade did not offer architects the same opportunities for interesting fenestration that

5.44. JAMES STREET
MARKET, BRADFORD, 1905
Market scene ca. 1930, just
before the market was
converted to a fish market.
The market was renovated
in 1988.

were available in multistory commercial office blocks, warehouses, and town halls. Sheer
size, bulk, and economy, therefore, made the market hall ideal for the simplicity and flatness
of elevation inherent in the classical revival and Renaissance styles.

The early giant market halls had remarkably similar façade designs: predominantly classical, they followed the trend in Britain as a whole, by mid-century leaning toward the classicism of the Italian Renaissance. The compact Italian arch could be integrated more func-
tionally into the exterior walls of the market hall than the cumbersome Greek colonnade.
The St. John's Market Hall in Liverpool established the pattern (see fig. 5.21). With only limited exterior architectural pretension, brick piers formed twenty-nine bays in which were
inserted two tiers of windows; the lower tier was semicircular and framed in stone, and the
upper tier formed a segmented brick arch. Thus, this simple utilitarian classical skin set the
precedent for what became the standard market hall façade, not only giving the hall a dignified face but complementing the bolder and more costly classicism being applied to other
public structures at about the same time. The St. John's Market Hall had eight entrances, the
principal of which were faced with Italian Ionic columns, and the entire building rested on a
stone plinth. More elaborate but similarly flat in both front and side elevations, Charles Edge's
Birmingham "Bull Ring" Market Hall (see fig. 5.26) was of Bath stone with imposing Doric
entrances at each end. A rusticated, closed loggia corresponded to arched bays above, which
were intercepted by broad and slightly extending entrance bays. In Blackburn the designer
Terence Flanagan, an engineer, used a triple-division roof plan to produce a three-gabled façade.
The 1848 hall (see fig. 9.3) is a variation on the standard classical elevation in that the decorative part of the elevation is raised to make a bold, continuous horizontal division of arched
upper windows in the Italian Renaissance manner. Flanagan out-designed his rivals by adding a broad, 72-foot campanile. Throughout the midlands, the north of England, and in parts
of Wales, a pediment was often added at the entrance. G. T. Robinson's massive
Wolverhampton market hall of brick and stone followed a similar pattern (see fig. 5.18). Built
in 1853, shortly after the town was incorporated, and not fully roofed until later, it was given

a Corinthian portico front with a five-bay blank arcade on each side, terminated by projecting wings. A simplification of the façade treatment is carried around to the other elevations (there are six entrances, one of which has a Doric portico). Between 1853 and 1856 Robinson reiterated some of these ideas in the design of the hall at Bolton, but on larger and grander scale (the building measured 218 feet by 300 feet). The hall was constructed entirely of stone, with a grand central portico, blank side arcades, and corner projecting wings, as well as a campanile and corner cupolas; the arcade bays extended along the minor elevations. Likewise, the new market hall of 1870 at Burnley (see fig. 5.40), although one-third the size of Bolton's, followed it in its Palladian Italian manner. The stone hall featured a notable projecting entrance portico with Doric columns, broken by square rustic blocks. Its standard recessed arched bays with semicircular windows gave Burnley's hall a heavy and monumental appearance. An eclectic variation on this theme was the Harrogate hall of 1874 (see fig. 5.41), where the triple-roof construction dictated the use of a massive triple-gabled front. It, too, had corner wings (one of which served as the stage for the tower) and a wrap of four bays

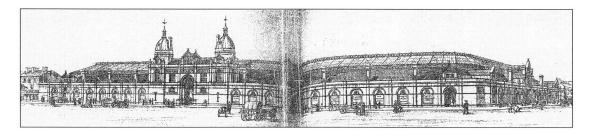

5.45. EXTERIOR OF MARKET HALL, SWANSEA, 1889

on each side of a large, carefully placed entrance for carts and pedestrians. Ashton-under-Lyne (1867), Stalybridge (1868), and Accrington (1869) all employed the familiar exterior classical wraps (all these halls still function as markets). Stalybridge's elaborately decorated brick market, with a French mansard roof tower, covered in fish-scale slate, had rusticated stone quoins, color-banded entrance arches, and polychromatic brickwork. Accrington, in reaching for an image worthy of the parliamentary status it sought, adopted the classical-

5.46. FITZALAN MARKET HALL, SHEFFIELD, 1856

wrap style of arched bays but with a more aggressive Italian façade and a central triumphal arch, the upper portion of which carried abundant sculpture on a central gable. Although Ashton-under-Lyne's hall had polychrome brickwork and a grand clock tower, and used the broad side of the parallelogram (with its 198 arched bays) as its façade, its form was little changed from that of most large halls built in the previous half-century. Carlisle's immense market hall of 1889 (see fig. 6.26), with its pioneering roof and old-fashioned façade, well illustrates the inability of nineteenth-century architects to invent an entirely new form which could accommodate both the old and new comfortably.

Thus, throughout most of the late nineteenth century, until the plate-glass shop fronts began to appear in the façades of the larger market halls in the 1870s, the classical wrapping remained standard. The large, single-level parallelogram offered few other stylistic possibilities—or at least, not at a price most towns were willing to pay. Even such later markets as Swansea (1897) retained the idea of a one-level face turned to the multibay recessed and blind classical archways to organize the whole façade into a single symmetrical composition (fig. 5.45). The Fitzalan Market Hall at Sheffield (1856) altered tradition somewhat with its two- and three-story front, but its long single-level extension carried on the arched bay classical-

5.47. KIRKGATE MARKET
HALL, BRADFORD, 1872

5.48. KIRKGATE MARKET
HALL, LEEDS, 1904

wrap form (fig. 5.46), while the triple-roofed market at Wigan carried on the traditional classical-wrap format but with an added covered portico around three sides.

The Shop-Front Façade

By the late nineteenth century, because of increasing competition from the department store and the cooperative shop, the market hall needed to reinvent itself. The solution was to adopt a multistory façade pierced with large plate-glass shop fronts. Although a number of early halls had incorporated shops into their exterior façades, opening the shops to the interior of the public market as well as to the street, it was not until the 1870s that the multistory shop-front façade became the common format for large markets. The first of the grand market halls to adopt this façade as part of a new market—in this case thirty-one shops along three sides of the building—was Bradford's Kirkgate Market (fig. 5.47) constructed in phases between 1872 and 1877. At about the same time Dundee put up the Victoria Market (1878), which included shops to the street front as well as within a long, wide glass arcade. But the best realization of the shop-front façade was the Kirkgate Market of 1904 at Leeds (fig. 5.48), which greeted shoppers with a front that was the rival of any department store in Britain at the time.

Indeed, the craze for the glass-fronted department store which swept Britain and Europe (beginning in Paris) was much of the inspiration. Also influential were the plate-glass-fronted "warehouses" (actually giant retail outlets) of a decade earlier in Glasgow and elsewhere. In Glasgow, one of Europe's leaders in retailing, the plate-glass craze came with great panache with Wylie and Lockhead's enormous "Crystal Palace of commerce"—although the earliest addition of plate-glass shop fronts to a large retail space was to Glasgow's Bazaar Market in 1843.

Whatever the concept's source, clearly the plate-glass impetus rested on the imperative to keep the market hall abreast of the competition. The shift in design from the bland and dull classical-wrap façade to the plate-glass façade reflects a shift in consumerism, for consumption was becoming more and more a social activity. As the architect Alfred Waterhouse noted, an important consideration in market hall design was to maximize the market hall's competitive position. The market hall's plate-glass front became the poor people's Bon Marché—an essential factor in keeping working- and middle-class shoppers loyal to the market.[12]

Historical Styles, "Freely Interpreted"

Its widespread popularity notwithstanding, the classical wrap was never the universal solution for market hall design, particularly outside of the industrial midlands and the north. Smaller halls enjoyed greater stylistic leeway in that scale was on their side: they simply had less area to cover. Such was the case with Stockport's classically fronted produce market of 1851 (fig. 5.49) and the 1892 Bilston market with its "Jacobean" façade (fig. 5.50). Even though market hall design was influenced by national discussions—often referred to as the "battle of the styles"—over whether to cloak the nation in Gothic or classical dress, market hall design was dictated as much by local needs and self-perception as by anything else. Durham's market hall façade, for example, was linked with that of the Guildhall to form a Gothic

5.49. Produce Market, Stockport, 1851

5.50. MARKET HALL,
BILSTON, 1892

5.51. MARKET HALL,
WIGAN, 1877
View of front section with
entrance and covered ex-
terior portico.

mirror of the nearby St. Nicholas's Church—and a complement to the medieval character of the town as a whole. The cathedral city of Litchfield used local tradition as a rationale to build a new market in the "Elizabethan" style, while in Wigan (fig. 5.51) and Darwen, both working-class towns, it was questioned whether "domestic Gothic" was an appropriate style to exemplify the town character and stature. Darwen locals expressed their concern that "any display of towers and turrets, pointed and elaborate details would appear to be ridiculously out of place in this somber working town." Conversely, the Gothic rejected by working-class Darwen and Wigan was adopted by Wokingham (fig. 5.52) in a project with a market arcade on the ground floor of a Gothic Revival town hall (1860), and in the new market of 1883 for Newark (fig. 5.53), which used pointed windows and interior buttresses in an attempt at a Gothic interior. The Gothic was exactly what was needed by the working people of London's East End as well—or, at least, so thought the promoters of the Columbia Market scheme, who contracted with architect H. A. Darbishire to build one of Britain's most outstanding (although an economic failure) Victorian market halls in the Gothic style (fig. 5.54).[13]

If the Columbia Market (1869) was Gothic pastiche par excellence, the Chester market hall (1863) stood as its equal in the Baroque (fig. 5.55). This was Chester's first covered market; it outdistanced most market design in its flamboyant use of the Baroque, which *The Builder* called an adaptation of the Flemish Italian, "treated with freedom." But rather than being a participant in the national battle of the styles, this hall was a result of local persuasion. It was Victorian Chester's way of redeeming itself from the sins of its fathers: the old

5.52. TOWN HALL AND MARKET, WOKINGHAM, 1860

markets, it was said, were "nothing to rivet the attention of the sightseer," and so the new market was meant to take Chester in quite the opposite direction.[14]

It was providential that at precisely the time the form of the market hall changed from single- to multistory, the nation had become enraptured with freestyle or eclectic architecture. Thus, a merger of new form with new style led to more flamboyant façades. Bradford's revolutionary multistory shop-front façade of 1872 therefore marked a major change in market hall form—from the flat and blind façade which depended on windows in the roof for its light to the tall ornamental façade which could accommodate large expanses of plate glass

5.53. MARKET HALL,
NEWARK, 1883

5.54. Columbia Market
Hall, London, 1869

5.55. MARKET HALL,
CHESTER, 1863

(see fig. 5.47). Concurrently, the architectural thought was that market hall façades, to realize their potential as communicators of the new public values, should be more elaborate and expensive than were necessary for mere marketing purposes. As a result, Gothic, the freestyle Renaissance, and an increasingly popular eclecticism were embraced with vigor.[15]

Several Yorkshire and Lancashire market halls illustrate this development. With its multistory front on three elevations, the Bradford Kirkgate Market (1872), by Lockwood and Mawson, is in a Venetian palazzo style common to much fashionable street architecture of the time. Its counterpart in Huddersfield in 1880 (see fig. 4.7), built on the site of the old market shambles, was in what *The Builder* called "Domestic Gothic." Both the Bradford and Huddersfield halls repeated the façade on the side elevations—in the case of Huddersfield, by way of a long arcaded row which made up the new butchers' shambles. In the front of the Huddersfield hall is a grand gabled entry which extended upward to the 106-foot-tall tower (with spire and four-faced clock). Huddersfield's first enclosed market, its multifaceted, light stone façade and green slate roof made it an imposing presence on the urban landscape and its surrounding region. The hall goes some distance to symbolize not only the town's victory in a long and costly battle with Sir John Ramsden over market rights but also the desire on the part of the town's leaders to ameliorate the "dull form of Huddersfield buildings" of the past.[16]

In 1882 Darwen adopted the shop-front market hall form as well (fig. 5.56), not in the Gothic style but with a projecting gable, arched entrance, and cupola in a modest Italian Renaissance interpretation. Here the shop-front façade was continued on only one elevation; the other side was assigned to a covered wholesale market.

Whatever the size of the market or its exterior style, by the 1880s the multistory shop-

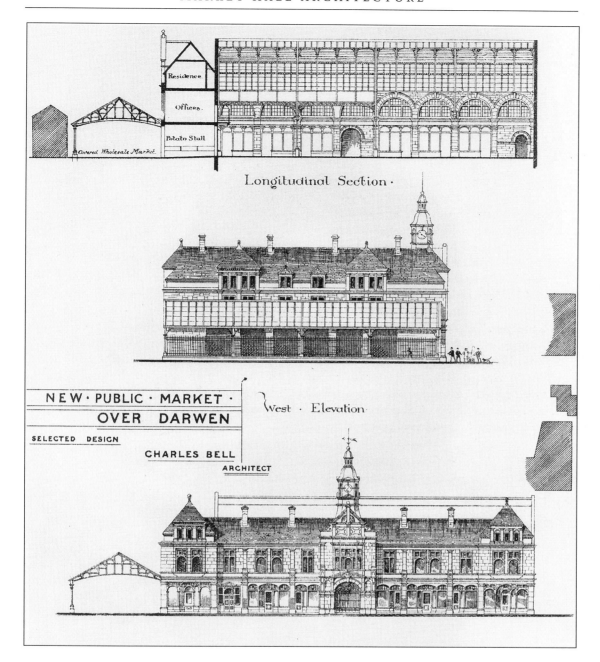

5.56. MARKET HALL,
DARWEN, 1882

fronted market hall had gained equal footing with the department store, the town hall, and in some instances even the railway station as an integral component of urban life. But did the market hall as a nineteenth-century building type have architectural forefathers? If so, they were John Foster at Liverpool, Charles Edge at Birmingham, John Dobson at Newcastle, George Dymond and Charles Fowler at Exeter, and Archibald Simpson at Aberdeen, who set forth the basic parallelogram patterns which were to become basic to market hall design, after

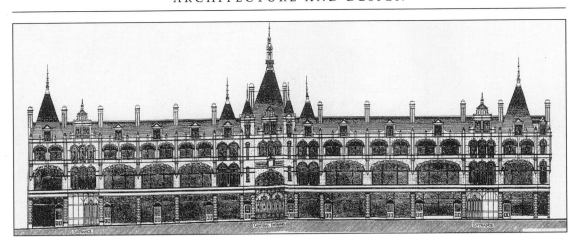

which the engineers Fox and Henderson at Birkenhead took the early plan and form of the market hall and gave it its modern glass-and-iron structure. Most of all, there is little doubt that what Leeming and Leeming accomplished in their native Halifax represents, in many ways, the apex of market hall planning and design. With its grand arcade leading into an unrivaled glass-roofed market with a domed hexagonal transept at the end of an extraordinarily long nave, its imposing interior clock, and its elegantly fitted-up stalls and shops, the Halifax Borough Market Hall of 1896 is, in essence, the quintessential market hall (fig. 5.57). Here Flemish gable, Baroque thin turret, Venetian palazzo windows, and French mansard roof commingle with plate glass and grand entrances to create a pastiche which provided the modern townscape with a new and distinctive addition in an expanding repertoire of monuments to commerce and consumerism.

CONSTRUCTION, SITE, AND MATERIALS

PERHAPS MORE THAN ANY OTHER NINETEENTH-CENTURY BUILDING TYPE, THE market hall speaks to the functionalist tradition of Victorian architecture. Because of their size, pioneering roof designs, innovative plans, and use of materials, the market halls of the decades after 1820 were a noteworthy departure from most existing public or private buildings. Although the planning and construction of market buildings did not produce the same level of national interest as did the planning of such other new public building types as town halls, prisons, and hospitals, market hall building proposals often generated enormous local excitement as to site, construction and materials, interior plan and fixtures, and sanitary arrangements.[1]

Market hall form and plan were dictated less by the sometimes wasteful engineering and architectural novelties applied to railway stations than by factors like sanitary arrangements, developments in mass retailing, the needs of increasingly convenience-oriented buyers and sellers, and the configuration of the site in which the market was to be placed. The market had to be built at a low enough cost to both maximize its value as a source of town revenue and guarantee that rents would be cheap enough to attract tenants. An examination of some features of market hall organization and design enables us to better understand this uniquely modern aspect of nineteenth-century building and architecture.

The Importance of Site

The decision on the part of a town to replace or remove its ancient open-air market offered considerable risk. The traditional market was usually ideally placed in the center of the most heavily traversed paths of the town—a fact well appreciated by market sellers. To change the venue of the public market could easily drive its customers and vendors to privately owned shops or to another town's market. A successful public market depended upon a site which was in good proximity to local transportation terminuses, the town's commercial center, and perhaps most important, the residential district. Furthermore, in most towns a large central market was preferred to multiple markets scattered throughout the town. Exeter built two markets, one on either end of the town, only to close one of them later, and Liverpool found that its newly built district market halls were both unpopular and unprofitable. An overwhelming majority of new markets were sited in virtually the same space that the market had stood on for centuries. Indeed, by not moving the marketplace, some towns made the wrong decisions. Failure of a public market to follow shifts in population, for example, led to the demise of many a market—such as in Aylesbury, in Buckinghamshire, where the market was abandoned because the population moved to a distant part of the town.[2]

Several factors worked to keep the market in its ancient location. First, the town was often legally bound to provide a market at its traditional site. Even when this was not the case, market relocation was risky because often market users—both buyers and sellers—refused to change their habits and switch their allegiance to a site away from the traditional marketplace. This seems to have caused the downfall of a number of less-than-successful markets, such as the new market hall at Bromwich, pulled down because it had been moved to an inconvenient site away from the town's center and its main thoroughfares.

6.1. STOCKPORT MARKET
HOUSE, CA. 1913

Finding space for the new market was usually difficult. Sometimes space for a new or expanded market was found by moving the ancient cattle market and slaughterhouse from the town center to the outskirts of the town and taking over the site. Often, new market space was found by covering over the old open-air area with a new market building. This was a particularly attractive solution because it was generally acknowledged that market buildings should stand independent of other buildings so as to have access from all sides. Understandably, then, the normal practice was to take over the traditional marketplace, as was done in Stockport, where a new market house built in 1861 and called the "glass umbrella on stilts" virtually covered the old marketplace (see fig. 1.3) area up to the entrance of the parish church (figs. 6.1, 6.2). Some observers viewed such decisions as reckless, and considerable public debate accompanied marketplace relocation. Soon after Warrington was incorporated as a borough, the town council decided to erect a market hall on two-thirds of the market square, a decision which aroused the wrath of some councillors and citizens who were strongly opposed to covering over the square. In Darlington, protest over the enclosure of the ancient open-air marketplace led to a poetic lamentation which ended with a call to the citizenry of Darlington:

> For less than this have Freemen fought, have
> heroes bled and died.
> Arouse my Townsmen! meet the foe,
> and beard him face to face
> Resolve that bricks and mortar
> shall not block your Market Place;
> Up, and be doing! guard your rights,
> though recreant souls may frown.
> And our Grand Old Healthy Market Place
> for aye shall bless the Town.[3]

To the bard's consternation, the town fathers decided to fill a part of the marketplace with a new market hall—a decision with some merit, as it turns out, because the Darlington hall remains to this day one of the most vibrant in England.

Until the advent of urban rail transport systems, which could move people quickly to suburban fields, nineteenth-century towns grew intensively rather than extensively. This meant new streets and new structures—including the market—were crowded into existing alleys, yards, gardens, and other open spaces. The Haslemere marketplace had become so encumbered with shops built up around it that town officials finally swept away the entire

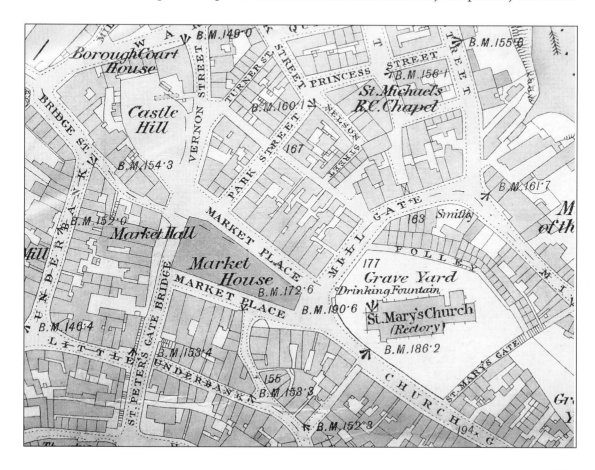

6.2. MAP OF STOCKPORT, 1872-75, SHOWING MARKETPLACE AFTER ERECTION OF NEW MARKET HOUSE IN 1861

The earlier (1851) produce market, the "Market Hall," faces the new Market House—itself occupying nearly the entire space of the old marketplace.

mess and built a new, enlarged market house in the same space. In providing for their new market hall, Doncaster officials mandated the demolition of the Butchers' Shambles, the removal of the Butter Cross, the destruction of the Town Hall and Grammar School, and the closing of the streets Meal Lane, Shoe Lane, and Rotten Row, which crossed the proposed site. When Huddersfield purchased the town markets from their manorial owner, it left the old marketplace intact but used an adjacent meat shambles as the site of its new market hall. While this site was highly desirable in terms of proximity to market users, its size dictated that the new building could not be larger than 270 feet by 102 feet—a figure that seemed large but that soon proved to be too small to accommodate Huddersfield's burgeoning population.[4]

Other towns were not so fortunate and had to find nearby spaces to clear away. Hanley market trustees placed the new market hall on the site of the principal public house and an adjoining bowling green. In 1817 Glasgow also built its new market hall on the site of the bowling green, called Candleriggs. An inventive adaptation to site occurred in Edinburgh, where a new bazaar market (later called Waverly Market, 1876) was designed for a steeply declining site adjacent to Princes Street (the principal shopping street). Here the architect, Robert Moreham, created a huge market on the lower level, with maximum access for pedestrians and carts. The roof of the market, on the same level as Princes Street, was supported by cast-iron columns, and was part skylight, part garden promenade. Princes Street, therefore, got both garden and market (fig. 6.3).

6.3. EDINBURGH, WAVERLY MARKET HALL, EXTERIOR AND ROOF GARDEN, 1895

Here the roof of the market hall served as the Waverly Gardens at street level. The market below was partially lit by a number of skylights at the edges and center of the roof garden, which in turn were protected with iron railings. At floor level, the market was adjacent to the principal railway station. The market no longer exists, but a new Waverly Market, in the form of a shopping center, retains the roof-garden concept.

The Market as Commercial Link

The most successful market sites were those used to link prominent points of commercial activity. The success of the traditional marketplace, after all, was its access from all points of the town. The linking of thoroughfares with a market hall was first done on a major scale in Birmingham between 1828 and 1835, when all the structures between the old marketplace, the "Bull Ring," and a major town thoroughfare, Worcester Street, were demolished and a vast market hall of 365 feet by 108 feet was erected in its place, with entrances on all sides (see fig. 5.26). Barnstaple followed a similar course. It built the new market hall between two of the town's main thoroughfares, High Street and Boutport Street, thus providing convenient market access for both local residents and visitors from outlying villages. The Barnstaple planners added to the new market's strategic attractiveness by building a new street (complete with a string of new butchers' shops) along the side of the market (fig. 6.4). Kidderminster's market hall was a "linking" market as well, as were the large market halls at Birmingham, Glasgow, and Pontypool (fig. 6.5).

The coming of the railway transport to many towns (see Chapter 8) provided opportunities as well as problems for market planners. How could the market be linked to the railway? Salisbury residents debated whether the new market should be built in the old town square or moved to the edge of the town at the railway terminus. Ingeniously, the new market remained in the town square, and a special "market railway" was laid out from the terminus directly to the rear of the market hall. In other towns, such as Edinburgh and Southport, the market halls were fortunate to be adjacent to the railway station. Accrington and Bradford laid out their new tramway systems so that the suburban populations would have convenient access to the central market; it was said in Accrington that tramway linkage to the market (the terminus was placed adjacent to the market hall) increased the number of people who used the market to more than twice the population of the town itself.[5]

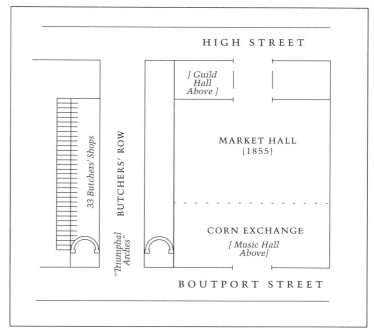

Market Site and Urban Redevelopment

Changing the location of the public market often had a major effect on urban land use. Despite the costs and problems involved with land acquisition and site clearance, it was often found that the only way to acquire a new or larger market site was through the expensive and controversial process of condemning existing urban structures. Unlike many town-center redevelopment schemes after the Second World War, wherein private commercial development was given site preference over redevelopment of the public market, nineteenth-century urban reformers usually gave the public market preference over private shops and other commercial property (and in some cases, private dwellings). And the need for a new market site in many crowded towns frequently led to substantial rearrangement of urban land use. This was often accomplished by leaving all or most of the town's marketplace intact and locating the new market nearby, by demolishing adjacent property. As a result, a new market from time to time acted as the catalyst for extensive infrastructure projects—not the least of which were slum clearance, new bridges, new streets, and new mass-transportation systems. This was the case in both Bristol and Darwen, where a section of a river was covered to create a new market site. When building a new market in 1877 on the site of its old marketplace, the town of Wigan built new streets extending through to the market, making it possible for more than a third of the population to walk there directly. Similarly, in order to give as wide and grand a pathway to its new market hall as possible, Lancaster swept aside an entire block of buildings, while Oldham opened a new street in front of its new hall by removing several existing buildings (fig. 6.6).

The Lancashire towns of Burnley, Bolton, and Liverpool illustrate how some market hall projects purposely (and successfully) drew the commercial heart of the town toward a new center—and how the centralized market blocked suburban sprawl. In 1870 Burnley had three designated market spaces in the old town center: a partially covered shambles called the

6.4. BARNSTAPLE, NEW MARKET SITE CONFIGURATION, 1855

The new market, 445 feet in length, was placed between the town's two main streets after the town destroyed a number of houses and workshops and opened a new thoroughfare (Butchers' Row) between Boutport and High streets. Where Butchers' Row met Boutport was marked by "triumphal arches" and a fashionably bracketed sidewalk overhang to protect the street's thirty-three new butchers' shops. The Boutport Street entrance gave market access to a large number of people from new residential streets opening onto Boutport Street. The new butchers' market replaced various street markets and slaughterhouses. Both the market hall and Butchers' Row still exist, although the arches at the end of the row have been removed.

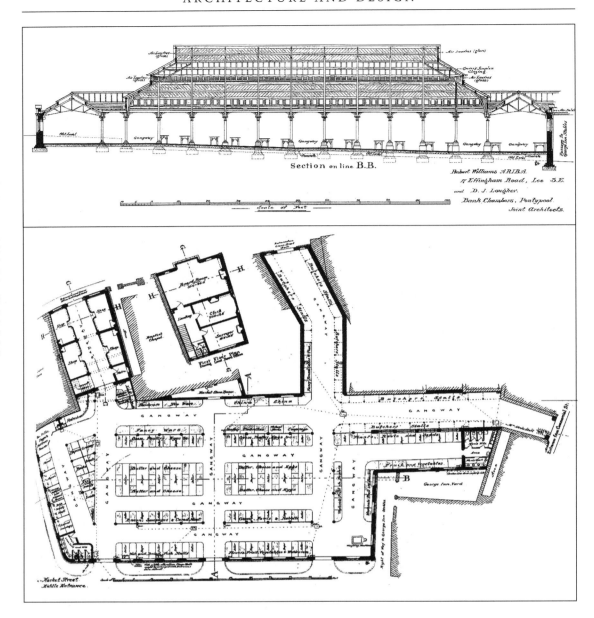

6.5. PONTYPOOL MARKET
HALL, ROOF CROSS SEC-
TION AND FLOOR PLAN,
1893

Here the architects were
faced with the task of
designing a market to fit two
site irregularities—a steep
incline and lack of access
from the principal street.
The solution was to slope
the floor (thereby avoiding
steps) and extend three
corridors out from the
market to reach the two
principal streets. As a result,
the tall, three-division roof
has three low appendages
which extend the market to
the edges of the site. The
roofs were a mixture of glass
and slate. See also figure
6.20.

market house, built in 1829; a covered market shed called Victoria Market; and the ancient
open-air marketplace near St. Peter's Church. Unable to keep up with the times, these poor
facilities had forced most of the town's market activity to spread up and down the main street,
St. James's Street, as far as the Hall Inn (fig. 6.7). As Burnley and its surrounding cotton-weaving
district grew, the town initiated an act of Parliament to allow the council to purchase the
markets and the market rights from the private Burnley Market Company. Then in 1870 it
erected a new central market hall into which all the street marketing would be placed (see
fig. 5.40). This led to the demolition of the old market house and all the property on four
adjacent streets (Poke Street, Fountain Street, Fountain Court, and Rodney Street). Thus at
one stroke the town recentralized the retail industry, removed all marketing from the streets,
and eliminated some of the worst, most unsanitary slum property. The new market hall had

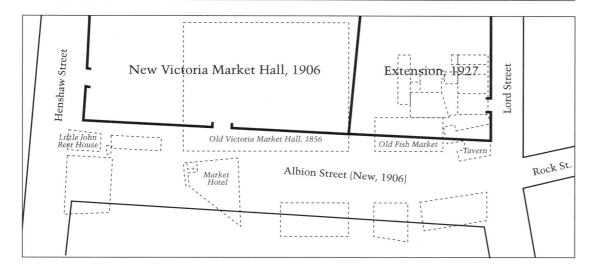

the added advantage of being in convenient proximity to the railway (which entered the town just north of the market) and the tramway (which passed along the bottom of Market Street).

The design and construction of Bolton's grand market hall (1½ statute acres in size) took place under somewhat similar circumstances. The site, as provided through a locally initiated parliamentary "improvement act" in 1850, was a stretch of uneven land adjacent to a number of notorious damp, dark streets of slum dwellings. The market-relocation plan became the catalyst for one of Britain's most ambitious municipal street and sanitary improvement schemes, a plan which swept away 1,700 slum dwellings and led to new street construction, a sanitary system, and the first bridge to connect the neighboring town of Little Bolton with Bolton (fig. 6.8). Thus the new Bolton market hall not only centralized urban retailing for the townsfolk, it also became the first physical link between the two Boltons.

Burnley and Bolton illustrate that moving the market was sometimes the wisest policy. Liverpool had discovered the same thing in the early nineteenth century. As the population moved outward from the old market near the docks, market officials stopped the policy of sending the market to the people rather than bringing the people to the old market. The St. John's Market of 1822 was placed on a full square block of land (a former rope works) along Great Charlotte Street, a considerable distance from the old town center. It was extremely successful; and in a stroke of either good luck or good planning, a waste area became a thriving center of retail activity from that time to the present.[6]

Awkward Elevations

Because many markets were legally restricted to a particular location, market architects had little choice but to place new markets on a hill or some other awkwardly configured site. Darwen's market hall of 1882 was built on reclaimed land, created by covering over a river; in Hanley, the principal frontage of the new market hall in 1849 was set on a severe slope by piercing the façade with shop fronts and entrances of varying heights (fig. 6.9). In Bolton the site on which the market was placed sloped nearly 50 feet down to the bank of the River Croal. Here the architect, G. T. Robinson, cleverly designed a vast vaulted lower storage level to support the new market and bring it up to street level. The Yorkshire town of Batley built its first enclosed market in 1878 on a steep hill, as did the towns of Bacup and Bideford. The Batley market failed, but Bideford's architect successfully addressed the market's dramatic elevation change by placing the hall and the arcade for butchers' shops at different levels. The two had separate entrances but a wide interior central stair to join them.

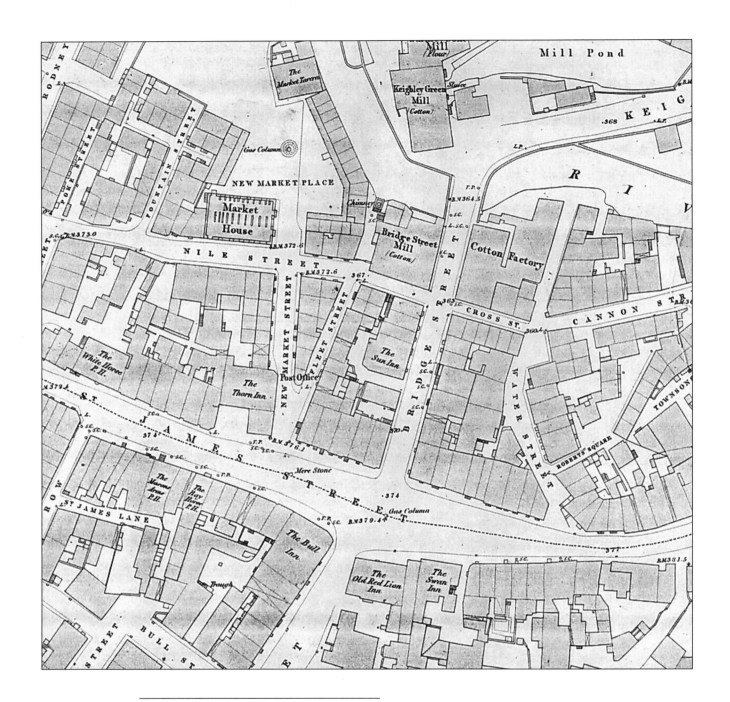

6.7. Maps of Burnley, Before and After Market
Redevelopment

By the second half of the nineteenth century the market
house was too small for the town's marketing, and hence
much of the market activity had spread along St. James's
Street. A new market hall built in 1870 occupied the space
of former slum dwellings from the point of the old market
house all the way to what was formerly York Street.

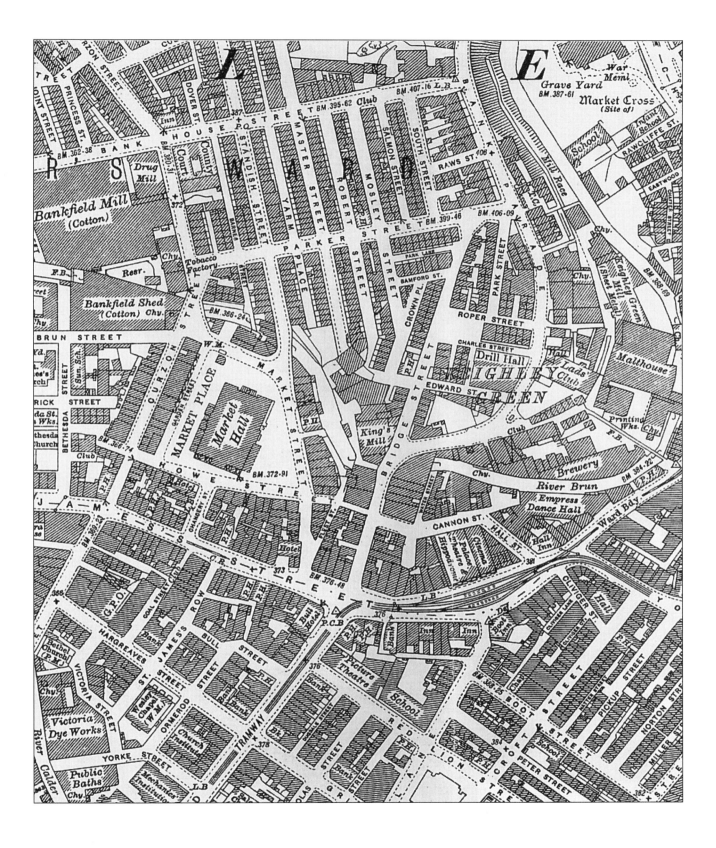

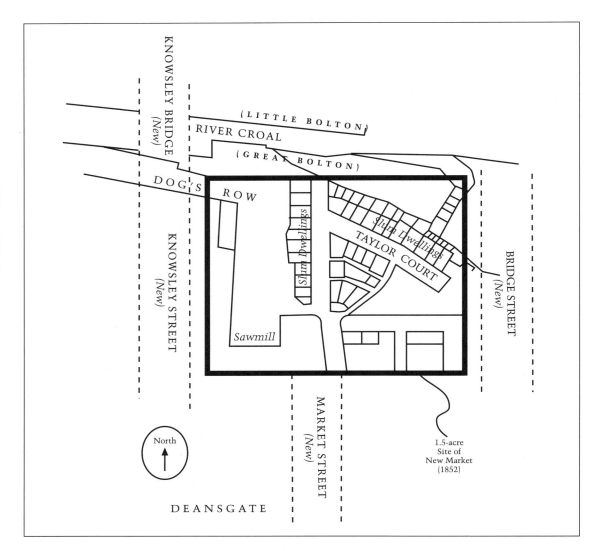

6.8. BOLTON, SITE OF THE NEW MARKET HALL, 1850

Site showing proximity to River Croal. The heavy line indicates the approximate location of the new hall. When designing the new market, planners included a road and a bridge, making the new market district the link between Little Bolton and "Great" Bolton (now Bolton).

KNOWSLEY BRIDGE *(New)*

(LITTLE BOLTON)

RIVER CROAL

(GREAT BOLTON)

DOG'S ROW

Slum Dwellings

Slum Dwellings

TAYLOR COURT

KNOWSLEY STREET *(New)*

BRIDGE STREET *(New)*

Sawmill

North

MARKET STREET *(New)*

1.5-acre Site of New Market (1852)

DEANSGATE

6.9. HANLEY, MARKET HALL ELEVATION, 1849

Convenience, Arrangement, and Plan

The nineteenth-century market hall partakes of the Victorians' obsession with comfort, cleanliness, and efficiency. Until the later appearance of the cooperative store, the department store, and the twentieth-century supermarket, the market hall was the pioneer in creating an environment which maximized comfort and service for both consumer and seller—initiating a virtual revolution in the way people bought and sold food and other goods. Market officials, planners, and architects sought to turn the old dirty, wind-swept public market into the town's most progressive retailing establishment. At Burnley this improving spirit was mixed with wise planning, and the market thus created became a "great boon to the town." The markets committee had announced that it would carefully oversee all aspects of the market, so as to make "arrangements as shall be of advantage to the shopkeepers and stallholders, and be a comfort and convenience to those who come to buy."[7]

Unfortunately, unlike railway stations, where money was often no problem and site arbitrary, market hall designers were limited by economic factors and a fixed and often restrained site. A market that was too small, such as at Hanley, where the aisles were inconveniently narrow, could lead to abandonment by either consumers or vendors, as at Newark-on-Trent, where market sellers left the hall and returned to the streets because the market was drafty and "badly built." On the other hand, the market hall had to pay for itself, so an oversized or overdecorated building would drive up rental costs, which in turn would defeat the purpose of the public market: to be a cheap source of food for the largest number of people. Needless to say, the quality and level of planning and construction varied considerably from town to town. In general, the market halls of the 1870s and later were more sophisticated in plan, materials, and services than the pioneer halls of the 1820s and 1830s, although the early halls were often larger. Architects and public officials spent countless hours planning and replanning the public market. Leeds was fortunate to have a former market stall keeper as mayor, with a self-proclaimed "mania for markets," who "liked to see how people get on with them." Mayor Archibald Scarr visited and studied the markets of Yorkshire and Lancashire to get a sense of how market layout and facilities affected consumer behavior, and his market at Leeds became one of Britain's most progressive and popular markets. Like Scarr, many town officials visited and inspected markets elsewhere as a prerequisite to planning a new market. Over time, in Leeds and elsewhere, written reports on markets piled up, and a number of general objectives were identified in the planning process: a central and visually striking entrance with an opposing exit and numerous subsidiary entrances to encourage regular shopping patterns, efficiency of arrangement, ease of movement within the market, abundance of light, careful ventilation, standardized and functional selling space, and attractive architectural space. Alfred Waterhouse, one of Britain's foremost architects, argued in 1877 that the most important features to be considered in planning a market hall were its value as a source of revenue, how to isolate the fish market from the rest of the market, the inclusion of a basement, sufficient light and ventilation, and the suitability of the design to the general architecture of the town.[8]

Arrangement of Interior Space

The placement of stalls and shops and the layout of aisles were critical in establishing retail patterns as well as social market behavior. For all practical purposes, the shape of the market, as determined by the site, was often such that certain stall or shop positions had a locational advantage over others. Likewise, the placement of the pillars supporting the roof influenced interior arrangement by breaking the market up into alleys or sections. The popular parallelogram-shaped building with its three-division roof construction favored a traditional three-aisle layout, while other roof arrangements led to different section patterns. The ar-

6.10. BILSTON, MARKET HALL, STALL AND SHOP DESIGN, 1892

6.11. BOLTON, MARKET HALL, 1856

The amount of natural light coming into this market was exceptional. Here we see the intersection of the two central transepts, framed above by iron screen trusses to give the hall an "arabesque" look. The building today looks very much the same (see fig. 11.11).

rangement of the supporting pillars in Lancaster's large, square market hall had the effect of breaking up the market into eleven distinct shopping alleys.

Ease of movement within the market was of great importance, not only to encourage the greatest amount of business but also to ensure health and safety. Narrow passageways could lead to overcrowding and even brawling. Glasgow's city architect remodeled the Bazaar Market building in 1855 so that even when crammed with people it could be emptied in ten minutes in case of a fire. Since the largest proportion of goods in the market were perishable, quick handling and easy transport in and out of the market were imperative. At the same time, allowing transport carts into the market at the very moment the townspeople were making their purchases was to be avoided, so interior storage facilities and convenient cart entrances were essential. Except at those market halls with separate interior shops, customers stood in the aisles to make purchases, and unless stalls offered space behind the counter for over-the-counter service, sellers stood in the aisles in front of their stalls, as was the case at Bilston and Bolton, with their low wooden stalls (figs. 6.10, 6.11).[9]

6.12. LANCASTER, NEW MARKET HALL, 1912

Interior arrangement, showing some of the thirty-three shops and sixty-five stalls. Constructed in 1880, the building was refurbished in 1909 and again between 1961 and 1975.

The architect also had to arrange the internal space without giving undue prominence to any particular stall or shop. This meant that stalls and shops needed to be standardized, and the market required wide aisles and frequent cross-aisles to direct the stream of traffic to all the stalls equally. The old open market usually had the advantage of not having a principal entrance—a fact appreciated by market traders. Equality of access also depended upon the placement of entrances and, of course, the type of interior traffic encouraged by the site of the market itself. Aisles in the Halifax market were a generous 10 feet wide, but many markets settled for narrower aisles. Stall layout varied from market to market, as did the number of interior shops. Lancaster's Market Hall interior in 1912 presented a scene of irregularity and disarray (fig. 6.12), particularly in contrast to the formal arrangement found in the Bolton market. Bilston's market of 1892 had forty-five "lock-up" shops, forty lock-up stalls, and fifty-five open stalls. Darlington's market offered its sellers four types of stalls: shuttered, box, open, and butchers'. Over the course of the century the typical market stall evolved from a rather primitive descendent of the open-sided outdoor market stall arranged in straight lines along

6.13. MARKET STALLS, VARIOUS DESIGNS

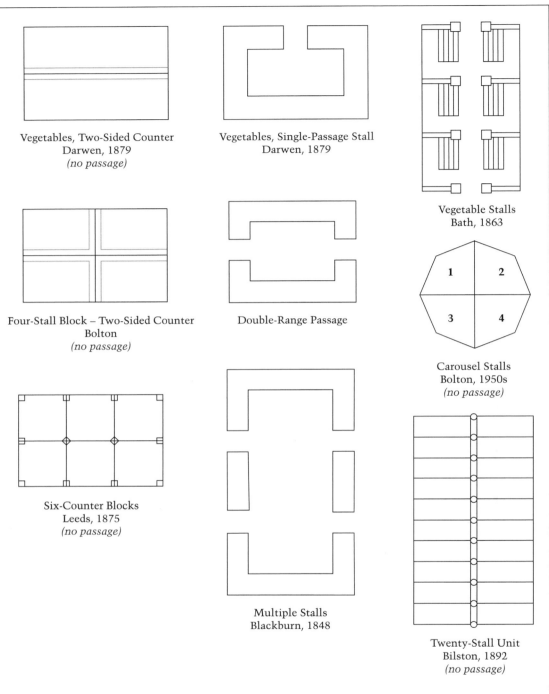

Vegetables, Two-Sided Counter
Darwen, 1879
(no passage)

Vegetables, Single-Passage Stall
Darwen, 1879

Vegetable Stalls
Bath, 1863

Four-Stall Block – Two-Sided Counter
Bolton
(no passage)

Double-Range Passage

Carousel Stalls
Bolton, 1950s
(no passage)

Six-Counter Blocks
Leeds, 1875
(no passage)

Multiple Stalls
Blackburn, 1848

Twenty-Stall Unit
Bilston, 1892
(no passage)

the market floor to the "two-front" stalls, in which four stalls were carved out of a square block, often walnut or deal, thus giving each stall two fronts and access to two aisles, as can be seen in the Halifax interior today. Even more sophisticated, the "double-range-and-passage" stalls gave the stallholders access to two aisles with the added advantage of a passageway traversing the stall (fig. 6.13). Although some stallholders and shop owners objected, stalls and shops were increasingly standardized as much as possible: they were given the same type of shutters, the same style signage, similar lighting and other fixtures, the same kind of roof, uniform painting or staining, and identical overall construction. Bradford's Kirkgate Market

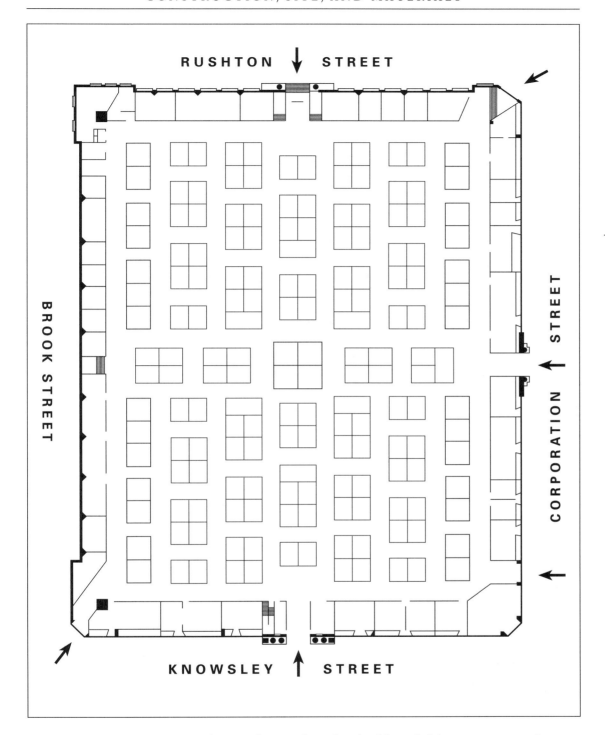

RUSHTON ↓ STREET

BROOK STREET

CORPORATION STREET

KNOWSLEY ↑ STREET

6.14. Bolton, Market Hall, Layout of Stalls, 1938

fit four stalls into an octagonal, providing each with a double-sided front. In 1938 Bolton replaced its stalls with fifty-one new stall "blocks," a system which arranged stalls in two to five units per block. Blocks were of varying size and modern design. Each had counter space on at least two sides, but the clerk still stood in the aisle (fig. 6.14). The blocks and the passages between them were arranged so no direct communication was possible from one side of the hall to the other, "to ensure as far as possible that the public circulated over the whole floor area." In Wolverhampton, twenty years after its market hall had opened, two new avenues were cut through several lines of stalls to move customers in the direction of under-

6.15. FOWLER'S PROPOSED
PLAN FOR THE
HUDDERSFIELD MARKET
HALL, 1877

frequented stalls. Southport's architects arranged the twenty-four double-range-and-passage stalls of its greengrocers division "so as to give them a fair chance of equal patronage by each occupying a corner." In the traditional pannier-type market building, as is the case at Bideford Market Hall today, the stalls are simply tables or benches, with the advantage of being movable, which allows a large open space to be created for other uses.[10]

The most important design issue was the appearance and position of the market entrances. Customers had to be drawn into the new market hall as easily as they were drawn into the old open-air marketplace. Lancaster's market hall of 1879 had seven entrances, Blackburn's six, while the Eastbank Market Hall at Southport (1881) had thirteen. It was generally agreed that markets with clumsy or concealed approaches were destined to fail: thus the market's entrances had to be visible from as many of the main streets as possible, and the central entrance had to be marked by a prominent tower or imposing sculpture. By mid-century most markets had at least one wide entrance opening onto an equally wide interior avenue.

Most markets were built with an understanding that shoppers disliked having to move up or down flights of stairs. Upper-floor and mezzanine galleries tended to fail as selling spaces.

Likewise, entrance steps could completely ruin a market, although it was not uncommon, considering the often irregular elevation of the market site, for at least one entrance to need steps. But it was generally acknowledged that elevation changes were best dealt with by means of a sloping floor rather than stairs. When Carlisle's market committee insisted that there be no steps going up to the market, the architect's answer was to create a 1 in 50 slope to the market floor. On the other hand, the market hall at Huddersfield ended up with a cumbersome staircase at its severely sloping main entrance. In 1877 Huddersfield's market committee rejected an ingenious plan by the eminent Charles Fowler which would have handled a 7-foot grade change in the market site by lowering the floor, so that the market contained a two-level shop front on the lower side and a single-level shop front on the higher (fig. 6.15). On the main front Fowler inserted an entrance with a recess which sloped according to the street grade, and for the side entrances he provided ramps, giving carts access to the market as well.[11]

Opening the Market Shops to the Street

With the addition of modern plate-glass fronts to the once blank market hall façade, market officials cleverly provided themselves with both an additional source of revenue and an enterprising way in which to draw more customers into the market. Indeed, the addition of the exterior shop window implied a welcome to the market which was absent in earlier markets, and it helped the market hall continue to appear up to date. The visual result was that the market hall front was transformed from the usual classical wrap to a plate-glass-fronted building, such as the hall at Hanley in 1849 (see fig. 6.9) even before the department-store craze arrived from France in the late 1850s. In reality, the only change to many of the older market halls was that exterior walls were simply punctured to allow direct access to the shops. It was in this manner that Bolton's exterior shop fronts were cut into the market's blank classical wrap in 1894.

Many of the newer market hall exterior-fronted shops had rooms above as storage or showrooms or, as it was common for tradesmen to live on the premises, apartments for the shopkeeper. Leeming and Leeming's Oldham Market Hall of 1904 had shop fronts on two sides of the market, each having windows and doors opening onto both street and market interior. There the architects ingeniously inserted independent stalls between the interior shop fronts that shared interior walls with the shops. Each of the sixteen Oldham shops, approximately 16 feet by 13 feet, had basement storage (with skylights to the sidewalk), a stairway to an upper floor, which could be used as either a showroom or living quarters, and walk-through access from street to interior market hall. These glass-and-iron-faced shop fronts provided an interesting modern façade for the market hall interior.

Other Plan Features

Poor ventilation and insufficient lighting could easily drive buyers and sellers away from the market. Architects sought to include lighting and a ventilation system to carry off both the excessive heat and the often undesirable smells of the market. Although few market halls were centrally heated (the grand Halifax Hall of 1896 was not centrally heated until 1954), by the 1880s most of the new buildings had some kind of individual heating system for stalls and shops. Ventilation, heating, and lighting were, along with stall rearrangement, the aspects of markets which were most often updated. Harrogate's stallholders used individual charcoal burners in their stalls, but because the fumes became so bad, market officials installed a central heating system based on a number of large stoves; Leeds addressed the ventilation problem of its 1857 market by simply replacing the entrance doors with large open iron gates. Elsewhere, the ventilation problem was tackled with the installation of louver clerestory roof openings or a special ventilation shaft at the roof's peak.

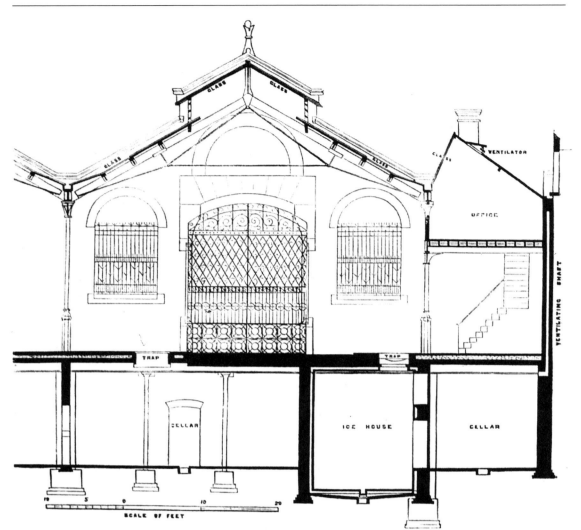

6.16. MANCHESTER FISH
MARKET, 1873

This new market, for both
wholesale and retail sale of
fish, was a part of the
gigantic Shudehill public
markets complex. Below the
2,000-square-yard building
were eight ice storage rooms
and eight cold cellars for
fish.

Before the modern shopping center, the department store, the cooperative store, and the
later chain store, the market hall pioneered in several design features which transformed
everyday shopping into an up-to-date, safe, and convenient experience. These included base-
ments with ice cellars for fish and meat storage, restaurants and snack bars, rooms for the
market inspectors (often placed to give a full view of the market), offices for market clerks,
public lavatories, weighing machines at the cart entrance, and various special interior meeting points for customer convenience, particularly, the fountain and an often grand interior
clock. "Under the clock" in the market hall of Halifax was a popular rendezvous. The exterior clock often became part of the language of urban life as well. Batley's market hall clock
was the first public clock in the town (1878), and Huddersfield's clock was regarded by its
townsfolk as so sophisticated that it became the standard timepiece for the town and surrounding district. Fountains were also popular. Birkenhead's market (1845) had two interior water
fountains, built of Portland cement, which sent up columns of water at the intersections of
the entrances. Birmingham's interior fountain gave the hall an imposing central focus, as did
the fountain in the Halifax Borough Market Hall. The fountain in St. Helier's market hall of
1882 had a unique 15-foot, three-tiered fountain over a circular pool decorated with ceramic putti.

The market hall tower served as a way to distinguish the market at a distance. It could
also house a capacious water tank that supplied a network of fire hydrants near all the entrances and in convenient places within the market itself. The first market hall to have a
sophisticated basement storage system was the Birkenhead hall of 1845, which had a vaulted

basement supported by 115 cast-iron columns: brick arching was supported on cast-iron pillars and girders to form the bed for the main floor. Manchester's fish market (fig. 6.16) had cold-storage rooms below the market, and the Bradford Rawson Square Market of 1899 had a cold-storage basement with a hydraulic lift that extended to the main (ground) floor and the first-floor balcony. Flooring varied from market to market and decade to decade. Early markets were flagged with thin stones of various lengths and breadths, usually laid in sand so that they were open to dirt and water. Bideford's market hall of 1884 had a much more sanitary yellow brick floor, and the Carlisle Market of just five years later had the latest in floor treatments—a concrete floor known as a "filler joist" floor, whereby small reinforced steel joists were covered with concrete. Most common by mid-century were various asphalt floors, which were preferred not just for sanitary reasons but because asphalt provided a quieter floor. Here a solid concrete foundation was covered by two or more inches of asphalt—often with indentations to give the user more secure footing. The Huddersfield Hall of 1880 was laid with patented Claridge's Seyssel Asphalt, a 1-inch thickness of asphalt on top of a concrete bed, which resulted in a floor that marketers could walk on "without the terrible clatter from wood or stone flooring."[12]

Lighting

The roof was the hall's principal source of both light and heat, but both needed to be regulated. Adequate lighting was important because it helped protect the consumer from fraud and deception. But while the market needed natural light, it could not tolerate the overheating which too often came with a fully glassed roof. Direct sun could be fatal to certain market products, particularly fish and meat, and as a result, many market authorities had to correct the architect's enthusiasm for too much glass. Yards and yards of calico had to be hung under the glass roof of the new market at Cardigan on its opening day because it was feared that the sun would damage the meat. Another problem for markets which relied on a central skylight or clerestory for their light was that all the available light fell in the center of the market, leaving the sides of the hall in darkness. The best light was obtained from the north side of the roof, and for this reason many markets were purposely positioned so that the roof extended on an east-to-west axis. The roof ridges were then glazed on the north side only, thus obtaining maximum light and keeping the interior cool in the summer. Another solution to the problem of too much sun entering the market was clouded glass, called "rough plate" glass, which gave the advantage of light but prevented the inconvenience of the sun's direct rays. Since many markets catered to urban working people who preferred evening shopping, artificial light had to be provided as well. Birmingham's hall had gas lighting from the day it opened in 1835, as did the 1822 hall at Liverpool, which boasted 144 gaslights. Redruth's hall was lit by electricity in 1888, while the Rochdale Market Hall was electrified in 1896. Few urban scenes impressed observers more than that of the gigantic gaslit market halls filled with throngs of well-behaved working-class families.

Materials and Roof Construction

After Edwin Chadwick's famous 1842 report on the sanitary condition of towns argued that a link existed between disease and unsanitary public and private space, architects, town officials, and planners concentrated on providing the public market with improved garbage and sewage facilities, better ventilation, clean and washable surfaces, and a plentiful supply of water. By 1880 it was common for new market halls to provide the lock-up shop with running water. Glazed tiles, salt-glazed bricks, terrazo, glazed slate, and glass were regularly employed because they were nonabsorbent and could be washed down. By the mid-nineteenth century the use of white glazed tiles, particularly in meat and fish stalls, was commonplace in new market halls, largely for sanitary reasons but also because they reflected light. Each of Southport's thirty-five permanent stalls had glazed white brick that went 5 feet high. Other materials, such as the enameled slate partitions in the butchers' market of Bristol's Exchange Market (1849), helped take the public market interior a long way from the filth and discomfort of the old street market. Most markets provided water and sewage disposal for their users as well as a garbage disposal system.

Exterior façade design innovation also drew on glazed (often polychromatic) brick. Once regarded as too common, brick construction was made stylish by the critic John Ruskin in the 1850s and afterward; but brick of the glazed sort was also appealing for functional reasons, for it kept the building free of the staining caused by air pollution. Glazed and polychromatic treatments can still be seen on the towers at the markets at Stalybridge and Ashton-under-Lyne, the market building at Bridgnorth, with its four-color brick front and tower, and at Barnstaple, where the market hall was dressed in red brick and trimmed with glazed dark blue and yellow bricks for the quoins and arches.

And what about the use of glass? Durham's citizenry was promised in 1850 that the new market would be covered with glass "much in the fashion of the great building in Hyde Park [being constructed] for the Exhibition of 1851." Although railway-shed architecture and the Crystal Palace were important archetypes for market hall roof design, few of the market halls imitated that structure's exterior glass-screen façade. The great glass façade of the Kirkgate Market at Leeds—which was built only a few years after the Crystal Palace by Paxton himself and looks quite at home with Paxton's earlier glass-and-iron "Victoria Regina" plant house at Chatsworth—is exceptional. While the glass-and-iron roof was nearly universal in market hall construction after the Birkenhead market hall of 1845, the exterior glass screen for the principal façade was not. Except when used on hidden sides, as was the case in the market hall at Louth, glass-and-iron screen façades were seen by most architects as temporary and wholly utilitarian building designs and not worthy for one of the town's principal monuments.[13]

Market halls were revolutionary, if for no other reason than because of their size, site innovation, and convenience. Most important, the market hall as a building type contributed much to the sweeping changes taking place in iron-and-glass construction during the nineteenth century. Like the late eighteenth-century textile mills and the later railway stations and glass conservatories, the market hall encouraged the use of new construction methods and materials, and in so doing, provided testimony that Victorian architecture had kept pace with its changing society. This was particularly the case with regard to the iron-and-glass roof. Indeed, the work of many market hall architects in the early and mid-nineteenth century was exceptional, even though some presented the character of mere tradesmen-architects rather than the traditional artist-architects. Most important, the history of the market hall illustrates the significance of the collaboration between the engineering and architectural professions. Because of this partnership, architecture indeed kept pace with society.[14]

Inhibiting architectural extravagance was the fact that architects and engineers were confined in their designs for public markets by the replacement of the individual, often aristocratic, patron by committees and councils less interested in architectural or engineering marvels and more interested in function and cost. Furthermore, most towns lacked the vast budgets for municipal markets that railway owners had for their stations, and market halls did not require the same level of innovation that train sheds or exhibition halls did. Although market planners would have liked to create a roof that allowed maximum floor space unobstructed by pillars, in reality, because of the necessity of grouping stalls and interlacing the market with aisles, the market floor could accommodate a more irregular and frequent placement of supporting pillars than could the roof over railway tracks. Indeed, from the late 1840s on, market hall roof construction owed much more to railway station engineering than to innovations by market hall architects. Blackburn's market improvement committee selected

Terence Flanagan, not an architect but a railway engineer, to design the Blackburn Market Hall of 1848.[15]

Market hall architects excelled in adapting the roof to a fixed and often inordinately large and peculiarly shaped building—usually at a low cost. In most towns, the market was the largest roofed space in the town. Cast-iron supporting columns had been used successfully in a strictly functional sense in late eighteenth-century textile mills and later as supporting columns for churches. Curiously, however, although iron-and-glass roof construction was a child of the industrial revolution, it had its earliest widespread application not in the industrial belts of England or Scotland but in the arcades, bazaars, and market halls of early nineteenth-century France, reaching its zenith in the great Halles Centrales of Paris, begun in 1854 (fig. 6.17).

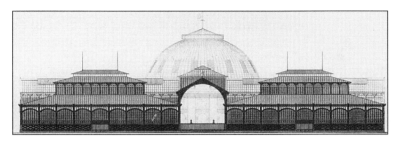

6.17. HALLES CENTRALES, PARIS, 1854-70

From the beginning, British centers of wealth (such as London and Glasgow) followed the French example, and by the 1830s, designers and proponents of architectural innovation like John Claudius Loudon were promoting iron-and-glass roofs for large conservatories and other public structures. By the late 1840s the popularity of iron and glass was ensured by such buildings as the Palm House at Kew Gardens (which attracted 64,000 visitors in its first year), and the Crystal Palace, which introduced the idea of prefabrication and standardization of parts. By the second half of the nineteenth century, large ironworks like McFarland of Glasgow were able to supply vast amounts of relatively cheap and standardized ornamental iron for the construction of such large buildings as market halls and railway stations.

Several types of roof construction were used in the building of market halls, but the two most common were the traditional frame or "truss" roof, made of wood or iron or a mixture of the two, and the more advanced arched roof, made of steel, which was, in essence, the building's wall as well. Most of these roofs relied on cast-iron columns, many of which, like

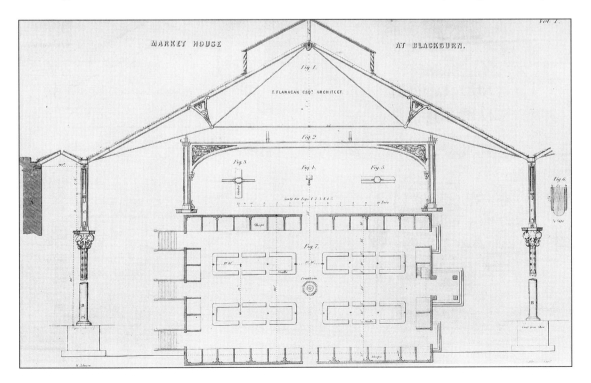

6.18. DETAIL OF COLUMNS AND SUPPORTS, MARKET HALL, BLACKBURN, 1848

those in Flanagan's modest-sized Blackburn Hall of 1848, served a decorative function as well (fig. 6.18). Iron trussed roofs place the tension of the roof in a vertical direction, while the tension thrust of the arched roof is in a horizontal direction. The iron truss construction was more widespread in part because it was cheaper, and in part because markets did not need the same large open spaces underneath that railway stations and exhibition halls did. In the earlier part of the century trussed roof "principals" were usually of part-timber and part-iron construction. Most markets adopted some variation of a multiple-span truss roof construction (that is, trusses side by side), with the result that many market floors were broken into divisions which corresponded to the divisions formed by the trusses and their iron supporting columns. The normal span for iron trussed roofs was in the range of 60 to 70 feet—much less than the span achieved in railway sheds.

Arched roofs were generally more costly but had the advantage of creating very large spans and thus freeing the building from lateral roofs, which created problems with water drainage and snow lodging in the valleys. The stability of an arched roof increased with its weight and size, so the roof was better suited for large spaces. Both types, trussed and arched, were commonly covered with some combination of thin wooden boarding, slate, lead, or (later) corrugated iron sheeting. By the 1890s some roofs had steel (rather than iron) principals. This was the case with Llanelli's market hall (1894), which had **T**-bar purlins of steel and timber screwed to the top on which to attach the roof boarding. This roof was covered with 3/4-inch white boarding, over which was a layer of felt and galvanized corrugated iron sheeting laid on and screwed to 2-inches-by-1-inch battens at suitable distances.[16]

The Higher Market at Exeter, designed by George Dymond and supervised by Charles Fowler, was a significant example of very early roof innovation wherein a combination of huge granite pillars supported a wood-framed roof (with plastered interior ceiling). From the center of this rose a cast-iron upper roof with partial glazing. The Exeter market is a good example of the transition from traditional materials and forms to the "modern" iron-and-glass roofs of the nineteenth century (see fig. 5.30) and forms an interesting contrast to the later and more modest iron-and-glass shedlike Market Hall of 1855 at Barnstaple (see fig. 7.1).

6.19. GRAINGER
VEGETABLE MARKET,
NEWCASTLE-UPON-TYNE,
1835

Here the wooden hammer beams make an interesting contrast with the classically arched butchers' market, which could be entered through the passageway on the right (see also fig. 5.23). The roof is noteworthy for its beauty and size.

The forerunners of iron truss roof construction in markets were the enormous early halls in Liverpool (1822), Birmingham (1835), and Newcastle (1835), all of which had a series of timber trusses stretching across the breadth of the building and were supported by cast-iron columns—in the case of Liverpool, there were a total of 116 cast-iron pillars 25 feet in height. Liverpool's roof was constructed in five spans or divisions,

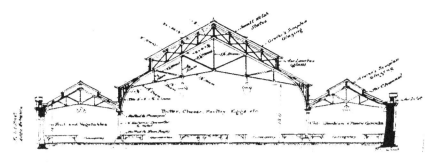

6.20. SIMPLE THREE-DIVISION IRON-TRUSS ROOF, MARKET HALL, PONTYPOOL, 1893

two of which were raised to form two vast clerestories, which in turn provided ventilation and interior light. Birmingham had a three-division roof, which included one central clerestory and several skylights, also on wood trusses and supported by cast-iron columns. Perhaps the most picturesque of the early market roofs was the one created for the Newcastle vegetable market hall in 1835 by John Dobson (fig. 6.19). Here forty-five square iron pillars carry longitudinal beams supporting a magnificent timbered roof which stretches the 338-foot length of the market. Side spandrels are fixed to the walls, and horizontal beams are supported by spandrels adorned with massive corbels.

The most innovative of the giant truss roofs was that at Birkenhead. Birkenhead had a utilitarian three-division roof carried on cast-iron columns; what was pathbreaking was that the roof was constructed of iron trusses with glass-roofed clerestories serving as skylights (see fig. 5.29). A modest but more typical market roof was the iron truss construction at Blackburn (1848) designed by Flanagan: three divisions (spans) of 36 feet each, supported by outside walls and two rows of cast-iron columns and longitudinal girders. The roof itself was a simple kind of iron truss introduced during the early days of railway construction: a single central strut held into place by tie-rods. The longitudinal spacing from truss to truss is 19 feet 10 inches, and the height from the floor to the top of the column is 25 feet and to the peak, 34 feet—all in all, making the market somewhat low compared to later markets, but typical

6.21. SHUDEHILL MARKET HALL, MANCHESTER, 1854

The four-span ridge-and-furrow roof was designed by a Mr. Wheeldon of the Heywood Phoenix and Derwent Foundries. Originally open on three of its sides, the market was eventually fully enclosed. Together, the four spans provided a market surface of 440 feet by 244 feet. The ends were finished with ornamental elliptical glass screens.

of a medium-sized mid-century market hall (see fig. 6.18). By the 1890s this iron-truss-roof formula had become common—used with simplicity and inventiveness at Pontypool (fig. 6.20; see also fig. 6.5). The span is relatively short, but when placed together, the three spans create a roof that is more than 100 feet wide. The floor plan shows how the roof dictated the layout of the market: the supporting columns became the locus for the stall organization.

The most typical market hall roof construction was an iron version of the traditional timber truss roof called the queen-rod (or queen-post) roof, in which the truss is supported by suspending rods that act as inclined struts and vertical ties. This can be seen in the three-division roof of the Pontypool Market, an ingenious roof in which one of the smaller of the two side divisions extends in two directions to cover the highly irregular site. Here the architects, Robert Williams and D. J. Lougher, were faced with the problem of designing a market to fit two site irregularities, a slope and limited access from the principal street, which came only by way of a narrow passageway through some buildings. The second problem was solved by extending roofed arcades out from the central building. The three-division roof, a mix of glass and slate, therefore has two appendages which extend it to the edge of the site.

Smaller than the Newcastle Grainger Market, but with a single roof (the Grainger Market really contained two roofs side by side), the Manchester market boasted an immense four-division trussed iron roof that was the largest market roof of its day. It covered a market floor of 440 feet by 244 feet (107,360 square feet). The roof consisted of two central spans of 72 feet each, with side spans of 50 feet. At the apex of the Manchester roof was a long skylight of rough plate glass. There were also louver-framed ventilation shutters on the sides. The ends were finished with ornamental elliptical glass screens, filled with rough plate glass and springing from large square pillars (fig. 6.21). This market at Shudehill, originally open on three of its sides, was eventually given side façades.

The most complex of the early iron-framed, queen-rod, truss roofed markets was that built at Bolton between 1852 and 1855. This enormous, seven-division roof (which survives) has two central 50-foot-span transepts, which cross each other to form a 76-foot-tall octagonal central hall, and six side aisles. Its iron trusses have inclined struts and vertical rod-ties extending from the truss, and, in addition, rods extending from the truss to the iron girders atop the supporting columns. A tall wood-framed clerestory sits atop the central nave, carried on arches and four massive Gothic hammer-beam iron screen trusses, which frame the central hall. All of this combines to create an extremely light and almost ecclesiastical space. A later but more elaborate version of the great market hall octagons was carried out for Bradford's Kirkgate Market (1872) by Lockwood and Mawson (see fig. 5.36); at St. Helier, which contains eighty tons of glass, in 1882 by T. W. Helliwell; and in Leeming and Leeming's Kirkgate Market in Leeds. This market has a central octagon encircled by a lower, narrower glass nave, with a trussed roof with circular ribs, all of which is fitted inside a five-story shop façade (fig. 6.22).

6.22. Cross Sections of Kirkgate Market Hall, Leeds, 1904

Arched-roof construction for markets in Britain began with Fowler's use of thin sheets of laminated timber bolted together in a curve in the Exeter Lower Market Hall of 1837. But the arched roof, with its greater potential for wider spanning, was used less for markets than for railway sheds, and it is not until after mid-century that the arched roof became common in markets. Two impressive arched-roof markets were constructed in 1866. The roof at Coventry's market is a single, 90-foot span formed by semicircular wrought-iron rib principals, springing from the floor line and passing through massive braced columns that are about 12 feet high. The roof is 46 feet high

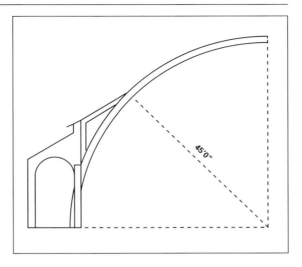

6.23. COVENTRY MARKET HALL, 1867

This was an unusually large arched roof; it permitted an uninterrupted market floor of 90 feet in width. The thrust of the arch springs from the ground rather than from a wall or support column and is conveyed through a side arch to the main wall of the building. The principals are tied together by trussed iron purlins.

to the center, covered with equal portions of glass and zinc, and the principals are connected by iron purlins set 8 feet apart (fig. 6.23). Derby's market hall roof (recently refurbished), taking its cue from Paxton's hipped-roof conservatory at Chatsworth, is an impressive single-span arched roof with large skylights (figs. 6.24 and 6.25). It is similar in construction to the roof of St. Pancras Station, London. It covers a rectangle 86 feet 6 inches by 192 feet, and the iron arch principals are supported on columns 22 feet high. The roof is divided into eight bays of 24 feet each. The principals consist of wrought-iron arched ribs, the inner and outer curves being true circles struck from the same center, with radiuses of 43 feet 9 inches and 41 feet 5 inches, respectively, the springing of the rib being 7 feet 6 inches above the center. The rib is of the same depth throughout, and consists of a $5/16$-inch thickness of web, with holes punched for sake of ornament (as at Paddington Station), connected with top and bottom flanges formed of two angle irons $3 1/2$-inches by $7/16$-inch. The rib carried wrought-iron lattice purlins at intervals of 6 feet 9 inches. At every alternate supporting place of the purlins, the web of the main rib is joined by a plate 1 foot 9 inches-by-$10 1/2$-inches thick, which plate

6.24. DERBY, MARKET HALL, EXTERIOR, 1866

is also riveted onto the web at the other purlins as a strengthening plate. The roof is hipped at both ends, so there are only five ordinary principals of 81 feet 5 inches of clear span. No provision is made for any additional horizontal thrust, such as would arise from pressure of wind or snow, but the roof offers great resistance in its longitudinal direction.

Certainly, the most advanced arched roof to be found in a nineteenth-century market hall is that covering the Carlisle Market Hall of 1889, designed by A. T. Walmisley and constructed by Robertson and Co. of Workington (fig. 6.26). The building was placed on a ground of irregular shape that is more than 60,000 square feet and has limited access to a principal thoroughfare (Fisher Street), so the task of the roof designer was difficult. Walmisley's solution was to roof the market with a three-division roof, each span being 70 feet 6 inches. The principal arches were tied arches—that is, lightweight arches 18 feet 9 inches high from their base to the apex of the ribs, which were tied together by round bar-iron ties that allowed no thrust on the walls or columns; the tying occurred only on the main ribs. To provide maximum open space, only alternate main ribs are anchored to a massive (four-ton) column, so that the distance between columns is nearly 40 feet. Maximum light is obtained by overhead glazing and by allowing the end gable screens to be filled in with glazing on wrought-iron astragal bars. The ventilator section is carried by the intermediate ribbing (fig. 6.27). The roof surface was covered with 1¼-inch wood boarding, with two glass openings and with the columns acting as the conduit for 6-inch stoneware piping to carry the roof water.[17]

Fixing the glass to the roofs, trussed or arched, presented difficulties; the process was the subject of much debate. The old system of setting the glass roof was to place the glass on zinc roofing and use screws and solder to fasten it. However, because of expansion and contraction of the zinc, the solder cracked, and the screws tore the sheets, causing leakage. The more modern ridge-and-furrow system was one of a number of innovations whereby putty was used for setting the glass, making it easy to repair. While putty was the preferred adhesive, over time it hardened, cracked, and caused leakage. As a result numerous new glazing systems were

6.25. DERBY, MARKET HALL, INTERIOR, 1866

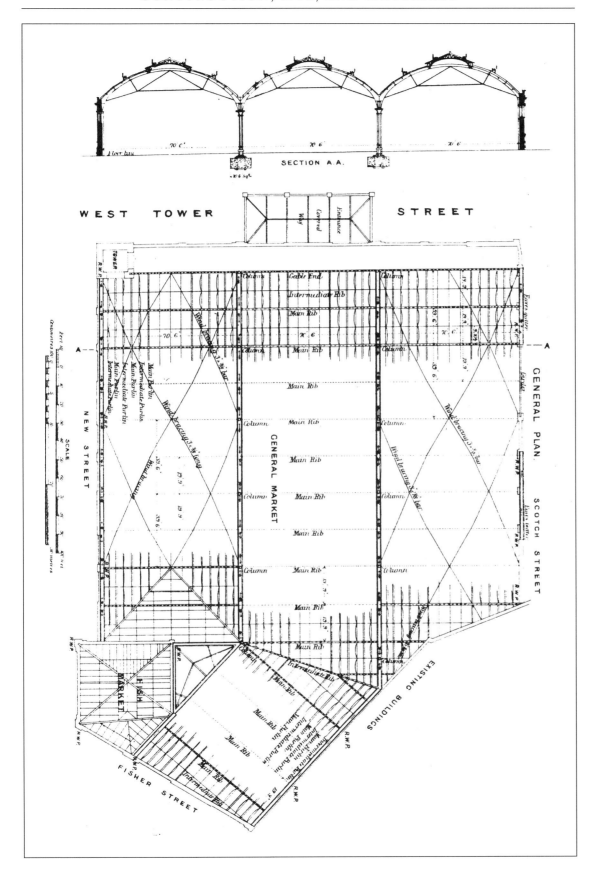

6.26. Cross Section and
Roof Plan of the
Carlisle Market Hall,
1889

6.27. CARLISLE MARKET
HALL, 1889

marketed and tried. One was a "thermoplastic" putty system, which was used in the covering of the new roof of King's Cross Station. It hardened in a few hours; when exposed to the sun's heat it became plastic, and on cooling again it returned to its original firmness. Other systems were tried in which putty was avoided altogether—the best being a method of fixing the glass to metallic sash bars, instead of wood, such as in the Helliwell system, in which a zinc or copper bar has a double gutter on top of which is screwed a zinc or copper cap for holding the glass down. The Helliwell system allowed play in every direction, and could be used on curved roofs.

PART THREE

THE MARKET HALL AND SOCIOECONOMIC CHANGE

❦

FOOD, THE MARKET HALL, AND THE STANDARD OF LIVING

LITTLE IS KNOWN ABOUT HOW AND WHERE FOOD WAS BOUGHT AND SOLD, its abundance, or what sorts of fare were typically found on the tables of nineteenth- and early twentieth-century urban dwellers. Historians have identified, amid considerable debate, general trends in per capita consumption. In very broad terms, by the 1750s British society faced general improvement with regard to the supply and distribution of food. This was because of considerable increases in domestic production and imports, which had begun in the late seventeenth century (in Scotland, from about the mid-eighteenth century). Overall, the actual quantities of foodstuffs brought into the marketplace and the town shops were greater than ever before; in fact, it is generally believed that until the late eighteenth century (with some exceptions during dearth years), the food supply actually grew at a more rapid rate than the urban population itself.[1]

But by 1790 a less optimistic view dominated the marketplace: that food consumption per capita saw little or no improvement (or perhaps an actual decline) for as much as a quarter of a century, that food quantity decreased for many urban dwellers, and that most towns faced overwhelming food-supply problems. Overall, after about 1790 many towns found that the rate of increase in the food supply was much less than the rate of increase in population and that wartime inflation reduced expendable income. Indeed, the population of England grew 72 percent between 1791 and 1831. Some towns grew even more rapidly. Between 1801 and 1851, Bradford grew from 13,000 to 104,000, and Leeds from 53,000 to 172,000. In Scotland, Glasgow grew from 32,000 in 1750 to 202,000 in 1831. Overall, then, it appears that from about 1790 until the 1820s, population increase, inflation, war, periodic scarcity, and an inequitable distribution of wealth meant that supply fell below basic needs, so that while most town markets had more food, many people faced an ongoing food shortage that left them with less rather than more food. To make matters worse, shifts from a local to a regional food-distribution system often worked against the average consumer and hence set off protests in the form of food riots, which became traditional in many towns. In particular, hundreds of food riots occurred in British towns in the period from 1756 to 1801. Although some argue that per capita food consumption picked up after about 1800, and real wages began to pick up by 1815, nevertheless, the urban food supply was insufficient and precarious, the quality was often unacceptable, and the mode of distribution was primitive and unsettled—so much so that the food riot was still a feature of the urban marketplace into the 1810s.[2]

What happened to the standard of living between about 1820 and 1850 is still a puzzle. Recent scholarship has centered on evidence of a decreasing average height for both males and females born between the 1820s and the mid-1850s, a change that proves that many people suffered significant decline in nutritional status. Increased unemployment and an unequal distribution of wealth further widened the food gap. A more optimistic (and popular) recent view holds that from 1820 the decline in the supply of food was halted and incomes rose: in the subsequent twenty-five years, the average skilled worker in England and Wales saw gradual improvement in the quality and quantity of food, particularly in the north of England, where bread had come to replace oatmeal as the working-class diet staple. In Scotland, as well, there seem to have been more gains than losses. In Britain, the average urban worker in the 1830s still ate an enormous amount of bread compared to animal products, although by this time sugar, vegetables (including potatoes), and animal foods, including cheese and meat, were becoming more common fare. Members of poor working-class families in Bath in 1837, for example, would have subsisted on a weekly diet of 8.5 pounds of bread and a pound each of meat, potatoes, and cheese. About the same time (1841), a typical semi-skilled worker's family ate slightly less animal fats and half the bread but eight times the potatoes (table 7.1). Another kind of fat, margarine, became a staple in the working-class diet in the 1880s.[3]

Despite references to "hungry forties," the most reasonable guess is that at least from the mid-1840s, overall the food supply increased sharply—partly because of the lowered tariffs on sugar, imported meat, wheat, and other imported items. For a growing number of men and women of the working classes, the prospect of severe food crisis had abated considerably by mid-century, and a modest improvement could be enjoyed. In the first half of the century, meat was a luxury for most working people (particularly women and children), but with the removal of government bans on meat imports in 1842 and the coming of railway transport, the meat supply increased; by 1850 meat prices had fallen 50 percent and the better-paid skilled laborers enjoyed more meat than had their counterparts in previous generations. For those working people below the income level of a skilled worker, "meat" often meant bacon and offal (and later, pork and imported frozen meat), with higher quality "butchers'" meat consumed only occasionally. A majority of engineers' families ate animal food daily, while common laborers and their families ate it two times a week or less. By 1864 even low-wage (semi-skilled) working-class families were eating nearly two pounds of meat and other animal fat a week (table 7.2), with fewer potatoes but still a great quantity of bread. However, while the level of consumption for many may have improved somewhat in quantity, by 1864 the diet had not changed much in terms of variety: the standard was still a bread-potato-meat diet supplemented by a little tea—and a goodly amount of beer. Overall, as one observer noted, it was too little for health and strength.[4]

Beginning in the 1860s the arrival of foreign tinned meat, improved transport of cattle, improved slaughtering facilities, and vast new supplies of grain from abroad contributed to a revolution in the working-class diet. American bacon was cheaper than British, but it had to be fried rather than boiled. New processed and packaged foods entered the marketplace in remarkable quantities, not the least of which were the prepared cereals which ushered in the "cornflakes revolution." Beginning in the 1870s meat could be chilled or frozen, which contributed hugely to smoothing out the problems of meat distribution and availability. Meat consumption per capita rose by 33 percent between 1880 and 1909. By then the average person ate more meat than bread, and skilled workers and their families were consuming two pounds of meat per person per week, although the differences between the diets of the skilled and the unskilled workers and those of men and women were still considerable. Beginning

Table 7.1 Weekly Diet of a Semi-Skilled Worker's Family of Five, 1841	
Bread	20 lbs.
Meat	5 lbs.
Beer	7 pints
Potatoes	40 lbs.
Tea	3 oz.
Sugar	1 lb.
Butter	1 lb.

Source: S.R. Bosanquet, *The Rights of the Poor and Christian Almsgiving Vindicated* (1841), 51,52; cited in Burnett, *Plenty and Want*, 68.

Table 7.2 Weekly Diet of a Semi-Skilled Worker's Family, 1864	
Bread	9.82 lbs.
Meat & Other Fats	1.90 lbs.
Potatoes	3.45 pints
Tea	0.50 lbs.
Sugar	0.50 lbs.
Milk	18.50 lbs.

Source: Burnett, *Plenty and Want*, 153. (Calculated from an average of accounts of returns of silk weavers, needlewomen, kid glovers, shoemakers, stocking weavers by a Dr. Smith in 1864.)

in the mid-1870s food prices began a steady decline which lasted until the mid-1890s. For the typical working-class family, food prices fell by 30 percent between 1877 and 1887; in the Black Country, for example, it has been estimated that the price of a basket of commodities (bread, butter, cheese, meat, sugar, tea, and bacon) fell by about 20 percent between the mid-1870s and the mid-1880s, and continued a steady decline for another decade. In London the so-called quartern loaf (4 pounds) fell in price from 7s4d in 1881 to 5s9d in 1896, and a basket of nine food items in 1900 in London would have cost 51 percent less than the same basket in 1877. Part of this improvement came about because during a depression that began in 1873, some British farmers switched from grain to fruit and dairy production and market gardening. This brought more cheese, milk, jam, eggs,

Table 7.3 Weekly Diet of an Urban Worker's Family of Three with a Weekly Income of Less than 25s, 1904		
Bread and Flour	28.40	lbs.
Meat	5.30	lbs.
Potatoes	14.00	lbs.
Tea	0.48	lbs.
Sugar[1]	3.87	lbs.
Butter	1.10	lbs.
Cheese	.67	lbs.
Rice, Tapioca, Oatmeal	2.54	lbs.
Coffee, Cocoa	.15	lbs.
Milk	5.40	pints
Currants, Raisins	.42	lbs.
Eggs	5.75	pence worth
Other	1s2	pence worth

Source: Memorandum on the Consumption and Cost of Food in Workmen's Families, 1904, P. P. [Cd. 2337]; quoted in Report of and Enquiry of the Board of Trade into Working Class Rents, Housing and Retail Prices . . . 1980, P. P. [Cd. 3864], xxvi; cited in James Treble, Urban Poverty in Britain, 1830–1914 (New York, 1979).

[1] Approximately 150 percent of the amount spent on sugar was spent on jam, marmalade, treacle, and syrup.

butter, and vegetables into the market. Overall food consumption increased by 150 percent between 1860 and 1880. In addition, increased real wages did not lead to a decrease in the proportion of family income spent on food; in fact, extra income appears to have been devoted to improving the variety and level of diet. The weekly diet of a skilled worker's family (table 7.3) shows this improvement. Gains in the diets of less-skilled workers were more modest, and despite this optimistic picture, a large segment of the population—probably a majority of working people, particularly women and children—still suffered from protein deficiency.[5]

The rural picture in the nineteenth century is much less rosy, particularly for agricultural workers of the south and the southwest, where meat was seldom consumed, for whom bread, potatoes, a little cheese, and some bacon made up the average diet. Even in the so-called Golden Age of British agriculture (1850-73) many farm workers were paid with decayed meat and inferior cheese, and they had no access to land allotments on which to produce a portion of their own food supply. But while the fortunes of the landowners fell in the period 1874-1896, those of agricultural laborers, particularly in the north, rose. Their diet improved in terms of nutrition and variety. Meat consumption became an everyday occurrence; the price of sugar, tea, bread, and other products fell; and more rural people gained access to land allotments. Food prices may have been lower for northern agricultural workers because the urban public market system was better developed in the north. It is clear (if ironic) that in the course of the nineteenth century, rural society was becoming increasingly dependent on the urban economy for its food supply.[6]

For the people of the middle and upper classes, the story of food and diet is quite different and less controversial. Throughout the nineteenth century, not only did their diet steadily improve in quantity, variety, and nutrition, but food consumption became a status symbol in the same way that consumption of clothing and household goods had. The lavish upper-middle-class dinner party became an institution, and, as popular cookbooks of the age suggest, an abundance of market products was available for middle-class larders. Indeed, the working class's share of the nation's food supply most certainly fell in proportion to the share of the property-owning classes.[7]

Regional Differences

Working people in London not only paid more for a basket of food than working people in, for example, Macclesfield, but the food itself was also of considerably lower quality and had less variety. A geographic study of food also shows that people in certain regions had greater access to a patch of garden or to a more protein-rich diet. This was the case for the thousands of families of handloom weavers in Lancashire villages who kept pigs and hens alongside their gardens. It has also been argued that nutritional levels were higher in the north of England because of greater availability of fuel for cooking. That is to say, more hot meals were eaten in the north of England than in the south, where coal was at least double the price. In addition, the coming of the railway encouraged a regional food bias. By the 1860s, for example, the railway had made three towns, Aberdeen, Edinburgh, and Leeds, the principal railheads for meat distribution. Those with access to these markets thus enjoyed a cheaper and more abundant supply of meat.[8]

The Local Market and the Urban Food Supply

Historians have remained surprisingly uninterested in how the character of the local market—its size, location, and attractiveness—affected the urban food supply. This want of attention to the local marketplace may be due to the paucity of quantitative data, but it is also a result of a common inclination to dismiss the public market as a last holdover from a disappearing traditional society. The argument has even been advanced that the public market was not an important source of food for the average town resident and that the independent shops provided nearly all urban household provisions—including tea, sugar, candles, cheese, butter, and even some meat.[9]

Our study of hundreds of local public markets, however, suggests otherwise. First of all, throughout the nineteenth century, most urban dwellers regarded the independent shop as an extravagance; indeed, working-class people (except those very poor workers who were tied to a system of credit at the corner shop) bought a majority of their food in the public market. Furthermore, into the twentieth century the public market was a major source of food for the middle classes as well. As late as the 1880s in Cockermouth most of the foodstuffs (potatoes, butter, eggs, fish, and meat) that were sold in the town's covered market were not available in shops. In the 1880s, for example, 90 percent of Great Yarmouth's poultry was purchased in the market, and it was estimated that in the 1850s, 20,000 of Durham's population of 31,000 drew its food supply from the town market; in Barnstaple in 1851 about 1,200 of the town's 2,000 households used the market every week for their principal shopping; and in Sheffield in the late 1880s half the population of 300,000 shopped in the two market halls. Soon after Accrington opened its municipal tramway system (which extended to towns in the adjoining district), estimates were that the market served a number more than twice the size of the population of the town itself. In Barnstaple's Pannier Market, for example, the number of carts carrying foodstuffs into the hall increased from 73,000 in 1873 to more than 200,000 in 1883 (fig. 7.1). And on an average Saturday as recently as the 1960s the Kirkgate Market in Leeds attracted more than 100,000 shoppers.[10]

Hundreds of local market histories tell us that there was probably much more variety in the nineteenth-century urban diet than generally supposed, in part, because many of these foods never appear in conventional measurements of standard of living. In 1843, for example, Liverpool's St. John's Market is recorded as providing not only the customary butchers' and "provision" shops for the sale of beef, mutton, lamb, venison, pork, ham, and bacon but also stalls for the sale of such cheap meat products as tripe, pigs' feet, salted and pickled ham, sausages, sheep trotters, and pickled pork. Also available were pigeons, plovers' eggs, birds,

cheese, dried and cured fish, vegetables, bread and biscuits, butter, catsup, and so on. Although the stock-in-trade of the typical market was perishable foods, particularly meat, fish, poultry, eggs, butter, fruit, and vegetables, most markets also offered a vast array of other groceries: flour, spices, tea, coffee, and confectionery. On the other hand, by the early nineteenth century, bread seems not to have been as important a market commodity. Some markets offered an impressive variety of foods. On an October day in 1853, for example, Torquay's market hall offered, among other items, mutton, pork, beef, butter, eggs, potatoes, rabbits, hares, turkeys, geese, ducks, partridges, pigeons, fowls, nuts, fruits, and a greatly admired portable machine which that day made nearly 600 pounds of sausage. Aberdeen's market hall, in the 1870s, offered its users, among the usual goods, English apples shipped in small sailing vessels from the Tay and two dozen different kinds of candy. Covering an entire city block, Glasgow's Bazaar Market offered "every conceivable commodity," but it was particularly famous for its fruit of every description "in great abundance."[11]

A considerable amount of market space was given over to the sale of food items other than meat, vegetables, or dairy products. They could include anything from rabbits and fish to eggs and confectionary. In Bolton in 1855, 37 of the 185 food stalls and shops were devoted to products other than meat and vegetables, and in the late 1880s nearly a third of Darlington's stalls were occupied by vendors selling something other than meat and vegetables. Bolton's market had more than 400 table spaces for farm women and others selling eggs, butter, and fruit, and in Liverpool, 500 sellers were accommodated at long tables for their country products like eggs, rabbits, and fruit.

Thus, while we know much about per capita sugar and tea consumption, we have no way of knowing how many baskets of mushrooms, eggs, or chickens and rabbits were brought to the market by farm women, or how many carts of vegetables or pints of strawberries showed up in a particular market in a particular week. No accounts were kept of actual market sales, but as we know that the floor space of the public markets more than doubled between 1800 and 1850, we can be sure that the amount of goods offered for sale increased proportionately.[12]

How Market Improvements Increased the Standard of Living

We have argued that the character of the public market—its facilities, location, ownership, and the like—had much to do with the expansion or contraction of the town's food supply. Some towns found themselves facing a precarious imbalance between food and population because their inferior market facilities left them on the wrong side of the local and regional distribution and transportation system. Insufficient public market facilities, for example, discouraged nearby country producers from increasing productivity or developing new products. As late as 1868 in London, for example, more than three-quarters of a million pounds of fish rotted because of primitive methods of storage and distribution. Improvement in market management and facilities (including efficiency in distribution and storage) affected the amount, quality, and variety of food reaching the consumer, so that overall, it is probable that the diet of the average family in many towns improved more and at an earlier date than has been previously assumed.[13]

Until Britain was unified by a national food-distribution network in the 1920s and 1930s, the quality and quantity of the average diet were largely determined by the town's proximity to regional and local producers and by the ability of the town to encourage those producers (and others) to bring their goods into the local market. Smaller towns in grain-producing regions like Winchester and Salisbury were faced with the problem that local farmers were moving away from market gardening and dairy farming, while many large cities, like Manchester, were locked into very small food-supply zones—Manchester's food-supply zone did not extend beyond a 15-mile radius in the 1840s. It was not uncommon at the beginning of the industrial age for people of one town—even a relatively large town—to have to travel to another for some or all of their food. Such was the case for the folk of Aberystwyth, who had to go elsewhere to purchase meat. Ashton-under-Lyne did not have a market at all between 1760 and 1827; and the market at Bacup in the first half of the nineteenth century consisted of a mere two stalls. The cotton-weaving district around Burnley, stretching from Padiham to Colne and including the townships of Burnley, Haversham, and Eaves, had more than forty thousand inhabitants but only a single market in 1870; and Leicester's market was the only one serving dozens of surrounding towns. The economy of Cornwall was strong in tin and copper production and fishing but relatively weak in agricultural production; thus most Cornish towns adopted the notion that market reform would lead to improvement in the food supply. The new industrial towns frequently found themselves in a similar predicament but for different reasons: having no historic links with the countryside left them with only a few shops and no market for their citizens. Swindon, whose population in 1855 reached nearly 7,000, was faced with this dilemma.[14]

Price, availability, and quality were often wildly disparate from town to town and region to region. The railway frequently increased this gap because it provided new access to certain town markets and created new regional retail and wholesale markets (for such items as "dead meat," potatoes, eggs, cheese, and fish), while leaving other markets isolated. Local farmers could now carry dairy, fruit, and vegetable products quickly to more local markets by rail before they spoilt. This made goods more available and prices more equal—and some housewives had to travel to neighboring towns to supply the family food stocks. This is why many new public markets were situated near the railway station. At the same time, the consumer-producer link became weaker, as intermediaries combined new transportation, storage, and preservation methods to purchase large food stocks directly from local producers and then resell them to local, regional, or national (even world) retailers. Wholesaling was generally against the law in the medieval and early modern market because it was felt that the practice would break the link between consumer and producer—and this is exactly what happened on a massive scale in the nineteenth century. Some towns became giant wholesale and retail distribution centers, while in other towns the decline of the public retail market forced the populace to shop elsewhere. Thus, while bestowing prosperity on towns well placed in the distribution network, both the railway and the wholesaling industries also brought about a contraction in the food supply to those towns situated outside the new rail system. Emerging as a major railway center in the north, Carlisle became a principal market town with a better-than-average food supply, while the small traditional market towns of Howden in East Yorkshire and Wooler in Northumberland, which were bypassed by the railway, lacked the eggs, butter, cheese, and vegetables which once filled their market squares. The gainers were the people who lived in towns which served as wholesale centers or which had good railway access. In the mid-nineteenth century, then, there was an anomaly: some towns were food-rich and others food-poor.[15]

Food Economics and Food Politics: The Importance of Local Control

An equally important factor in determining whether a town would be food-rich or food-poor was the degree of local government promotion of the retail and wholesale markets. To be sure, since the beginning of the town itself, local government had sought to control its food supply. Notwithstanding some instances in which a town's food was distributed in order of social rank—with the poor coming last—the goal of most towns was a distribution of food that was equitable enough to preserve public order. Local government initiatives in securing the food supply reached new heights in the late eighteenth and early nineteenth centuries and contradict twentieth-century claims that the Victorian age was a time of laissez-faire alone. Indeed, the period preceding the Municipal Reform Act of 1835, which is regarded as a time of municipal lethargy and corruption, was, in the case of food policy, one of considerable action on the part of local governments.[16]

Local authorities had always regarded the availability of a steady supply of food, particularly wheat (oats in northern England and Scotland), at a moderate price to be indispensable for the maintenance of domestic peace and good order. This regular supply was sought by a number of means: the establishment of a public monopoly on grain through so-called meal markets, special taxes to support the poor, town council grants and public subscriptions for the purchase of food for the poor, special subsidies for bakers, and even encouragement of road building. In Kent the "badness of roads" was one factor that made it difficult for the small freeholders to send their goods to the local market, whereas improvement of Scottish roads led to better-supplied markets at such towns as Haddington, where a good road allowed farmers to use the "double carts" that increased their freight loads eightfold.[17]

The most popular early modern food policy was the prohibition of food speculation, hoarding, or sale outside the public market by retailers, intermediaries, or others. These were the so-called forestalling, regrating, and engrossing laws which sought to prevent individuals from gaining a corner on the market in wheat or other commodities and reselling it. These laws had existed for hundreds of years in an effort to enforce what was called firsthand buying, that is, direct sale between consumer and producer. It was believed that intermediaries, conventionally called hucksters and higglers, were speculators who not only caused harmful disruptions in supply by exporting local food to another town but also violated the notion of the "just price." In times of scarcity, it was believed, the poor should have priority in the distribution of grain.[18]

In Lancaster and elsewhere, municipal officials restricted the entry of hucksters and higglers into the market until midday so that ordinary householders could purchase for themselves "at first hand" at the best price (fig. 7.2). Buying grain outside the market was still a crime in Harwich in 1808, and new bylaws for the market at Tiverton in 1825 established a five-shilling fine for anyone buying food before it reached the market and then selling it again in the market.[19]

7.2. NOTICE FROM THE
MAYOR OF LANCASTER,
1796

The mayor gives notice that
"hucksters and higglers"
would not be allowed in the
market before 11 A.M., in
order to give the towns-
people better access to the
food supply.

Borough of Lancaſter.

WHEREAS several Hucksters and Higglers,
have made a Practice of buying up Fruit,
Eggs, Butter and other Provisions, in this Market,
in order to sell the ſame again, to the great inconvenience and Detriment of the Inhabitants of the Town
who ought firſt to have an Opportunity of ſupply-
ing themselves therewith, from the Market.

Notice is therefore hereby given,

THAT if any HUCKSTERS or HIGGLERS, shall in
future presume to buy any of the above-mentioned
Articles in the Market before the H O U R of 11
o'Clock in the Forenoon, they will be prosecuted,
with the utmoſt Rigor of the Law.

By Order of Mr. MAYOR.

JANUARY 30th, 1796.

Further, to keep consumers from being placed at a disadvantage, town governments often mandated that bread prices be set by law (an "assize"), or that a specified amount of grain be set aside at a fixed low price for the poor. This was often the reason for creating a meal market. Glasgow was typical in that its meal market was regularly held in a fixed open and public space under town council surveillance because officials saw it as their duty not only to provide a market for the poor but also to prevent hoarding and speculation. Nonetheless, abuses remained common, and the market was often the scene of food riots. In fact, by the late eighteenth century, engrossing, forestalling, and regrating were fast becoming ordinary business practices. Increasingly, the nation's grain supply came to be sold by auction to speculators and dealers in "sample markets" that were closed to the consumer, and often in a building known as the Corn Exchange.

At the same time, town officials and merchants sought to repeal the protectionist Corn Laws, which, by keeping grain at an artificially high price, could anger the laboring population and cause disturbances of the peace. Still another solution was to eliminate tolls in the market or to offer bounties, premiums, and other forms of price supports that would lower the price of food, particularly bread. The town of Market Drayton, for example, eliminated tolls on grain sales as early as 1743, hoping to bring farmers to the town. More than a century later, Winchester's mayor argued that by abolishing its market tolls the town would encourage more farmers to come to the Winchester market. Glasgow subsidized bakers by providing them with cheap flour, while Bristol's town government offered premiums for potatoes and promised interest-free loans to fishermen who expanded the local fleet.[20]

Yet by the end of the eighteenth century it had become clear to many that these traditional ways of managing the urban food supply were no longer either practical or workable, and municipal authorities turned to a more radical (and costly) solution: the creation of an enlarged and enclosed public retail market. Through the building and management of vast new municipal market buildings, local authorities, along with a reform-minded public, sought to increase and cheapen the town's food supply. They also hoped to encourage the consumption of more nutritious foods and to improve consumers' knowledge about food use and preparation. The idea was that how much and what quality food came from the local and regional growers and producers were determined by the size, location, comfort, and aesthetics of the local public market. Durham is a case in point. Durham's market, long in a declining state, was said to be the worst market in County Durham; the food supply was reviled as not as cheap as it ought to be because it lacked the facilities many of the neighboring towns possessed. "So long as they were exposed to the dirt, filth, and sludge of that miserable place which they called the market," argued one citizen, "it was quite impossible that they could expect to be supplied either cheaply or abundantly with the necessaries of life."[21]

The lesson was clear: towns with good market facilities, both retail and wholesale, would see regional foodstuffs come into their market. A small reduction in prices at a given market—because of larger turnover or lower rents—or increased competition owing to attractive facilities could mean that some consumers would have more disposable income for other (perhaps more extravagant) items. The size of the town often had little to do with the quality of the market, as was discovered by market-poor Wakefield when the regional food supply began to move to more-attractive market facilities in smaller neighboring towns. Indeed, the allure of outside sellers and buyers was the reason private shopkeepers' interests were generally regarded as secondary to the interests of the town market. In Stockport and elsewhere, shops were demolished to enlarge the market. Such food economics was one reason many towns made a greater fanfare over the opening of the new market than about almost any other civic event. Southport was undergoing acute economic depression when construction was begun on the new market hall in September 1879, but a huge spectacle was made of laying the cornerstone, complete with parades, fireworks and other special events, free entertainment, and lofty speeches.[22]

Cheaper Food

Thus, in an age which ardently debated the pros and cons of state intervention, the municipal regulation of food became politicized in a way it had never been before. Typical of this was the argument of the mayor of Carlisle that the municipal government must take responsibility for providing food for its working people. The mayor of Winchester was speaking of the town's new market when he stated that it was desirable for Winchester's inhabitants to have a greater supply of food than hitherto; and Manchester's market committee argued that only by building better market facilities could Manchester reverse the transfer of its trade to other towns. Few individuals better illustrate the link between politics and food than Archibald Scarr, mayor of Leeds and champion of the public market, who argued that it was the duty of town government to promote its markets so as to supply the public with good and cheap provisions. The same sentiment was expressed in Huddersfield, where a new market hall was erected to bring the townspeople food as cheaply as residents of Leeds could get it; and in Burnley it was announced that the new market hall would bring about a wholesome system of competition among the various trades. Similarly, approximately a century after the construction of its first market hall, the Liverpool market committee stated its belief that the value of the public market to the ratepayer could be judged not only by its earnings but also by the degree to which it brought savings to consumers. This goal of price reduction was reinforced, in Liverpool, through the publication of a weekly food price list, "The Housewife's Guide," in the local press. The list was designed to show customers that shopping in the public market was cheaper than in the shops.[23]

Price disparity was a matter of public debate. In Hull it was questioned whether, as some merchants claimed, Hull's food was more expensive than that in Manchester, Leeds, or Bradford because of the town's inadequate market facilities; and in Taunton it was argued that food was cheaper in nearby Bridgwater. It was maintained in Huddersfield that its population, which consumed a hundred tons of potatoes daily, paid between 30 and 40 percent more for them than did people in other towns, while the mayor of Winchester lamented that food was comparatively expensive in his city. In all these towns there was strong public sentiment in favor of a large and attractive public market hall as the best way to draw local and regional suppliers to town. Lancaster's town officials proposed a new public market partly in order to attract back to Lancaster the "country people" who had gone over to Preston, which had a new covered market.[24]

Much evidence suggests that in Huddersfield, Liverpool, and elsewhere this is exactly what happened: towns with the best market facilities had the largest, most varied, and cheapest food supplies. The high concentration of market halls in the industrial northwest may well explain the fact noted earlier: that a basket of goods purchased in Lancashire and Cheshire in 1905 cost considerably less than the same basket of goods in the southern counties. The new market building in Ipswich was claimed to have brought in a larger supply of provisions from the country and lower prices than ever before remembered, and it was noted in 1835 that a new market building at Kidderminster in the midlands "appears on the whole . . . to have increased competition in the market by inducing the country people to attend, in consequence of the increased room and accommodation." Butter in Harrogate sold for less in the market hall than in the local shop, a boon to the poor and lower middle classes; and in some towns, such as Reading, the public market provided so much of the food consumed by working people that it was acknowledged that "it is the working classes we are providing for . . . in carrying out a market scheme." Some market halls, such as those at Doncaster and Sheffield, were known for selling the best class of goods at a lower price the town shops. "I am speaking on behalf of the poor," said Watford's medical officer, who sought an improved public market, "and it would be for the good of the poor people to obtain things cheap without going to buy them in shops." Prices, particularly of the less-desirable joints of meat, were lower in the Rochdale market hall than in the shops. In Liverpool not only were public market prices lower than shop prices, but in areas near the public market the prices in local shops were lower than those of shops in other neighborhoods.[25]

Thus the market hall could offer the seller faster turnover and lower rents; this was the case in Bolton, where public market tenants paid 50 percent less rent than shopkeepers. Furthermore, the public market could guarantee lower prices, as Taunton's did for at least a hundred years after 1768, by forcing members of certain trades to sell only from the public market. In Taunton the restricted item was meat, while in Aberdeen until about the same time it was milk; and even in the 1880s, the only meat available in Oxford was through the public market because butchers' shops were prohibited by a local market act.[26]

Better Supplies

An examination of several food items further illustrates these developments. It appears that reformed public markets meant a more abundant supply, lower prices, and higher quality in meat and poultry. The demand for poultry is typified by the rapidly growing city of Harrogate, whose desire for a poultry market generated public demand for a new market hall in 1847. Although poultry is seldom considered in discussions of diet, public markets devoted such a large amount of space to it that we must conclude that poultry was an important component of the average person's diet. Typical of the market hall customers in Sheffield in 1864 was the skilled ironworker who "carries off the fattest capon, the plumpest goose and the biggest turkey the market affords."[27]

The market hall made possible the sale of enormous quantities of meat. Well into the twentieth century, a large number of the butchers who served town needs were country butchers who lived some distance away (often kept out of the local trade by the organized tradesmen) and had to be induced to bring their supply to town. To attract them to the market, enormous sums were spent on special markets for cattle sales, public slaughterhouses, and new, centrally located, attractive, clean retail markets with low rents. Providing a convenient public cattle market was one way to encourage regional farmers to sell their cattle in one town rather than another, and the new market hall likewise increased the availability of butchers' meat, particularly inexpensive pork, for the retail sector. Although it is commonly assumed that working people did not eat much meat in the 1820s, the public market in the Cornish mining town of Redruth boasted between thirty and forty butchers who sold only pork. In 1844 Truro had ten butchers, some selling from stalls in the street and others from shops; three years later a new market hall opened with thirty-four butchers, thus conceivably tripling the town's meat supply. Manchester's market committee, unhappy with the fact that the poor could not get any cheap meat but the low-grade waste products called mixed meat that were sold in private meat shops or the dirty meat shambles, built a new meat market and slaughterhouse to encourage country butchers to bring more meat to the city. Indeed, for most public markets, cheap, good-quality meat (including poultry and even inexpensive rabbit in season) was the mainstay of the market. In 1890, twelve of Britain's largest market halls devoted approximately 38 percent of their space to butcher sales. The Newcastle Grainger Market, built in 1835, was divided into two shopping areas, a vegetable hall of fifty-five shops and a butchers' hall with four long avenues that provided the people of Newcastle with a total of 196 butchers' shops, in which it was said the amount of meat for sale exceeded anything previously known in the north of England (see figs. 5.23 and 5.24). Swansea's hall of 1892 had eighty butchers' stalls (see fig. 5.42), while in Halifax the Borough Market Hall housed forty-three butchers' shops (see fig. 5.33). As late as the 1930s, Bradford's households relied on the municipal market for a significant portion of their meat (fig. 7.3).[28]

It is often argued that before the 1870s, fruits and vegetables (other than potatoes) did not make up an appreciable portion of the average diet. Even before the increase in imported citrus fruits in the second half of the nineteenth century, however, local market histories tell of an abundance in the quantity and variety of fruits and vegetables. Edinburgh had so many vegetables and "garden stuff" that it was able to supply, unexpectedly, an entire fleet of 20,000 for seven weeks in 1781 without seriously interrupting the town's food supply. It was known in Sheffield that the skilled laborers who flocked to the market came for early peas, winter salads, and the first asparagus.[29]

How does the statistician convert "garden stuff" into a measurement of the food supply—including a field of mushrooms picked by an enterprising young boy and his father?

> Tommy Cornthwaite owned this here field. He meadowed it and cut it and it was just going green again. We dropped into this field and dad said, Look here Jack its been snowing. Does thou know, we gathered that many mushrooms it took him all his time to carry them? . . . there was 40 pound. Forty pounds of buttons. He went to Charlie Parkes and said, What is em running at? He said, Ill give you 3d a pound. Forty threepences, which was ten bob. He [Charlie] had them on the train to Leeds Monday morning and he was getting 7d a pound. However dad was satisfied.[30]

To measure the significance of vegetables and fruits to the market one may look at the physical ordering of many market halls. From their beginnings, market halls sought to attract producers of fruits and vegetables from the surrounding area, so it became imperative to set aside considerable attractive, efficient market space for them. A study of the layouts of the markets of Liverpool (1822), Birmingham (1837), and Exeter (1837) shows that an astonishing amount of space was devoted to vegetable—including potato—and fruit sellers. Darwen's architect provided for three types of vegetable stalls in the new market of 1882 (fig. 7.4).

7.3. BRADFORD, RAWSON PLACE MARKET HALL, BUTCHERS' AVENUE, CA. 1930

The abundant display here points to the continued importance of the public retail market as a principal source of meat in the twentieth century.

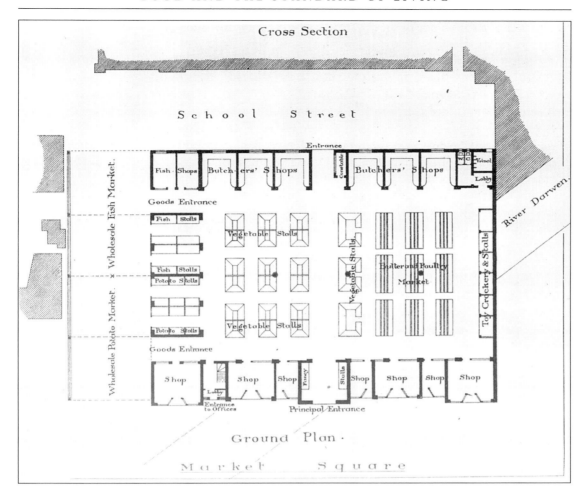

7.4. Layout Showing Vegetable Sales Space, Market Hall, Darwen, 1882

It was remarked of Worcester's Market House in 1819, "the quantity of fruit sold in the market at the proper season is astonishing." It is even doubtful that the highly nutritious potato would have become so popular in English towns without the public market. Indeed, it was the nineteenth-century market hall that educated the British public about the merit of a variety of fruits and vegetables, which continued to be popular in the twentieth century (figs. 7.5, 7.6).[31]

The public market also taught the British people to eat more fresh fish. Indeed, the concern of local governments about the diets of their constituents is best seen in the case of fish. Before about 1850 most fresh fish that were intended for urban consumption went to London's Billingsgate market, where they often rotted away; with the exception of London and a few coastal towns, therefore, the only fish available to the urban masses in the first half of the nineteenth century was dried or cured. The town of Dorchester, for example, was only seven miles from the sea, but its market had little fish for sale because Londoners would pay higher prices for fresh fish than locals, so it was all exported. In addition, Dorchester had only primitive market facilities for the storage and sale of fish. But during this period it was generally known that fish, already recognized as nutritious, was going to waste in many parts of the country while people were starving in others.[32]

Beginning in about 1850 the railway, improved storage and shipping methods, and the steam fishing trawler resulted in the availability of a vast new supply of cheap fresh fish for urbanites—"food for the millions," as it was described by *The Builder* magazine. But because of its perishable nature, fish depended more than most foods on the availability of good market facilities. Although in some coastal towns like Hastings and Torquay fish could easily be sold right on the beach or from the dock, in most cases the buying and selling of fresh fish for widespread consumption depended upon a sanitary, strictly regulated, and covered marketing facility. The absence of a covered market, it was claimed, was the reason for Peterborough's short supply of fish; and in crowded London the story was oft repeated of a van loaded with fish being driven round and round Billingsgate market for eleven days, with the same load of fish, waiting for access to the notoriously congested market. Thus it was argued up and down the land that improvement in the supply of cheap fish and the end to the "wanton . . . wicked, waste of fish" was possible only if an improvement in market facilities accompanied the advances in transportation and storage.[33]

This problem was met in several ways. In some towns, local governments subsidized fishermen directly. When Newcastle paid for tugboats to tow fishing smacks to the market, the price of fish for the poor fell to a fraction of its former cost. Between 1800 and 1803, the Bristol government paid more than £970 in bounties for fish brought into the town. Most important, public market authorities all over Britain entered the retail fish business by building public retail and wholesale fish markets, as separate buildings or as divisions of a larger general market hall or even, as at Salisbury, by building a Special Fish Express railway link to the market hall. Although numerous towns including Liverpool and Manchester erected market buildings for fish in the early decades of the nineteenth century, the great boom in fish-market building began in Birmingham in the mid-1860s, when the Birmingham Mar-

7.5. VEGETABLE SALES, ST. JOHN'S MARKET HALL, LIVERPOOL, CA. 1955

KELLY'S

High-Class Florists and Fruiterers

For Everything in Floral Art
Wreaths and Bouquets a Speciality
Daily Deliveries to all parts

Good Selection of Choice Seasonable Fruits,
Vegetables, etc.

TELEPHONE 7200

Market Hall, Blackburn

7.6. FLYER FOR KELLY'S
HIGH-CLASS FLORISTS AND
FRUITERERS, MARKET
HALL, BLACKBURN, 1948
From their beginnings,
market halls specialized in
the sale of fruits and
vegetables. Attractive stalls
and shops became standard.

7.7. THE FISH STALLS, BIRMINGHAM MARKET HALL, 1870

The women on the left are probably housewives buying the family fish, while the woman with the cart on the right probably intends to resell the fish door to door or on the street.

kets and Fairs Committee contracted for a regular supply of fish from Torbay and built in 1869 a huge fish market alongside its market hall. By the 1880s Birmingham had become one of Britain's major exporters of fish—even to seaside towns. It is a curious fact, wrote one observer at the time, that Birmingham was better supplied with fish than either London or Liverpool (fig. 7.7). Other towns followed suit. By the 1880s Bradford was also importing fish on a scale greater than London. Saturday-night sales in Bradford's fish market were described as extraordinary because the fish for sale was cheaper and of higher quality than that sold in the private shops, and the twelve fish stalls in Durham's market were described as being more benefi-

7.8. GREAT CHARLOTTE STREET FISH MARKET, LIVERPOOL, 1945

This retail market, built in 1835 just opposite St. John's Market Hall and enlarged with new front in 1873, served as a major source of fish and game for Liverpool households until it was gutted by bombs in 1940.

cial to the inhabitants of Durham than almost anything else. More than half a dozen new fish markets were built in Lancashire between 1872 and 1874, and the large number of fish shops and stalls in general markets suggests that fish had become a regular part of the urban diet. The amount of space reserved for fish sales in Darwen's market in 1879 was only about a third less than that devoted to meat sales (see fig 7.4). Liverpool's new market in 1822 had thirty-six fish stalls, but by 1835 market officials had opened a large (19,800 square feet) Retail Fish Market on the opposite side of the street (fig. 7.8). By 1873 the number of retail fish sellers in the public market had risen to nearly a hundred. In an effort to provide cheap food for the people, Manchester followed the practice of Aberdeen, Hull, and Grimsby of providing fish stalls in the public market free of charge to fishermen, thus bypassing intermediaries. By the 1870s increases in the urban fish supply were astounding. Fried fish had become a standard component of the working-class diet.[34]

To increase their food supply, many towns needed to do something about the explosion in wholesale marketing that pulled goods away from the local retail market and toward high-volume retailers. Wholesalers were striking deals with local farms, particularly large ones, to buy their output, which they then sold largely to the increasing number of cooperative shops and chain stores. So big public wholesale markets like those in Liverpool, Manchester, Glasgow, and Birmingham came to monopolize the output of all but the small growers, crowding out the small and mid-sized public retail markets. Many of the towns with these markets did not have a public wholesale market of their own, so much of the food supply was bypassing the town altogether.

To address this problem, town officials built their own wholesale markets, often attached to the retail markets but required to be open certain hours for retail trading. In 1879 Darwen attached wholesale potato and fish markets to the market hall. Burnley and Sheffield officials established a wholesale market for fruits and vegetables within the public retail market to save the retailers the costly trip to Manchester, and to give the people a chance to buy cheap produce in the wholesale market (fig. 7.9). This curious blurring of the distinction between wholesale and retail, although controversial in its day, was not unusual, as a large

7.9. CASTELFOLDS WHOLESALE FRUIT MARKET, SHEFFIELD, CA. 1890

Like many wholesale markets in the nineteenth century, this market was built adjacent to the public market hall to give the townspeople an opportunity to purchase at the lowest possible price from local growers.

number of small and large public wholesale markets, including those of Leeds, Bolton, Southport, and Manchester, gave the poorer classes limited access to wholesale markets, often after ordinary business hours. Southport's working people made extensive use of the town's wholesale market on Saturdays, when tolls were low and farmers were given free space. In Bolton, it was said, it was not unusual to witness a worker purchase a half-load of potatoes (84 pounds) in the wholesale vegetable market. Allowing the poorer classes into the wholesale market reinstated, it appears, some direct contact between the producer and the consumer, and overall improved the bargaining position of the customer.[35]

Finally, an examination of the urban standard of living from the perspective of the market hall points to two forgotten (and largely immeasurable) ways the public market changed the nation's dietary habits. First, prepared food purchased (and often eaten) in the market became increasingly common. Much of this "fast food," as we would call it today, had regional origins and was of marginal nutritional value, but its popularity suggests that the diet of working people was more varied than commonly supposed. Prepared food had always been part of street hawking, but it took on new life in the market hall, where the offerings could become standardized. The smell of oatcakes, hot meat pies (like Yorkshire trunnel pie—tripe filling topped with peas), hot green peas, black pudding, tripe, cow heels, sheep trotters, and whelks, most of which were eaten at the stall, was a feature of many of the enclosed markets. In 1893 the Pontypool market hall had two stalls set aside for tea, coffee, pork pies (called "faggots"), and hot green peas, and the Stalybridge market in the later 1880s had three ice-cream stalls in addition to two refreshment shops. Dozens of markets in the later nineteenth century included (often using "gallery" space) separate tea rooms, dairy bars, and refreshment rooms (fig. 7.10).[36]

7.10. ADVERTISEMENT FOR
TAYLORS' REFRESHMENT
ROOMS AT THE MARKET
HALL, BLACKBURN, 1948

FOR A GOOD MEAL, CALL AT —

TAYLORS'

(TOM PROCTOR)

REFRESHMENT ROOMS

Hot Meat Pies and Meat and Potato Pies a Speciality.

Roast Beef, Pork, Boiled Ham, Ox Tongue, etc., all superior quality at a reasonable price.

HOT LUNCHEONS

CORNER CAFE

MARKET HALL, BLACKBURN

PHONE 5920   Telegrams: Eatough, Market, Blackburn.

Equally important, the price of food for the working classes was discounted significantly on Saturdays. Generally, most perishable goods, including meat, were sold at a reduced cost. Unlike today, when perishable goods are on sale for several days, before refrigeration, sellers of perishable goods did not close shop until they were "sold up." It was a fact of urban life that food prices in the public market declined by the hour after noon on Saturday, so watchful and thrifty buyers could hold out for the real bargains on Saturday night. There was not a single family in Truro, it was said, that would not come to the market hall on a Saturday night to purchase the next day's beefsteak. In 1857 Liverpudlians in pursuit of a bargain spent so extravagantly on their Saturday-night suppers of discounted beefsteak and onions or roast goose that they were accused of imprudence by some of their middle-class critics. Indeed, this aspect of the food economy explains, in part, why the Saturday-night market rivaled the Saturday-night pub as a center of working-class life.[37]

In light of these facts, we can conclude that there was more food coming into the average British town than has been suggested. The search for cheap food for the laboring family, particularly by women, was a routine part of nineteenth-century life. Through the public markets, local governments made a notable contribution to this search and to the urban standard of living in general. The quantity and quality of the food supply no doubt varied from town to town according to the degree of market reform undertaken by local authorities, but as the earliest significant modern mass-retailing development, the market hall stressed high volume, low prices, modern service, and low overhead. Municipal market policy improved the quality and quantity of diet through better facilities for sales, display, and storage and by improved sanitary arrangements. In so doing, it introduced consumers to new foods like fresh fish, facilitated the widespread distribution of potatoes, and increased the demand for meat, vegetables, and fruits, as well as for ready-made foods.

The history of the market hall also suggests that contrary to some claims, it is likely that the public market, as the expression of a fairly progressive municipal food policy, helped democratize the British diet, closing the gap between the rich and poor.[38]

CHAPTER EIGHT

PATTERNS OF GROWTH AND REFORM

MORE THAN SEVEN HUNDRED PUBLIC MARKET BUILDINGS HAVE BEEN CON-structed in Britain since 1750. As we have seen in the preceding chapters, there were a number of impetuses for building these markets. Unprecedented urban growth, improvement in both wages and the supply of food, increased powers of local governments, and new theories concerning the moral and physical arrangement of public space all revolutionized the position of the public market in urban society. However, the reform and building of markets varied considerably from town to town, region to region. As Asa Briggs reminds us, the world of Victorian cities was "fragmented" and without a uniform pattern. Indeed, it is hard to write generally of the public market because the market was a local institution, subject to little or no central accounting or regulation (with the exception of national sanitation standards), and reform was almost always connected to local demographic, economic, cultural, and political circumstances.[1]

Identifying national patterns in the distribution of the food supply on a local or even regional basis is further hindered by the lack of data. Two central government surveys (one done in the 1880s, the second in the 1920s) document retail marketing facilities for those two periods, but no accounting system existed that would allow us to do more than estimate either the actual quantity of food entering the local public market or the relative importance of the market (versus the private shop) in supplying the town. No local or central authorities kept track of the volume of goods sold in the public market; and national data on diet and food consumption have little to do with the local marketplace; they are largely concerned with aggregates of such imported commodities as tea and sugar or with grain (for bread) which were not sold retail in the public market.

Despite these limitations several general patterns of market use and activity are identifiable. Specifically, the timing and regional distribution of market reforms can be estimated by examining the 319 locally initiated parliamentary market-reform acts passed between 1801 and 1881. In addition, we surveyed actual market building activity between 1750 and 1950. We discuss the broad results of that survey in this chapter; the reader should also consult the Gazetteer for further details. Although far from statistically complete, this survey provides aggregate trends in the type, location, size, and timing of some 705 new markets constructed in nearly four hundred English, Scottish and Welsh towns.

Growth Patterns by Building Type

Market buildings evolved as appendages to the open-air market: first in a "traditional" market form, in which the market was a part of a multipurpose market house-town hall or a freestanding market house which held only a small portion of the market; then in an enclosed market which was usually a large, partially walled, partially roofed structure or group of structures that held the entire market; and finally in the fully roofed and enclosed market hall, which was a new building type. For many towns, the enclosed market represents the transition from open-air marketing to the modern market hall—and later to the shopping mall (fig. 8.1).

8.1. LEEDS, KIRKGATE
MARKET HALL, 1904

Few market halls better
illustrate the transition
from the traditional street
market to the municipal
market as does this hall, the
prototype for the modern-
day shopping mall.

Approximately 60 percent of all markets constructed in Britain between 1750 and 1950 were market halls, whereas the remainder was split between the traditional market house (about 26 percent) and the enclosed or covered building (about 14 percent; fig. 8.2). The traditional market-house form dominated market architecture and organization into the early nineteenth century and remained popular throughout the century. The innovative enclosed or covered markets (the prototype for the market hall) became increasingly popular after 1800. Forty percent of the enclosed markets were built before 1830, whereas fewer than 10 percent of market halls had been constructed by that date. Most important, by the 1830s the market hall had become the predominant market type. Nineteen market halls were built in the 1830s; twenty in the 1840s; and another twenty-nine in the 1850s. But the 1860s was the heyday of the market hall: 60 percent of all halls were built after that date.

8.2 MARKET BUILDING PROJECTS, BY TYPE, 1751-1950

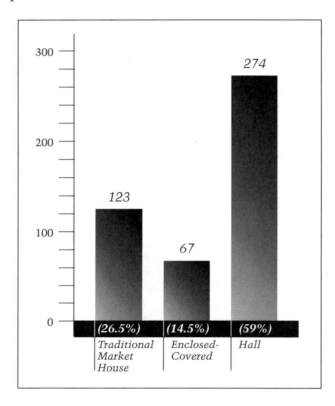

Market Reform and Construction

British market building flourished between 1820 and 1880, during which nearly half of all construction took place. Of the 591 new public retail markets built between 1751 and 1950 all but 46 were built before 1901 (fig. 8.3). Three overall peaks occurred in market construction: the 1770s and 1780s, the 1800s and 1820s, and the 1870s. The increased building activity in 1770s and 1780s was probably a result of the increased food supply and population—or even a response to food riots—it speeded up even more after 1801 and through the 1820s and 1830s. For the half-century after about 1820, the peaks in market building activity correspond to peaks in market reform activity. Altogether, building activity nearly doubled during the half-century beginning in the 1820s. This is particularly true in the southwest and in industrial cities like Liverpool, Leeds, Newcastle, and Birmingham where huge market buildings were constructed.

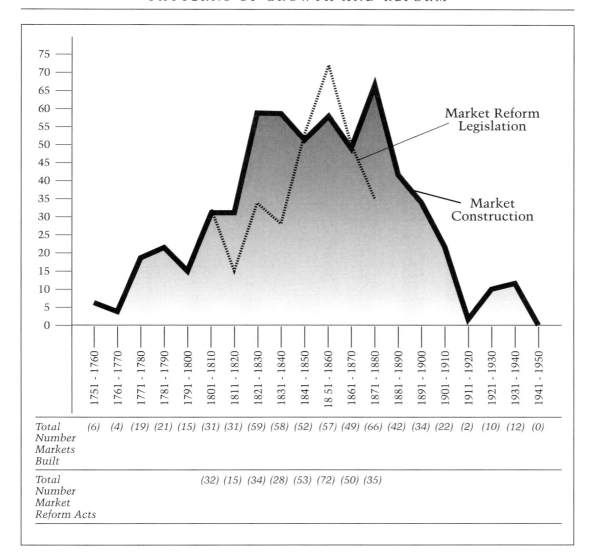

	1751 - 1760	1761 - 1770	1771 - 1780	1781 - 1790	1791 - 1800	1801 - 1810	1811 - 1820	1821 - 1830	1831 - 1840	1841 - 1850	18 51 - 1860	1861 - 1870	1871 - 1880	1881 - 1890	1891 - 1900	1901 - 1910	1911 - 1920	1921 - 1930	1931 - 1940	1941 - 1950
Total Number Markets Built	(6)	(4)	(19)	(21)	(15)	(31)	(31)	(59)	(58)	(52)	(57)	(49)	(66)	(42)	(34)	(22)	(2)	(10)	(12)	(0)
Total Number Market Reform Acts						(32)	(15)	(34)	(28)	(53)	(72)	(50)	(35)							

8.3 TIMING OF MARKET CONSTRUCTION (1751-1950) AND PARLIAMENTARY AUTHORIZATION OF MARKET REFORM (1801-78)

Inasmuch as the first booms in public market construction (in the 1780s and 1800-1830) came decades before national government initiatives in urban reform (such as the Municipal Corporations Act of 1835 and the Public Health Act of 1848), it appears that *local* governments led in market reform as an aspect of urban public services. This contradicts the standard notion that local governments before 1835 tended to be corrupt and ineffectual.

The building boom of the 1850s was most likely a result of rising real wages and hence, rising food demands. It is also probable that it was inspired by a sense of crisis following decades of perceived dearth and social crisis. While aggregate figures on certain foods show an upward spiral in the 1840s (see Chapter 7), other evidence indicates that some workers, such as handloom weavers, were on the brink of starvation; and society in general was much taken with what were seen as the related issues of violent revolution and the price of grain. Although historians have noted that popular complaints in the 1840s led to the repeal of the Corn Laws, they have said little about how local governments took up market construction in the 1820s as a way to address the urban food crisis.

After a slump in market building activity in the 1860s (a slump which corresponds to the national trend in public and residential building), market construction reached another peak in the 1870s. Sixty-six new markets were constructed—11 percent of all new market construction for the century. The 1870s surge (which corresponds to a national building boom)

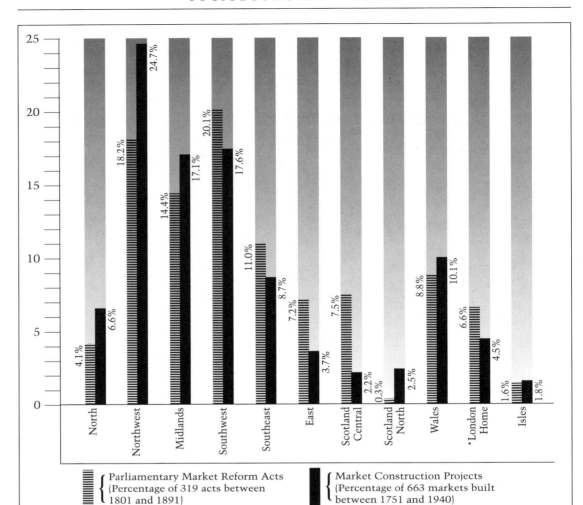

8.4 GEOGRAPHIC DISTRIBUTION OF MARKET CONSTRUCTION AND REFORM

▤ { Parliamentary Market Reform Acts (Percentage of 319 acts between 1801 and 1891)
Source: Royal Commission on Market Rights and Tolls, "Local Acts, Local and Personal Acts, and Provisional Order Acts (Passes Since the Year 1800)" (1888-91), vol. 1, appendix B.

■ { Market Construction Projects (Percentage of 663 markets built between 1751 and 1940)
Source: Gazetteer

*LH includes the "London Home Counties" (Kent, Surrey, Middlesex, Essex) but not the "London Metropolitan District" markets of London proper because the latter were exclusively wholesale markets (e.g., coal, hides, fish, meat) rather than public retail markets.

Market Regions

NORTH
Durham
Northumberland
NORTHWEST
Cheshire
Cumbria
Greater Manchester
Lancashire
Merseyside
South Yorkshire
West Yorkshire
Yorkshire
MIDLANDS
Derbyshire
Leicestershire
Nottinghamshire
Shropshire
Staffordshire
Warwickshire

West Midlands
Worcestershire
SOUTHWEST
Avon
Cornwall
Devonshire
Dorset
Gloucestershire
Herefordshire
Somerset
Wiltshire
SOUTHEAST
Bedfordshire
Berkshire
Buckinghamshire
Cambridgeshire
Hampshire
Hertfordshire
Norfolk

Oxfordshire
Suffolk
Sussex
EAST
Humberside
Lincolnshire
North Yorkshire
SCOTLAND CENTRAL
Fife
Lothian
Strathclyde
Tayside
SCOTLAND NORTH
Grampian
Highlands
ISLES
Isle of Wight
Jersey
Guernsey

WALES
Anglesey
Clwyd
Dyfed
Gwent
Gwynedd
Mid Glamorgan
Montgomeryshire
Pembrokeshire
Powys
South Glamorgan
West Glamorgan

LONDON HOME
Essex
Greater London
Kent
Middlesex
Surrey

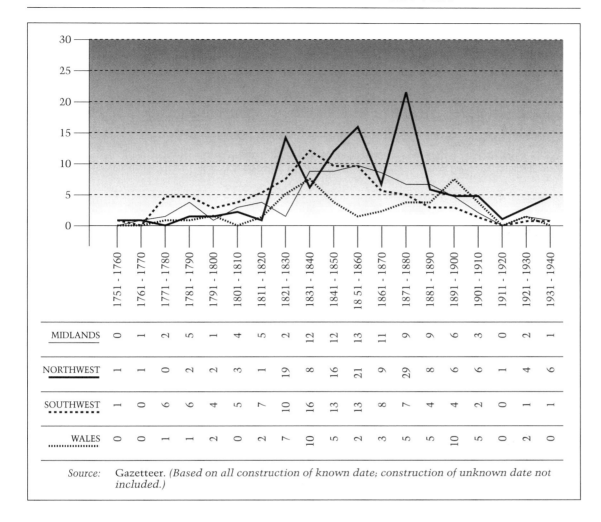

	1751 - 1760	1761 - 1770	1771 - 1780	1781 - 1790	1791 - 1800	1801 - 1810	1811 - 1820	1821 - 1830	1831 - 1840	1841 - 1850	18 51 - 1860	1861 - 1870	1871 - 1880	1881 - 1890	1891 - 1900	1901 - 1910	1911 - 1920	1921 - 1930	1931 - 1940
MIDLANDS	0	1	2	5	1	4	5	2	12	12	13	11	9	9	6	3	0	2	1
NORTHWEST	1	1	0	2	2	3	1	19	8	16	21	9	29	8	6	6	1	4	6
SOUTHWEST	1	0	6	6	4	5	7	10	16	13	13	8	7	4	4	2	0	1	1
WALES	0	0	1	1	2	0	2	7	10	5	2	3	5	5	10	5	0	2	0

Source: Gazetteer. *(Based on all construction of known date; construction of unknown date not included.)*

8.5 TIMING OF MARKET CONSTRUCTION, BY REGION, 1751-1940

was a result of a combination of factors, including cheaper and more plentiful food, railway expansion, rising real wages, continued urban population growth, and improved methods of public funding. Building continued at a high level into the 1880s, but by the 1890s, with the exception of Wales, construction declined precipitously. Although twenty-two new markets were built in the decade 1900-1910, by the early 1900s the market boom was over, at least until the age of urban redevelopment following the Second World War. Only twenty-four new markets were built after 1910.[2]

Geographic Distribution of Building Activity

The northwest of England accounted for a quarter of all market construction between 1750 and 1950, while the midlands and southwest each make up 17 percent of the total (fig. 8.4). Most significant, the three regions which make up the so-called industrial north (the midlands, the northwest, and the north) account for nearly half of all market building activity. Conversely, the populous and urban southeast and east (including London) were responsible for only a small proportion of the nation's market building, while Wales accounted for 10 percent of all building activity. Figure 8.5 shows the timing of the regional building activity for four regions. A boom took place in the northwest in the 1820s, followed by bursts in the 1830s in Wales, the midlands, and the four major regions southwest. The building in the northwest occurred in two more bursts, in the 1850s and the 1870s—a pattern which follows the economic depression experienced by the textile industry in the 1860s because of the Ameri-

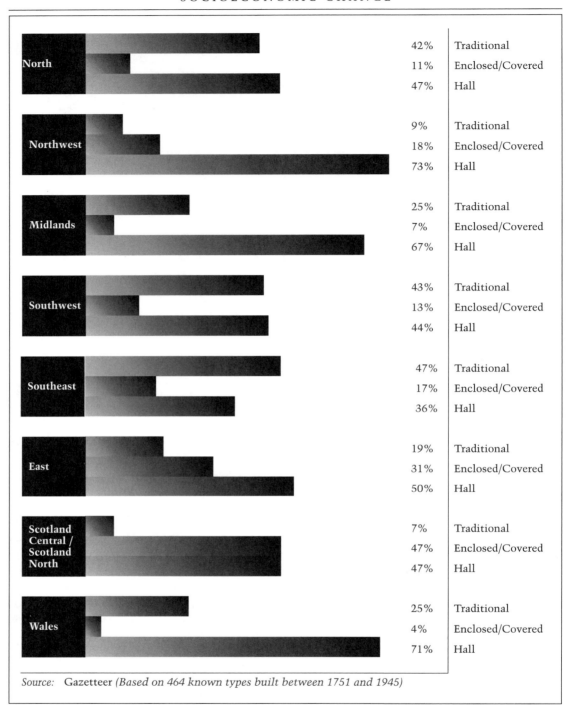

8.6 REGIONAL
DISTRIBUTION OF MARKET
BUILDING PROJECTS, BY
TYPE

North	42%	Traditional
	11%	Enclosed/Covered
	47%	Hall
Northwest	9%	Traditional
	18%	Enclosed/Covered
	73%	Hall
Midlands	25%	Traditional
	7%	Enclosed/Covered
	67%	Hall
Southwest	43%	Traditional
	13%	Enclosed/Covered
	44%	Hall
Southeast	47%	Traditional
	17%	Enclosed/Covered
	36%	Hall
East	19%	Traditional
	31%	Enclosed/Covered
	50%	Hall
Scotland Central / Scotland North	7%	Traditional
	47%	Enclosed/Covered
	47%	Hall
Wales	25%	Traditional
	4%	Enclosed/Covered
	71%	Hall

Source: Gazetteer (Based on 464 known types built between 1751 and 1945)

can Civil War. After an initial market-building spurt, the southwest failed to follow the subsequent northwest booms because it did not have the same urban population explosion, and because by the 1870s many southwest towns were beginning to feel the economic contractions that accompanied several decades of regional depression brought on by agricultural decline.

The market-building boom in England's northwest during the 1870s was also linked to the fact that before constructing a new market, many towns needed to purchase the market from its manorial owner; only after enabling legislation of the 1850s and 1860s (particularly

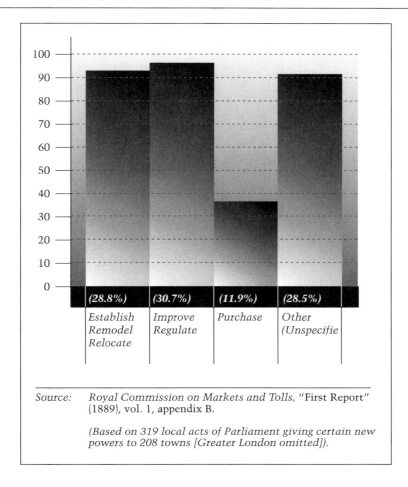

(28.8%)	(30.7%)	(11.9%)	(28.5%)
Establish Remodel Relocate	Improve Regulate	Purchase	Other (Unspecifie

Source: Royal Commission on Markets and Tolls, "First Report" (1889), vol. 1, appendix B.

(Based on 319 local acts of Parliament giving certain new powers to 208 towns [Greater London omitted]).

8.7 ACTS OF PARLIAMENT AUTHORIZING MARKET REFORM IN 208 TOWNS, 1801-78

the Local Government Act of 1858) could they do so. Midlands activity occurred earlier and on a more linear course; there was one boom in the 1880s. The Welsh pattern is quite different: peaks in 1831-40 and 1891-1910, with a period of inactivity between.

Just as the volume and timing of market building varied by region, so did market type. The new market hall type was most popular in Wales, the northwest, and the midlands. As figure 8.6 shows, towns in the northwest, the midlands, and Wales were more likely to build market halls than were towns in the east, southeast, and southwest. Construction of the traditional market, the old market-house form, appears to have all but disappeared in the northwest of England and in Scotland, whereas it remained strong in the south.

The dominance of the market hall in the midlands and the northwest (and urbanized Scotland and Wales) in the Victorian era reflects the fact that these were Britain's most rapidly growing urban and industrial areas. New markets in the northwest on the average had nearly double the floor space of the new markets of the southwest and two-thirds more floor space than midlands markets. Nevertheless, market type also varied within regions; in the southwest, where the traditional market was common, for example, the markets of Devon were predominantly of the market hall type.

Parliamentary Legislation as a Measure of Market Activity

Between 1801 and 1880, 208 towns initiated more than three hundred parliamentary acts to reform specific aspects of the market or local market activity. These acts authorized towns to establish a new market, to rebuild, relocate, or shut down an old market, to purchase the

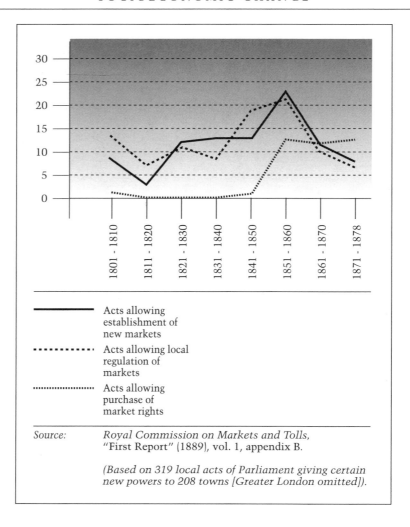

8.8 TIMING OF MARKET
REFORM LEGISLATION,
1801-78

Acts allowing
establishment of
new markets

Acts allowing local
regulation of
markets

Acts allowing
purchase of
market rights

Source: *Royal Commission on Markets and Tolls,*
           "First Report" (1889), vol. 1, appendix B.

           (Based on 319 local acts of Parliament giving certain
           new powers to 208 towns [Greater London omitted]).

market from its manorial owner, or to rearrange the market layout or enact new market regulations. Figure 8.7 indicates the frequency of the various reforms: ninety-eight acts allowed specific towns increased control over local market regulation; ninety-two acts allowed as many new markets to be built; and thirty-eight acts allowed specific towns to purchase their market from its private owner. In the early decades of the nineteenth century, a higher level of parliamentary activity was directed toward increasing local regulatory power over the markets, while parliamentary permits to construct new markets are fairly evenly spaced in the decades following 1820, with the exception of an unusual burst of construction in the 1850s (fig. 8.8). Permission to purchase markets was rare before the 1850s. All of this suggests that local governments relied most on parliamentary legislation during mid-century. Parliament-initiated market reform reached its peak in the 1840s and 1850s (more than half of all local market reform acts were passed between 1841 and 1860), but slowed down after 1860. The decrease was probably a result of broader powers being extended to local governments after mid-century, especially through the Local Government Act of 1858, which made it easier for local governments to purchase and finance public markets. Market reform activity between 1801 and 1840 had centered on activities other than market purchase. From the 1850s on, however, purchase of the market became increasingly important. Towns found it less necessary to seek parliamentary permission to regulate or move their market than to purchase it from a private owner. Roughly a quarter (23 percent) of all parliamentary legislative grants after 1851 empowered local officials to purchase the market from a private owner.

The region most affected by parliamentary reform was the southwest. The higher ratio of grants to construction projects for the southwest (see fig. 8.4) reflects, in part, the fact that more southwestern towns were bound by ancient charters that restricted market activity, even when they owned the market. The southeast was hardly affected by parliamentary reform. This region accounts for less than an eighth (11.6 percent) of the parliamentary grants, while the heavily populated London home counties of Surrey, Essex, Kent, and Middlesex (excluding Metropolitan London) were even less interested in parliamentary permission for market reform (6.6 percent of the total). There were no parliamentary petitions on behalf of public retail markets in Metropolitan London itself.

A Regional Divide?

Our market survey data confirm the conclusion of the market commissioners of 1888 that the public markets of the south and east were generally in a "languishing or decaying state," while those in the northwest and midlands were vibrant and successful. Of the nine nineteenth-century public retail markets built in Surrey, for instance, only three were built after 1830. Only one market was built in Essex after 1830. Only one market was built in Bedfordshire in the nineteenth century, two in Hertfordshire, three in Norfolk, and except for Hastings and Brighton, only four towns in Sussex built markets.

But the commissioners missed the impressive public market revival in the west and southwest of England and in Wales. For instance, the county of Somerset saw significant market building activity throughout the nineteenth century—much of it traditional market house-town halls—which was probably a consequence of Somerset's thriving agricultural industry, which was strong even during the nationwide agricultural depression of 1873-96. Even more impressive, thirty-six new markets were built in Devon over the course of the nineteenth century. While a number of the new Devon markets were smaller, traditional markets, such as those at Great Torrington and Brixham, most of them were large modern halls built for pannier marketing. This was the case at Newton Abbot, Exeter, Barnstaple, and Torquay, wherein considerable market hall floor space was made available to country sellers. Cornwall, which experienced a population growth of more than 50 percent between 1801 and 1831, built a great many new market buildings, but these tended to be in the traditional forms rather than pannier market halls.

These data on both building and reform activity allow us to divide England and Wales into two parts with regard to public retail markets: a market-rich north and southwest, and a market-poor east and southeast, including London (map 8.1). These regional divisions are particularly evident after about 1810, and by the 1880s they must have been a fact of British economic and social life.

There are two reasons for this division. First, market building was most spirited in areas (with the notable exception of London) with the greatest population and industrial growth. The new market halls were best fitted for regions with large working-class populations, whose food demands dictated large new market spaces. The midlands and the northwest (particularly Lancashire and the West Riding of Yorkshire) were, along with certain isolated pockets of growth like the south of Wales and the Tyne and Wear region of the northeast, the areas of greatest industrial and urban growth in the nineteenth century and, correspondingly, the regions with the most pressing needs for an improved food supply.

The other reason for the difference in market-building growth is the fact that the industrial and urban north, with its growing wealth, underwent a shift in consumer demand from bread to meat at the very time the west began to yield an extraordinary increase in meat, dairy products, and vegetables. This northwest-southeast division of markets is remarkably simi-

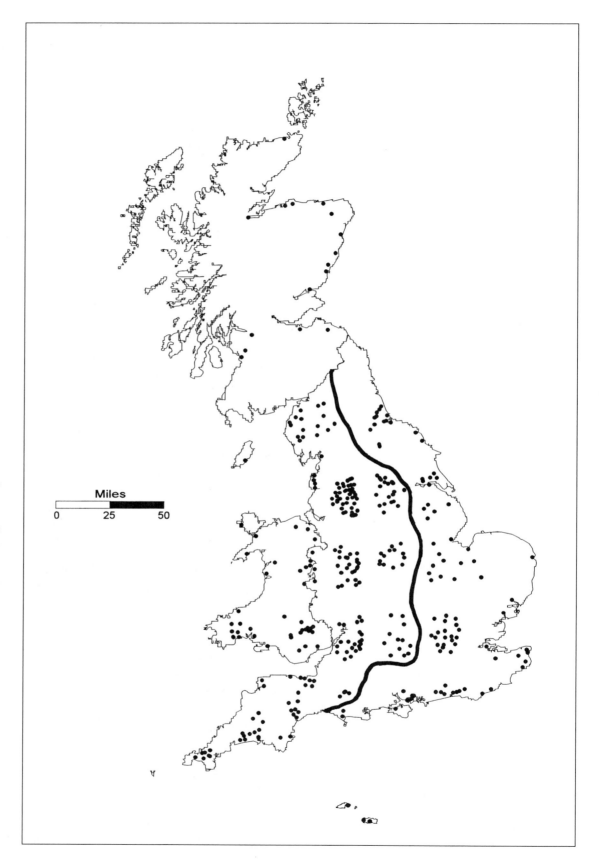

MAP 8.1. MARKET
CONSTRUCTION SINCE
1750

The heavy concentration of
public retail markets in the
west supports the conclu-
sion that England and Wales
can be divided into a market-
rich west and a market-poor
east.

Miles

0   25   50

lar to the historian James Caird's "Caird's line" of 1851, which divides the country into two agricultural regions: the north and west, and the east and south. The north and much of the west concentrated on dairy and meat, while the south, as far west as Dorset and Wiltshire, held to what was called "high farming": concentration on grain production. Indeed, by 1850 the country had become divided by crop: "down corn, up horn," as the saying went, and the high-rent meat and dairylands of the north and west were more profitable than the grain farms of the south and east.

Thus, it was in the industrial north that food supply and demand came together. The locally produced food offered a more nutritious range of foods in the north—the predominance of pastoral farming generally meant more meat, animal fats, and milk in those areas than in the south—and even agricultural workers were better fed than those of the prosperous, high-farming south. In Yorkshire, farm laborers could often afford to contribute to their own larders or the local market from their personal gardens; some even had cows and pastureland. Much of the west converted from grain to dairy and meat farming (particularly Somerset, Cheshire, and Cumberland), and as in the north suffered less from the fall in wheat prices.[3]

For the south and east it was different. From the Napoleonic Wars into the early part of the nineteenth century, the food supply for local consumption in the south and east actually contracted: as intensive wheat agriculture increased, agricultural wages fell. By the second half of the nineteenth century, southern farm villages were shrinking or even disappearing. Already by the 1830s, areas of poor soil in Staffordshire, Nottinghamshire, Norfolk, Suffolk, and Berkshire had reverted to sheep walks. In addition, the flow of population was from villages to small towns and from small towns to large ones. Rural depopulation was particularly felt in such places as Wiltshire after 1840; and in the country as a whole between 1870 and 1900 the amount of arable land decreased from 15 to 12 million acres. Generally then, with the exception of dairy farming in Somerset, the regions of slowest public market growth were those which had the most grain farming, the least mixed farming, and the greatest depopulation of agricultural villages.[4]

The Nation Divided in Habits

The northwest-southeast divide is also a demarcation of differences in national marketing habits. Outdoor street marketing remained the norm for London, while in the south and southeast the private shop emerged early as a more important supplier of goods than the public market; in fact, private shops replaced the public market in many towns. By 1800 the south and southeast had more than twice as many shops per person than the west, southwest, and north of England, which were tied to a modernized system of public markets. The south and southeast of England had a better system of shop retailing than elsewhere, which explains why these areas did not need the public market. Equally important, urban Scotland (particularly Glasgow) went in an even more modern direction as it moved to the forefront of a mass-retailing revolution that featured both multiple shops and big stores, thus lessening the importance of the public market.[5]

Conversely, well into the twentieth century, the people of the midlands, the north, and the southwest continued to buy and sell in the public market, despite the growth in the late nineteenth century of cooperatives and multiple shops. This conservatism was in part due to the inability of northern shopkeepers to meet the demands of the northern industrial-demographic explosion and in part because, compared to the market towns of the south, the sphere of influence for the typical market towns in the north was much larger (on the order of 70 square miles) than in the south. It is also probable that the evolution of a better system of canals and roads in the midlands and the north encouraged centralized marketing, as did the growth of handloom weaving. By 1800, for example, more than a dozen coaches traveled daily to and from Preston carrying the weavers' output, and by the mid-1820s more than a thousand handloom weavers traveled back and forth from their rural homes to Manchester on a weekly basis. In short, the nature of the region's industry, with its emphasis on outwork, encouraged rural and village folk to shop in manufacturing towns.[6]

The Public Market and the History of the British Town

The geography and timing of the reformation of public markets, particularly the building of market halls, suggests then that this reformation was a phenomenon of the industrial-urban revolution; and in spite of the current inclination to emphasize the continuity rather than the change produced by the Industrial Revolution, there was a significant change in how most people bought and sold their food.

But was this change in market environment a positive one or a negative one? To be sure, although market reform was not felt uniformly by all new industrial towns and by all classes, an examination of the nineteenth-century town from the perspective of the reformed public market calls for a change in the traditional view, upheld by Friedrich Engels and others, that the new "working-class towns" were simply unplanned and badly built towns in which no one cared or bothered about the workers or their families. In his influential study *The Condition of the Working Class in England* (1845), Engels claimed that the public markets in the new industrial towns were filthy and disease-ridden and that the market system worked against working-class interests: workers, he said, received nothing but leftover food largely unfit for human consumption. To Engels, the public market was the scene of class exploitation: "When the market opens, there is an ample supply of good food, but by the time the worker arrives the best has gone. . . . The potatoes purchased by the workers are generally bad, the vegetables shriveled, the cheese stale and of poor quality, the bacon rancid. The meat is lean, old, tough and partially tainted. . . . Food is generally sold by petty hawkers who buy up bad food and are able to sell it cheaply because of its poor quality."[7]

Considering what we now know about local markets, it is probable that Engels's portrayal of the town market as anarchic and exploitative was not even true to the experience of the average working-class family in the industrial Lancashire of which he was writing, and it was changing rapidly. Indeed, a closer look at the towns to which Engels refers—Liverpool, Manchester, and the eleven "working-class" towns surrounding Manchester (Bolton, Preston, Wigan, Bury, Rochdale, Middleton, Heywood, Oldham, Ashton, Stalybridge, and Stockport) suggests a much less gloomy picture. Although there is little doubt that public market reform was needed, what Engels neglected to mention is that most of these Lancashire towns had undertaken or were undertaking it; for at least some working people in the 1840s market conditions must have been improving rather than deteriorating. (In London, on the other hand, there was virtually no market reform throughout the nineteenth century.) The overall direction was toward a greater level of market organization, policing, and inspection; better products; and more appealing facilities to attract outside suppliers. Of the towns Engels describes, Wigan, Preston, Stockport, and Heywood seem not to have modernized their markets, but Manchester had a new fish market (1828) and a new general market. And significant reform began there in 1846 as well, when the town purchased the market rights from the local lord. Liverpool's giant new market hall of 1820-22 was revolutionary and almost immediately became the model for urban developments elsewhere. Middleton had built a new market house and shambles in 1791 (as part of a new town hall), and as a result of the dangerous condition of Rochdale's marketplace (where street sellers obstructed passageways), the town built its first market hall in 1823, and then a larger one with 24 shops and 180 stalls in 1844. A market hall (complete with clock tower) was built in Ashton on a site of 14,000 square yards in 1828; and although Bolton had no market building in 1844, when Engels singled it out as one of the worst of the new industrial towns, it had established a large new open-air marketplace in 1826, which was regarded as the finest unenclosed market in the county. And in 1853 the town began construction on the giant classical-fronted market hall, which is still in use today. At Stalybridge, where marketers were dependent upon nearby Ashton, a market improvements act of 1828 resulted in the appointment of the town's first market inspector and the erection of a new market house-town hall (built in 1831 and altered and expanded in 1843). In Oldham schemes to construct a market building failed until 1856, when the town's first market hall was built.

Market Building and Food Consumption Levels

No accounting of sales is known to have been undertaken by any market, but the increase in rental and toll income from the markets and the swell in market building in the four decades after 1850 suggest that significant user pressure was placed on market facilities at the very time that demand for food increased. The 1870s peak in market building corresponds exactly with what is known about improvements in food consumption. As noted elsewhere in Chapter Seven, the dramatic increase in food consumption which began about mid-century and hit its peak after the mid-1870s was probably a result of rising real wages for workers and new (and cheaper) foods coming into market and shop. By the mid-1890s, prices began to rise and real wages began to fall, which slowed down the spending increase.[8]

On the other hand, to posit such direct correlation is probably too simplistic. Growth in the supply and variety of processed foods continued well after 1890, and the national diet improved considerably between 1909 and 1934 (particularly in the period after about 1928), but these improvements did not result in an upswing in public market construction.[9]

Market Growth, Municipal Ownership, and the Local Government Act of 1858

The quality and timing of market reform had much to do with ownership of market rights and the ability of reformers, usually municipal governments, to improve or rebuild public markets. As we have seen, manorial ownership, combined with limited powers on the part of local government, often blocked even the smallest efforts to meet changing market needs. As important as they were, special acts of Parliament were often prohibitively costly. Aberystwyth's special act in 1872 to improve its markets cost the town between £1,200 and £1,500, a sum many times the yearly revenues accruing from the markets. Unable or unwilling to spend the customary large sums needed to obtain a special act of Parliament, many rapidly growing towns, particularly those that lacked a civic improvement commission to look after the town's environmental services, had to wait for permissive legislation or official incorporation as a borough, reforms that did not come until mid-century or later. Borough status was not achieved in Darwen, for instance, until 1878, and then was the town able to build what it regarded as adequate public market facilities. Oldham was incorporated in 1856, but it took nine years for the town to acquire the borrowing power to purchase the markets.[10]

Most important, perhaps, the Local Government Act of 1858 inaugurated a new era in market history because it gave local authorities the right to acquire, by purchase or lease, public or private market rights, property, and tolls, and to make bylaws and take (and set) rents and tolls. Indeed this legislation was important in encouraging market construction in England and Wales. The act allowed certain local authorities to borrow funds without recourse to a further act of Parliament. In the period 1884-87 alone, for example, Parliament, through its Local Government Board, allowed municipalities to borrow a total of £150,000 to build thirty markets, among which was the new Carlisle market (completed in 1889) made possible by a loan of £30,000. Because of the loan provisions of the 1858 act, the amount of outstanding loans for market building owed by town councils and other urban authorities, such as improvement commissions and market trusts, was £2,157,000 by 1887. It is difficult to estimate how many new markets this figure represents, but considering that the large Carlisle loan was twice the size of the average construction loan, and that some of the earlier loans had been partially paid off by 1887, then it appears that the loan provisions of the 1858 act may have been responsible for as many as a hundred new markets.[11]

The Railway and Tramway

The nineteenth-century mania for markets coincided with a passion for railways. Although wide-scale railway building had begun in the 1840s and it was said that by the early fifties the railway had "conquered Britain," it was not until the 1860s and 1870s that many towns and villages were able to celebrate the coming of railway service.

The railway furthered public market expansion in three distinct ways. First, it fostered an explosion in regional and national trading that in terms of the public market meant vast supplies of new and cheaper foods, especially meat, fish, and fruits, entering the town market. Second, the railway dispelled the long-held notion that it was desirable for each locality to have its own commercial center. In effect, the fact that the railway bypassed most towns meant that some towns (often large ones) would be market-rich and others market-poor. Indeed, improved accessibility to larger towns and cites contributed to an increasingly top-heavy urban system whereby more and more people congregated in larger urban areas. By drawing market customers from outlying villages, the railway and the urban tramway destroyed some towns as commercial centers. At Worksop, for example, people stopped driving their carts to the market because they could more easily ride the train to Mansfield. Indeed, one town in Hertfordshire pulled down its unused market house because everyone now shopped in a nearby town on the train line. The coming of the railway caused St. Aubin's market to give way to St. Helier, Devonport to Plymouth, Penrith to Carlisle, and South Molton to Barnstaple.[12]

Third, in those towns fortunate enough to have railway access, the railway and its urban counterpart, the tramway, furthered a centralized marketing system because they drew people from the suburbs and distant villages to shop in the town center; in this manner the railroad speeded up the centralizing process which had begun in many towns in the late eighteenth and early nineteenth century and made the city center more rather than less important.

All of this was particularly true after 1860 into the 1870s and 1880s, when the motorized tram (at first, horse drawn) became a common feature of life in large cities. Such was the case in Bradford, where as a result of a new tramway system connecting the town to the market, "the state of [the market] . . . was reversed, and now the center of the town is better than outside," and people "prefer to come to the central market instead of shopping at their own places." In Bradford and elsewhere, country vendors who hitherto traveled to town by foot or cart now used the railway or the tramway, and it was not uncommon for customers traveling by train or tram from one town to have their fare paid by grateful shopkeepers in another town. Certainly, the number of travelers on the local tramway on market day must have testified to the quality of a particular market, as well as to the quality of the local diet. The railway, in short, made it possible for people to shop in both cheaper and in more exotic markets. The wealthy classes of a southeastern town like Hastings could now go to London on a regular basis, just as the working people in towns nearby Accrington could now shop in Accrington with its modern and attractive market hall.[13]

It is certain that the coming of the railway inspired new market construction. Local officials, tradesmen, nearby farmers, and consumers in general were well aware of the connection between the local market potential and the railway, so it was not unusual for towns, in order "to keep money in the town," as they said in Accrington in 1869, to build new centralized markets. Similar developments occurred in Truro, Carlisle, and Tewkesbury, which all built new market halls to take advantage of railway services. The coming of the railway to Lytham in 1846 caused the outlying villagers to swarm into the town, which responded by building a new market house in 1848. As in Hull, Bradford, and Accrington, it was common to bring the tramway to the market hall. Oldham's tramway linked that market with consumers in nearby Shaw, Royton, Chadderton, and Lees; Accrington's market hall was linked by tram to much of the surrounding countryside; and Edinburgh's Waverly market was but a short distance from the main railway station. Even towns without railway access, like Batley in Yorkshire, built new markets to combat competition from nearby towns that had it. The market hall, then, was the reflection of a town's ambitions as well as its fortunes.[14]

THE GRAND AGE OF THE MARKET HALL, 1830-90

BE JUST AND FEAR NOT
—motto carved over Carlisle Market Hall, 1889

RISING UP IN THE HEART OF MANCHESTER, THE VAST SMITHFIELD MARKET, OR Shudehill as it was locally known, was for a century after it was erected in 1846 a feature of every worker's Saturday night out. A source of cheap food and free entertainment, it catered to a crowd that was as much in search of Sunday dinner as of a bit of frolic on Saturday nights. Led by an army of housewives amid a blaze of gaslights, thousands of families marched up and down the aisles and traversed the galleries, inspecting food and other goods, searching for bargains, and collecting a week's worth of news and sights.[1]

The scene at Manchester's Shudehill was typical of the drama being enacted in hundreds of towns all over Britain. The Saturday-night crowd was the most lively and heterogeneous of the week, making up a complete cross-section of townsfolk: families looking for bargains; young childless couples whose budgets allowed a little more extravagance; courting couples; single men and women; and groups of young people, all "strolling" the market. "Young lovers," said an observer of another market, "are the best buyers we have." In an age that predated mass spectator sport, cinema, and television, the market hall helped relieve the dullness and restrictiveness of everyday urban life, provided one of the few regularized public experiences in the nineteenth century, and was a "must" for tourists. In addition, the market hall provided links with the countryside of both past and present at a time of increased alienation for many who were making the transition from rural to urban-industrial life. The author of a local lyric illuminated this when he wrote of Liverpool's St. John's Market Hall:

> Perchance it is that good Saint John
> Has laid a special blessing on
> This buxom dear so strangely bred,
> Half town, half country
> That charms like hers are safely spread
> With such effrontery.[2]

Equally important, the market hall, like the later department store and shopping mall, introduced society to both a change in the scale of marketing and a wide range of new products, which in turn were transformed from novelties to essentials. Fish and tinned meat, for example, were among the many new foods that became dietary staples, and dozens of unfamiliar gadgets, from phonographs to bicycles, emerged as household requisites. A new consumer world was in the making, which mixed business with entertainment and which adopted the sentiment that material consumption would bring about human happiness, promote respectability, and nurture the nation's aesthetic sensibility.

Surely the visual form of the market hall itself supported such a view. Like the other pleasure palaces of the new industrial-urban world, the pub and the music hall, where cut-glass windows, polished brass accouterments, and wood paneling aimed at elevating the sensibilities of the clientele, the market hall ennobled the act of buying and selling by removing it from the muddy, windswept open market to its realm of the beautiful, the orderly, and the respectable. Here in the market hall the polychromatic brick decorations, soaring roofs

of iron and glass, groups of polished, varnished oak, and red deal stalls, painted and gilded girders, wrought-iron gas lanterns, and grand interior clocks and fountains all placed the visitor in an ambiance of beauty, excitement, and glamour. Newcastle's neoclassical market hall (see figs. 5.23, 5.24), with its series of splendid Roman arches, was likened to a set from a play. The Leeds Kirkgate market dazzled visitors with great wrought-iron painted dragons acting as buttresses for interior iron pillars. And shoppers at the Bradford and Halifax market halls could not help but be in awe of the iron-and-glass roofs towering overhead. Birmingham's indoor fountain attracted such great crowds that traders complained that business at their stalls was being obstructed by spectators (fig. 9.1). On the outside, many a market façade exhibited the Victorian penchant for the sublime and the picturesque as part of the fascination with architectural imagery. Indeed, the market building was frequently the town's most eye-catching structure. The public market, once the ugliest and dirtiest place in town, had been carefully transformed into a palace of myths, illusion, and expectations.[3]

Social Function

It is not surprising that the market hall was a social mecca for townsfolk of all ages and classes. Like the earlier open marketplace, the market hall was one of the town's principal promenades, often crowded with young men and women whose main intention was not to buy but to see and be seen. Bolton's great central aisle was turned into a "mashing" (flirting) parade for the

town's lads and lasses, while its upper gallery was filled with crowds of children who milled round the cages of puppies, rabbits, doves, and other small animals. Indeed, Bolton's refurbished market hall even today has the sort of festive character which permeated most market halls (fig. 9.2). Until the cinema drew them away early in this century, nearly all of Manchester's boys made the Saturday-night trip to the Shudehill Market, less to shop than to delight in the crowds and the entertainment. Indeed, market officials often debated whether to allow street and fair performers into the Friday- and Saturday-night markets. There were many spectacles inside the hall: ice-cream

9.2. BOLTON MARKET HALL, RENOVATED INTERIOR, 1990

vendors, match sellers, toys, hot ready-to-eat food, clog dancers, and jugglers; and as the Saturday market spilled out beyond the confines of the market hall into the open air, the spectacle was enhanced. Consider the Shudehill on a Saturday night in 1867: "In the outskirts of the marketplace you may have yourself accurately weighed and measured for one halfpenny. For the same sum you may receive a shock from a galvanic battery. You may then enjoy a few moments of sporting, by shooting at a target over a rifle range ... [and listen to] the strains of an energetic Scotch fiddler."[4]

Glasgow's market hall, the Bazaar, presented a similar scene of color: "Saturday night is the time to see the Bazaar and Candleriggs in all their glory. Pedestrianism is difficult, at some points impossible. In the streets, the pavement is lined with itinerant vendors, and both the roadway and footpath are crowded with passengers. In the Bazaar, especially in the southern passes, locomotion proceeds at a snail's pace; and the ... haggling of the customers [and a] continuous hum rising above all, have a peculiar fascination to those who love to study human life in a great city."[5]

A custom in the outlying country villages around Newcastle was for bride, groom, and wedding party to "leuk throo the Mairkit":

> To the student of character, the Saturday scenes in our market are often full of interest. Thousands pass and repass; buxom housewives and rosy lasses jostle against sisters who have only too clearly the wearing marks of poverty. Each tradesman, every saleswoman, is on the alert for customers, particularly if it be that the goods are perishable. One class of visitors always attract attention when they perambulate the

Market, namely, the brides, bridegrooms, and the bridesmaids from the outlying country villages. With these it seems to be de rigeur to "leuk throo the Mairkit." On their appearance they are the observed of all observers. The pot-pie lasses leave their customers to famish or not, as they please, whilst the bridal party sails past, in all the conscious pride of matrimonial honours: nor do its members seem to care a button for the good-humoured chaff which is occasionally addressed to them, especially if any of the party are recognized as acquaintances or customers. Indeed, they rather seem to like the obtrusive attention thus paid them. What wonder? Why should they be angry or we surprised? Was there ever a woman yet that wouldn't turn her head to look at a bride, and then to criticise the husband?[6]

Because of its size and location, the market was frequently the center of the town's social and political activities. Newcastle's market was used informally as a promenade, as well as for tea parties, the annual assemblage of Sunday-school children, and as a hall for public assemblies. In 1902 Batley's market hall provided the backdrop for the town's celebration of

9.3. BATLEY MARKET HALL, 1902
With its 90-foot-high clock tower, the Market Hall at Batley provided a backdrop for occasions of importance—and acted as a reminder of the town's stature in West Yorkshire.

Edward VII's coronation (fig. 9.3). Stockport's market hall of 1850 had a balcony on the front of the hall from which electioneering speeches were delivered to crowds in the marketplace, while Newton Abbot's market hall was the scene of the town's first demonstration of the wireless. Edinburgh's Waverly Market had, for public viewing, an aquarium, and in 1879 the market itself was packed with 20,000 people to listen to the M.P. and Liberal Party leader, William Gladstone.[7]

Going to Market

As the market and marketing changed, it was inevitable that some of the natural links people had to place and season would be broken. The old-fashioned, small local market, with its close proximity to the countryside, in which products were locally grown and sellers and buyers often knew one another, gave way to large urban market halls which disrupted these traditional connections. This happened not simply because of urban growth but also because new forms of transportation allowed buyers and sellers to go considerable distances to regional market centers, which offered foreign goods that had been shipped from afar. The convenience of the local market and locally produced goods was traded for an expansion in the quantity and variety of goods available at more distant markets but, as was the case with much of urban life, in increasingly standardized forms.

This change can be seen in Devonshire. In the fourteenth century the county had seventy-three towns with regular markets (and in most cases a fair as well), but by the nineteenth century the marketing was largely accomplished in a dozen or so towns. For Britain as a whole, there were many so-called market towns which no longer had a functioning public market; their markets had been absorbed by a few retail centers. Eight roads converged at Helston, Cornwall, for example, making it the hub for a large number of villages in the district, ensur-

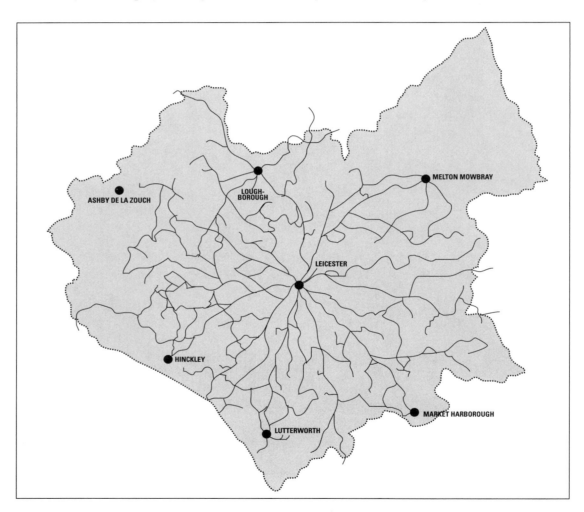

9.4. ROUTES TO THE MARKETS OF LEICESTERSHIRE, 1884

Each market day hundreds of horse-drawn carts made up a remarkable county-wide transport system which carried thousands of marketers from 300 towns and villages to the seven market towns, including the principal market in Leicester.

ing its prominence as the district's market center. Likewise, in east Lancashire, some 40,000 people from several dozen towns stretching along the valley from Padiham to Colne looked to Burnley as their market center. In Yorkshire, before the railway brought new and cheaper products to Barnsley, the people around the nearby town of Wombell traveled by horse-drawn wagonettes to the Wombell Saturday-night market. But with Barnsley transformed into a retail mecca, Wombell's town market was abandoned, and the wagonettes were used to take people to Barnsley. In 1842 one of Liverpool's markets was served by sixteen coaches coming from outlying villages, while the success of Accrington's market hall, it appears, was partly due to a municipal steam tramway linking the town to the surrounding countryside. Until their own market was built in 1882, people from Darwen regularly undertook a tram journey to Blackburn's market hall for their weekly shopping. Oldham was linked to towns in the surrounding countryside by tram, and it was to keep people in those towns coming to Oldham that the town built a new market hall in 1906. Leicestershire's thirty markets of 1500 declined to thirteen in 1700 and dwindled to a mere seven by the 1880s.[8]

Yet while many market towns marveled at the goods and people pouring into their market by railway, it was the old-fashioned carrier cart which continued to transport the mass of both customers and goods to the market. Indeed, modern transport had encouraged the growth of old-fashioned ways. In Leicestershire, four hundred cart-and-wagon carriers, making scheduled stops along the way, brought marketers from more than three hundred towns and villages to that county's seven market towns each week (fig. 9.4). The center of this system was the market at Leicester, which served some 90,000 persons each week. It was said in Hull that on Saturday nights one could count two hundred goods-and-passenger carts from more than one hundred villages lining the streets around the market. Bideford market was linked to numerous nearby villages by several dozen regularly scheduled carriers, usually horse-drawn covered vans in which passengers sat on wooden benches along the sides. From the village of Bradworthy, the journey to Bideford was a distance of about twenty miles and took three to four hours. In addition to passengers, the cart contained bags and baskets of eggs, butter, and other produce, belonging to women "wearing neat clean aprons" who regularly "sat at the market." For some it was the trip home which was the most memorable, when the chatter and laughter rose to crescendo, and many of the passengers were "well oiled from their visit to the Inns." Until the 1930s the travel patterns remained the same, except that the motorized omnibus now supplemented the horse-drawn carrier cart: the Bideford Motor Bus Company operated busses on dozens of the same routes to and from Bideford on market days.[9]

Social Distinctions and the Market

Because the market appealed to all classes of people, it is difficult to define the market hall in terms of social class. It is noteworthy that although the Victorian world was unusually stratified and hierarchical, its reinvented market did not encourage social separation but rather led to even more social mixing than had the open markets of a hundred years earlier. But the social mixing it fostered was usually on middle-class terms. Indeed, the reformed public market assumed a rather middle-class character, as the middle classes used it as a venue for imparting their values to the working classes. Unquestionably, one of the motives behind market reform was to reverse the direction of social emulation which took place in the marketplace. In the Victorian market, behavioral standards were set not, as in former times, by the lower-class roughs of the street but by the respectable middle classes. Indeed, one of the principal functions of the new market was to provide an acceptable place for middle-class women to do their shopping. Scarborough citizens wanted a new market hall similar to that in Southport so that "ladies could go through and order anything they pleased," and in Warrington it was said that ladies who refused to visit the uncovered market could be found shopping in the town's new market hall. Blackburn's market was popular with many ladies because it had many dry goods and drapery stalls. Indeed, the reformed public market may have been one of the few places where the increasing formality of public life included rather than excluded women.[10]

Still, despite the increase in social mixing and the cultivation of middle-class standards, most market halls had certain class distinctions. The "respectable" classes tended to frequent the market in the early hours of the day, when the quality of goods was high, while the poorer classes could be found in the market later in the day and in the evening, when prices were lower. Working-class women did most of their marketing on their husbands' payday: in Aberdeen in the 1870s this was Thursday evening, so from Friday morning on, working-class women, "carrying large two-handled baskets to hold their purchases, flocked down to do business at the open green and especially the covered Market Buildings." Most days of the week at about 11 A.M., the avenues of St. John's Market in Liverpool were "thronged with elegantly dressed ladies, and persons of the highest respectability"; they became less crowded toward the afternoon, until nighttime, when multitudes of workers poured into the market, even though the traditional working-class market day remained Saturday well into the twentieth century. In some large cities with more than one market hall, a particular hall might take on a particular social character: Liverpool's St. James's Market Hall was described as quiet and respectable, while St. John's was animated, particularly at night. The gallery in Dundee's Victoria Market of 1877, with its thirty-six shops and wide promenade, was regarded as a "fashionable resort."[11]

At various times certain market halls had a distinctly working-class character because of the products they sold. In Bristol in the 1880s, St. Nicholas Fish Market allowed only good-quality fish in the market, thereby virtually closing the market to the poor. In other places the classed nature of the market was a result of the proximity of the market to its users and the social makeup of the town itself. In the early nineteenth century, Dewsbury had scarcely any people of wealth, so almost everybody attending the market was working class; and by the late nineteenth century, the "bettermost people" had abandoned the market, as happened in Exeter. Similarly, the "best part" of the town of Sunderland in County Durham in the late nineteenth century had grown so distant from the old town center that the middle classes were cut off from the market. In the 1880s Windsor's small market near the castle was used largely by working people, but in Ashton-under-Lyne the market was described as not for the poorer folk.[12]

Shopping and Shoppers

At the market hall entrance, a shopper could hire a porter to follow her with a basket to carry her purchases, and to accompany her to her front door if desired (fig. 9.5). At the Shudehill Market in Manchester some 450 licensed porters (who paid the 2 shilling license fee) were available for hire. At many market halls, such as Glasgow's Bazaar, the market superintendent required proof of "good character" before issuing a porter's license. In Aberdeen the porters were called "hurleys" and wore blue-and-white striped aprons, while at Salisbury, market porters wore identification badges on their right arms to show that they obeyed public market bylaws.[13]

As we have seen, Saturday was the traditional market day for the working classes. If Arnold Bennett's fictional characters are typical of working-class pottery towns, then it is noteworthy that some men had the habit of "going forth on Saturday mornings to the butcher's or poulterer's, and buying Sunday's dinner." Whether done by men or women, Saturday shopping was connected to two exigencies of working-class life: most wives worked at some point in their lives, and Saturday was payday. Little is known of how working women accomplished their shopping, except that middle-class observers were critical of their supposed ignorance of household management and proper diet. But probably, the reformed market encouraged working-class women in a multitude of ways—from sanitation to product selection—to become consumers in a modern sense, that is, more aware of food and dietary issues.[14]

Certain shopping practices were common throughout Britain. While the more modest-sized halls held to the traditional practice of opening only on certain appointed market days (usually one day in addition to Saturday), the large market halls responded to the needs of urban growth (and a decline of household garden plots) by opening five or six days a week. This

9.5. BOYS IN THE MARKET HALL, INVERNESS, 1870

The boys in this photo are probably market porters, who carried purchases for the customers while they were shopping and then accompanied them home with the basket.

encouraged what we would consider "modern" shopping patterns. In addition, most market halls were open on Saturday nights, but many larger markets opened their doors on other nights as well, primarily as an accommodation to working people. Unlike London's street markets, the typical town market was never open on Sunday. The opening and closing of the market were usually announced by the market bell; on Saturday, the closing bell was normally rung at 11 P.M. or midnight. Liverpool's St. John's Market opened at 8 A.M. in the winter and 7 A.M. in the summer, with special opening hours on Wednesdays and Saturdays of 6 A.M. and 5 A.M., respectively. Year round, St. John's Market closed at 8 P.M. every night but Saturday, when the bell sounded at 11 P.M. In all markets the normal Saturday-night price reductions caused a great rush and bustle, reaching a crescendo by about 10 P.M., as the shoppers who gambled on lower prices snatched up bargains. But keeping the market open late on Saturday night generated considerable debate. Some opposed the practice because of the noise and congestion, and they were joined by others who regarded midnight as too late an hour to be up if the marketers were to live up to their church-going obligations the next day. But the late-night hours were firmly entrenched, and indeed, for many in the working classes they were regarded as a right. Exeter's town council debated a proposal to shorten Saturday-night hours for thirty-six years, finally setting back the closing by a half an hour.[15]

Most shoppers were attracted to the market hall because of its great diversity of stalls, the products to be had, and, of course, the cheap prices. The process of selection, however, required an education. It would never do for a shopper to go directly to a stall and make a purchase. Unlike buying in the shops, where one stepped up to the counter and placed an order, buying in the market hall was based on the notion of "shopping around"—or, as it was called, "the voyage of inspection." Hence the market was departmentalized so as to allow the buyer to survey all the vegetable dealers' offerings, for example, before going on to the butchers or the dry-goods sellers. Hence, separate areas were delineated for butchers, fish sellers, vegetable sellers, farm women with cheese, butter, and eggs, and so on. Often the gallery would be used for the sale of "fancy goods" or toys or candy. Many early nineteenth-century halls, such as the one at Brighton (see fig. 5.27), had an open layout: there were no permanent shops or stalls but rather, long tables or benches were set up each week. Poultry and meat sellers, it appears, occupied arcaded spaces along the exterior walls, which made it possible to clear the market for other uses. Increased market activity naturally caused this rather open, disorganized (or at least undefined) layout to give way to a design that featured a large number of fixed stalls and shops. Whatever the original design, however, predictable patterns of interior arrangement evolved, and shoppers grew familiar with the logical and functional organization of the halls.

In 1872 the pressure for space was so great in the crowded Shudehill Market in Manchester that farmers selling produce were asked to remove all goods and vacate their assigned spaces by noon so as to "make way for other market sellers"—millinery and provisions dealers, booksellers, and others. The plan of the Swansea Market Hall (see fig. 5.42) of 1897 reveals how a shopper would progress in the hall: entering by the main gate, one proceeded along the market circumference to inspect the various goods set out according to type, finishing up at the flower market which surrounded the grand octagonal fountain. Swansea's hall had the perfect layout: customers entered at one end of the market and emerged at the other with their week's provisions.[16]

The Pannier Markets

Markets in the southwest and Cornwall were principally of the pannier type. These rather simply arranged but often spacious markets had no fixed stalls or shops and provided only crude tables or benches on which the sellers could display their panniers. The pannier markets at Bideford and Barnstaple, for example, had vast open floor space arranged with what were called "sittings" (ordinarily a bench of 3-4 square feet), on which the farm women placed their baskets. The rental of these pannier benches at Barnstaple was ten shillings each per year to reserve the bench, and a fourpence toll each day the sitting was used, usually the regular Tuesday and Friday market days (fig. 9.6). Newton Abbot, among other pannier markets, charged only on a daily basis, and as time went on many of the larger pannier markets, such as that at Exeter, became daily markets with a mixture of pannier spaces and fixed lock-up stalls and shops.[17]

9.6. BARNSTAPLE, PANNIER
MARKET HALL, 1990

The primary function of a
pannier market is to provide
standing (or sitting) space for
farm people and, most
important, bench or table
space for their baskets of
dairy, vegetable, and other
goods for sale. Like many
Devonshire markets, Barn-
staple market was known for
selling Devonshire cream
from large earthenware
bowls. Today the markets
still offer locally grown farm
goods, canned goods, and
fresh fish.

Market Sellers

The public market was one of the town's major employers. The purveyors of goods in the original market halls, as today, fell into several categories. Every market had its regular army of sellers, among whom would have been a few local merchants who had private shops but also held a shop or stall at the public market primarily to unload perishable goods at week's end. Then there were the country people, who usually stood or sat at the benches and, as at Macclesfield, arranged their pats of butter on cabbage and rhubarb leaves. The rest were permanent market sellers, sometimes called "grafters," who had a casual or fixed stall or shop within the market. Market selling tended to be a family industry, in which all members of the family participated and the rights to the stall or shop passed down from family member to family member. One Liverpool market seller had not missed a day at the market between the time she was propped up in a basket as an infant under her parents' stall and her death at the age of ninety.[18]

The country people who brought locally produced goods into the market were also an important part of the market's economy. But as the nineteenth century progressed, many of the permanent stall- and shop holders became retailers in the modern sense: they did not produce what they sold but instead procured goods from wholesalers or producers. Some stall owners operated more than one stall in the same market; still others, taking advantage of the fact that market day or days varied from town to town, rented stalls in more than one market, moving themselves and their inventories from town to town. Some even found the market hall a starting point from which to begin a chain of market enterprises. It was from his stall in the Leeds Kirkgate Market in the mid-1880s that Michael Marks developed the unique retailing innovation of having all items in a special section of the stall sell for one penny; he went on to set up similar stalls, Penny Bazaars as they were called, in a number of other towns. By 1890, Marks operated Penny Bazaars in Leeds, Castleford, Wakefield, Warrington, and Birkenhead market halls; in the next decade he added stalls in nineteen other market halls, all operating under the slogan, Don't Ask the Price, It's a Penny. Out of these chains grew the giant Marks and Spencer retail department-store chain. Thus, in a real sense it was the market hall as a marketing phenomena that gave birth to the chain store, or multiple shop, and ultimately to the department store.[19]

Many professional market sellers were women. In the late nineteenth century, girls began to work in Sheffield's Norfolk Market Hall at the age of twelve for wages of one shilling a day, often keeping on until old age. In Liverpool's St. John's Market from 1900 to 1930, for example, approximately 40 percent of the nearly three hundred permanent market shop and stallholders or "occupiers" (not clerks) were women, and most casual country market sellers were women as well. Women dominated the fruit stalls and, as well, made up a sizable portion of owners of stalls and shops selling poultry, fish, and meat. In addition, in Liverpool and elsewhere (particularly pannier markets), a regular contingent of dairy women, farm women and girls, or village women marketed produce from their garden plots. Indeed, women had always sold in the public market, and some market tradeswomen, such as fish sellers, were notorious for vulgarity and harshness. With the coming of the reformed market in the nineteenth century, however, the image of "market women" moved in the opposite direction.[20]

Moving the market indoors from the streets changed market behavior and practice in a number of ways. With the advent of the market hall, buying and selling became more standardized and less haphazard. Market rules usually stipulated that articles brought to the market for sale be sold only in the designated sections. Selling surfaces were better constructed, more attractive, cleaner, and larger, and, in general, goods were better displayed and inspected—all giving the customer greater access to the product and more information, and the seller a more comfortable work environment as well as a better chance for a profit. Moving indoors meant for some sellers that better records could be kept; some even began to extend credit to their customers.[21]

Considering the general lack of improvement in work and living conditions for the eighteenth- and nineteenth-century farm workers who regularly sold in the town market, it is possible that the cleaner and dryer building which replaced the street market was one of the the few improvements they enjoyed in the course of their lives. Although the old custom of haggling over prices was discouraged by market officials, it was by no means eliminated, and the trend toward fixed pricing that had been pioneered by Michael Marks gave the buyer an advantage. Stall and shop sellers usually wore a uniform, generally a white apron or smock. A fixed and enclosed stall or shop allowed sellers to take advantage of modern advertising techniques, including signs to identify their shop or stall, elaborate displays of goods, and large advertising boards attached to the market's interior walls (fig. 9.7). Fixed indoor stalls made

9.7. ABERDEEN MARKET HALL, CA. 1880

The "advertising boards" shown on the walls of this market demonstrate how the municipal market hall kept pace with modern advertising techniques.

it easier for goods to be sorted, weighed, and packed. Overall, although the process of urbanization strained the age-old links between rural producer and town consumer, the new enclosed market made possible a more permanent and regularized relationship between the professional market retailer and the consumer. With allotted and fixed spaces, the market stall or shop holder became as established as the owner of the corner shop and more easily identifiable than had been possible in the old open-air market.[22]

It was for the art of salesmanship that the public market became best known. In an age of little national advertising, few brand names for foodstuffs, and little pre-packaging of goods (until the late nineteenth century), market salesmanship was of singular importance. Indeed, sales talk, or "pitching," as it was called, was one of the special differences between the public market and the private shop, which did not allow the kind of sales banter that characterized the public market. In both places, customers were not encouraged to handle the goods: this was part of the over-the-counter service offered by the shop clerk or stallholder. But unlike the private shop, where goods were often out of sight, visual inspection of goods was encouraged and consequently displaying them to best advantage became the consummate market hall art.

The finest public speakers of all, it was said, were the sellers in the public market. Every town market had its fast-talking, colorful salespeople, who convinced their customers that they were getting a special bargain. Some became famous for their showmanship; a regular feature at the Rugeley market was a crockery salesman who threw platters at his audience if he was not getting the prices he asked for. Indeed, one of the aims of market reform was to eliminate bellicose sales practices—including "hawking" goods within the market. One sales technique popular with some market sellers but a scourge to market officials was the so-called Dutch Auction, in which the salesperson continually lowered his or her prices until a buyer was snared. The goal here was to draw large crowds, but because the auction interrupted the ordinary tranquility of the market, the practice was usually prohibited. It was partly for this reason that Glasgow's market bylaws stipulated that no stanceholder or tenant of the market "shall attempt, beyond the limits of his stance or occupancy, to induce any person to make purchases."[23]

9.8. THE PET STALLS, BIRMINGHAM MARKET HALL, 1870

9.9. ACCRINGTON MARKET HALL, ALFRED SMITHIES GREENGROCER STALL, 1902

Flags, paper lanterns, and palm fronds are used to decorate a greengrocer's stall to commemorate the coronation of Edward VII in 1902. Even without the special decorations, the stall has an inviting and tidy appearance that encouraged the market hall voyage of inspection.

The Market Hall and the Age of Mass Consumption

The market hall helped create what is commonly called the age of mass consumption. Not only did the market hall offer greater consumer choice, but owing to improved market facilities, generally lower prices, and rising real wages, the acts of choosing and selecting became more cultivated and ritualized, both as a necessity and a pastime for shoppers of all classes. In Swansea it was said that on winter nights it was pleasant "to turn in from the cold and wet . . . to the cheerful warmth of packed crowds and to browse awhile in search of riches at the

9.10. CYCLE STALL, ACCRINGTON MARKET HALL, CA. 1910

Bicycles and phonograph records point to the role of the market hall in fostering a new world of consumer products for working- and middle-class customers.

second-hand bookstall." A major attraction in Birmingham's market hall was the pet stalls (fig. 9.8). Indeed, new market facilities, along with advanced merchandising and sales techniques, encouraged consumption well beyond simple need. As a result, the display of goods in the market hall shop and stall became legendary: meat, poultry, vegetables, and flowers were exhibited with a fanfare that gave the market hall a festive appearance (fig. 9.9). By the late nineteenth century the market hall had come to offer such a variety of goods that it could rival the twentieth-century shopping mall. Thus, the market hall emerged as an early instru-

9.11. WILKINSON'S DEPOT FOR PHONOGRAPHS AND RECORDS, NORFOLK MARKET HALL, SHEFFIELD, CA. 1900

ment in recruiting consumers for the mass consumption explosion. Durham's new market of 1852 provided accommodation for butchers, clothiers, hatters, ropers, potters, booksellers, coopers, tinmakers, shoemakers, bacon and cheese factors, glovers, worsted dealers, basket makers, gardeners, quack medicine vendors, confectioners, blacking makers, hardware merchants, sellers of implements of husbandry, and sellers of fish, potatoes, and fruit. Blackburn's new market hall (1852) included the usual butchers' and greengrocers' stalls, but had as well milliners, furniture dealers, dressmakers, shoe and clog makers, and straw hat and bonnet dealers (which suggests that the market hall was where Blackburn's mill girls, known for their clogs and shawls, shopped). By mid-century some market halls were so crowded with goods that more room was sought, and in most large towns, fish and often meat sales were relegated to separate (typically adjoining) quarters. In 1852 complaints were registered by Birmingham's Markets and Fairs Committee that the "avenue" for manufactured goods in the hall was not large enough. For the next three years the hall was rearranged, and seven new shops were added.[24]

By the end of the century, most market halls offered the latest in durable decorative and "artistic" goods, such as cheap porcelain, decorated pottery, and glassware, as well as leisure products like bicycles, phonographs, records, postcards, and musical instruments (figs. 9.10, 9.11). Dewsbury's turn-of-the-century market hall had both a doll stall and Betty's Tuppenny Stall, which specialized in cheap toys. The halls at Wigan and Stalybridge sold sewing machines as well as tinned biscuits and ready-made clothing. Bradford's grand Kirkgate Market Hall was celebrated for the variety of products offered: musical instruments, crystal, jewelry, confectionery, ironmongery, crockery, baskets, cutlery, and drapery, and by the 1920s the Rochdale Market Hall offered sewing machine repairs, optical services, and American magazines and comics.[25]

This consumer revolution was, in effect, a cultural revolution. To unprecedented numbers of men and women of the middle and working classes, the market hall offered the possibility of aesthetic choice and encouraged the fulfillment of what has been called "the very human desire" to possess objects of art. For the first time in Western history the arts no longer validated only the powerful few but now gave respectability to the many—in the form of books, cheap parian sculpture, decorated porcelain, stoneware and earthenware, musical instruments, decorated brass and cast iron, electroplated silver, cheap printed and woven fabrics, and even cheap prints and postcards. Bourgeois respectability, it was learned, could be purchased in the public market, and beginning in some places as early as the 1820s and 1830s the public market became an agent in the democratization of taste and an important cultural bridge between classes. In Oldham's market hall, "Cheap Jack" the bookseller attracted crowds to his book auctions. Arnold Bennett's fictional hero Edwin Clayhanger found a new world of richness in the bookstall of the covered market of his working-class "pottery town." Books, for Clayhanger, did not simply satisfy a thirst for knowledge; in addition, the book, with its beautiful cover, "might be a bibelot, a curious jewel, to satisfy the lust of the eye and of the hand." The traditional dichotomy between daily life and high art was broken. As the Scottish popularizer of taste John Loudon noted, "We feel that the source of all improvements has its origin in the desire of . . . that individual . . . who endeavors to raise his taste, and give evidence [of it] to his friends and the world. . . . We therefore cannot but approve of displaying this taste, in a preeminent manner, on houses, gardens, furniture, and every thing connected with the home."[26]

In this context, the market hall encouraged shopping as a respectable leisure activity; in addition, for many in the working and middle classes, it represented the point of confluence of consumption and culture. The market hall mixed social goals, cultural ideology, and consumerism under one roof, and by doing so taught people what they ought to desire. Unlike the ancient fairs and outdoor markets that the market halls replaced, which were notorious for their vulgarity and socially unacceptable activities like dog fighting and bull baiting, the market hall made consumption honorable.

Space, Order, and Respectability

The market hall was more than simply an economic enterprise. As noted earlier, much of the political and cultural activity of nineteenth-century urban society grew out of an effort to reconstruct the "fossilized" town according to the new moral ideals of the Victorian middle class. The problems, in the eyes of market reformers, were many and daunting—and as diverse and far-ranging as contaminated water supplies and the perceived immoral behavior of young people who danced in the streets on market days. The market hall building itself, with its modern materials, planned spaces, ordered arrangement of stall, shop, entrance, and exit, and its architectural embellishment, was designed to elevate thought and action—as well as to intimidate the incorrigible. Public marketing thus became separated from other street activities. When compared to the street market of old, the new market hall, as a "town within a town," was inordinately peaceful. Markets had a high moral tone: they represented a place for civility and fair prices.[27]

The decision to build a new market building was often a justification to launch an assault on the traditional custom of street selling, or hawking. From the late eighteenth century on, the goal of most market authorities (reinforced by the Public Health Act of 1875) was to permit marketing only inside an enclosed and regulated space. Opposition to street hawking arose, in part, out of a desire for cleaner, safer, and more respectable streets; the practice was also attacked by shopkeepers and market traders, who argued that to allow it was unfair because hawkers seldom paid tolls (and thus paid nothing toward the town rates). In town after town, street hawking was prohibited, and the proportion of the nation's food supply purchased from costermongers declined, although the prohibitions were often not fully enforced, and many towns, particularly London, relied heavily on street hawking as a principal form of food distribution. In Castleford, it was said, street hawking was a convenience for the upper classes because it eliminated the need to send their servants to the market; instead, the servant could meet the vendor at the doorstep or a street corner. At one point it was argued that the reason Exeter's two market halls were in decline was that door-to-door hawking had become so entrenched, and in Torquay the market hall found it difficult to compete with licensed hawkers who took goods from door to door. Whether to allow street hawking was a subject of much local debate, and in some towns it became a major political issue.[28]

The market hall was also the means by which to enforce new behavioral standards of buying and selling. Market officials, backed up by disgruntled town councilmen, market buyers, and sellers, established new standards of acceptable salesmanship. "There must be order kept in the market," said Burnley's town clerk. And the enclosed and isolated nature of the new market halls allowed for greater market policing. A new building usually meant new bylaws. The bylaws fixed the rules of proper market behavior and use and in so doing delineated standards for many aspects of market trading: wholesomeness of goods, weights used, cleanliness, and so on. Bylaws set standards for the use and storage of carts during market hours, the amount of rents and tolls, the inspection of provisions by market officials, the arrangement of stalls, and the general decorum expected of buyer and seller. Bylaws were printed and distributed among market sellers, published in the local press, and placed on the market walls. For instance, on display in the Torquay market hall today are excerpts from the parliamentary act which gave the market a virtual monopoly on sales of goods outside town shops, and five of the provisions of the Market and Fairs Clauses Act of 1847.[29]

Typically, Salisbury's market hall bylaws of 1858 forbid swearing, noise disturbance, offensive language, indecent or vulgar behavior, and smoking. The regulations of the Dundee market hall specified that "rude language" was not allowed and persons under the influence of drink could not enter the market, and in Burnley, where the town clerk mandated that the market be orderly, the market inspector was given the authority to eject persons who used "disgusting language," were abusive, violent, or drunk, who created an obstruction, or who engaged in quarreling. Market officials threw sellers out on account of bad language, drunkenness, and even improper attire. Some market sellers looked to market authorities to guarantee that the public market be "a fair field of competition" by rigorously enforcing market bylaws. As a result, Liverpool's bylaws forbid any market seller to attract persons by "handselling or by elevating himself or herself upon a platform or upon anything raised above the floor level of the market." The ancient custom of "bawling" or "crying" fish or other goods was banned in indoor markets, and Newcastle's new Sandhill Fish Market of 1823 came to a premature end because all the women fish sellers were banished for unacceptable behavior. Soon after the Darlington market hall was opened, the inspector began to fine stallholders for bawling their wares. In that same year Launceton's citizens boycotted their market in protest against the "extreme filthy . . . appearance of that market's butchers," while a few years later Birmingham's market officials censured stall keepers for abusive and insulting conduct. In Leeds, Marks and Marks, the fruit sellers, were reprimanded by the Market Committee for their "habit of making a great noise and wearing an objectionable costume in front of their shops, causing annoyance to the other tenants, and unduly attracting customers." Similarly, in Ashton-under-Lyne, William Gibson, a pot seller, was fined for "shouting his wares for sale," and it was not uncommon for a stallholder to be denied further tenancy for using bad language.[30]

In addition, the elimination of "strife and contention" in the market hall was sought through routine policing and a vigilant market committee. Most towns of size had a regular market police force or used local constables to monitor market behavior. Market inspectors, or "market bobbies" as they were called in Birkenhead, found that unacceptable behavior was not confined to market vendors; indeed, as the prereformed market made frighteningly apparent, market customers were potentially as troublesome as market sellers. Most market officials were suspicious of any suggestion to allow entertainments (including theatrical exhibitions) back into the public market, largely because of the danger of encouraging unruly crowds. As late as the 1820s, the Newton Abbot market still had a lock-up cell in the marketplace for drunk and disorderly buyers and vendors, and Redruth's town constable was given the task of suppressing vagrancy and ballad singing in the market. Nevertheless, the records of market officials suggest that theft, drunkenness, and fighting in the market hall were rare, and when they occurred, they were followed by demands for greater police action. Indeed, the most common of the market disciplinary problems seems to have been keeping unruly children and roaming youths out of the market hall. When Wolverhampton tenants complained that their hall had the stigma of being the "worst conducted Market hall in England," the markets committee responded by employing a market policeman to rid the place of boys and others who attended the hall only to loiter.[31]

Respectability within the market was also sought by allowing only the right sort of products in the hall. In Peterborough, for example, market officials sought to keep the susceptible public from toys and "the most trumpery rubbish of every sort of description," which filled the market and debased "one's notions of decency." The selling of coconuts in the Burnley market was prohibited because "it attracts rough people," and in Bath it was argued that Mrs. Barnett's tea and coffee stall in the market hall was an asset to that town because "it is keeping people from drinking beer and spirits."[32]

The Fight Against Fraud, Adulteration, and Unsanitary Conditions

The crowd attending the opening of the Wolverhampton market hall cheered when it was announced that goods would henceforth be sold by weight and not by measure, such as a "bunch," a box, or a basket. Selling by measure was generally regarded by the market user as the bane of the marketplace because it led to fraud. What was adopted in Wolverhampton was adopted all across Britain as town officials became increasingly serious about the prevention of fraud and unsanitary conditions in the public market. Indeed, the attack on market fraud was the earliest instance of consumer protectionism on the local level and represents a gradual shift in economic power from seller to consumer. It is also probable that improvement in the quality and quantity of the urban food supply was partly responsible for the general decline in the death rate in Britain in the second half of the nineteenth century.[33]

There was much to reform. The absence of a regular and sufficient diet was a fact of British life and was often aggravated by unsanitary conditions, adulteration, and fraud. The weak physical condition of the poorest of the urban population and the high rate of mortality in certain urban areas were to an appreciable degree due to the historically poor quality of the urban diet. Early nineteenth-century handloom-weavers in Lancashire villages, for example, preferred their own home-grown poultry and vegetables to "town food." Adulterated and unwholesome food, often sold amid the "filthie and noysome stink of the streets," was a common feature of the old marketplace and continued well into the nineteenth century.[34]

In fact, with the growth of industrialization and urbanization in the late eighteenth and early nineteenth centuries, the predicament of food fraud became a great deal worse before it became better. In the early stages of industrialization and urban growth, most British towns abandoned food controls and did little to address the problems of urban environment—particularly the problem of sanitation, which was a major issue before the municipal and sanitary reform legislation that began around 1835. As the distance between producer, seller, and consumer grew and became more impersonal, more and more wholesalers and middlemen took the opportunity to adulterate their products. In an age that disdained regulation, the rise of the anonymous intermediary encouraged ingenious food adulteration schemes, and the absence of refrigeration and national standards of weight and measure, inadequate packaging, and the end of self-regulation by the guilds and corporations of tradesmen all led to a rise in food fraud. Unfortunately, even improvements in transportation were as likely to lead to the deterioration as to the betterment of food quality. A large quantity of old and diseased meat, for example, was sent to Glasgow because the steamship and railway could transport cows that in an earlier age would never have reached the market on hoof.[35]

The foods most subject to adulteration were milk, ale, bread, tea, coffee, spices, and flour; the class of people most subject to such fraud was the poor of the large manufacturing towns. As late as 1875 a third of Manchester's milk supply was adulterated, a fact which helps explain why Manchester suffered so many epidemics. In London, it was claimed in the final decade of the century that it was scarcely possible for the poor to buy pure food. A mid-century chemical analysis found that of fifty-five samples of food in Birmingham, twenty-one were adulterated, as were twenty-two of eighty-four in Liverpool, twenty-five of seventy-three in Manchester, and twenty-one of sixty-three in Leeds. Coffee commonly had varying amounts of additives, including potatoes, burnt sugar, roast corn, or chicory. Sugar was often adulterated with treacle, sawdust, lime, starch, and even animal blood. Spices were often packaged with red lead, red earth, salt, or ground rice. Various kinds of ground leaves were added to tea, and bread was frequently made of flour containing bean meal and alum. It was said in 1861 that 10 percent of all meat sold in London was unfit for human consumption, and that unnatural color was frequently added to fruit. Food adulteration had become such a national scandal that many producers were careful to advertise their products as pure and wholesome.[36]

How does the public market fit into this grim picture? Was the public market a source of wide-scale food adulteration and consumer fraud? In fact, the battle against fraud, lack of sanitary conditions, and adulteration was well under way on a local level in most town markets in the early decades of the nineteenth century, long before adulteration became a "national" issue in the 1840s. Behind this was a political assumption that there was a direct connection between bad health and bad markets. Voters in Hull, for example, expressed the fear that the "wretched" state of the market was the source of "some severe disease." Early attacks on declining food quality took the form of enforcement of market cleanliness, elimination of street selling with its rat-infested stalls, bylaw revision, and food inspection. Attracting particular attention was the perceived relation between the spatial arrangement of the market and the level of cleanliness. Lack of sanitation, of course, was a major reason for enclosing the market in the first place.[37]

Selling indoors automatically brought about a change in the way goods were handled and sold and made it easier for the consumer to judge the quality of the products: food was frequently displayed and dispensed on white-tiled or marble counter tops or even behind glass; vegetables were washed and weighed on clean, accurate scales. The enclosed market offered better drainage and flooring, a supply of running water, good roofing and lighting, and regular market cleaning. Furthermore, the creation of local boards of health after 1848 led to improved market planning—including hygienic ways of displaying food. One of the attractions of building a new market at Harrogate, for example, was that buyers would be relieved of the uncertainties they faced when purchasing food in the old open-air market. Liverpool's 1822 market hall had forty-four stone compartments for potatoes—each 9 feet wide—and the market authorities claimed that the sanitary arrangements of its new fish market of 1837 were "all that can be desired." By the 1850s numerous market halls could boast ventilation systems, lavatories, tiled walls and metal counter tops, and advanced water and drainage systems. With glass roofing, the introduction of first gas and then electric lighting, paved flooring, permanent stall and shop facilities, in-market water supplies, and, particularly, a modern inspection system, the reformed markets were more comfortable, better lit, and better organized, and they offered more wholesale food than the markets of old.[38]

Another check to unsanitary conditions, adulteration, and fraud was the creation of tighter standards of inspection and weighing. From ancient times, markets had established standard weights and measures by which incoming goods were scrutinized and disputes settled. "He who seeks to find eternal treasure must use no guile in weight or measure," was the inscription chiseled on Truro's old market house. Manchester's prereform markets had an army of twenty-four market inspectors whose job it was to check, by taste if necessary, meat, fish, beer, bread, and other products. How well such consumer protection efforts worked is difficult to say. Most town records document attempts to halt market abuses. As in many towns, adulteration and incorrect weighing of bread in Edinburgh was so difficult to control that officials once threatened to deprive the bakers of their town citizenship. Soon after its purchase of the market from Lord Mosley, Manchester's town council found that the "irregularities and disorder" at Shudehill disappeared with the appointment of a uniformed inspector. In 1828, Truro's constables weighed the butter offered for sale in the market and found large amounts of underweight butter, which was then confiscated for distribution to the poor. The ingenious nature of one butter seller, a woman named Brown, is indicative of the kind of deception confronting both market buyers and market inspectors. The woman took a piece of butter which weighed about an ounce and a half and stuck it to the bottom of each half-pound of butter, as she passed it from her basket to the official scales. She then dexterously removed it after the butter was handed back, to stick on the next half-pound. "By this means all her butter was made weight. Unfortunately for her, the trick was observed by a thrifty housewife who watched the process, and communicated the result to the constables."[39]

Chemical analysis of food was not systematically taken up in the public market or elsewhere in the nineteenth century. Most municipalities did not begin food sampling by chemical analysis until the early twentieth century, and in general, market officials were slow to appreciate the value of chemistry in detecting adulterated food. It took nearly twenty years of public outcry and debate over adulteration of foodstuffs, largely milk, bread, and beer, before it became customary for town officials to appoint analysts to test for and report on adulterated food. Soon after Manchester appointed a public food analyst in 1873, the quality of the town's food improved. Significantly, most early chemical evidence suggests that the main source of adulterated food in Manchester and elsewhere was not the public market but the private shop. Of the four foods most often tampered with—meat, bread, ale, and milk—only meat was commonly sold in the public market. All of the chemical-analysis surveys in the 1850s found contaminated food in shops but none in the public market.[40]

Sanitary reform seems to have touched the market at an earlier point than it did other aspects of urban life. As the pace of market reform sped up, town officials expressed their awareness of the connection, if only implicit, between disease, diseased and unwholesome food, and a dirty market. Edwin Chadwick's influential report of 1842 on the intolerable sanitary conditions of most towns no doubt had a direct influence on market reform—although the fact that Chadwick made no reference to the public market suggests that it was in a better condition than the rest of the town's amenities, such as water supply and waste drainage. Nevertheless, there is little doubt that the health crisis of the 1830s and 1840s and the ensuing sanitation movement, including Chadwick's own work, encouraged a more watchful eye's being cast on the public market and the public slaughterhouses. Truro's impressive new market of 1847 was built in part through the influence of the town's sanitation reformer, one Dr. Carlyon. Twelve years later in Salisbury, the idea for a market hall was first introduced by another sanitation reformer, Dr. A. B. Middleton, who envisaged a new market as one of a number of projects for a more healthy town. Market architects, working with expanded market-bylaw powers, become ever more intent on providing the market with refuse disposal and sewage facilities, washable surfaces, and a plentiful supply of cold and hot water. Glazed tiles, salt-glazed bricks, terrazzo, glazed slate, and glass were ideal materials for markets because they could be washed down. Indeed, one of the goals was to create a shopping environment which not only was clean but looked clean. In the new Oldham market, iron-and-glass market hall shop fronts, light iron columns, and glazed brick, it was claimed, would have "a clean and effective appearance."[41]

The rule in the public market was that vendors were responsible for inspecting their own goods. Any vendor who brought unwholesome or adulterated food into the market risked immediate confiscation and destruction of the product. The Glasgow market bylaws mandated that no unwholesome meat, fruit, vegetables, provisions, or commodities of any description could be brought into, kept, or exposed for sale in the Bazaar, and any such meat, fruit, vegetables, provisions, or commodities so brought, kept, or exposed for sale would be seized and destroyed or otherwise disposed of by the superintendent or his assistants, or dealt with under the provisions of the Glasgow Police Act of 1866.

Naturally, such self-policing could be effective only if backed by rigorous bylaws and inspection systems. In 1847 local food inspection and sanitation bylaws and ordinances were supplemented by various national public health, food and drug, contagious diseases, and slaughterhouse and unwholesome food acts—most of which were permissive or "enabling" acts, in that they encouraged greater local regulation. In 1858 Birmingham's markets committee, in order to protect the poor against "fraud and deceit," undertook a rigid inspection system, and within twenty years it was annually conducting 100,000 in-market inspections of weight and measuring practices. Although it is not clear how much the Birmingham experience was duplicated elsewhere, or even how far the Birmingham experiment went in reducing fraud and adulteration, some market traders complained that inspection was too rigid and rigorous.[42]

The caliber of inspection improved. By the late nineteenth century, food inspection, food analysis, and general market administration, once undertaken by citizens as market "lookers" (in Southampton they were called "discreets of the market") on a voluntary basis had evolved into recognized professions. In Birkenhead the market "bobbies" were trained professionals, dressed in black suits, swallow-tailed coats, and top hats. Nearby in Liverpool, St. John's Market had, by 1890, a staff of market constables (nine of whom were trained food inspectors) who were apparently equally well dressed (fig. 9.12). In large and medium-sized towns such as these, administration was usually in the hands of a market superintendent or supervisor appointed by the town through its market committee. Superintendents were charged with overseeing the work of dues collectors, weighers of provisions, and inspectors. With their inspectors, market superintendents, as professional municipal servants, recommended numerous changes and reforms in the municipal marketing system, such as the establishment of national grading standards for certain foods, for example, produce and eggs.[43]

9.12. LIVERPOOL MARKET OFFICIALS, ST. JOHN'S MARKET HALL, 1885

PART FOUR

DECLINE AND RECOVERY

CHAPTER TEN

❦

THE PUBLIC MARKET AND THE RETAIL REVOLUTION, 1890-1939: DECLINE OR MODERNIZATION?

BY THE 1890S THE PUBLIC MARKET WAS FACING CONSIDERABLE COMPETITION from the new-fashioned department store, the chain store, and the cooperative shop. It is difficult to measure the popularity of the public market with urban consumers except to say that these new avenues of consumerism offered strong competition. The boom in market hall building had passed by 1890 and, in fact, a number of public markets either went out of business or entered into a period of decline. The market in Maidstone, for example, was out of business by 1890, and the town was left dependent on the local shops, while in Glasgow at about the same time the public Bazaar Market was closed to retail trading because the "great extension of Glasgow in every direction . . . and . . . its equally plentiful supply of shops of all kinds . . . seem to supersede the usefulness of the Bazaar as a general retail market." Having done much to promote progressive market design in the past, by the turn of the century even the architectural and building periodicals began to view the public market in a highly romanticized manner that harkened back to a pre-industrial world (fig. 10.1). After the First World War this process of decline accelerated—partly because many of the halls were half a century old, in disrepair, and had a depressingly backward air about them.[1]

One factor deflecting popular sentiment away from the public markets was the fact that by the end of the nineteenth century, many governments downgraded the priority they had earlier given to improving the public food supply. In addition, food prices were falling and supplies were rising. Also, towns refocused their resources on sanitary reform, gas and water services, slum clearance, and (during the interwar years of the twentieth century) public housing. As a result, some public markets were allowed to deteriorate to the point of public embarrassment, remaining only as a shabby reminder of an age of want. Many were pulled down or reduced in size for the convenience of street alterations or other public services. Thus at

10.1. BUILDING NEWS DESIGNING CLUB, "A MARKET HALL FOR A COUNTRY TOWN," 1903

By the turn of the century, the architectural press had lost interest in the market hall as an experiment in urban efficiency and progress and had turned to the romantic pre-industrial market house for its inspiration. This was a winning entry in a market design competition sponsored by the *Building News*.

10.2. Howden, Market
Hall, 1871

A noble attempt to keep the
town market eventually
failed because of changes in
transportation, in particular
the opening of the Hull and
Selby Railroad around 1850
which bypassed the town. A
half-century later a new
bridge at Goole drew more
customers away from
Howden market. The build-
ing sill exists, but the
market was closed in 1905.

Bath, for example, the movement of middle-class families to the distant suburbs and the pressure for additional space to serve growing municipal business led to a downgrading of the market façade and a shrinkage of market space in favor of new municipal offices.

At the same time, many growing industrial towns witnessed the first serious beginnings of suburban sprawl, brought on in part by the tramway and the new underground, which carried a growing population away from the town center and toward the new suburban shops. Now the local High Street grocer, greengrocer, butcher, fishmonger, and florist shops, along with street hawkers, replaced the old public market. Indeed, after about 1890, and particularly after the end of the war in 1918, the earlier *intensive* urban growth patterns of many towns changed to *extensive* explosions. Suburban property development created new neighborhoods which relied less heavily on the city center to satisfy consumer needs. Local shops were served principally by deliveries from regional and national wholesalers, thus widening the gorge between local and regional farmers and the local population. For instance, by 1918, the public market buildings in Winchester and Chichester, as in other towns in the south, had been converted into retail shops or deteriorated into markets for old clothing and junk.

The fortunes and misfortunes of the East Riding Yorkshire town of Howden is instructive. Howden was a prosperous market town until it was bypassed by the canal- and then the railway-building booms. It grew little in the nineteenth century; in fact, growth actually declined during the agricultural depression years beginning in the early 1870s. In 1871 the town attempted to regain its former prosperity and status as a market center by building a market hall (known later as the Shire Hall) in the old marketplace (fig. 10.2). This interesting combination market house-town hall of red brick, with a tiled roof, arched entrances, crow-stepped gables, and clock tower, was reminiscent of the Gothic markets of the Low Countries with which East Riding had strong historic ties. But by the 1900s the market was dead. Howden's decreasing population, the agricultural depression, the coming of motorized transport (particularly the bus), and a new bridge to Goole—and its market—made the nearby towns of Hull and Goole attractive alternatives to Howden's dark little Victorian market hall; the market closed in 1905.[2]

Some market halls were never particularly flourishing concerns, especially in towns in the southeast of England that had a sizable middle-class population connected to high-fashion shop retailing, both locally and in nearby London. By 1900, Maidstone was one of many towns in Kent where the market had long given way to good shops in town. Here it was simply impossible to buy meat or vegetables or fruit in a general public market. Similarly, only five years after it opened in 1858, the Weston-Super-Mare market hall was little frequented and "scantily supplied"—allegedly due to the fact that this growing seaside town had many well-stocked shops. Bristol's St. Nicholas fish market had to be reconstructed because it was too large, and similar market overbuilding could be seen in other towns.[3]

The Expansion of Modern Wholesaling

A general perception by 1918 was that the public market had seen its day. Indeed, a particularly threatening retail revolution had already begun. Most noticeable in the new way of doing business was the replacement of the direct link between local farmer and urban shopper by large regional and national food marketing firms which bought directly from specialist farmers or from commission salesmen or wholesale distributors (fig. 10.3). Even local market retailers found that their contacts with the country producers were being usurped by wholesalers. Although most towns were still surrounded by belts of intensive cultivation for local markets, overall, the trend was in the opposite direction. By contracting to purchase the farmer's goods directly, on a regular basis, and for predictable prices, dairy, fruit, and vegetable wholesalers made it more profitable and convenient for many farmers to sell their entire crop at the gate rather than carry it to the public market. Farming for the regional intermediaries rather

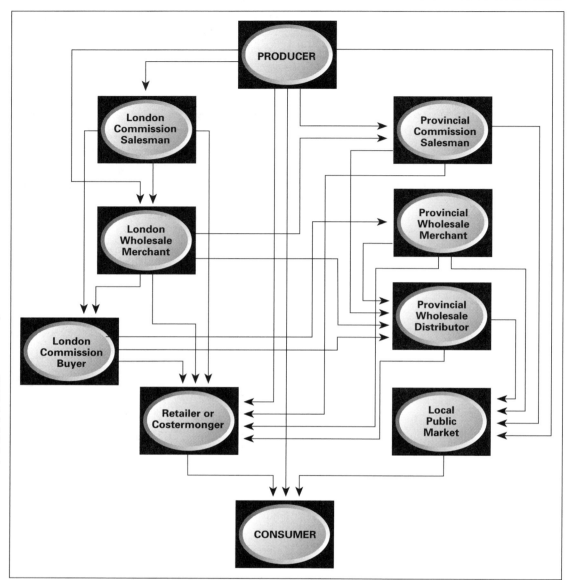

10.3. FROM PRODUCER TO CONSUMER: THE PATH OF FRUIT AND VEGETABLE SALES

A variety of intermediaries or "middlemen" interposed between the producer and the consumer. It was in the nineteenth century that the traditional path of goods from producer to consumer via the public market became a complicated system.

than for the local market sometimes meant that customers were offered a higher quality and more variety of fruits and vegetables, but it also meant that sometimes they had to make do with prepackaged items.[4]

It is estimated that in some instances as many as six intermediaries were interposed between the grower and the consumer. Most fruit for Scotland, for example, reached the consumer by way of a vast wholesale fruit auction for provincial commission salesmen in Glasgow; it was then carried by a wholesale distributor to a retailer, who would place the items in a stall in the public market or local shop. In the early 1920s, about 25 percent of the Cambridge area vegetable crop and 70 percent of the Cornish potato crop were sold directly to wholesalers, who in turn resold them at giant wholesale markets, or even bypassed the wholesale market and went directly to retail chains. The egg market was dominated by intermediaries known as higglers, who called at farms with a motor van or a one-horse carriage once or twice a week, and then resold the eggs to retailers and wholesalers. By 1890 dairy products were increasingly supplied through national and regional wholesale dairy companies. Much of the cheese and milk produced in Wiltshire and Cheshire, for example, was organized by large dairy retailers.[5]

Further accelerating the elimination of direct exchange between farm producer and public market was the arrival of commercially processed and cheap imported foods. Farm curing of bacon, for example, had given way to bulk factory-cured bacon, and canned corned beef, fish, and even Scotch broth became regular household staples in the 1870s and 1880s. The importation of cheap (sometimes called colonial) meat, particularly pork from America and Ireland, was so considerable (and popular) that in some parts of the country, butchers found it impossible to get rid of the less-desirable cuts of beef and mutton that previously would have been sold at the end of the week at a reduced price.[6]

New Competition: The Cooperative and the Chain Store

These changes in distribution and product meant that an increasingly large share of the food supply was sold by way of large-scale chain stores and cooperative-society shops, which were more closely integrated into the new large-scale distribution schemes than were the independent market stallholders. Still, for at least a half-century, the public market was able to benefit from the new food distribution system, in part because some local wholesale markets remained vibrant, and in part because the public market was able to provide a home for the chain stores and the cooperative shops.

The idea of the cooperative shop arose in the early nineteenth century, but its real influence came with the creation of the North of England Co-Operative Wholesale Society in 1863, and a kindred society in Scotland five years later. The chains followed in the next decade. The imported-meat chains like James Nelson and Sons, the tea and grocery merchant's chain Lipton's, and the Home and Colonial Stores grocery, along with Templetons, Massey's, and Cochranes, began in the 1870s and 1880s, but it was not until the 1890s that they became widespread. Initially, the chains were regionally based, like Dyson's in Dewsbury, but Lipton's, which had its beginnings in Glasgow, provided a model for the nationally based chain store.[7]

Retail chains like Lipton's took business from the public markets. Geared to providing better prices, products, and service, the chain stores and the cooperative shops competed with the market hall for working-class custom. Chains and cooperative shops, like the market halls, were established on the principles of low price, high turnover, and cash-only sales; but unlike the market hall, they often offered their own brand products, presented a more modern image and outlet, and relied heavily on imported products at rock-bottom prices. At the outset, Lipton's, for example, was able to offer tea and imported ham at half the price of the ordinary shop or less. Lipton's also started selling margarine in the early 1890s and jam in 1892. In many cases the chains bypassed the wholesale distribution chain by intervening in the production process. Until the public markets could catch up, the chains and co-ops pioneered in providing goods that were not originally available in the average market hall—tinned food, cheap tea, and cheap imported meat (often pork or frozen beef).[8]

In the early years of this retail revolution, the cooperative movement had a more damaging impact on the public market hall than did the private chain stores. By 1901 there were 1,229 cooperative societies trading in England and Wales. The cooperatives were heavily concentrated in the same northern manufacturing districts which boasted numerous large and popular market halls; more than 65 percent of cooperative business activity took place in the north and northwest. The Lancashire wool town of Bacup, for example, boasted a cooperative society housed in a palatial building, with seven additional branches in town. As at Rochdale, where the cooperative movement had its beginnings, the Bacup cooperative pulled business away from the public market. There, too, it was not uncommon, as in Pontefract market hall, for the local cooperative to keep a stall in the public market hall. Nationally, by 1914 the chains and the cooperatives commanded about a fifth of all retail grocery sales. The continued growth of the chains and cooperatives between the world wars was considerable. Immediately following the Second World War, the chain-store and cooperative share of the retail trade had risen to about a third.[9]

The Market and World War I

World War I greatly disrupted marketing habits. Unrestricted submarine warfare by the Germans from 1916 onward highlighted the nation's seemingly dangerous dependence on imported food supplies—a fact which was borne out by the widespread potato shortages and ensuing food lines in the spring of 1917. During the war the number of retail traders in Liverpool's public market contracted so considerably that a portion of the market was turned over to wholesalers. The government responded to the country's food shortages by establishing a Ministry of Food, which, in turn, guaranteed Britain's wartime food needs through enforcement of price controls, regulation of consumption, and increase in home production.

The war unwittingly speeded up the decline of the public market. National prices and consumption controls had disturbed the standard trading patterns. High wartime wages and currency inflation completely changed traditional consumption habits, as many people moved up the dietary scale. Furthermore, wartime use of food coupons tied consumers to particular retailers and broke the age-old custom of shopping around. After the war British housewives were criticized because instead of purchasing from a single market, they preferred to go from shop to shop, each with its own services and overhead.[10]

The Interwar Years and Changing Consumption Patterns

A multitude of events in the interwar era worked against the small retailer and the public market. The most hidebound element in the food-distributive system in the interwar years was the retail market. It was the slowest to adjust to postwar conditions and was the area where costs were highest and an abundance of small establishments gave way to an extravagant method of distribution. For the most part, government food policy ended with the war. The Ministry of Food was disbanded in 1921. The policy of the national government was to return to international free trade—a disastrous policy from the farmer-producer's point of view. Local governments, on the other hand, more or less abandoned the public market, while the national government encouraged the organization of central wholesale markets in large towns (to save energy and fuel), thus killing the retail business in many smaller towns. Further, postwar deflationary policies and postwar slumps saw a shrinkage of farm acreage put under cultivation but no return to livestock farming at the prewar level. Free-market agricultural policy was only ended with the introduction of statutory marketing boards for potatoes, milk, bacon, and pigs after 1933, barely in time to establish itself before the outbreak of war again in 1939. Beginning in 1928, standardization of products, encouraged by the Ministry of Agriculture "National Mark" schemes, prescribed quality grading (and hence marking) of such products as eggs, making it even more difficult for local farmers to sell directly to their local markets.[11]

The interwar era was a period of changing personal consumption habits. The market day no longer featured a great convergence of folk from the surrounding countryside. Much of the shopping which had previously been done at the public market was increasingly accomplished in shops or by mail order, whereby "the money goes off to the big cities." This was, after all, the age not only of football, the radio, the cinema, suburban housing schemes, and the automobile, but equally important, the age of imported butter, tinned beans, and tinned meat. Great fluctuations in trade and manufacturing brought periodic and often long-term economic insecurity and deprivation for many working people in certain declining industries like cotton textiles and shipbuilding, while for many people the 1920s brought a more comfortable life. One result of this is that the market hall in some towns began to be a specifically working-class institution.[12]

Appropriately enough, the market hall was now and then converted to the mass-entertainment passions of the new modern world. Haverfordwest's market became a sports hall, largely for boxing tournaments. During the First World War the market hall at St. Austell in

Cornwall was closed and converted into a cinema. When the market reopened after the war, the layout was completely changed: the meat market was never reopened, the dairy benches were never used again for eggs, butter, and poultry, and the market fell into disuse. The word was that the market hall had had its day.[13]

The grand Victorian market halls, now blackened with the soot of a past most postwar residents wished to forget, were increasingly regarded as an eyesore, a blot on the townscape. Many markets were at least half a century old and were viewed unforgivingly by a modern world which took its aesthetic clues from the avant-garde utilitarian style of the German Bauhaus and the international style of design. The postwar world deplored the pre-1914 townscape as a relic of old-world inequality, moral rigidity, and hypocrisy. Town planning in Britain, which had its roots in the sometimes utopian works of Patrick Geddes and Ebenezer Howard at the turn of the century, was increasingly concerned with housing schemes that drew people out of the city. With some remarkable exceptions, where municipal governments took an interest, most markets were left to fend for themselves.

The New Transportation Revolution

Nothing abetted the decline of the public retail market in the interwar era more than yet another transportation revolution, this one the result of the internal combustion engine: the rise of the automobile, the bus, and the lorry (truck). Whereas fifty years earlier the railway had encouraged intensive urban growth and a centralization of marketing activity, the automobile, the lorry, and particularly the bus put millions of small-town and rural folk on the road, headed toward urban centers and away from their traditional markets. Small-town residents, in particular, seized the chance to travel to larger, more exotic, distant markets. Consequently, between 1914 and 1920, as the number of automobiles on British roads doubled, consumer allegiance to local public markets dwindled. For the people of South Molton, for example, a twelve-mile bus trip to the larger town of Barnstaple became a realizable shopping adventure, and the South Molton market suffered. How could the tiny provincial markets of Horwich or Farnworth compete with the allure of the large and interesting urban market in Bolton, which was only a short bus ride away?

Improved road transportation also encouraged tradespeople to bypass the small markets. The milk lorries of the regional marketers now traveled from farm to farm, picking up the surplus milk which once went to the local market in the form of clotted cream, butter, or cheese. This new world of dairying left little time for cream- and butter-making, and the small- and medium-sized public markets, particularly those whose principal draw was the pannier trade, lost much of their trade. To make matters worse for the local market, enterprising farmers and shopkeepers used lorries and motor vans (and even bicycles) to carry goods to the consumer's door or to the village shops. The butcher's van, the fish van, and the grocer's van took the products from shop counter and market stall to cottage and farm gates. By the 1930s small companies like J. R. Carter's Broad Oak Farm Sausage Company in rural Essex dispatched their products by van or bicycle to waiting customers. The market at Narberth, for example, gradually declined in the interwar period because numerous businesspeople purchased vans to carry goods to outlying customers who had traditionally trekked to the Narberth market. In 1939 Mrs. Thorley, the last person to stand in the Macclesfield Butter Market, ceased to attend the market, leaving it empty.[14]

The Return to Street Hawking and Open Markets

The public market was further weakened in the interwar era by a general return to street vending. To address the rise in the demand and supply of cheap foods and consumer goods, and to provide a substitute for unregulated hawking, many towns reversed their position and allowed—and even encouraged—the reestablishment of weekly open-air markets, usually in conjunction with the enclosed market. In addition, numerous vendors set up unauthorized stands, often on wastelands at the town's outskirts or in suburban areas. Already in the last years of the nineteenth century it had been observed that street hawking and open-air marketing were on the increase because shops and the public market could not meet the needs of the population. This practice was now seen as a convenience to suburban households and a way to avoid costly financing for public marketing. The number of street hawkers of fruits and vegetables in thirteen large towns increased on the order of one-third in the years following the First World War (table 10.1).[15]

Street selling was already on the rise in Reading by 1890, where the town had outgrown its crowded and inconveniently located (and only partially covered) market building of 1854. Such was also the trend in Bath, Cambridge, Bolton, and Torquay, where street hawking of food, particularly in the newer suburban districts, made a comeback. Cambridge market stallholders pleaded with town officials to counteract the door-to-door suburban hawking by building a warmer and drier market to draw shoppers back. In Manchester, it was claimed, one could do quite well by hiring a cart for fourpence, then purchasing unsold produce from the Shudehill wholesale market and hawking it around the town. In Bolton it was not uncommon to find dozens of hawkers' carts lined up in front of the wholesale fish market.[16]

Table 10.1 Street Hawkers of Fruits and Vegetables		
TOWN	ESTIMATED NUMBER OF STREET HAWKERS OF FRUITS AND VEGETABLES	
	1913	1923
Bolton	360	470
Bradford	1,060	721
Brighton	85	145
Dundee	24	36
Eastbourne	40	38
Edinburgh	90	124
Leeds	800	1,000
Liverpool	600	1,500
Manchester	1,000	1,500
Newcastle-upon-Tyne	179	229
Oldham	100	150
Sheffield	460	525
Swansea	80	100
Total	4,838	6,538
Overall Increase		35%

Source: Ministry of Agriculture and Fisheries, *Departmental Committee on Distribution of Prices of Agricultural Produce, Interim Report on Fruit and Vegetables,* (London, 1923), 69.

The revival of the open-air market was in part due to the lack of space in the market buildings (particularly for casual traders) and municipal financial restraints, and in part a way for the town to promote employment opportunities in a time of recession and increasing unemployment. Financing a market addition or even a new public market was something many towns could not undertake after 1900, and even less after 1918. Dewsbury's open market was shut down in 1937 after a runaway lorry accident in the Market Place. It was reopened at a new open-air site despite proposals for a new covered market. Liverpool established two open-air markets in 1923, not just to meet consumer demand but also to set up a large number of unemployed ex-servicemen as market traders. And so the crowded enclave of wood and canvas market stalls once again became a commonplace weekly scene for many urban dwellers. The weekly outdoor markets surrounding the Accrington Market Hall and in Dewsbury's Market Place tell of how the open-air market had once more become a part of urban life (fig. 10.4).[17]

Market Hall Revival

These changes in retailing, consumer expectations, transportation, and government policies from the late nineteenth century into the 1920s did not necessarily result in fewer people or less food entering the public market. In spite of all the forces working against it, the market hall continued to thrive between 1890 and 1939. Around 1900, when local government investment in market construction was coming to a virtual standstill, many market halls were overflowing with both customers and goods. Despite their conspicuous intrusion onto the streetscape, butcher and grocery chain stores accounted for only about 10 percent of the gro-

10.4. ACCRINGTON, OPEN MARKET, CA. 1912
The twentieth-century comeback of street marketing occurred in part because market demand outgrew market buildings. Here the street market fills the space at the entrance to the Market Hall (right).

cery trade in 1910, and in some towns all or a portion of this took place in an outlet inside the public market hall. So, notwithstanding the challenges the market hall faced from the modern world of retailing, the public market was still regarded as an institution of considerable merit. When the suggestion was made in Swansea in 1921 that the public market hall be converted into a meeting hall, an alderman replied that "no one will ever touch a brick of Swansea Market while I'm alive."[18]

Indeed, one of the most neglected facts of late nineteenth-century working-class life is that by the 1890s the market hall had become a working-class department store. In many towns, it was thus in the forefront of the mass-retailing revolution. New products, such as bicycles, phonograph records and players, pianos, and electrical appliances, all found their way into the market hall—which was the perfect venue for introducing them to the customer. No longer was the market hall primarily a source of perishable foods. In the Aberdeen market hall in 1860, two out of three vendors were butchers, but by 1890 the ratio had fallen to one in eight. Meanwhile, the number of market shops and stalls specializing in ready-made clothing and other drapers' items increased twofold. Old luxuries replaced new. Of the fifteen shopfronts in the Hull market hall in 1888, only one had anything to do with the sale of food—the fish shop. And between 1900 and 1919, the six confectionery stalls in Harrogate's market hall had decreased to two, while the Harrogate Incandescent Lighting Company established two stalls there to sell electric lamps and lighting fixtures. Increasingly less space was occupied by the pannier women with their eggs and cheese, as the transitory market was subsumed by permanent stall- and shopholders, some of whom were part of the chains or cooperative societies. British Traders (a grocery chain) had a shop in Scarborough Market Hall.

Dyson's Fent and Remnant Stores, Marks and Spencer's Penny Bazaar, and W. H. Smith, the newsagent, set up businesses in many market halls. By 1890, Archie Scarr, the mayor who started as a Leeds Kirkgate Market Hall vendor and whose sales talk and manner of dress had become legendary, was a wealthy man with thirty shop assistants. The Scarr family vegetable stall in the Kirkgate Market had added confectionery, grocery, hardware, and crockery to its offerings and had grown into a chain of eight shops, in the Kirkgate hall itself and in branches in Bradford, Burnley, and elsewhere. Despite his transformation from small-scale trader to mass retailing figure and mayor of Leeds, Scarr still presided as monarch of the Leeds market.[19]

Because of its low overhead, high turnover, links to local producers, emphasis on advertising, and alluring display of goods, the market hall was in many ways the first and the most successful of the retail venues to respond to demand for cheap food and consumer goods. Well into the 1920s the market hall was idealized as both a thriving trading ground for ingenious small traders with small capital assets and a place which would "afford consumers an opportunity of buying their food more cheaply." Indeed, many of the sales techniques celebrated as the innovations of the chain-store and cooperative revolution were in reality first practiced in the market hall: fixed and clearly marked prices, self-selection, and using low prices to achieve high turnover. As already noted, the retail innovators Marks and Spencer used their market stalls to test out their mass-retail concepts with considerable success. In 1900, twenty-four of Marks and Spencer's thirty-six retail outlets were in market halls (fig. 10.5).[20]

Cooperative store competition was weaker in large towns like Bolton, Blackburn, Birmingham, and Liverpool, which had established, large-scale public market systems. Even in Leeds, Newcastle, and Manchester—which all had significant numbers of cooperative shops—

10.5. MARKS AND SPENCER'S MARKET HALL STALLS, HUDDERSFIELD, 1901

By the 1880s the market hall had become a prototype for both the more economical department store and the shopping mall. The Penny Bazaar concept of fixed pricing and self-selection grew out of Michael Marks's stall in the Leeds Kirkgate Market Hall. By 1900 the greatest number of the firm's branches were in market halls in the north of England. This view of the Huddersfield stall shows how the firm pioneered in the prepackaging and prepricing sales practices which were to become the hallmarks of the modern supermarket.

the proportion of the population trading with the cooperatives was low. Conversely, cooperative trading seems to have been most successful in towns like the northern mining district towns, which had the weakest municipal programs for public marketing services.

The public market tended to retain its monopoly on perishable goods. Most cooperatives and chain stores, for example, chose not to compete with the public market in the sale of fruits and vegetables. Well past 1914 the greengrocer trade remained in the hands of small shopkeepers in private shops, with street hawkers, or with market hall stall- and shopkeepers. This is less true of the egg and poultry trade, but generally, small producers throughout the country still brought their eggs weekly to the local market.

In addition, and despite the rise of an array of middlemen, local and regional farmers continued to be a major attraction on market day in the public markets as they offered a range of goods from fruits and vegetables to meat, sausages, fresh butter, eggs, poultry, and rabbits. In Liverpool, St. John's Market Hall was one of the town's major industries, with its 632 shops, stalls, and farmers' tables. All in all, St. John's Market accommodated 2,000 persons employed in the retail trade, many of them producers from the country. In Blackburn as late as 1948, more than 1,500 persons were employed in the public markets. "The markets stimulate competition," argued the market manager from Liverpool, "and if properly organized, prove a great aid to trade expansion, in addition to which there is afforded full opportunity of rigid inspection of food by the Public Health Authorities, which otherwise could not be so effectively carried out." Thus, while it had to give up some of its share of the retail trade to newer types of retail outlets such as the chain store and cooperative (and the department store), the typical municipal public market probably experienced an actual rise in the volume of goods it provided for urban households. Unfortunately, public markets kept no records on sales volume, nor have sufficient stall- and shopholder records survived to allow historians to determine market growth patterns. The only existing growth indicators are figures on revenue arising from the rental of market space, the number of markets in operation, and general qualitative observations about the amount of goods entering the market. All of these suggest that the public market boomed. While St. John's Market suffered a fall in market rental revenues during the war (a drop from £21,015 in 1901 to £12,759 in 1917), market use rebounded to prewar levels by 1921 (£22,216) and then rose to a record level in 1927 (£25,661).

The population of Britain nearly doubled between 1851 and 1901, as did per capita income, particularly from the 1870s to the 1890s. The proportion of per capita expenditure on food remained roughly the same—one-third of income. This means that most people were using increased resources for an expanded and more varied diet. By 1904 meat, poultry, and eggs accounted for one-third of the total food expenditure for the average urban working-class family, while another third was divided evenly between dairy products (cheese, milk, butter) and bread and cereals; the remaining third was spent on vegetables, fruit, and an increasing supply of luxury prepared foods like jam, syrup, cocoa, pickles, tinned foods, and biscuits. During the interwar period, the most striking changes in diet were a 30 percent decrease in bread and potato consumption, a 45 percent increase in meat consumption, a 40 percent increase in sugar consumption, a 50 percent increase in tea and butter consumption, a more than 50 percent increase in vegetable (other than potato) consumption, and a 300 percent increase in fruit consumption. All in all, more food was being delivered to the tables of ordinary folk. And the public market continued to be a major source of the urban food supply. In the words of an Oldham market official: "The growth of the Chain and Multiple store, has not justified the fears of many that markets have had their day, as the revenue is today greater than ever it has been. Increased revenue is the outcome of good business, and a bright Saturday afternoon produces at the markets of Oldham a shopping crowd which rivals that of the Football or Rugby field."[21]

The Question of Modernization

Unlike earlier decades, when town market officials spent lavishly on "modernizing" market halls by installing elaborate shop fronts to their once plain façades, in the decades before and after the First World War, market maintenance and renovation were often performed piecemeal; and in some towns, the markets were grossly neglected. Many of these markets, it appears, were in towns, such as Reading and Cambridge, which did not have a history of progressive municipal market reform or strong consumer support for the local market, but equally, they were often found in towns where market business was thriving and profits were considerable. Often market profits were not reinvested in the market but instead were routinely applied to reducing the town rates. The income to the city from the Glasgow Bazaar for the years 1878-82, for instance, was £3,118—nearly two and a half times the £1,306 average yearly expenditure on the market. Ironically, this was at the very time the city was making the decision to shut down the market. "It was indeed a sad day for the poor folk of Glasgow," noted one Glaswegian, "when the market ceased to exist." In Liverpool between a third and a half of St. John's Market Hall income was used to reduce the town rates, while a comparatively meager amount was used for market improvement and modernization. Income for 1921, for example, was £22,216, out of which approximately £2,000 was used to replace the carbon-lighting system with a modern electric system for the shops and add ninety new 500-watt lamps to the hall. The surplus went to relief of local taxes.[22]

Many town authorities failed to fireproof their aging and half-timbered market halls, and devastating fires were not uncommon, often resulting in a return to an open-air or partially enclosed market or the construction of a building which was inferior in size and architectural distinction to the hall it replaced. In Southport, for example, a 1913 fire destroyed the grandiose Eastbank Market Hall (fig. 10.6). It was not until 1931 that the town authorities con-

10.6. SOUTHPORT, EASTBANK MARKET HALL, DESTROYED BY FIRE, 1913

10.7. Newcastle-upon-Tyne, Grainger Market Hall, the New Vegetable Market Hall, 1883

structed a new market, a "retrograde," small, "very simple one-story structure," whose principal entrance was removed from its prominent position on Eastbank Street.[23]

On the other hand, beginning in the 1880s there was some building of new markets and considerable modernization of old market buildings. Owing to the challenge of the retail revolution and the growth in quantity and variety of foods and other consumer goods, many overcrowded and outdated market halls were rebuilt, modernized, and in some instances expanded. The huge vegetable hall of the Grainger Market at Newcastle was replaced by a single-span arched-roof building of iron and glass (fig. 10.7). Although the great market building boom was over by 1890, seventy-four building projects were undertaken between 1891 and 1940. The two decades before the beginning of the First World War featured several new giant market halls—most notably at Swansea (81,000 square feet), Leeds (24,000 square feet), Oldham (18,421 square feet), Cardiff (16,200 square feet), and Wolverhampton (16,461 square feet), and smaller markets like those at Goole and Hull in East Riding, Yorkshire; and Aberavon, Abertillery, and Tredegar in Wales; the Borough Market at Gravesham in Kent (1902); and new fish markets in Barrow-in-Furness, Dundee, Edinburgh, Leeds, and Manchester. Then, after the war and despite the difficulty of obtaining capital for municipal projects, new construction was carried on in a number of towns, some of which had not previously had an enclosed market. The Welsh towns of Crymych and Ellesmere Port constructed their first covered markets, as did the Lancashire town of Hyde; and Wrexham built a vegetable market in 1927 to supplement its two other market buildings. After considerable public debate, Nottingham relocated its market by building a new hall in 1928, and Bolton added a second public market hall, the Ashburner Street market, in the early 1930s, several blocks from its giant central market hall. In a rare instance in which a preexisting structure was adapted to market hall use, the town of Luton closed its old street market in 1925, moving it to the "plait hall"—the building which had been built by the Board of Health to house buyers and sellers of straw plait. Plymouth, like many other markets, replaced its large, popular, but physically antiquated market with a more efficient one, and at Lancaster, market officials proposed that the old Corn Exchange be converted into an extension of the public fish market.

Most market building activity came in the form of alteration and renovation projects, some of which proved as innovative and modern as those of the cooperative and chain stores. When Ashton extended its market hall in 1930, the architect introduced the stained-glass windows which continue to impress visitors to this day. In 1894 Bolton's huge but aging market hall was losing its share of the retail trade, so the town undertook a costly reorganization and modernization scheme: the hall was altered by the addition of modern exterior shops fronting onto the two main streets running alongside, thus giving it the same modern glass frontage that the town's cooperative and department stores had. A generation later complaints were again heard that the market was becoming antiquated: "There could be no question that if the Market Hall were to be adequately representative of a town of Bolton's standing," argued Bolton's market committee in 1933, "and if it were to compete successfully . . . with multiple stores, extensive improvement was urgently required." Again the municipal government responded. A new cold-storage system was installed, a red concrete floor replaced the old stone flags, and an internal delivery system which used small trucks and an electric lift to move goods from the basement storage level to the market floor was installed, as was a new overhead lighting system, an electric heating system, a new fire-protection system, polished oak doors to replace the original iron gates, new laboratories, a new hot water system, and a new layout of shops and stalls.[24]

In the past, stallholders had been permitted to erect their own stalls and follow individual ideas of display and layout; in the interwar era, the emphasis was on uniformity in design and style. The stalls at Bolton, for example, were arranged in fifty-one blocks with two to five stalls per block (all of which had selling space on at least two sides); the stalls had walls of metal-faced panels, glazed roofs, standardized lettering, and electric lighting. With the thirty shops along the sides, the modernized market accommodated a total of 199 market shops and stalls: "The blocks of stalls and the passages between them have been arranged so as to not admit direct communication from one side of the market hall to the other, and to ensure as far as possible that the public will circulate over the whole of the floor area" (see fig. 6.14). Although Bolton's stalls were modernized in 1955, the layout of the market remained the same as in the 1930s.[25]

Perhaps the grandest interwar modernization scheme was that in the Lancashire cotton town of Blackburn, where the interior of the old Victorian market hall was transformed into a shopping complex not unlike an up-to-date department store—proclaimed to be a "modern, useful, and artistic store" (fig. 10.8). Likewise, from the late 1880s to the 1920s, Liverpool's aging and overused St. John's Market Hall was reorganized and renovated with the erection an elegant red-stone-and-granite pilaster shop-front façade, with three entrances to the market. This necessitated removing eight small shops and a number of farmers' tables in favor of two large shops (41 feet deep by 19 feet wide) and four smaller shops, all with rooms above, toilet facilities, and storage cellars. Each shop front was made of glass "so as to give as much display as possible to the stocks," all of which would "adapt the Markets to modern requirements." This "mania for pulling down or building up," as some tenants regarded Liverpool's market policy, was part of a highly successful effort to maintain St. John's position as the hub of Liverpool retailing in an age when the market hall was facing serious competition from the private shops. In the 1920s, St. John's Market was so popular with traders and the public that city profits on it nearly doubled.[26]

In addition to its two hundred regular traders, St. John's Market had sixty-two small stalls reserved for country people, who on Saturdays provided a big attraction with their sausages, butter, eggs, rabbits, poultry, and vegetables. A waiting list existed for stallholding, and storage areas were let out for retailing. In an effort to keep up with the modern trend of the age, the old arc lights were replaced with a new electrical system, stalls were rebuilt, and new

10.8. Blackburn,
Market Hall, Interior
After Alteration, 1935

kiosks put up for tobacco, chocolates, and French cakes. The main entrances were given neon signs, and market tenants installed their own refrigerators. If the market officials had problems, they were not those of a shrinking market but of how to restrain stallholders from piling their goods into the avenues and how to keep certain tenants from "calling their wares in unduly loud voices." Nevertheless, pressure from the markets committee led to a plan in 1935 to replace the old market hall with a public auditorium to seat more than 5,000 persons, a restaurant, and a public parking garage. Although never built, the proposed building would have reduced the size of the market and set it under a public auditorium. The proposal represents a shift in local sentiment away from the primacy of the public market in public life. Following the protest of the market's stallholders, the city and many of its merchants took the broader view that the old market was more valuable than the ratable value of the land, and hence it remained standing and in use until 1964. In fact, it was widely recognized that the ability of the market to attract crowds of potential customers had always been what gave the neighborhood its residential and commercial value. "There is feeling in the minds of the shopkeepers," wrote the market manager in 1920, "that their properties for business purposes would deteriorate in value, and in the case of buyers that the cost of food would tend to rise if the Markets were removed."[27]

In Liverpool and elsewhere, the belief that the public market existed to provide cheap food for the masses had changed but little from that of one hundred years earlier: market officials continued to argue that it was only through a giant public market, attracting "large concourses of people," that competition would be stimulated so that the greatest quantity of wholesome food was offered at the lowest possible price. In fact, erratic prices and the boom and bust nature of the British economy of the 1920s had made the cost and distribution of food—not the least of which was maintaining adequate marketing facilities—a "nerve centre of many post-war economic problems." Wildly fluctuating food prices concerned public market officials, who were alarmed that the local food supply was so closely tied to the national economic trends. Some officials regarded these fluctuations in supply and price as being due to irregular distribution and inadequate market facilities rather than overproduction. "Real competition," argued the manager of St. John's market, "can only be set up by vendors selling commodities side by side under one roof." A town without a strong public market, it was held, had higher-priced and poorer-quality foods, not just because of the goods in the market but because of the market's influence on shop prices: meat prices in private shops in nonmarket towns were as much as 60 percent higher than in towns with public markets.[28]

Nevertheless, the Liverpool proposal of 1935 to shift the market site's primary use from marketing to recreation and parking was a portent of the change in public priorities which were to come in many towns in the years after the Second World War.

THE PUBLIC MARKET IN THE AGE OF THE SUPERMARKET, 1939 TO THE PRESENT

PERHAPS THE BEST INDICATOR OF THE RETURN TO NORMAL URBAN LIFE AFTER the Second World War was the restoration of the public market to its former vitality. Despite continued food shortages and rationing, within a few years of the war's end many markets experienced a greater volume of trade than at any time in their history. Indeed, postwar shortages of food, clothing, and household goods led consumers to spend much of their time inspecting shops and stalls. St. John's Market in Liverpool had suffered a 75 percent decline in stallholdings during the war, but within a few years it had reverted to the "compact little world of its own"—a noisy and bustling place of good humor and better prices; a shoppers' paradise that included everything from chocolate bonbons, cocktail wafers, French bread, and meat "fit for a Queen" to toys, beads, bags, and hats. Likewise, the markets at Stockport and Ashton-under-Lyne boomed as market activity returned to its prewar level, and the Sheffield markets were so crowded that the market committee considered finding new accommodations. Although the open-air street market had made a comeback during the war and attracted large crowds of both buyers and sellers in places such as Mansfield, Barnsley, and Bridlington, for many the old Victorian market hall continued to be the place to shop. From the southwest of England pannier-type market halls to the halls of the midlands and the north of England with their Saturday trading tables, the public market still offered goods directly from the land and, overall, the lowest prices in town.[1]

In spite of this return to normal, however, one could also see that market halls were beginning to move in an unwelcome direction. Beginning in the mid- and late 1950s dozens of market buildings were abandoned and then razed in the name of urban redevelopment. In effect, the Second World War had set in motion a train of events and attitudes which worked to the disadvantage of the public market: namely, the breakdown of traditional shopping and dietary habits, a widespread cultural rejection of the past and the historic townscape, and the adoption of wartime and postwar planning which gave the public market a secondary place in most redevelopment schemes.

The Impact of the War

The war, as Arthur Marwick has observed, "cracked many of the conventions of British society." A number of markets had been destroyed by German bombing, including the relatively small market space connected to the town hall at Cowes and large market halls at Hull, Birmingham, and Swansea. Of the markets left intact, St. Aubin's Market Hall was open for only four hours a day to sell local produce, and some markets were closed because they had been requisitioned for "war work." Part of the Newcastle Market Hall was closed down and the area dug up for air-raid shelters. Oswestry's Crossmarket was requisitioned for war use, and Blackpool's market was moved into the open air because the market building was requisitioned for war purposes. After the first winter, only about a half-dozen traders were left.[2]

During the war and for nearly a decade afterward, a changing and lessened food supply and a food-rationing system (many food controls were still in place in 1953) led to forced shifts in diet that prepared postwar generations for both new foods and new food-preparation ideas. In fact, compared to the wartime market, the nation's food supply actually worsened rather than improved in the years immediately following the war. For shoppers the immediate postwar years were spent coping with shortages and juggling with points and coupons. Not until the mid-1950s boom in living standards could consumers and market traders alike say that "we are recovering from the devastating effects of the war. Food and goods of all kinds have become more plentiful and many controls have gone or have been relaxed."[3]

But at the same time the war had interrupted the custom of shopping in the public market and had introduced the consumer to an awareness of improved nutrition. Vegetables, particularly potatoes, onions, and carrots, were promoted during the war for their nutritional value, as was milk. Milk consumption increased dramatically during the war, as did that of fish, but meat consumption declined (tinned meat consumption increased), and consumers switched from fresh to dried eggs and fruits. The government also compelled egg vendors, including farm women, to sell their eggs to egg-packing stations rather than to the nearby market, a policy which led to the closing of some public markets, such as Liverpool's poultry and egg market, during the war. The rationing system, because it required the consumer to register with a single retailer, discouraged the customary market hall hunt for the best price, and government wartime food distribution regulations discouraged direct exchange between farmers and urban consumers.[4]

Wartime society had become more attentive of food hygiene, and consequently many consumers looked more critically at the sanitary state of the postwar market. Market authorities responded by adopting new standards for food selling and display. Although new hygiene legislation was directed more to the open-air market than to the indoor market, the national statutes were subject to considerable local interpretation and were therefore often used by town officials and property developers as a justification for closing market buildings. For many years Dartmouth's town council refused to make the necessary repairs and alterations on its sadly deteriorated market, and after the market was in a state of disrepair, the council recommended closing and replacing it because of the high cost of bringing it up to the standards required under new food hygiene regulations.[5]

Postwar Urban Redevelopment

Even before the end of the Second World War many towns had adopted, partly under encouragement from the central government, plans for redevelopment after the war was over. In these and the plans which followed in the two decades after 1945 (particularly after the Festival of Britain in 1951), British towns exhibited their pride not in what was considered an outdated obsession with architectural pastiche but in vast new utilitarian urban redevelopment schemes, undertaken to redress several serious problems, some of which grew out of the war and some that dated back to the nineteenth century. More than half a million homes were either destroyed or made uninhabitable by enemy action during the war, and as many as three million more were seriously damaged. Still other homes were due to be replaced because they were part of vast slums which went back fifty or more years. All in all, it was estimated that Britain needed six million new homes. Equally important, the central marketing areas of some towns, such as Hull, Plymouth, and Coventry, were destroyed by enemy action, while in most towns the intensified competition between automobile, bus, and pedestrian for urban space reached new and often unsafe levels. In Peterborough it was claimed that public market congestion was responsible for doubling the accident rate. Concern over pedestrian safety and lack of public parking mounted as many concluded that city center congestion and the lack of parking facilities were not only causing trade to vanish but were making the city center a dangerous place. At the same time most towns regarded town-center retail trade as a principal economic barometer. As had been argued a century or so earlier, it was felt that the future of the town, including its ability to attract new industry and retain and expand existing industry, rested with its ability to entice both retailers and consumers to the town.[6]

This postwar crisis in urban space was the catalyst for wide-scale rebuilding and urban reorganization. It was accepted in most quarters that only through massive demolition, reorganization, and rebuilding according to a unifying plan could the endemic problems of the past be corrected. For the first time in British history, urban planning was not only initiated by the government at Westminster but adopted a set of universal planning concepts which were thought to be more or less applicable to local circumstances. Accordingly, although British towns and cities had a history of being designed and redesigned much according to local needs and local visions, most postwar urban redevelopment schemes accepted the general principle—set forth by the 1947 Town and Country Planning Act—of "comprehensive" redevelopment of the town center. As it was understood at the time, comprehensive redevelopment rested on the idea of rebuilding large sections of the town center "as a whole," according to a unified plan. This redevelopment, it was advised, "should be applied to any area which in the opinion of the planning authority suffered from extensive war damage, conditions of bad layout, obsolete development, or were in need of the relocation of population or industry." Although some multi-activity space was eventually favored, the earliest planning advice from the professionals to the town officials was that the central zone of the town should be as single-functional as possible, largely retail shopping, and that outer zones should absorb new, high-density housing. In this manner, the reformed town would avoid the overlapping of activities which prevailed in the prewar town.[7]

Postwar planning contained an inherent disregard for either existing structures or the human need for links with the past. Its frame of reference was not "place specific"; it emphasized "sociological analogs," which reflected current social thought. The guidelines for the redevelopment of central urban areas suggested a uniformity. Planners proposed retaining old street patterns and existing buildings when feasible, but when possible, they suggested eliminating noncommercial buildings and adopting vast rebuilding schemes, with "modern" tower blocks, department stores, new, wide streets and pedestrian walkways, "shopping zones," and giant parking lots, much of which were to be on multilevel surfaces with restricted vehicular traffic. It was "undesirable" for the reconstructed town to "perpetuate the pre-war conditions under which the principal shops tended to be located on a single street, or a small number of streets." Inefficient layout of streets and "confusion of building uses" in the city center were to be replaced with a uniform and orderly regrouping of blocks to fit vehicular and shopping needs. Further, and of particular consequence for the public market, it was advised that retail markets should be so placed "in order to ensure that they will not break up the continuity of main shopping streets and the vehicular traffic to which they give rise will not cause congestion in neighbouring streets." Arguing for the demolition of the old market hall and for the "pedestrianisation of our whole city center," one Bradford official predicted that "we shall have a reasonable city, where you can move about safely in the next 20 or 30 years, while other cities have to shut up shop." Furthermore, to ensure that development would infringe as little as possible on the ratepayer, town projects were increasingly placed in the hands of private developers, who had little experience or understanding of how public markets functioned and who looked only to maximize short-term profits through high rents—an unrealistic prerequisite for the public market, whose very existence relied on modest rents.[8]

What was proposed was, in effect, a recentralization of urban marketing that was more ambitious than the nineteenth-century schemes, which sought to fuse the traditional market or town square with the new market hall. The mid-twentieth-century redevelopment ideal centered on replacing the entire town center with private retail shopping facilities in the forefront, often, as in Aberdeen, with a department store as the centerpiece of a new covered market or, as at Oswestry, with a Woolworth's in place of the market. Wholesale rebuilding made it difficult to retain specific buildings or any semblance of the existing townscape or even particular traffic patterns on a piecemeal basis. It was clear that the working of the whole took precedent over the working of the parts. Form was to precede, not follow, function. A new urban landscape was in the making, which, in the end, was to leave a drab legacy of uniform and anonymous cubic boxes designed in the worst of the twentieth-century modern or international style. This new landscape had little regard for the history of the town or even its historical center.

The rearrangement of the towns and cities of Britain was devastating for both the position and the concept of the public market. Arguing for redevelopment, Llanelli town officials claimed that the market hall was located on one of the most important commercial sites in south Wales, and unfortunately for Bradford's architectural heritage, its Kirkgate Market Hall stood on "the plum redevelopment site in the country." The old public market was no longer given preference over private stores; it was not seen as being a social and economic institution worthy of such treatment. And it now had to compete not only with other retailers—the co-op and the big-name multiples—for the sites but also with parking lots, traffic plans, and pedestrianization schemes. "You can leave this monstrosity in the city center," said the chairman of Bradford's Development Committee of the town's Kirkgate Market Hall, "and let the traffic snarl up, and see hypermarkets built to take shopping out of Bradford, or you can make the city a reasonable place for shopping and for the pedestrian."[9]

The Argument for Market Replacement

The immediate justification for replacement of market buildings was the belief that they had outlived their useful physical life. Indeed, many public markets were unsightly and in a sorry state of repair. Part of this was because local governments had invested only a fraction of their market revenue in market improvement and upkeep between 1919 and 1939; and the war had brought a near-total neglect of the market's physical needs. In 1945, three-fifths of English, Welsh, and Scottish market buildings had been in use for more than half a century, and many were shabby and worn. Besides basic structural problems, many markets had antiquated heating and cooling systems and inadequate refuse disposal and water facilities. For those markets which remained open during the war, wartime restrictions on building, materials, and capital expenditure often led to an ignominious fall into disrepair. Although a few markets were scheduled for modernization in the first decade after the war (such as Doncaster's, where new "tubular aluminum" stalls were installed), the continued restrictions on construction materials and investment capital delayed repairs for so long they fell into an even more acute state of dilapidation. One of the Sheffield markets still had a temporary canvas roof four years after the war. At Bradford the portion of the Rawson Square Market Hall which was gutted in an air raid was not repaired until 1958, and the postwar market at Goole was described as a bare-looking church hall, lit by gas, unheated, with a "higgledy-piggledy" arrangement of stalls and inadequately displayed goods. To make matters worse, local urban redevelopment planning encouraged postponement of short-term repairs and maintenance. Thus even if market officials and traders were keen to modernize archaic market premises, too often they were prevented or discouraged by the expectation of wide-scale town redevelopment.[10]

It is ironic that while most public postwar markets experienced an unprecedented boom in activity and continued to generate substantial revenue for the town, they remained mired in lethargy and uncertainty. Although in some instances, such as at Cardigan and Dartmouth, market supporters were able to reverse local government plans to bulldoze public market buildings, the general pattern was otherwise. Wolverhampton's Reconstruction Committee in charge of town planning expressed the popular view that the market hall had "passed its useful structural life and its retention would involve extensive and costly repairs"—an opinion which eventually led to its destruction. The repair of Royton's market hall roof was deemed so costly that the town council decided to "pull the hall down"; Worcester's High Street

11.1. SHEFFIELD,
DEMOLITION OF NORFOLK
MARKET HALL, NOVEMBER
1960

Market Hall of 1857 (with its 1805 stone façade and interior that "vied with any other of its size in the kingdom alike for its elegance of design and accommodation") was closed in 1955 because the council voted not to repair the roof; and Sheffield's Norfolk Market Hall was demolished in 1960 (fig. 11.1). Market traders and consumers in Sheffield opposed the closure (and eventual demolition) by collecting 10,000 signatures and even petitioned the queen for her support in saving the market. In Newcastle it was felt that the vast Grainger Market Hall of 1835 should be pulled down because it was "out of date" in comparison to the nearby shops which had been "modernized." Action on the part of traders, consumers, historians, and preservationists kept the Newcastle Market Hall standing—and functioning just as it did a century and a half ago.[11]

Like dozens of other markets, two of the early giants, Aberdeen's Market Hall of 1842 (rebuilt after a fire in 1888) and Liverpool's St. John's Market, were all demolished, as was one of the greatest of the late Victorian market halls, Bradford's Kirkgate Market. Despite its post-1945 popularity with the consumer and the considerable rental income of £20,000 per year (a 50 percent return on expenditure for the town), Liverpool market authorities allowed the St. John's Market structure to deteriorate to the point of being a health hazard, a shabby reminder of century-old municipal pride. "The general market facilities are still more in keeping with 1822 than with 1955," argued one critic. Only seven washbasins were provided for the hundreds of men and women who worked in the market, and there were only four hot-water taps remaining in the entire market. Rubbish was pushed through a hole in the floor into a waiting cart which was emptied only when it overflowed, and the announcement that the "rat population" was at an all-time low was ironic rather than encouraging. City officials estimated that refurbishing the market would cost £100,000, and they argued that the value of the land was too high to invest such sums for a market that could not possibly withstand competition from supermarkets of "modern design." A scheme of redevelopment was drawn up and approved, and, as one supporter of the old market reflected, "yet another market is doomed to be replaced by a shopping center."[12]

As Liverpool's market history reveals, it is misleading to suggest that the nation's market buildings were no longer economically viable. Public market rents and tolls still brought in a notably high income for the town. When Sheffield authorities decided to demolish Norfolk Market Hall in 1949, it was providing the town with a revenue of more than £14,000. What had changed was that in Sheffield and elsewhere, the economic viability of the market was measured more by the value of the land on which it stood than by the principle that the public market was an essential public service. Therefore, as postwar redevelopment schemes pushed up city-center land values, the public market tended to be regarded as a poor investment. Indeed, urban redevelopment was costly, and in the early years it was underwritten by town governments, not, as later, by private developers. Selling off the market was a way to finance new streets and parking lots. Local planning authorities were forced to calculate how redevelopment schemes could be financed through higher rents, and it was for this reason that the Ministry of Town and Country Planning advised (in 1947) local planning authorities to encourage the erection of buildings (such as popular chain stores, hotels, restaurants, or cinemas) which would attract other private investment. The traditional market arcade, said the planners, "is almost always unsuccessful."[13]

Times had changed. Although in some towns, like Tavistock, it was thought that the town needed the drawing power of the public market, officials and urban planners no longer saw the public market as the hub of the town's retail economy. Since the interwar years, supporters of the public market had seen the idea of the public market as a public service disappear, a change of heart which is rather ironic considering the popularity of collectivist and sometimes socialist wartime and postwar thinking about how to improve urban life in Britain. "Why should ratepayers have to provide this palatial market hall and the means for a small minority to make a good and easy living?" asked one critic of the Wolverhampton Market Hall in 1958. As the cost of public services increased, some council members suggested that the town was not getting a proper financial return from its market lease; thus it was proposed in Richmond, Yorkshire, that the old market hall should be "put to better use" by turning it into an indoor shopping center which would bring in higher rents. The Richmond market was saved but Royton's market hall was torn down in the mid-1950s, partly because, as some council members saw it, the market was simply subsidizing sellers from out of town and there was little need for a market when there were good markets in nearby Rochdale and Oldham.[14]

Also working against the postwar market hall was the fact that the war's physical and psychological damage led to widespread disillusionment with the past and a general abandonment of history as a guidepost and architecture as a language for the present and future. As a result, the mood of urban planners and government officials in particular, as well as of much of the public, was against preserving the past in favor of a future that avoided it. "The problem," noted novelist Vera Brittain, "is that we have had too much history." Such antihistorical views, encouraged and enforced by a great postwar victory by the political left as well as by a growing public attachment to things "American," did not bode well for the Victorian townscape. The architectural language of the nineteenth-century town, including that of the market hall, was ridiculed and forgotten. Neither solitary buildings nor the townscape as a whole had a secure future unless they were of undisputed historic significance—which in most instances meant they had origins in the eighteenth century or earlier. While the Ministry of Town and Country Planning advised that consideration be given to "buildings which should be retained because of their architectural value, historic interest or special association with the life of the community," it also suggested that "buildings which have outlived their period of usefullness . . . should be replaced as soon as circumstances permit." The public market faced a serious disadvantage in this respect because it was identified with a particular architecture—an architecture which was both misunderstood and out of fashion. "To imitate antique styles because we are building in a University town or Cathedral city is an insult to the very architecture we hold in such respect," said one influential architect, "but where necessity demands that we rebuild . . . to have the courage of our own convictions, allowing us to build frankly for our own time, is the only true way of maintaining the traditions we have inherited." The bashing of Victorian architecture which took place from the 1950s to the 1970s was unrelenting, and in the process the old market halls were humbled. "Utterly artless and tasteless," "of the grossest design" was the assessment of Bridgnorth's 1855 market. Once the pride of Accrington, its flamboyant market hall was deemed "not irreplaceable," and Bradford's dramatic Kirkgate Market Hall was called a "monstrosity," both "pretentious and dull." Ludlow's market hall, even in its own day called "Ludlow's bad luck," was similarly derided: "There is nothing that could be said in favour of its fiery brick or useless Elizabethan detail."[15]

Depopulation of City Centers

By removing large numbers of people from the city center, urban development schemes often made the declining market a self-fulfilling prophecy. When residents were relocated, either to new outlying suburban developments or to new towns even farther away, their marketing patterns changed, and their loyalty to the old market became tenuous at best. Birmingham, for example, lost 8,000 of its population in 1957-58, Liverpool 6,300, and Manchester 5,100. In England and Wales, more than 877,000 houses, largely in the old city centers, were demolished in the twenty years following the Town and Country Planning Act of 1947. Many of those who left the old neighborhoods had been the people who were most attached to the public market; in Sheffield it was claimed that 75 percent of the people who were moved out of the city center and relocated in outlying housing developments had been regular customers of the public market. Although many families attempted to maintain their link to the city— often shoppers returned to their old haunts in the city center by automobile or, most likely, by bus—over time, the trek to the historic public market was replaced with one to the nearby shops and supermarket.[16]

The Supermarket and the Self-Service Revolution

For a number of years after the war the multiples, or chain stores, within the market halls acted as a draw to the hall itself. In fact, for the first decade national retail chains such as the butchers James Nelson and Sons, dry goods merchants Marks and Spencer and Woolworth's, as well as regional chains like Brown Brothers clothiers and Redman's cafes opened so many branches in public market halls that some feared that the multiples would eventually take over. Woolworth's took over a portion of the Oswestry market, and in Plymouth the old-time pannier traders were actually moved outdoors in order to make room for the retail chains. What would happen, it was asked, to local farm people who sold in the market only one or two days a week or to the independent traders, many of whom were local families who had served customers in the market halls for generations?[17]

But by the early 1950s in Plymouth and elsewhere another trend was under way, as many of the multiples moved out of the market and into larger, modern premises, where new retailing practices could be implemented. By 1960 the only Marks and Spencer branch remaining in a market hall was the one in Newcastle's Grainger Market.[18]

About this time (mid- to late 1950s) another wave in retailing battered the market hall and forever changed the nature of both diet and food distribution in Britain. The supermarket was normally a chain or multiple store which took the concept of self-service and low prices to new heights. Self-service was, of course, nothing new to retailing and can be traced back to the Leeds Kirkgate Market Hall, where Michael Marks first invited his customers to make their own selections from baskets of presorted, prepriced goods. But the 1950s version of self-service was on a vastly broader scale. Here the customer, with cart in hand, was given free rein in an immense modern market, with wide aisles and long shelves from which a variety of brand-name goods, nearly all prepackaged, could be selected and presented for a single payment, or checkout.

"The modern idea" of shopping, as one observer in Liverpool lamented, "seems to be to get away from the genuine market idea and go in more for supermarkets." Indeed, something genuine about shopping was being lost. Alone in the supermarket, the consumer had considerably more control over the shopping process, but choice and selection were actually influenced more by advertising and brand names and less by direct communication between seller and consumer. Moreover, when it came to durable goods, such as kitchen wares and small electrical appliances, the shopper was being taught to make purchasing decisions not just according to function but also according to "design." "The housewife of the future and particularly the young matron," it was noted, "will demand that not only must the household utensil, whether it be the refrigerator or the cooking pan, be useful but it must also be designed on pleasing lines. It must catch the eye." Such notions made it necessary for shop- and stallholders not only to offer a wider variety of goods but also to pay greater attention to display.[19]

Further, the supermarket self-service revolution led to prepackaging of goods on a scale never before seen. This was immediately popular with the consumer because it meant that the tasks of selection, weighing, and grading were largely taken care of before the time of the sale. Tea was first packaged in the 1890s, and packaged milk, biscuits, and other goods arrived after the First World War, when road transport allowed national distributors to reach every village and farm rapidly and directly. Yet it was only after the Second World War that packaging was extended to almost every conceivable consumable product and was made a central part of self-service shopping. Prepackaging potatoes, for example, began in 1955. Before this, all potatoes were sold over the counter according to the customer's order. By the mid-1950s even meat and fish were being sold prepackaged. Packaging encouraged "branding" goods because the consumer was now left to rely on the brand name on the package as a guarantee of quality. Through advertising, consumers were educated to believe that brand-named packaged products were of higher quality and more sanitary than goods on display loose in the market, and for this they were willing to pay a little more.

These trends made the traditional market trader obsolete. The modern shopper was encouraged to ignore personal salesmanship, cheapness, and individual attention. Products were less identified with a particular shop or stall than with a name on a package. Individual salesmanship would never again have the same influence it did in the market hall era, and the consumers behind the shopping cart were left to judge merchandise on their own. As product names and the design of the package became supreme, lamented the market traders, "the article will more or less be sold before the customer enters the shop."[20]

In this manner, then, the homely and friendly atmosphere of the old public market, with its individual stalls overflowing with goods, its crowded aisles, and its customary animated exchange of both goods and gossip, rapidly gave way to the world of swift, rather impersonal, and homogenized assembly-line shopping. Shopping became less and less a social act and more a private and isolating activity driven primarily by economic considerations. Not until the concept of the shopping mall did something akin to the social atmosphere of the market hall once more arise.

A few supermarkets were built as early as 1949 but because of a shortage of building materials the supermarket boom was delayed in Britain until the late 1950s. The building wave was at first localized in Greater London where (perhaps not inconsequentially) the public market system was most primitive, and gradually crept northward from the mid-1950s on. To be sure, old shopping habits were slow to die. Some modern shopping centers—such as Seacroft's new town center—saw their anticipated public still traveling to nearby Leeds, which had long supplied their wants in the old-fashioned manner. With many such exceptions in mind however, between 1950 and 1959 the average grocery and meat shop increased its annual self-service sales from £17 to an estimated £340. The number of self-service shops increased from fewer than 500 in 1950 to more than 3,500 in 1957 and 5,000 in 1959. The first "self-serve" (supermarket) grocery chain in Kidderminster in the midlands was Tisdale's, which opened in April 1954; and the Lancashire town of Burnley had one supermarket in 1961 and six in 1964. Cooperative societies were some of the first retailers to enter the supermarket field, and by 1957, 2,000 of the 13,000 cooperative societies' grocery branches had self-service shopping. Large multiple retailers pushed into the self-service field and claimed 800 such shops by 1957. Woolworth's, regarded as the "keenest competitor of the [public] market," began to convert to self-service in 1955, and the Whiteley's chain converted their premises to self-service in the early 1950s, although the Home and Colonial Stores did not believe that self-service would ever catch on in Britain as it had in America.[21]

In the late 1960s the self-service supermarket concept took still another turn in the form of the out-of-town superstore, such as Woolco, a Woolworth's store that carried a vast number of goods including food, footwear, fashions, furniture, and fancy goods under one roof. Superstores were usually near thruways on town and city outskirts. The first such store was opened in 1967 and it was predicted that forty others would follow. Then twenty years later, a new retail wave swept the nation, the giant malls which, as in America, pulled shoppers away from town centers and to suburban plots surrounded by parking lots. The age of the automobile and the suburban home had transformed shopping habits once again. Modernism, once on the side of the public market hall, was now on the side of the private shop. Consumers who once bypassed the shops because market traders could undercut the shopkeepers were now bypassing the old market for the same reason.[22]

Just as public authorities had tipped the scale in the past in favor of what was then a public food and marketing system, they now came down in favor of private retailing. The "chromium-plated palace," as some called the new supermarket, with its offer of self-service shopping, was "the most serious competitor" the markets had yet known, and represented a reversal of the historic principle that the food-distribution point should be established principally for the benefit of the customer and not for the benefit of the seller. "Deplorable development schemes will so well provide the younger consumer with supermarkets," it was feared, "that only old people will continue to use the market as the younger generation adopts the supermarket."[23]

As a result, the coming of the supermarket significantly lessened the place of the public market in providing the supply of food and other goods. By the early to mid-1950s there were increasing reports of specific public market halls or open-air markets in serious decline. By the 1960s many public markets were in worse shape still.[24]

Fighting Back

For the most part, market hall supporters were on the losing side. Market traders found it difficult to influence town planners and officials. For more than a century they had had the upper hand in the retail world only because local officials gave preference to the public market. Now that private retailers and central planning were favored, they had no protector. Compared with the modern supermarkets the old Victorian buildings looked, to many, rather silly, and the market trader's trade association, the National Market Traders Federation (NMTF), was weak, for it represented only a fraction of the nation's traders. In fact, at the local level, market traders had only limited organization or none at all. Most market traders looked to the national federation only in times of crisis—usually, when a local government proposal came to move, alter, or close a market. The NMTF itself was skeptical of town planning schemes, arguing that their higher rent potential led town councils to favor private shops, particularly the multiples and the supermarkets, over the public market. Federation leaders sought to educate market traders in the need to modernize their marketing practices and to organize in the face of redevelopment schemes. They lobbied and negotiated, often successfully, on behalf of local traders before government groups, but overall, NMTF intervention was usually too little, too late. By the time the NMTF took up the question of redevelopment in a particular area, either the market had deteriorated to such bad physical condition that federation protests seemed obstructionist, or local officials were already committed to a particular redevelopment plan.

Market traders realized that they had much to lose with redevelopment schemes. Their greatest fear was that new developments would give locational preference to the supermarket and multiple-store giants, many of which were newcomers. It was also feared that new market facilities, particularly as a result of expensive redevelopment schemes, would mean higher rents, which in turn would ruin their long-standing competitive edge over the newcomers. Even sensitive market-rehabilitation schemes such as the one put into effect at Bolton caused a rise in rents which, in turn, drove traders with low profit margins out of the market. Modernization could be a trap any way market traders approached it. A stall or a shop in a new market hall could turn out to be a retailing nightmare.

The first battle between market traders and town officials was over rent increases. Rents had risen little during and immediately after the Second World War, but by the 1950s market authorities became obsessed with the notion of bringing public market rents up to a level which better reflected real or potential property values. Some market traders took their protests to the Prices and Incomes Board or to their M.P.s, but most adopted the tactic of negotiating reductions once a new rent had been established. But market rents continued to rise. Indeed, it was not unusual for market rents to increase by a third or even to double. In the late 1960s both Huddersfield and Cardigan raised public market rents by a third.[25]

It was also often the case that market officials sought to maximize their return on town infrastructure investment by demanding that market stalls pay rent for a five-and-a-half-day week. In most of the giant public markets, like Liverpool and Birmingham, this was already the case, but many medium- and small-sized markets were open less than five days a week or simply required traders to pay rent on the days they were actually present. Many small-time market traders held to the custom of "casual" trading, whereby they opened a stall in one market on one day and at another market the next. Indeed, the livelihood of many market traders rested on their ability to pull in profits from more than one town. Trying to work more than one market full-time meant hiring sales assistants; it led to the age-old dilemma of the small shopkeeper: What to do about all those days the shop is virtually empty?

Under the circumstances, market stallholders had little choice but to accept higher rents, which meant, inevitably, a reduction in profits. Naturally, only those markets which could offer low rent and allow casual rentals while providing an attractive environment for the consumer thrived. The models for success, then, were the older markets which were not touched by redevelopment schemes, like the pannier markets of the southwest of England (such as Bideford and Barnstaple) and older markets in the north like Ashton-under-Lyne, Todmorden, or the Ashburton market at Bolton.

Linked to rent was the broader issue of urban redevelopment. Most traders in the public market deplored government redevelopment policies and argued that something had to be done to meet the increased competition such policies promoted. Some fought to block redevelopment schemes, but many felt that the supermarket was just an American craze which would never take serious hold in Britain. For the most part market hall retailers were slow in trying new marketing techniques or appreciating the enormity of the combined threat from the new self-service supermarkets and urban redevelopment. Many market traders, it was claimed, didn't really put up a fight, although it is only fair to say that their main recourse was the landlords who were the same town officials urging redevelopment in the first place.[26]

In the battle against the new and the modern, market hall retailers were at a disadvantage because one of the products they sold was an intangible: character and tradition. Many market traders held that to emulate the big multiples such as Marks and Spencer or the grocery supermarkets would be to destroy the very essence of the public market. "The council is supposed to represent the people," wrote one opponent to demolition in Stockport, "but they refuse to get it into their heads that the people do not want a modern market. They prefer to shop in the old friendly atmosphere created by local traders." One thing that many townsfolk, including "preservationists" and market traders, recognized was that the new, sanitized market halls, which were too often incorporated into modern shopping centers, lost much of the charm of the public market. The lowered ceilings, harsh lighting and equally harsh surfaces, bland, boxlike interiors, and ungraceful and boring exteriors of the new markets had a present-mindedness and dullness which mirrored the malaise and alienation of contemporary life. The grandly flamboyant Victorian market at Chester may have been bitterly cold in the winter and hot in the summer and a dust trap to boot, but it imparted to its users a character and sense of place which the new plain-fronted, windowless, air-conditioned replacement could not provide. Although since its inception the market hall had become increasingly standardized in terms of stall size, layout, and general design, it retained an individual character, which the supermarket could not match: a sense of competition, variety, and individuality; the excitement of price bargaining, fresh goods often brought by locals from the nearby countryside; and goods that were less likely to be graded or standardized.

This "character" factor made it difficult for most public market traders to adopt more than a superficial measure of supermarket marketing techniques. "The multiple stores and the co-ops are all out to capture as much trade as they can," and they had the advantage of mass buying, big advertising campaigns, and strong financial support. Against these, it was advised, "the small independent man must use his individuality, his personal attention and knowledge of his customers and aim to turn his money over many times." So while some urged the stall owner to try such steps as giving up the "sacrosanct display" which discouraged self-service, and to be sure that all goods were clearly marked, the typical public market stall was too small and the amount of capital outlay prohibitive to provide the same level of prepackaging and self-service as the supermarket. The public market was, after all, based on the idea of many traders competing within a single space, and the flamboyant stall displays of dry goods and foodstuffs were now out of date, because national advertising had trained consumers to make their selections from a wide variety of brand names—something which space limitations made physically impossible for most market traders to provide. The days were gone when the market trader's stock could be wheeled into the market in a small cart or hamper. Unlike shopping at the supermarket, the market hall shopping routine was for a resolute shopper to go from stall to stall comparing quality and price. This took not only considerable time but also considerable social energy and, for some, a canny economic sense; in fact, in many ways, it was the supermarket and not the market hall which better fit the postwar image of the passive and dutiful modern (and middle-class) housewife. Besides, for many of the postwar generation, the humorous pitch of the market seller "no longer appeals in a era when first-class entertainment is available in one's own home at the touch of a switch."[27]

One response of market traders and others who championed the preservation of the public market was to venerate it in the context of the history and tradition of town life. The market hall, as it was claimed in Kidderminster, was part of "the character of the town." To alter the market was to alter a way of life. These people looked to the market hall not only as a bastion against the onslaught of modernism but also as a way to create an outdoor atmosphere indoors. Some even claimed that too many markets were becoming more like ordinary grocery stores and less like the old market halls. "The new market with its artificial light and low ceiling will look just like another supermarket with the exception that the counters will be run by different businesses." Hence, the traditional market hall became increasingly revered. In Stockport it was said that the market hall presented a scene which "survives only on the front of greeting cards," and but for the modern dress of the stallholders and shopkeepers the market "could have been [in] 1853 instead of 1953." It was in this spirit that in 1959 the *Market Trader*, the monthly trade journal of the National Market Traders Association, began a regular series on the history of markets which focused on the ancient rights and functions of the town market and described the civic pride which went into the building of the great market halls of the nineteenth century. Each month a particular market was featured, reminding traders, consumers, and public officials that the public market was one of the town's most ancient and venerable institutions.[28]

Market traders used historic preservation as a means of blocking development schemes which threatened the market at the same time that local officials were arguing that modern market buildings could be designed to preserve the traditional market atmosphere. The tenants of the Newport, Wales, market in 1967 expressed the hope that the proposed town redevelopment scheme "would not be so drastic as to completely alter the character of Newport, which had been essentially a market town for centuries," and in a long public debate, which eventually saved the town's small but historically and architecturally important market, a Dartmouth citizen warned the town council that "we have a unique building which must be preserved," not "converted into a chromium-plaited matchbox three storeys high."[29]

The New Market Halls

For some towns the new age called for new market halls. The first large-scale postwar market hall was a costly (£385,000) but highly successful modern circular concrete hall (276 feet in diameter) at Coventry, opened by the Coventry Corporation in 1958. It had two hundred teakwood stalls and shops with brass and galvanized steel fittings, a terrazzo floor, and a rooftop parking lot. Forty of the stalls were placed in the traditional manner of the one-sided shop set into the perimeter wall. The circular plan was adopted as the best means of providing access for the shopper at numerous points around the perimeter and giving the stallholders equal locational advantage (fig. 11.2). The new Plymouth Pannier Market Hall, which opened the following year, was equally large (but approximately the same size as the earlier market hall which was demolished), with a barrel- or shell-shaped roof which created a large central hall unencumbered by vertical supports. As one of Britain's largest market halls (the central hall is 224 feet by 148 feet), it has 16 lock-up shops, 144 fixed stalls, and 64 bench stalls for farmers trading in the old pannier manner. Neither the Plymouth nor Coventry market halls were built as extensions of a shopping center, and both were striking enough architecturally to make them recognizable institutions and notable structures in their day.

Many new market halls, although retaining the concepts of personal service and direct contact between buyer and trader, took their design cues from the modern department store and supermarket. Rather than building an unattached new market in the old manner the builders incorporated a new market hall into a larger town-center shopping complex, or, as in Kidderminster, moved a large and thriving market away from the retailing center of the town altogether. Well-meaning town officials were attracted to these schemes because higher rents

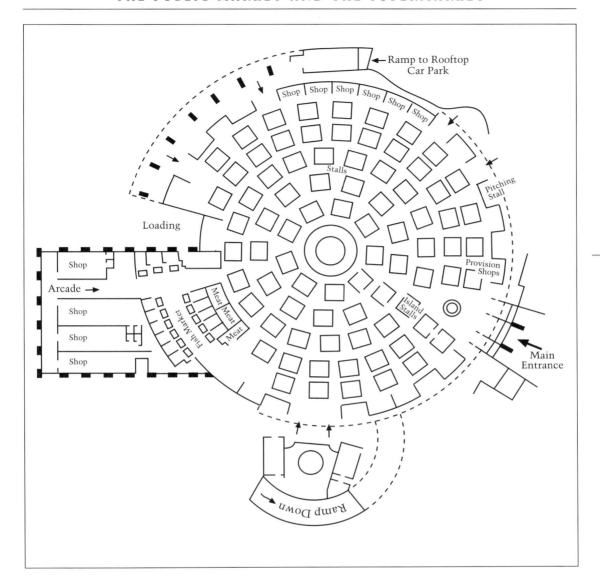

11.2. COVENTRY, NEW MARKET HALL, 1958

could be had from the big department stores, the multiples, and the supermarket chains. Wigan's town council first reversed its decision to demolish the market hall, one of Lancashire's largest, and undertook a program of renovation, but then the hall was destroyed after all in 1988 to make way for a new hall within a shopping complex called the Galleries. In Luton a new 39,000-square-foot market hall, complete with a central heating and ventilation system, and metal-framed stalls with formica counters, was included in a large shopping center. With its limited pedestrian entrance (by escalator) and its attached parking lot for 800 cars, the new Luton market hall boldly announced that it was a market for the automobile age (fig. 11.3).

Although conventional market-planning wisdom of the past century operated on the premise that neither consumer nor trader liked multilevel shopping facilities, in postwar planning the temptation was to stack the market as a multilevel building. This was done, for example, with the modest market at Hyde, where the three floors of a new "space age" market were connected by stairways and ramps. Further shrinking the market hall's presence on the street was the practice of placing the new hall inside a shopping center. Birmingham's new market hall (replacing a hall that was partially destroyed during the war) was positioned inside the new Bull Ring Shopping Center, thus making the public market only one of more than a hundred retail shops. Manchester's colorful Shudehill Market was tucked inside the "vast, gloomy" multilevel Arndale Center; and Liverpool's historic 140-year-old market hall was replaced by a new, "dreary" looking multilevel market hall inside a giant, multipurpose shopping center. Overall, by incorporating the public market into the larger and rather dull and homogenized new shopping centers, often set next to ugly parking lots, the new markets at Liverpool, Manchester, and Birmingham, like many others, lost much of their former aesthetic appeal and social uniqueness. They became, instead, a part of what one historian has called "a kind of dead urban heartland."[30]

11.3. PLAN, LUTON MARKET HALL, 1972

At the time of its construction, Luton Market Hall was the largest within an eighty-mile radius of London. Located within the vast Arndale shopping center, like many of the new postwar market halls it offers its users a supermarket atmosphere—with principal emphasis placed on the car and car park.

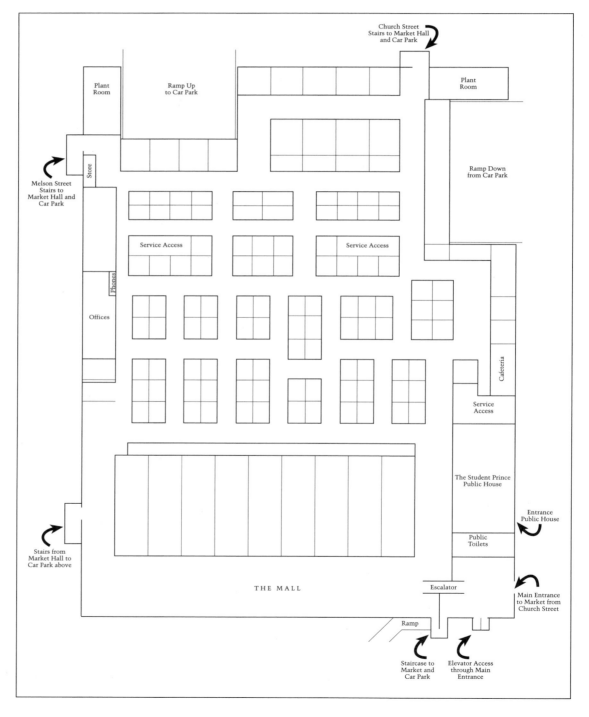

Proposals to remove the public market to a less desirable site were so frequent that one observer noted, "one can almost forecast it in advance." Typically, in Nottingham the new market hall was placed on two levels and behind a group of new shops, and in Wolverhampton, where the widely used and kindly regarded market hall of 1853 was demolished, the new market was transferred to a site some distance away (at the edge of a ring road) and into what some contemporaries called a box-and-blocklike complex (fig. 11.4). The town could have spent the funds (£685,000) on rehabilitating the grandly theatrical cast-iron market hall (fig. 11.5), but it was the wrong age for Victorian architecture, and such an idea did not fit into the town's reconstruction plan. Rugeley's Gothic Revival market hall, with its elegant stained-

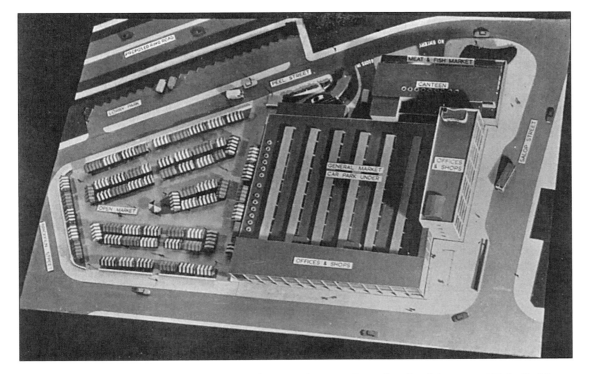

11.4. VIEW OF THE PROPOSED NEW MARKET AT WOLVERHAMPTON, 1953

Once occupying a position in the traditional town center and catering to pedestrian traffic, the proposed new market is surrounded by parking lots and a new ring road.

glass windows, was pulled down to make way for a parking lot for fifty cars. Wakefield authorities proposed moving the market to a new building nearby in order to redevelop the old market site into new shops, and Darlington city planners won over the town council with a plan to move the market to another part of the town and convert the old site to a car park. In Darlington, however, objections by market traders prevailed, and Waterhouse's grand tower and market hall were refurbished in 1978 and still stand at the center of Darlington's shopping district. But market halls in Huddersfield and Sheffield were demolished and the markets resited in large, drab, cheap-looking utilitarian boxes (figs. 11.6, 11.7). The Huddersfield Gothic Revival hall and its Shambles Lane were likened to Montmartre and recognized as the "essence of the town," but council members had been to Blackburn and were convinced that the stately Victorian building had to give way before "modern retailing standards." Although the new building of 1970 was hailed as "design for the seventies," it was also termed "strange and impersonal" and one "th' owd folk ull tak a bit to get used to."[31]

In many cases it was the car park which won the day. In both Dudley and Kettering it was proposed that the marketplace be converted into a car park, and one of Sheffield's two market halls was demolished in order to relieve traffic congestion. Architecturally, the most tragic market hall loss of the postwar era was the demolition of the magisterial Kirkgate Market Hall at Bradford in 1973 at the hands of planners who were more concerned with pedestrian space and car parks than with the architectural heritage of the town. Bradford's proposal to

11.5. WOLVERHAMPTON,
INTERIOR VIEW OF MARKET
HALL OF 1853, CA. 1960
The old market hall on the
eve of its demolition.

11.6. SHEAF MARKET
HALL, SHEFFIELD, 1963

11.7. HUDDERSFIELD
MARKET HALL, 1970

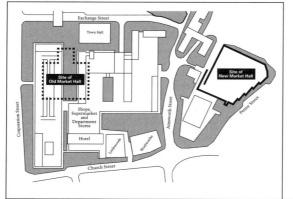

11.8. BLACKBURN, MAP OF
NEW TOWN CENTER
REDEVELOPMENT SCHEME,
1964

The market hall lost its
prominent position in the
town center in 1964—as the
new market hall was shifted
to the edge of the commercial district in order to give
place to a new shopping
mall.

destroy its century-old Victorian market
hall (listed as a grade 2 national monument)
because it interfered with a redevelopment
project, "caused more controversy than any
other in the city's history." Despite overwhelming financial, architectural, and social arguments in favor of retention, the
Bradford city council decided, in a clandes-
tine manner, to incorporate the market site

11.9. BLACKBURN,
DEMOLITION OF THE
MARKET HALL TOWER,
DECEMBER 1964

Shoppers stop to witness the
destruction of the stone
market tower, which had
been part of the townscape
their whole lives.

into a huge redevelopment scheme which contained an entirely new market of approximately the same size.[32]

Events in Blackburn illustrate how a thriving public market lost out in the redevelopment process by removal to a new site. In the years following the Second World War the Blackburn Market Hall (with its imposing tower), built in 1848 and standing next to the town hall, dominated the city skyline and retail marketing activity. It was, however, grossly overcrowded. Shops and stalls were fully occupied, and a large number of traders were on a waiting list for available space. As a result, the open-air market which grew up around the market hall had become increasingly crowded, with more than 7,000 stalls. The Blackburn Development Committee, facing the problem of a crowded market and a crowded city center, adopted an approach which in the end was ruinous to the historic position of the market hall. "Blackburns," it was announced by its planners, "is going to have the sense and the courage to knock down its whole town center, re-plan it, and build it in accordance with modern needs and ideas." To do so more than a hundred acres of the town center were cleared, the old market hall was demolished, and the new market hall was placed on a site at the edge of the development area. Locational preference was given to a vast array of new shops, supermarkets, and department stores, in a design its opponents termed "second-rate" and "out of date," and in an arrangement and form that were unrelated to either the town's traditional pattern of buying and selling or the physical and aesthetic patterns of Blackburn's townscape (figs. 11.8, 11.9).[33]

Renovation and Rehabilitation

The alternative to demolishing the old market building was to renovate it. Yet this course was often difficult because it meant sorting out various, seemingly chronic structural and material defects and solving the mystery of how to fit twentieth-century services into a nineteenth-century building. Nevertheless, market hall renovation was widespread and in many

11.10. DERBY, RESTORED MARKET HALL, 1989

instances highly successful, particularly after the concept of comprehensive urban redevelopment went out of fashion in the late 1970s. Renovation and rehabilitation restored medium-sized markets in Wrexham and Barnstaple, and smaller markets in Chichester and Richmond, Yorkshire. In Gloucester and Kendal, the Victorian market halls were retained by incorporating them into a town center shopping center. This was done successfully in Preston, where city planners considered the covered market too profitable to destroy; an earlier redevelopment scheme that left the market undisturbed was resurrected. Modern public health demands led Lancaster to renovate its market hall between 1955 and 1975, with new butchers' shops, a fish sellers' arcade, new stalls throughout, a new balcony, and a costly mosaic at one of the main entrances. In 1978, after four years of debate between town councillors, the community, and planning and architectural experts, Stockport's impressive mid-Victorian market hall, the "glass umbrella on stilts," was saved from demolition. The Stockport council reversed an earlier proposal to replace the building and instead spent more than £500,000 to repair the corrosion and general deterioration of years of inattention.[34]

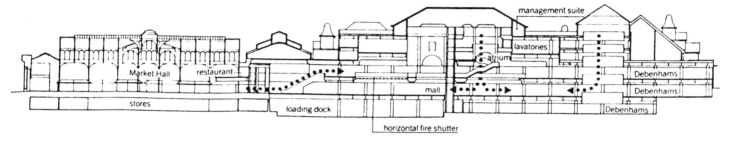

11.11. BOLTON, CROSS SECTION OF MARKET HALL AND NEW CENTER, 1989

This stone and cast-iron hall of 64,000 square feet was restored and incorporated into a shopping center in such a fashion as to retain the Victorian hall by making it the centerpiece for a new shopping center.

Renovation of market halls has brought about a renaissance in city-center shopping in a number of towns. The Halifax Borough Hall was successfully refurbished; and, on a more ambitious scale, Derby officials undertook a building program which restored the giant, centrally located Derby market hall to its original glory for its original use (fig. 11.10). During the course of the renovation, it was found that the supporting columns were out of line vertically and the foundation had sunk. These and other structural problems were corrected, and the whole of the nonstructural interior fabric was gutted and rebuilt in sympathy with the original style. Similarly, Bolton's huge classical-wrap stone market hall by G. T. Robinson (1855) was carefully restored much to its original form so as to remain a stallholders' market, but at the same time, it now acts as a dramatic entrance to a new shopping center built in a style to complement both the old market hall and the historical character of the town center (fig. 11.11; see also fig. 6.11). The revitalized Bolton market of 1988, along with the renovated halls in Derby and Darlington that acknowledge the historic townscape, offers an antidote to the banal and dull modernism of urban redevelopment schemes of the 1950s and 1960s, and a testimony to nineteenth-century market hall design.[35]

By the 1990s the public market hall had come full circle. In towns like Bolton and Barnstaple where the old market halls survived, they not only prospered, they contributed to a new appreciation of urban life and a new sense of town pride.[36] The economic and social advantage of the market hall once again became clear to the consumer, while its aesthetic and historical importance contributed to the new thinking about town and townscape.

NOTES

INTRODUCTION

1. *Southport Visiter*, 8 Sept. 1881.

2. The Gazetteer lists sources for further inquiry for the markets in more than three hundred towns.

3. See the source notes in the Gazetteer. Nikolaus Pevsner treats the subject of the market hall only briefly in his *A History of Building Types* (n.p., 1976; reprint, 1986), 235-240. A large number of existing market halls are included in Julian Orbach's *Blue Guide: Victorian Architecture in Britain* (London, 1987). Typically, H. A. N. Brockman's *British Architect in Industry, 1841-1940* (London, 1974) treats market halls not only in a cursory manner but with considerable disdain. C. W. Chalklin, in his chapter "Country Towns" in *The Victorian Countryside*, vol. 1, ed. G. E. Mingay (n.p., 1981), gives no attention to town retail markets except to say that they were, by 1888, in decline in importance and number and were being superseded by the village shop; likewise, public market buildings are given scant attention in Jonathan Brown, *The English Market Town: A Social and Economic History, 1750-1914* (Marlborough, Wilts., 1986), 47. A welcome study of the market hall is found in Thomas Marcus, *Buildings and Power: Freedom and Control in the Origin of Modern Building Type* (London, 1993).

4. The only exceptions to this are a late nineteenth-century inquiry into food adulteration and one into urban market tolls. See the introductory essay on sources in the Gazetteer. Surprisingly, most historians of early nineteenth-century social reform, particularly in public health, miss important market reforms because there is little evidence of effective central government action. See, e.g., E. C. Midwinter, *Victorian Social Reform* (London, 1968). These histories omit the actions of local government.

5. For a discussion of Sunday marketing in London see the report of the Royal Commission of the House of Lords on the Observance of the Sabbath Day, "Minutes of Evidence" (1850), qs. 1535-49.

CHAPTER 1: The Traditional Market

1. On market days, for example, early nineteenth-century Godalming had a weekly market on Wednesday, whereas Southampton had three market days a week, and its fish market was open every day. Coventry's market was on Wednesday, Friday, and Saturday. Parliamentary Papers, *Report of the Royal Commission on Municipal Corporations* (London, 1835-39, hereafter *Municipal Corporations Report*), vol. 2 (1835), 738, 867, 1807-08. For examples of market rights, see Maggie Colwell, *West of England Market Towns* (London, 1980), 40. The City of London held a monopoly over markets within seven miles of city limits: see David Owen, *The Government of Victorian London, 1855-1889* (Cambridge and London, 1982), 244-47.

2. *The History of the Market in Abergavenny* (n.p., n.d.), 1. For the market at Plymouth, see *Market Trader*, 22 Aug. 1959, 21.

3. Quoted in *History of the Market in Abergavenny*, 2.

4. For the lack of covered market space, see *Lewis's Topographical Dictionary* (n.p., 1831), vols. 1-4; quotation from "The Market Cross," *Department of the Environment Survey, Malmesbury*, ST9387 1/45 I; for Hemel Hempstead, see *The Victoria History of the Counties of England: Hertfordshire* (London, 1908), vol. 2, p. 219.

5. *Free Market Committee Minutes*, Leeds, 25 Oct. 1841. (Although in 1835 municipal corporation commissioners throughout England uncovered some questionable market practices, such as mayors who used toll collection as a prerequisite of office, their reports do not indicate any significant level of corruption in the local administration of markets.) J. D. Marwick, ed., *Extracts from the Records of the Burgh of Glasgow* (1781-95), vol. 8, pp. 26, 282, 587; Coventry town officials acted in 1719: see Benjamin Poole, *Coventry: Its History and Antiquities* (Coventry, 1870), 330.

6. Sidney Webb and Beatrice Webb, *The Development of English Local Government, 1689-1835* (London, 1963), 6; for numerous descriptions of overcrowding in the public market see Parliamentary Papers, *Royal Commission on Market Rights and Tolls*; George Penny, *Traditions of Perth* (1836; reprint, with introduction by A. Cooke, 1986), 15.

7. "Scotland—Dundee," in *Municipal Corporations Report* (1835), 299; Cris Howell, *Some of Our Old Pictures of Midsomer Norton, Paulton, Chihampton, and Radstock* (n.p., 1979), unpaginated; for the Derby incident, see W. Alfred Richardson, *Citizens' Derby* (London, 1949), 175.

8. E. P. Thompson, "The Moral Economy of the English Crowd in the Eighteenth Century," *Past and Present* 50 (1971): 47, 53; Robert B. Shoemaker, "The London 'Mob' in the Early Eighteenth Century," *Journal of British Studies* 26, no. 3 (July 1987): 301; and Roger Wells, "Counting Riots in Eighteenth Century England," *Bulletin for the Society for the Study of Labour History* 37 (1987). Wells argues that for the period from 1600 to 1850, the number of food riots has been considerably underestimated. See also John Bohsted, *Riots and Community Politics in England and Wales* (Oxford, 1986). The *Annual Register* is quoted in G. D. H. Cole and A. W. Filson, eds., *British Working Class Movements: Select Documents, 1789-1875* (London, 1967), 21.

Chapter One
cont'd

9. On street entertainment, see Gordon Jackson, *Hull in the Eighteenth Century: A Social and Economic History* (Oxford, 1971), 286; on bull baiting, see Robin Bush, *The Book of Taunton* (n.p., 1977), 56; for Newcastle, see S. Middlebrook, *Newcastle-upon-Tyne: Its Growth and Achievement* (2d ed., n.p., 1968), 126; for Barnsley, see *Market Trader*, 16 Jan. 1960, 23; for Petworth, see Roger Turner, "The Great George Inn, Petworth," *Sussex Archaeological Collection*, vol. 19, p. 137; we are indebted to Mrs. Marion Ogden for information on Wokingham; the Penzance reference is quoted in R. M. Barton, *Life in Cornwall in the Early Nineteenth Century* (Truro, 1970), 54.

10. David Robertson and Margaret Wood, *Castle and Town: Chapters in the History of the Royal Burgh of Edinburgh* (Edinburgh, 1928), 270; David Diaches, *Edinburgh* (Edinburgh, 1978), 122-23; see also [Gilbert Elliot], *Proposals for Carrying out Certain Public Works in the City of Edinburgh, 1752* (Edinburgh, 1752).

11. For complaints, see W. J. Lewis, *Born on a Perilous Rock* (Aberystwyth, 1980), 137; the Dundee description refers to the period from 1746 to 1799. See *Dundee Delineated, or A History and Description of that Town* (n.p., 1822); for Glasgow, see *Glasgow Herald*, 11 July 1817, 1; see also *Glasgow Corporation Minutes*, 5 Mar. 1846, 16; St. Helier complaints are in A. E. Tagg, *A History of the Development of the Jersey Markets, 1882-1982* (States Department of Public Buildings and Works Bulletin, n.p., 1982); on pigs, see *Glasgow Herald*, 26 Oct. 1866, 2; for well-bred ladies' complaints, see *Royal Commission on Markets and Tolls*, vol. 3, "Salisbury."

12. John A. Longford, *A Century of Birmingham Life, 1741-1841* (Birmingham, 1868), vol. 1, p. 373; *Directions for Walking the Streets of Manchester* (Manchester, 1809), 6-7; William E. A. Ason, ed., *The Annals of Manchester: A Chronological Record from Earliest Times to the End of 1885* (London, 1886). See, for example, the entries for 4 June 1821 and 2 July 1821; *Glasgow Herald*, 14 Oct. 1872, 4; *Bury Times*, 10 Jan. 1971, Manchester Central Library newspaper clippings, box 255.

13. *Bridgwater Official Guide* (n.p., 1935) 17; for "college of bad language," see David Owen, *The Government of Victorian London, 1855-1889* (Cambridge and London, 1982), 244; Charles A. Wilson, *Aberdeen of Auld Lang Syne* (Aberdeen, 1948), 194; sentence of Mary Windsor cited in Isaac Watkin, *Oswestry* (n.p., 1920), 182.

14. From Barton, *Life in Cornwall in the Early Nineteenth Century*, 89.

15. "Icharletoni" [R. J. Charleton], *The Streets of Newcastle* (Newcastle, 1885-86), 104; Robertson and Wood, *Castle and Town*, 271; the *Magazine*, 28 Aug. 1975, 33; for Oswestry markets, see *Shropshire Magazine*, 31 Dec. 1978, 26; for brawling, see W. M. Laren, "Old Edinburgh Markets,"

Evening Dispatch, 29 July 1942; Manchester quote is from Alderman McCake in 1905, unattributed newspaper clipping of 9 Dec. 1909, Manchester Central Library, box 225; Edward Bradby, *The Book of Devizes* (n.p., n.d.), 51.

16. See Dorothy Whitaker, *Auld Hawkie and Other Glasgow Characters* (Glasgow, 1988); Alexis de Tocqueville, *Journeys in England and Ireland*, trans. George Lawrence and K. P. Mayer, ed. K. P. Mayer (London, 1958), 57; Alexander Pearson, *Annals of Kirkby Lonsdale* (Kirkby Lonsdale, 1930), 173; for Gloucester, see "The Opening of the New Market," *Gloucester Press*, 3 May 1856; for Scarborough, see William Rowntree, cited in "The Opening of the Scarborough Market Hall," *Scarborough Gazette* 11 Aug. 1853; on Manchester, see "Memorial Received from Shopkeepers in the Old Market Place," *Proceedings of the Council*, Borough of Manchester (2 May 1888), vols. 1887-88, p. 361.

17. The first opinion was that of the Clevedon local board. Cited in Jennifer Capp, "Clevedon," in *Bristol and West Country Illustrated*, August 1980, 38; the second is from "Proceedings of the Society—Food Committee," *Journal of the Society of Arts* (10 Jan. 1868): 124.

18. Letter from Chief Constable McCall to the Town Council Finance Committee, printed in the *Glasgow Herald*, 16 July 1872; the Manchester Town Council instructed its Market Committee in 1847 to discover what steps could be taken to remove the nuisance arising from the existence of a peddlers' market at the corner of Swan Street and Rochdale Road. See *Proceedings of the Council*, Borough of Manchester (1847-48). See also Improvement Committee Report of July 1852 in *Proceedings* (1852-54); this report led to the prohibition of selling in certain streets.

19. "Keith," in *Municipal Corporations Report* (1835). The outdoor market often contained shooting galleries and merry-go-rounds. See *Royal Commission on Markets and Tolls*, "Accrington," vol. 9, p. 464; *Dundee Advertiser*, 10 Dec. 1881; *Royal Commission on Markets and Tolls*, vol. 9, "Oldham," James Donnan, *A Sketch of the History of Dundee* (n.p., 1853), 40. Similarly, in seventeenth-century Taunton, riotous behavior at the Saturday-night market was a town issue: see Robin Bush, *The Book of Taunton* (n.p., 1977), 56. See also the letter to the editor, *The Builder*, 9 Jan. 1869, 35, and *The Municipal History of the Royal Burgh of Dundee* (n.p., 1878), 135.

20. *Victoria History of the Counties of England: Wiltshire* (Oxford, 1970), vol. 9, p. 132. Market accommodation was provided in 1852. On the temptations of the public house, see "Opening of the New Market House at Bacup," *Bacup Times*, 24 Aug. 1867; the Harwich Quarter Session for 1765, for example, records forty-four persons who have been charged with using deficient weights and measures: see Leonard T. Weaver, *The Harwich Story* (n.p., 1975), 102.

CHAPTER 2: Inventing the Market Hall

1. Parliamentary Papers, *Royal Commission on Market Rights and Tolls*, 14 vols. (London, 1888-91, hereafter cited as *Royal Commission on Markets and Tolls*), vol. 8, "Brighton"; *Royal Commission on Markets and Tolls*, vol. 8, "Loughborough"; "Opening of the Market Hall," *Bacup Times*, 24 Aug. 1867; *Scarborough Gazette*, 11 Aug. 1853; *Royal Commission on Markets and Tolls*, vol. 9, "Bolton."

2. On definitions of public space, see Paul M. Hohenberg and Lynn Hollen Lees, *The Making of Urban Europe, 1000-1994* (2d ed., Cambridge, Mass., 1995), chap. 9, and M. J. Daunton, "Public Place and Private Space: The Victorian City and the Working-Class Household," in Derek Fraser and Anthony Sutcliffe, eds., *The Pursuit of Urban History* (London, 1979). Although Daunton identifies a shift from participatory to passive use of public space, we find it coming at the beginning rather than at the end of the nineteenth century.

3. Llewellyn Jewitt, *The History of Plymouth* (n.p., 1873), 487-88; Sylvester Davis, *A History of Southampton* (n.p., 1883), 127-28; for Coventry, see *The Victoria History of the Counties of England: Warwickshire* (Oxford, 1969), vol. 8, p. 291.

4. James Ogden, *An Historical Description of Manchester* (n.p., 1887), 70-71; Arthur Redford, "Manor and Township," in Arthur Redford and I. Russell, *The History of Local Government in Manchester* (1939), vol. 1, pp. 131-49; see Manchester Corporation Market Committee, *The Manchester Markets, 1846-1946* (n.p., 1946), 12-13; Kevin Grady, "Profit, Property Interests and Public Spirit: The Provision of Markets and Commercial Amenities in Leeds, 1822-29," *Thoresby Society* 54, no. 122 (1976): 165-67. We are grateful to Maurice Beresford for this citation.

5. See Henry Mayhew's accounts in *London Labour and the London Poor*, 4 vols. (1861-62. Repr., New York, 1968); *Royal Commission on Markets and Tolls*, vol. 8, "Loughborough"; Doncaster Civic Trust, "Market Place Conversion Area," *Newsletter*, Nov. 1986; J. Jeffrey, *Hints for a History of Birmingham* (n.p., 1853). Jeffrey describes conditions in the year 1769.

6. *Royal Commission on Markets and Tolls*, vol. 9, "Market Harborough"; the account of the mountebanks is from Kingston-upon-Hull and is found in *The Victoria History of the Counties of England: Yorkshire* (Oxford, 1969), vol. 1, p. 409. The Scottish town with the flogging was Inverness: *Glasgow Herald*, 6 Mar. 1817, 4; poem from an anonymous pamphlet, "Short History of South Molton Guildhall and Museum" (South Molton, 1987), 2.

7. James McCall, *Glasgow Ancient and Modern* (n.p., n.d.), vol. 2, p. 879; J. D. Marwick, ed., *Extracts from the Records of the Burgh of Glasgow*, 12 vols. (Glasgow, 1876-1918); R. K. Dent, *Making of Birmingham* (n.p., 1894), 137; *Royal Commission on Markets and Tolls*, Appendix: "Returns," 2-34.

8. *Royal Commission on Markets and Tolls*, vol. 4, "Sunderland," vol. 3, "Halifax" and "Cockermouth"; W. J. Lewis, *Born on a Perilous Rock* (Aberystwyth, 1980), 137.

9. See the 1886 survey of 242 municipal boroughs: *Royal Commission on Markets and Tolls*, vol. 14, "Return Giving Particulars in Respect of Each Municipal Borough in England and Wales," 2-35.

10. The quote about Hereford is from John Shane, *The Celebration of the Butter Market* (n.p., 1976), 7, that on Winchester, *The Hampshire Chronicle*, 3 Oct. 1857, 3.

11. Marwick, *Extracts*, vol. 10, 28 Feb. 1817, 4 Sept. 1817, 20 Nov. 1817, 11 Feb. 1822.

12. *Royal Commission on Markets and Tolls*, vol. 11, "Final Report," 54, 86.

CHAPTER 3: Ownership, Tolls, and Market Reform

1. Alan Everitt, "The Primary Towns of England," *Local Historian* 11, no. 5 (Feb. 1975), 270. The seven-mile stipulation was a fourteenth-century ruling; its rationale was that a reasonable day's journey was considered to be twenty miles. When divided into three parts—time to walk to market, time to do market business, and time to walk home—the traveling was determined to be six and two-thirds miles each way, or roughly seven miles. See Maggie Colwell, *West of England Market Towns* (London, 1980), 11.

2. For Manchester's battle with Lord Mosley, see William Axon, ed., *Annals of Manchester, 1781-1803* (n.p., 1886). The relationship between the private shopkeeper and the publicly owned market was generally congenial. One of the more frequent debates in the economic history of many towns was whether the public market—be it an open-air market, a market hall, or a scattering of costermongers— benefited the town's shopkeepers. Most merchants appear to have supported improving the public market because they saw it as the most effective way of drawing customers into the town. In addition, many private shopkeepers found in the public market an ideal opportunity for creating additional trading venues for themselves, particularly on market days, when they could open a stall or shop within the public market and, among other advantages, rid themselves of perishable goods. In a few towns it was claimed that shopkeepers were vehemently opposed to the market—to the point of blocking improvements or ensuring that market tolls were set high enough to keep market prices level with those of the shops. Such claims are rare and difficult to substantiate, although the Bridgnorth market hall of 1854 was never used because local shopkeepers won a legal judgment preventing the board of health from removing the market from the street to the new hall. Presumably, it was about this time that local citizens took steps to remove market traders from the old market under the town hall by driving a pony and cart through them. See "Bridgnorth Market," *Shropshire Magazine* 27, no. 12 (June 1975). This is set out in a letter to the *Journal of the Society*

Chapter Three cont'd

of Arts (7 Feb. 1868), 237, suggesting that local opposition to the market was also the case in Reading; see also C. Bradlaugh, "Market Rights and Tolls: How They Make Food Dear," a leaflet published by the Cobden Club in 1888. For views that the market offered positive support for town business, see Parliamentary Papers, *Royal Commission on Market Rights and Tolls*, 14 vols. (London, 1888-91, hereafter cited as *Royal Commission on Markets and Tolls*), vol. 9, p. 217.

3. For example, see Parliamentary Papers, *Report of the Royal Commission on Municipal Corporations* (London, 1835-39, hereafter *Municipal Corporations Report*), vol. 2, pt. 3, "Walsall" (1835), 2048; "Markets and Fairs" (typed m.s., n.d., Macclesfield Library) n.p.; C. Stella Davies, *A History of Macclesfield* (Manchester, 1961), 62; for Chard, see *Royal Commission on Markets and Tolls*, vol. 11, "Final Report," 60.

4. For a discussion of the legal origins of market rights, see *Royal Commission on Markets and Tolls*, vol. 11, "Final Report," 2-31.

5. *Municipal Corporations Report*, pt. 3, "East Redford" (1835), 1864.

6. The argument (and its history) is sketched out in David Cannadine, *Lords and Landlords: The Aristocracy and the Towns, 1774-1967* (Leicester, 1980), 391-95, 414-16.

7. For Wakefield, see *Royal Commission on Markets and Tolls*, vol. 11, "Final Report," 72.

8. The Winchester case is found in the *Hampshire Chronicle*, 4 Feb. 1856, 3; for Carlisle, see the *Carlisle Journal*, 4 Oct. 1889, 5.

9. These figures are from *Royal Commission on Markets and Tolls*, vol. 14, Appendix B: "Return Giving Particulars in Respect of Each Municipal Borough in England and Wales," 2-34.

10. *Royal Commission on Markets and Tolls*, vol. 11, "Final Report," 69.

11. *Royal Commission on Markets and Tolls*, vol. 1, First Report, Appendix B, "Local Acts, Local and Personal Acts, and Provisional Orders, Passed Since the Year 1800," 225-30; The purchase-transfer costs are from returns received by the market commissioners in 1886. Of forty-three market purchases, all but one (Wells in 1779) took place in the nineteenth century. See *Royal Commission on Market Rights and Tolls*, vol. 14, Appendix B.

12. *Municipal Corporations Report*, vol. 2, "Maidstone" (1835), 7; Roy Hewett, ed., *Maidstone of 1549-1949* (n.p., 1949), 48; for Taunton, see *Royal Commission on Markets and Tolls*, vol. 11, "Final Report," 19-20.

13. "A Record of Municipal Developments From 1847 to 1947" (n.d., Warrington Central Library), 5.

14. *A History of Darwen Market Hall, 1882-1922* (n.p., n.d.), 1.

15. "New Life for Clevedon's Market," *Bristol and West Country Illustrated* (Aug. 1990); *Huddersfield Weekly News*, 3 Apr. 1880, 36; "The Opening of the Market Hall," *Huddersfield Daily Chronicle*, 1 Apr. 1880, n.p.; Robert. K. Dent, *The Making of Birmingham* (n.p., 1894), 137, 307-08, 375-76; Birmingham Market and Fairs Committee, "Birmingham Market Hall, 1835-1935" (1935), 5-8.

16. *Royal Commission on Markets and Tolls*, vol. 2, "Minutes of Evidence," 5740-55, 5825-5906.

17. See Tom Devine, "Introduction," to Hamish Fraser and R. J. Morris, *People and Society in Scotland*, vol. 2 (Edinburgh, 1989), iv.

18. R. J. Morris, "Urbanization and Scotland," in Fraser and Morris, *People and Society in Scotland*; how widespread exclusion of outside merchants was is unclear, although until the early nineteenth century, Glasgow merchants used this ancient custom to keep certain country vendors out of the town; the Glasgow Bazaar Market, for example, was held as part of the common good until its official transfer to the corporation in 1905. See John Lindsay, *Municipal Glasgow* (n.p., n.d.), 301, and City of Glasgow, *Municipal Glasgow, Its Evolution and Enterprises* (Glasgow, 1914), 139; for Dundee's expenditures, see *Municipal Corporations Report: Scotland* (1835), 299-300.

19. Francis W. Steer, "The Market House, Chichester," *Chichester Papers* 3, no. 27 (1962), 1-3; *Carlisle Journal*, 4 Oct. 1889, 5. For Harrogate, see Harold Walker, *The History of Harrogate Under the Improvement Commissioners, 1841-1884* (n.p., 1986), 328-30.

20. Axon, *Annals of Manchester*, 22-23 Oct. 1883.

21. *Municipal Corporations Report*, pt. 3, "Coventry" (1835), 1807-08; Liverpool Markets Committee Minutes, "Report on Manchester Markets," Report One (1872); before its conversion in 1968, a British pound consisted of 20 shillings ("s"), each of which had 12 pence ("d").

22. The reference to Manchester's tolls is from Liverpool Markets Committee Minutes, "Report on Manchester"; see also *Royal Commission on Markets and Tolls*, vol. 2, "Minutes of Evidence," 834-929.

23. *Royal Commission on Markets and Tolls*, vol. 11, "Final Report," 59, 91, 98, 107.

24. The Lancaster citation is from 1886; see John Catt, *A History of the Lancaster Market* (n.p., n.d.).

25. The charge that market tolls led to increased food costs in Liverpool was made by Charles Bradlaugh, M.P., who appears to have had considerable influence on the tone of the royal commission's questioning in 1891 but not on its final recommendations. Bradlaugh published a pamphlet entitled "Market Rights and Tolls: How They Make Food Dear" through the Cobden Club in 1888. With regard to the charge of "excessive profits," no indication is given of what is meant by this term. W. A. Casson of the Local Government Board named thirty-one markets as having large profits in his responses to the Royal Com-

mission on Markets and Tolls. They were Chester, Stockport, Derby, Plymouth, Stockton-on-Tees, Bristol, Hereford, Maidstone, Ashton-under-Lyne, Chorley, Warrington, Leicester, Norwich, Northampton, Henley, Wolverhampton, Brighton, Birmingham, Middlesborough, Halifax, Huddersfield, Blackburn, Bolton, Burnley, Liverpool, Manchester, Oldham, Bradford, Cardiff, Swansea, and Leeds.

26. For a discussion of market profits, see *Royal Commission on Markets and Tolls*, vol. 11, "Final Reports," 49-68, and vol. 2, "Minutes of Evidence," 770-77; The revenue estimates are based on earned revenue. Privately owned markets or markets in rural districts received an average income of £484 compared to £1,084 for markets belonging to or rented by town councils or other local government bodies: see *Royal Commission on Markets and Tolls*, vol. 56, "Minutes of Evidence," 66-93.

Using market profits to reduce the town rates was a widespread practice well into the twentieth century. On the one hand, the practice may appear unfair because the result was that market users, particularly working class people, thereby subsidized the propertied classes; on the other hand, applying market revenues to the rates was a way to force market stall- and shopholders to pay the same the town rates ordinary shopkeepers were.

27. The reference to Cannock's return on market investment is from Roger H. Whiting, "The Cannock Market Hall Company Limited" (typescript; Cannock Library, n.d.), unpaginated.

CHAPTER 4: Great Expectations

1. "Market Buildings," *Building News* 34 (1 Feb. 1878): 121; Paxton's views on ornament are in George F. Chadwick, *Paxton* (London, 1962), 161, 203; for the destruction of Paxton's market in Leeds, see: "Proposed Reconstruction of Leeds Markets," *The Builder* (8 Feb. 1896): 122.

2. Hugh Meller, *Exeter Architecture* (Exeter, 1989), 49; Alexander Clifton-Taylor, *Six English Towns* (London, 1978), 168; the reference to the "crude" city was by Glasgow architect Alexander Thomson in his *Art and Architecture: A Course in Four Lectures, 1874*, ed. Thomas Gilard (Glasgow, n.d.), 17; for an example of town guide promoting urban beautification, see James Donnan, *Alectum: or, A British Sketch of the History of Dundee* (n.p., 1853), 42-43; the Middlesbrough reference is cited in G. E. Mingay, *The Transformation of Britain, 1830-1939* (London, 1986), 6; the reference to the town as ornament is found in "The New Market Hall," *Rotherham Advertiser*, 28 Jan. 1889; for Bradford, see Parliamentary Papers, *Royal Commission on Market Rights and Tolls*, 14 vols. (London, 1888-91, hereafter cited as *Royal Commission on Markets and Tolls*), vol. 2, "Bradford," and for Huddersfield, see *Huddersfield Weekly News*, 3 Apr. 1880, 36.

3. For examples of concern over population control, see Parliamentary Papers, *Report of the Royal Commission on Municipal Corporations* (London, 1835-39, hereafter *Municipal Corporations Report*), Scotland, "Dundee" (1835); the reference to the Chartist years is from F. C. Mather, *Public Order in the Age of the Chartists* (n.p., 1959, 1971), chaps. 1 and 3; the complex relationship between food riots, industrial disorder, and politics in the 1760s is the subject of Walter J. Shelton, *English Hunger and Industrial Disorders* (Toronto, 1973); Godwin's views are from his book *Town Swamps and Social Bridges* (London, 1859; repr. Leicester, 1972).

4. John Claudius Loudon, *Encyclopedia of Cottage, Farm and Villa Architecture and Furniture* (London, 1833; rev. ed. 1836), 94; for further discussion of this aesthetic revolution see James Schmiechen, "The Victorians, the Historians, and the Idea of Modernism," *American Historical Review* 93 (April 1988), 287-316; for Bolton, see "Opening of the Bolton New Market Hall," *Bolton Chronicle*, 22 Dec. 1855, 6.

5. Charles Wilson, "On the Formation of Provincial Museums and Collections of Works of Art," *Transaction of the Architectural Institute of Scotland* (n.p., 1854-55), 57, 358; the reference to market design is from *The Architect*, 1 May 1869, 235; the Burton-on-Trent sculpture was the work of a Mr. Roddis of Birmingham: see "New Market Hall, Burton-on-Trent," *The Builder* 47 (15 March 1884): 385; "Southport and Its Markets," *Southport Guardian*, 25 Mar. 1903 [in Southport Library, Lancashire News Clippings File, vol. 1]; "Opening of the New Market," *Gloucester Journal*, 3 May 1856; *Carlisle Journal*, 4 Oct. 1889, 6; the poem is from P. A. Whittle, *Blackburn As It Is* (Preston, 1852), 123; the Scarborough reference was the opinion of Mr. William Rowntree: "Opening of Scarborough Market Mall," *Scarborough Gazette*, 11 Aug. 1853; "Opening of Bolton's New Market Hall," *Bolton Chronicle*, 22 Dec. 1855; the fears of the middle class are expressed in "Report of the Food Committee," *Journal of the Society of the Arts* 16 (1867): 92, and in a letter by "C. S." to *The Builder* 39 (13 Nov. 1880): 598; the reference to Sunday diets is from Barrie Trinder, ed., *The Industrial Revolution in Shropshire* (n.p., 1981), 205-06.

6. *Royal Commission of Markets and Tolls*, vol. 9, "Oldham," 366; the reference to the public house is from "The Opening of the Market House," *Bacup Times*, 24 Aug. 1867; the reference to crying of fish is from Birmingham Markets and Fairs Committee, "Minutes and Reports, 1851-1878," vol. 2 (1 May 1856); *Royal Commission on Markets and Tolls*, vol. 4, "Reading"; "strict adherence" quote from *Dundee Advertiser*, 10 Dec. 1881; the reference to women in Manchester is from an unidentified newspaper cutting, dated 9 Dec. 1905, from box 255, Manchester Central Library.

Chapter Four
cont'd

7. "Manchester As It Was," *Bradshaw's Manchester Journal*, 16 Oct. 1841, 386. I thank Susan Pyecroft for this citation. The reference to respectable women needing to wash is from W. M. Bowman, *England in Ashton-Under-Lyne* (n.p., 1960), 296; Borough of Barnstaple, "Proposed New Market House: Report of Committee" (1851) [NDA box 5, no. 3, Barnstaple Library].

8. The "happy family" and "greatness and glory" references come from "Opening of the New Market," *Gloucester Journal*, 3 May 1856; the citations on protecting the poor are from Birmingham Market Committee, "Minutes and Reports, 1851-78," vol. 2 (29 Oct. 1858), and the "Leeds Free Market Committee Minutes," 19 Jan. 1871.

9. For the reference to the town's "honourable reputation," see "Opening of the Bolton Market," *Bolton Chronicle*, 22 Dec. 1855; for an example of the market being an asset to an energetic mayor, see the letter to the *Tenby Observer*, 3 Nov. 1878, 2.

10. The reference to the benevolent parent is from "Opening of New Market at Batley," *Batley Reporter*, 11 May 1878; W. Fordyce, *The History and Antiquity of the County Palatine of Durham* (Durham, 1857), vol. 1, p. 360.

11. Pete Williams, *Warrington in Camera* (Warrington, 1981), 27; "Manchester As It Was," 386; on Darwen's self-sufficiency, see the Lancashire Library, *A History of Darwen's Market Hall, 1882-1982* (Darwen Library, 1982), 7; P. A. Whittle, *Blackburn As It Is: A Topographical, Statistical, and Historical Account* (Preston, 1852), 123; *Dundee Advertiser*, 30 May 1872; the Darwen reference is in *The Builder*, no. 2056 (31 July 1882): 31; the Launceton citation is in *Royal Commission on Markets and Tolls*, vol. 3, "Launceton"; *The Salisbury and Winchester Journal and General Advertiser*, 28 May 1859, 6; "Proposed New Market House: Report of Committee," Borough of Barnstaple (12 March 1851) [NDA, box 5 no. 3, Barnstaple Library].

12. H. W. Gwilliam, *Old Worcester*, vol. 1 (n.d., typed m.s., Worcester City Library), 48; Salisbury's new market hall (1859) was also promoted as being "somewhat after the style adopted in the Crystal Palace" (*The Salisbury and Winchester Journal*, 28 May 1859, 6.); Kenneth H. Rogers, *Book of Trowbridge* (n.p., n.d.), 118-19; "The Laying of the Cornerstone of the New Market," *Accrington Times*, 23 May 1868; *Carlisle Journal*, 4 Oct. 1889, 6; for Truro, see *West Briton and Cornwall Advertiser*, 5 Nov. 1847, 2.

13. The Accrington references are found in *Blackburn Times*, 30 Oct. 1869, 31; for Aberystwyth, see *The Builder* 28 (3 Sept. 1870): 704.

14. For Halifax, see Eric Webster, *Under the Clock: The Story of the Victorian Borough Market, Halifax* (Halifax, 1983), 16; Arthur C. Ellis, *An Historical Survey of Torquay* (Torquay, n.d.), 291.

15. *South Devon Journal*, 13 Sept. 1850, 5.

CHAPTER 5: Market Hall Architecture

1. *The Builder*, 15 Feb. 1851, 100.

2. For Petworth, see P. Jerome, *Tread Lightly Here* (n.p., 1991), 166; for Horsham, see A. Windrum, *Horsham: An Historical Survey* (n.p., 1978), 62.

3. Francis Steer, "The Market House, Chichester," *Chichester Papers* 3, no. 27 (1962): 4, 11-13.

4. The "new school" claim was made by J. C. Loudon in 1831. See Louise Melanie, *Loudon and the Landscape: From Country Seat to Metropolis, 1783-1843* (New Haven, 1988), 142-43.

5. The Bristol descriptions are found in John Latimer, *Annals of Bristol in the Nineteenth Century*, vol. 2 (n.p., 1887), 253, and *Lewis's Typographical Dictionary*, vol. 1 (London, 1831), 240.

6. "J. A. P," "A Short Account of St. John's Market," *Architectural Magazine and Journal* 2 (1835): 133.

7. W. Collard and M. Ross, *Views of Newcastle* (Newcastle, 1841), 7.

8. The references to Birkenhead are from W. W. Mortimer, *The History of the Hundred of Wirral* (n.p., 1847), 364, and "The Rise and Progress of Birkenhead," *Civil Engineer and Architects Journal* 8 (1845): 257.

9. The quote is from Bridgett Cherry and Nikolous Pevsner, *The Buildings of England* (2d ed., Devon, 1955), 93; a description and plan of the Exeter market is found in *Architectural Magazine and Journal* 3 (1836): 12-13.

10. The reference to Bolton's renown is found in Parliamentary Papers, *Royal Commission on Market Rights and Tolls*, 14 vols. (London, 1888-91; hereafter cited as *Royal Commission on Markets and Tolls*), vol. 7, "Bolton."

11. The Southport market hall was constructed at a cost of £25,000. *Royal Commission on Markets and Tolls*, vol. 4, "Scarborough."

12. For a discussion of the plate-glass shop front, see *Building News* 33 (21 Dec. 1877): 656; Waterhouse was making reference to Southport's new market. See "Southport," *Building News* 33 (14 Dec. 1877): 602.

13. The Darwen citation is from *Building News* 37 (15 Aug. 1879): 177; for a similar view of Wigan, see *Building News* (9 Apr. 1875), 397.

14. *The Builder* 21 (7 Feb. 1863): 97; the reference to Chester is from Thomas Hughes, *The Stranger's Handbook to Chester* (n.p., 1856; repr., 1972), 97.

15. *Royal Commission on Markets and Tolls*, vol. 2, "Bradford."

16. "New Market Hall," *Huddersfield Weekly News*, 3 Apr. 1880.

CHAPTER 6: Construction, Site, and Materials

1. In fact, it was not until the 1870s that the leading architectural journal, *The Builder*, began to feature articles and illustrations on market hall building plans. Several articles on market hall building were included in John C. Loudon's influential *Architectural Magazine and Journal* in the 1830s. See articles in Loudon's *Architectural Magazine and Journal* (1834-39), vol. 1: "Hungerford New Market, London"; vol. 2: "Liverpool Food Market: St. John's Market"; and vol. 3: "Exeter Higher Market."

2. For a discussion of market design see S. H. Brooks, *Select Designs For Public Buildings: Consisting of Plans, Elevations, Perspective Views, Sections, and Details . . .* (London 1842), 34, 69, 89; the reference to Aylesbury is found in Parliamentary Papers, *Royal Commission on Market Rights and Tolls*, 14 vols. (London, 1888-91, hereafter cited as *Royal Commission on Markets and Tolls*), vol. 8, "Aylesbury."

3. The Warrington debate continued for four years—with the victory going to those who wished to cover the square with a new market hall. See [Warrington] "A Record of Municipal Developments from 1847 to 1947," (Warrington Library), 4; for the Darlington debate, see R. Scarr, "The Shaping of Darlington Centre: Origins of the Clock Tower, Covered Market, and the High Row," *Scarce Cuttings* (book 1, Darlington Library), 24.

4. *Royal Commission on Markets and Tolls*, vol. 4, "Huddersfield."

5. *Royal Commission on Markets and Tolls*, vol. 4, "Accrington."

6. A history of the Liverpool market is found in *Architectural Magazine and Journal* 2 (1835): 130.

7. "Opening of the New Market Hall," unidentified newspaper, Jan. 1870, Burnley Library Newspaper File.

8. *Royal Commission on Markets and Tolls*, vol. 2, "Newark"; "Herbert Yorke" [Archie Scarr], *A Mayor for the Masses: History and Anecdotes of Archibald William Scarr* (Leeds, 1904), 17-18; Waterhouse, quoted in "Southport New Markets Competition," *Building News* 33 (21 Dec. 1877): 656.

9. The reference to "brawling" is from *Royal Commission on Markets and Tolls*, vol. 4, "Reading."

10. *A History of Bolton's Markets* (Bolton Public Library, n.d.), n.p.; [G. T. Rostance], *Centenary of the Opening of the Retail Market Hall, 1853-1953* (County Borough of Wolverhampton, 1953), 7; "Improvements at Southport," *The Builder* 36 (1 Oct. 1881): 433.

11. George E. Street, who was hired by the committee to judge the entries, found Fowler's layout, and his fresh-looking Queen Anne design, to be superior (see *The Builder*, 4 Oct. 1877), but it was rejected by the committee.

12. Proper flooring was much discussed. The Huddersfield experiment with flooring can be found in "New Market Hall, Huddersfield," *Huddersfield Weekly News*, 3 Apr. 1880, 36.

13. The Durham citation is from *The Builder*, 15 Feb. 1851, 100.

14. The reference to the architectural profession is from Frank Jenkins, "The Victorian Architectural Profession," in *Victorian Architecture*, ed. Peter Ferriday (Philadelphia, 1964), 45.

15. Despite a recent positive reassessment of Victorian architecture, the general twentieth-century opinion of the design of Victorian public buildings has held that most of it was little more than application of a neoclassical formula and that function was neglected. Architectural standards for public buildings were low and reflect the so-called barbarism of burgesses (the mayors and members of the town corporations who ran the towns). "Mayors, corporations, and vestries, invited designs for what they wished to build with little more thought of architecture than when they invited tenders for building it" (H. S. Goodheart-Rendel, "Victorian Public Buildings," in *Victorian Architecture*, ed. Ferriday, 87-91, quote on 88). Generally, town officials turned to local architects for public buildings. This purported decline of good architectural taste was intensified, it is argued, in the building profession in the 1830s by the rise of the general contractor, who was a businessman rather than a master craftsman and who had supplanted or replaced the architect. See Jenkins, "The Victorian Architectural Profession," 45. A good, positive reassessment of Victorian building and the history of building types is Thomas A. Markus, *Buildings and Power: Freedom and Control in the Origin of Modern Building Type* (London, 1993).

16. Unpublished memorandum, "Specification for New Market Buildings at Llanelly [Llanelli]," St. Vincent Iron Works, Bristol, to the Chairman, Local Board of Health, Llanelli, 4 Apr. 1894 (Llanelli Library Collection). The memorandum provides the following information with regard to "Quality of Materials":

"The whole of the materials and workmanship to be of good quality to the satisfaction of the Local Board and their Surveyor. The steel to be of the sizes and dimensions given on the Drawing and capable of standing a tensile strain of 24 to 31 tons per square inch with 20% elongation in 8 inches. The sheets to be of contractor's own manufacture and of the best quality. The timber used in the Buildings to be of best quality Baltic red deal or pitch pine, or other approved equal quality, well seasoned, free from sap, shakes, large or loose knots. The roof Boarding to be of best quality Swedish or Norwegian white or other approved brand. The glazing to be of a patent non-putty system."

17. For a discussion of the Carlisle Market Hall see *The Engineer* (13 Apr. 1888): 300-305; and Arthur T. Walmisley, *Iron Roofs* (n.p., 1900), 66-67.

CHAPTER 7: Food, the Market Hall, and the Standard of Living

1. For a general discussion of an "optimist" view with regard to standard of living after about 1750, see Peter Lane, *The Industrial Revolution* (New York, 1978), chapter 14; for the Scottish standard of living see James Treble, "The Standard of Living of the Working Class," in T. M. Devine and Rosland Mitchison, eds., *People and Society in Scotland*, vol. 1 (Edinburgh, 1988); for some working people, real wages appear to have fallen in the 1760s, but the 1770s and 1780s were decades of wage improvement for most people. See G. Holderness, "Agriculture and Industrialization in the Victorian Economy," in G. E. Mingay, ed., *The Victorian Countryside*, vol. 1 (London, 1981), 184; L. D. Schwarz, "Trends in Real Wage Rates, 1750-1790: A Reply to Hunt and Botham," *Economic History Review* 43, no. 1 (1990), 90-103. Schwarz finds that certain Lancashire and Yorkshire workers were spared falling wages in the 1760s.

2. Gregory Clark, Michael Huberman, and Peter H. Lindert argue in "A British Food Puzzle, 1770-1850," *Economic History Review* 48, no. 2 (1995), that all available data on foodstuff supplies show per capita stagnation or even decline from 1770 to 1850—although these estimates, they claim, underestimated the actual supply. One recent claim is that real consumption per capita rose slowly between 1761 and 1770 and 1811 and 1820. See Charles Feinstein, "Capital Accumulation and the Industrial Revolution," in R. Floud and Donald McCloskey, eds., *The Economic History of Britain Since 1700*, vol. 1 (Cambridge, 1981), 136; For shifts in dietary preference see Carole Shammas, "The Eighteenth-Century English Diet and Economic Change," *Explorations in Economic History* 21 (1984), 254-69; For a summary of the arguments with regard to food riots, see John Bohstedt, "The Moral Economy and the Discipline of Historical Context," *Journal of Social History* (Winter 1992), 265-84. John Bohstedt's *Riots and Community Politics in England and Wales, 1790-1810* (Cambridge, Mass., 1983), 211-13, is an excellent study but gives little or no attention to the influence of the local market system on the character of the riot. The estimated number of riots is from Roger Wells, *Wretched Faces: Famine in Wartime England, 1793-1801* (Gloucester, 1988), 98. See also Feinstein, "Capital Accumulation and the Industrial Revolution," and M. W. Flinn, "Trends in Real Wages 1750-1850," *Economic History Review*, 2d ser., vol. 27 (1974). Historians debate whether a "Malthusian crisis" was incipient. Most recently, John Komlos has set forth the argument that such a crisis existed. See Komlos, "Further Thoughts on the Nutritional Status of the British Population," *Economic History Re-*

view 46, no. 2 (1993): 363-66; for the opposing view, see Roderick Floud, Kenneth W. Wachter, and Annabel Gregory, "Further Thoughts on the Nutritional Status of the British Population," *Economic History Review* 46, no. 2 (1993): 367-68. Earlier N. F. R. Crafts argued that it is unlikely that agricultural consumption grew with population; more likely is that in the period 1700-1831 only the top 10 percent of the population enjoyed increased consumption levels. Crafts, "British Economic Growth, 1700-1831," *Economic History Review* 36, no. 2 (1983). See also Roderick Floud, Kenneth W. Wachter, and Annabel Gregory, *Height, Health, and History* (Cambridge, 1990).

3. The Bath diet for 1837 is taken from R. S. Neale, "The Standard of Living, 1780-1844: A Regional and Class Study," *Economic History Review* 19, no. 3 (1966): 599; John Burnett, *Plenty and Want: A Social History of Diet in England from 1815 to the Present Day* (London, 1979), 23-27; Wentworth L. Scott, "On the Supply of Animal Food to Britain and the Means Proposed for Increasing It," *Journal of the Society of Arts* (21 Feb. 1868): 256, 257. Even in mid- and late Victorian Britain it was generally acknowledged that the average person was underfed; indeed, some observers were shocked by the poor physical appearance of the laboring population. The optimist notion of substantial growth after 1820 is based particularly on real-wages data presented in G. N. Von Tunzelmann, "Trends in Real Wages, 1750-1850, Revisited," *Economic History Review*, 2d ser., vol. 32 (1979), and more recently in Peter H. Lindert and J. J. G. Williamson, "Reinterpreting Britain's Social Tables, 1688-1913," in *Explorations in Economic History* 20 (January 1983), and Jeffrey G. Williamson, *Did British Capitalism Breed Inequality?* (London, 1985); on the pessimist side, J. E. Williams's claim of little improvement until after the 1840s is based on the use of aggregates, including national income, capital formation, and capital consumption: see Williams, "The British Standard of Living, 1750-1850," *Economic History Review* 19 (1966); more recently, Joel Moykyr has argued, based on consumption data, that little improvement in consumption occurred before 1850. See Moykyr, "Is There Still Life in the Pessimist Case? Consumption During the Industrial Revolution, 1790-1850," *Journal of Economic History* 63 (March 1988). His argument is based on per capita consumption of tea, sugar, and tobacco. The argument that claims height for evidence of improved diet is challenged by a recent contention that height is conditioned by the disease environment. See Hans-Joachim Voth and Timothy Leunig, "Did Smallpox Reduce Height?" *Economic History Review* XLIX, 3 (1996). See also Paul Johnson and Stephen Nicholas, "Male and Female Living Standards in England and Wales, 1812-1857: Evidence from Criminal Height Records," *Economic History Review* XLVII, 3 (1995): 470-81. For a new pessimistic interpretation in the standard-of-living debate, see Simon Szreter and Graham

Mooney, "Urbanization, Mortality, and the Standard of Living Debate: New Estimates of the Expectation of Life at Birth in Nineteenth-Century British Cities," *Economic History Review* LI, 1 (1998): 84-112. The bread/meat ratio estimate is based on the Shumpeter-Gilboy Index and the index R. S. Neale has constructed for Bath: see R. S. Neale, "The Standard of Living, 1780-1844: A Regional and Class Study," *Economic History Review* 19, no. 3 (1966), 599. Barnsby argues that meat and dairy prices in the Black Country actually rose in price from the 1840s to the mid-1870s—although this estimate is based on purchases for the Poor Law union and not that of the average working-class family who probably took greater advantage of the larger supplies of cheap meat in the market; See George Barnsby, "The Standard of Living in the Black Country During the Nineteenth Century," *Economic History Review*, 2d ser., 24 (1971).

4. The survey was conducted by Dr. Edward Smith, the Medical Officer of Health, in 1864. The evidence is summarized in "The Lives and Deaths of the People," *All the Year Round*, 8 Oct. 1864; John Burnett, *Plenty and Want*, 101.

5. Public health legislation after 1848 gave a boost to wholesale meat firms, which came to dominate much of the distribution trade. See Gareth Shaw, "Changes in Consumer Demand and Food Supply in Nineteenth-Century British Cities," *Journal of Historical Geography* 11, no. 3 (1985); "The Lives and Deaths of the People," in *All the Year Round*, 8 Oct. 1864, 202-03. Meat prices actually rose during the 1850s and 1860s. See W. L. Scott, "On the Supply of Animal Food to Britain," *Journal of the Society of Arts* (21 Feb. 1868): 257. The Black Country estimate is based on purchases made by the local Workhouses in Stourbridge and Wolverhampton; it is not known if those making the purchases took advantage of new lower-priced commodities like frozen meats, as would have been the case of the average working family. See Barnsby, "Standard of Living in the Black Country During the Nineteenth Century"; the nine items were flour, potatoes, bread, beef, mutton, bacon, butter, tea, and sugar. See *British Labour Statistics*, table 87, and Gareth Shaw, "Changes in Consumer Demand and Food Supply in Nineteenth-Century British Cities," *Journal of Historical Geography* 11, no. 3 (1985): 284. On the switch from grain, see G. E. Mingay, ed., *The Agricultural Revolution: Changes in Agriculture, 1650-1880* (London, 1977), 66-68; David Taylor shows that milk production was the largest (and fastest-growing) single sector in English agriculture in the last quarter of the nineteenth century. Small-scale butter making grew, but cheese production fell by two-thirds between about 1870 and 1890: David Taylor, "The English Dairy Industry, 1860-1930," *Economic History Review*, 2d ser., 29 (Nov. 1976), 589-91. The 150 percent estimate is from Roderick Floud and Donald McCloskey, *The Economic History of Britain Since 1700*, vol. 2 (Cambridge, 1978), 133;

the reference to less-skilled workers is from Burnett, *Plenty and Want*, 162. For a vast number of casual workers, the quality and quantity of the food on their tables was partly governed by the rhythms of the labor market: periods of unemployment meant that some or all family members had less to eat. Also, although the thesis is often overstated by middle-class observers, the working-class diet was likewise affected by the amount of the family income spent on alcohol.

6. See John Rule, *The Laboring Classes in Early Industrial England, 1750-1850* (London, 1986), 53-55; also Burnett, *Plenty and Want*, 117-29.

7. Middle- and upper-class consumption of meat had traditionally been very high: 20 to 30 percent of the middle-class family food budget was spent on meat in the 1820s, which was about one-half to three-quarters of a pound of meat per person per day. See Burnett, *Plenty and Want*, 64.

8. We know much more about tea, sugar, and tobacco than we do about other foods because they were imported and therefore the quantities were carefully counted. An alternative to this national accounting approach is to look at consumer demand in high-wage areas, such as the north of England. By the end of the nineteenth century, Lancashire wages were between a quarter and a third higher than Buckinghamshire wages, a situation which often led to substitution of, say, coffee for milk, and wheaten (white) bread for brown bread or porridge oats and oatcakes. The suggestion that regional standard of living inequalities were a product of wage income inequalities is set forth in E. H. Hunt, "Industrialization and Regional Inequality: Wages in Britain, 1760-1914," *Journal of Economic History*, 46, no. 4 (December 1986): 960-61. As early as the eighteenth century there appears to have been a shift away from calcium-rich foods (milk, cheese, and grain products) to wheaten bread, tea, and sugar, particularly in the south. See Carole Shammas, "The Eighteenth-Century English Diet and Economic Change," *Explorations in Economic History* 21 (1984): 254-69. For example, it is probable that concentration on bread and meat prices underestimates long-term improvement and misses an increased variety in diet—as some working people supplemented their diets with cheap fish. The absence of home-produced pork in calculating food-consumption levels is noted by B. R. Mitchell and P. Deane in *Abstract of British Historical Statistics* (Cambridge, 1962). Many other items could be added to this list. On regional variations in food prices see Ian Gazeley, "The Cost of Living for Urban Workers in Late Victorian and Edwardian England," *Economic History Review* 42 (1989): 207-21. Gazeley claims that regional variations were modest, being on the order of 5-7 percent at the most; Gareth Shaw, "Changes in Consumer Demand," 284; E. P. Thompson, *The Making of the English Working Class* (New York, 1966), 291, 305, 316; Dr. Smith estimated that the average cost of a week's food

in Bethnal Green and Spitalfields was 23 pence, while a more nourishing but equal amount of food in Macclesfield was got for 20 pence—a difference of 15 percent. Cited in "The Lives and Deaths of the People," in *All the Year Round*, 8 Oct. 1864, 210; on the relationship between fuel and the quality of the diet see M. Loame, *From Their Point of View* (n.p., 1908, repr. 1980), 159.

9. "With the exception of meat and vegetables, there seems little doubt that by the end of the 18th century the retail trade was largely in the hands of shopkeepers," H. C. Mui and L. Mui, *Shops and Shopkeeping in Eighteenth-Century England* (Kingston, Ont., 1989), 28; see also Burnett, *Plenty and Want*, 146. Burnett does not mention the public market at all. For an argument that the Muis have overestimated the importance of the shop, see the review of their book by S. D. Chapman in *Albion* 23, no. 3 (Fall 1991). In her book *The Impact of English Towns, 1700-1800* (Oxford, 1982), P. J. Corfield is correct in her claim that by 1760 the shop had not superseded the open markets but that, rather, shops complemented the retail markets. The most important study of the food supply of a particular town since Blackman's study of Sheffield is Roger Scola's study of Manchester, *Feeding the Victorian City: The Food Supply of Manchester, 1770-1870* (Manchester, 1992). Scola shows how the retail shop complemented rather than replaced the public market. See also Scola's "Food Markets and Shops in Manchester," *Journal of Historical Geography* 1, no.2 (1975): 153-68. Somewhat the same position is taken by Ian Mitchell in an important study which stresses the coexistence of shop and public market in eighteenth-century Cheshire. Ian Mitchell, "The Development of Urban Retailing 1700-1815," *Journal of Historical Geography* 5 (Spring 1990).

10. See Parliamentary Papers, *Royal Commission on Market Rights and Tolls*, 14 vols. (London, 1888-91, hereafter cited as *Royal Commission on Markets and Tolls*), vol. 4, "Cockermouth"; W. Fordyce, *The History and Antiquities of the County Palatine of Durham*, vol. 1 (n.p., 1857), 359; Borough of Barnstaple, "Proposed New Market House, Report of Committee, 1851," Barnstaple Public Library, NDA box no. 13; *Royal Commission on Markets and Tolls*, vol. 4, "Sheffield"; *Royal Commission on Markets and Tolls*, vol. 9, "Accrington"; the estimate for the Leeds market is from Steven Burt and Kevin Grady, *The Kirkgate Market: An Illustrated History* (Leeds, 1992), 78. For Barnstaple, see *Royal Commission on Markets and Tolls*, vol. 2, "Minutes of Evidence," 88.

11. It was not uncommon for slum dwellers to raise pigs, or for working adults and children to supplement the family diet by collecting nuts, berries, and fruits in the surrounding countryside. Although homegrown food may have declined in many rural areas, such as the south and southeast where enclosure had eliminated cottage plots, a considerable amount of food was still produced in towns themselves. For example, in Glasgow in 1816, 65 "cowfeeders" or dairymen kept 586 cows in the town which provided most of the town's milk; and it was common in the early nineteenth century for some urban dwellers to have their own garden plots (and perhaps a pig or a cow) to provide food for their own use or to be sold in the market. One investigator found an Edinburgh family sharing their quarters with pigs in the upper stories of a tenement; when the owner was asked how a particularly large pig had gotten up the stairs, the owner replied that "it never was down" (source: letter, Burton to Chadwick, 20 July 1840, National Library of Scotland). Many people in Yorkshire, including people in the slums, kept pigs. See Marie Hartley and Joan Ingilby, *Life and Tradition in East Yorkshire* (n.p., 1976), 112; "Memories of Devonport's Market," *Western Evening Herald*, 27 Mar. 1991, 4. Equally important, as fewer agricultural workers were allowed access to their own garden plots and as the practice of the farmer feeding his workers disappeared, rural people became increasingly dependent upon the nearby town market—although it appears that in the southeast of England the village shop, and not the public market, captured much of this new trade. For Torquay, see *Torquay Chronicle*, 4 Oct. 1853; the Glasgow quote is from *Tweeds Guide to Glasgow* (1874), 15.

12. This is based on a comparison of new market construction in the decade ending 1800 and that ending 1850, per Gazetteer data.

13. That market improvement resulted in shifting consumption patterns is suggested in Gregory Clark, Michael Huberman, and Peter H. Lindert, "A British Food Puzzle, 1770-1850," *Economic History Review* XLVIII, 2 (1995); with regard to London's meat and livestock markets, Richard Perren argues that inadequate facilities at the Smithfield meat and livestock markets did not affect the level of meat prices. Richard Perren, "The Meat and Livestock Trade in Britain, 1850-70," *Economic History Review* 28, no. 3 (1975): 385-400. The only study we know that claims that improvement in the public slaughterhouse led to an increase in the local food supply is Shaw, "Changes in Consumer Demand." But in concentrating on the wholesale meat market, Shaw misses the significance of the public retail market. With regard to the retail system, Shaw claims that by 1837 shops were already the major source of groceries—other than for meat and vegetables—for most urban consumers (291) because of the movement of population to residential suburbs. This is not necessarily the case, because in some large cities the urban tramway actually brought many suburban consumers to the central public market. The importance of the shop notwithstanding, the decline in the importance of food shops in the central city of Hull and elsewhere may well have been the result of the growth of the central public market as much as of that of the suburban shop. More than 30,000

square feet of new indoor public market space was built in Hull between 1887 and 1904; *Royal Commission on Markets and Tolls*, vol. 3, "Watford."

14. For Manchester, see Arthur Redford and I. Russell, *The History of the Local Government of Manchester*, vol. 1 (London, 1939), 140; for Aberystwyth, see W. J. Lewis, *Born on a Perilous Rock* (Aberystwyth, 1939), 133. For Bacup, see *Bacup Times*, 24 Aug. 1868; for Burnley, see "Opening of New Market Hall" (scrapbook, Burnley Central Library, n.d.); for Swindon, see "A Visit to Swindon New Town," *The Builder* (13 Dec. 1855): 209. It is also noteworthy that improved food supply was important to local manufacturers, who saw in falling food prices a good justification for cutting wages.

15. The coming of the railroad to Barnstaple brought lower prices and higher supplies: "When I was a boy my mother used to go to Barnstaple to buy butter . . . to lay a stock for the year because she could get it cheaper," remembered one witness: Testimony of Mr. Clements, *Royal Commission on Markets and Tolls*, vol. 3, "Bideford." Wooler's market, once served by wagons drawn by eight horses but then bypassed by the railroad, was described as a town "lost in a long day-dream," where the market was virtually dead and the shops dull and dingy (*The Builder*, 16 Dec. 1876, 1215).

16. Outhwaite has argued that government intervention diminished after the 1630s and that food rioting increased in the eighteenth century: R. B. Outhwaite, *Dearth, Public Policy and Social Disturbance in England, 1550-1800* (Basingstoke, 1991), chap. 4. For an example of distribution according to rank, see *Carlisle Journal*, 4 Oct. 1889, 5; with regard to the paucity of attention to nineteenth-century reform on the local level, a helpful synthesis of the subject of reform from the central level is Eric Midwinter's *Victorian Social Reform* (London, 1968). However, Midwinter does not look at local government reform initiatives before 1848 other than in public health.

17. For the desire to secure the town's food supply see: "15 June 1804: Petition of the Glasgow Town Council to Parliament," in J. D. Marwick, ed., *Extracts from the Records of the Burgh of Glasgow*, vol. 9 (Glasgow, 1876-1917); for Kent see Arnold Toynbee, *The Industrial Revolution in England* (London, 1883, rev. ed., 1908), 38; and for Haddington, see John Sinclair, ed., *The Statistical Account of Scotland, 1791-1799*, vol. 2, introduction by T. C. Smout (Edinburgh, 1975), 449-59.

18. Hucksters and higglers—wholesalers—are common today in some of the southwest pannier markets and can still be seen in markets (e.g., Newton Abbot) with stalls for eggs; the idea of the poor having access to the town's food supply is part of the argument of the so-called moral economy, set forth by the historian E. P. Thompson in "The Moral Economy and the English Crowd in the Eighteenth Century," *Past and Present* 50 (1971): 96-136. As Thompson notes, these assumptions were losing ground by the early nineteenth century.

19. For Lancaster, see "The New Market Hall," *Lancaster Guardian*, 29 May 1880. Higglers were blocked from the Bristol market until midday: see John Latimer, *Annals of Bristol*, vol. 2 (1893, repr. 1970), 193; on buying outside the market see Leonard T. Weaver, *The Harwich Story* (n.p., 1975), 102; for Tiverton, see "Market Medley," *Market Trader*, June 1964, 16. Testimony in a Manchester court in 1671 revealed the abuse perceived by the townspeople when "several persons living within the said town, and also others that come from remote places, in buying up of cheese, butter, eggs, bacon, pullen, and with all sorts of fruit, by ingrossing them to sell again by retail, so that the inhabitants are either forced to buy of them who so ingrossed them, or else be unsupplied." See *Manchester Court Leet Records*, vol. 5, p. 148 (cited in Redford and Russell, *Local Government of Manchester*, vol. 1, p. 136).

20. On local pressure to repeal the Corn Laws see James Cleland, *Annals of Glasgow* (Glasgow, 1816), vol. 2, p. 46; "Market Drayton," *Shropshire Magazine*, Aug. 1975, 33; for Winchester see "The Opening of the New Market House, *Hampshire Chronicle, Southhampton and Isle of Wight Courier*, 8 Oct. 1857, 3; this was about the same time that Glasgow deregulated the price of bread by eliminating the assize. See Marwick, *Extracts*, vol. 9, 2 June 1801 and 5 Nov. 1808; see also Sidney Webb and Beatrice Webb, *English Local Government from the Revolution to the Municipal Corporations Act: The Manor and the Borough*, vol. 3 (London, 1921), 513; for Bristol see John Latimer, ed., *The Annals of Bristol in the Nineteenth Century* (Bristol, 1887).

21. For a discussion of waste of nutritious food arising directly from the poor market facilities, see *The Builder* (11 Nov. 1882): 611; for the perception that only the highest classes knew how to prepare and serve food, see *Journal of the Society of the Arts*, 15 Feb. 1867, 190, and 4 Jan. 1867, 101; the Durham citation is found in W. Fordyce, *History and Antiquities of the County Palatine of Durham*, vol. 1 (Durham, 1857), 359-60.

22. *Royal Commission on Markets and Tolls*, vol. 4, "Wakefield"; the Stockport demolitions took place in 1824 and again in 1868. "Survey of the Market Place" (typescript, Stockport Library General Information File); "The Fete: Lord Derby in Southport," *Southport Visiter*, 19 Sept. 1879.

23. For Carlisle, see *Carlisle Journal*, 4 Oct. 1889, 6; for Winchester see the *Hampshire Chronicle*, 3 Oct. 1857, 3; for Manchester, see Arthur Redford and I. Russell, *The History of the Local Government of Manchester*, vol. 3 (London, 1939), 57; for Mayor Scarr of Leeds see the *Royal Commission on Markets and Tolls*, vol. 4, "Leeds," and also Scarr's autobiography (under the pseudonym

Chapter Seven
cont'd

"Herbert Yorke"), *Mayor for the Masses: History and Anecdotes of Archibald William Scarr* (Leeds, 1904); for Burnley see *The Builder*, 21 Sept. 1878, 996. See also *Huddersfield Daily Chronicle*, 1 Apr. 1880; and "Opening of the New Market Hall," Jan. 1870 (unidentified newspaper, Burnley Library news clippings file); for Liverpool, see City of Liverpool, *Report of the Manager of the City Markets, Liverpool*, Reports for 1920, 1921, 1930.

24. *Royal Commission on Markets and Tolls*, vol. 4, "Hull," and vol. 9, "Bridgwater"; *The Huddersfield Weekly*, 3 Apr. 1880, 3; for Winchester see *Hampshire Chronicle*, 9 Feb. 1856, 3; "Lancaster's Markets, 1193-1880" (typescript, Lancaster Public Library), Pt. 8854, 14.

25. For Ipswich, see R. L. Cross, *Ipswich Markets and Tolls* (Ipswich, 1965), chapter titled "New Market, 1810-1888"; for Kidderminster see Parliamentary Papers, *Report of the Royal Commission on Municipal Corporations* (London, 1835-39), Pt. 3, "Kidderminster" (1835); for Harrogate, see *Royal Commission on Markets and Tolls*, vol. 4, "Harrogate"; for Reading, see *Royal Commission on Markets and Tolls*, vol. 4, "Reading"; the reference to Doncaster and Sheffield is found in *Royal Commission on Markets and Tolls*, vol. 9, "Rotherham"; for Watford, see *Royal Commission on Markets and Tolls*, vol. 3, "Watford"; for Rochdale, see *Royal Commission on Markets and Tolls*, vol. 9, "Rochdale"; for Liverpool, see City of Liverpool, *Report of the Manager of the City Markets*, Reports 1925-1926, 1926, 1926-27.

26. For Taunton, see David Bush, *The Book of Taunton* (Taunton, 1977), 57, and the *Royal Commission on Markets and Tolls*, "Minutes of Evidence," vol. 2 (1888) q. 5590-99; for Oxford, see *Royal Commission on Markets and Tolls*, vol. 4, "Oxford," and "Final Report," 62. It is not surprising that some of the opposition to market building came from butchers who feared that a new public market might force them to give up their shops. See, for example, *Royal Commission on Markets and Tolls*, vol. 8, "Peterborough"; Charles A. Wilson, *Aberdeen of Auld Lang Syne* (Aberdeen, 1948), 70.

27. Poultry is not considered in assessments of diet because no workable statistical base exists for calculating poultry production, and hence, the meat component of the nineteenth-century diet is limited to beef and pork. The reference to Sheffield is from the author of a Society for Promoting Christian Knowledge investigation on Sheffield and cited in Sidney Pollard, "Sheffield," in Andrew Lees and Lynn Lees, eds., *The Urbanization of European Society in the Nineteenth Century* (Lexington, Mass., 1976), 202. In 1847 the residents of Harrogate had to travel to the weekly market at Knaresborough, three miles distant, or rely on street hawkers. The *Harrogate Advertiser* commented: "The whole town now has not a confectioner's, a fishmonger's or a poulterer's shop. . . . All the fish Harrogate ever

beholds is brought by a fishwoman who generally disposes of her principal stock at the hotels by ten in the morning and leaves the private boarding houses and the town to make what shift they can." Cited in Bernard Jennings, ed., *A History of Harrogate and Knaresborough* (n.p., 1969), 106.

28. For an example of efforts to bring "country butchers" to the town market, see J. D. Marwick, ed., *Extracts from the Records of the Burgh of Glasgow*, vol. 8 (Glasgow, 1876-1917), 28 Nov. 1782; the stated purpose behind the new Glasgow cattle market was to "ensure a more steady and plentiful supply of butcher meat of the best quality and in some cases, such as in Glasgow, to break the monopoly of the meat trade formerly in the hands of an elite group of [incorporated] butchers." See *Glasgow Herald*, 11 July 1817, 1, and James Cleland, *Former and Present Times* (Glasgow, 1836), 22-28; for Redruth, see Frank Mitchel, *Notes on the History of Redruth* (n.p., 1948), 101; for Truro see *Pigot's Directory, Cornwall, 1844* (n.p., 1844), and Williams's *Directory, Cornwall, 1847* (n.p., 1847); in nearby Yeovil, the number of town butchers increased after a new market hall was built, from thirteen in 1842 to sixteen in 1850. *Pigot's Directory, Somersetshire, 1842*, and *Hunt's Directory, Yeovil, 1850*; for Manchester, see Louis Hayes, *Reminiscences of Manchester from 1840* (London, 1905), 125; Newcastle's market is described in "Icharletoni" [R. J. Charleton], *The Streets of Newcastle* (Newcastle, 1885-86), 209; it appears, overall, that the proportion of Newcastle's meat sales in the public markets was at its highest in the 1860s and 1870s, after which many butchers began to set up in private shops.

29. For the discussion of the paucity of fruits and vegetables in the average diet, see Peter Ambrose, *The Quiet Revolution: Social Change in a Sussex Village, 1871-1971* (London, 1974), 20; see also D. J. Oddy, "Working-Class Diets in Late Nineteenth Century Britain," *Economic History Review*, 2d ser., vol. 23 (1970): 314; the argument is accepted by Elizabeth Roberts in "Working-Class Standards of Living in Barrow and Lancaster, 1890-1914," *Economic History Review*, 2d ser. vol. 30 (May 1977): 312; the Edinburgh citation is from Sinclair, *Statistical Account of Scotland*, 44, 212; The reference to Sheffield's vegetables is from Sidney Pollard in Andrew Lees and Lynn Lees, eds., *The Urbanization of European Society in the Nineteenth Century* (Lexington, Mass., 1976), 202.

30. Elizabeth Roberts, "Using Oral History," *Journal of Oral History* 3, no. 2 (1974): 17.

31. John Chalmers, "A General History of Worcester," 1819 (manuscript, Hereford and Worcester Record Office).

32. *Royal Commission on Markets and Tolls*, vol. 3, "Dorchester"; on the waste of fish see W. L. Scott, "On the Supply of Animal Food to Britain," *Journal of the Society of Arts* (21 Feb. 1868): 257.

33. *The Builder*, 19 May 1883, 664. Neither per capita fish consumption data nor retail fish price data are given serious consideration in most cost-of-living assessments. For example, Bowley's standard price indexes are based on sources which did not include fish, and recent studies make use of figures on salmon fish only. See A. L. Bowley, *Wages and Income in the United Kingdom Since 1860* (Cambridge, 1937), Ian Gazeley, "The Cost of Living for Urban Workers in Late Victorian and Edwardian Britain," *Economic History Review* 2 (1989), 218, and A. R. Prest and A. A. Adams, *Consumers' Expenditure in the United Kingdom, 1900-1919* (Cambridge, 1954). Barnsby's workhouse figures for the second half of the nineteenth century do not include fish: see Barnsby, "Standard of Living in the Black Country During the Nineteenth Century." The Black Country town of Bilston, for example, had eight fish shops and eleven butchers' shops in its new market hall of 1892—suggesting that not only was fish an important part of the local diet but also that it enjoyed a popularity akin to that of butcher meat. See Gazetteer, "Bilston." Also, the proximity of Black Country towns to Birmingham's important fish markets makes it probable that fish was an important part of Black Country diet: *Royal Commission on Markets and Tolls*, vol. 8, "Peterborough"; The Billingsgate fish story first appeared in the *Quarterly Review* (Fall 1888): 444, and then in *The Builder*, 11 Nov. 1888, 611.

34. Fish prices in Newcastle fell from a range of 9-20 pence to a range of 1-1$^1/_2$ pence per pound. *Royal Commission on Markets and Tolls*, vol. 4, "Newcastle"; for Bristol, see John Latimer, *Annals of Bristol in the Nineteenth Century* (1887), 6; for Birmingham, see Birmingham Markets and Fairs Commission, *Minutes and Reports*, vol. 4, 349-56; *Royal Commission on Markets and Tolls*, vol. 2, "Birmingham"; on Birmingham's fish supply compared with that of London, see *The Builder*, 25 Oct. 1884, 573; for Bradford, see *Royal Commission on Markets and Tolls*, vol. 4, "Bradford"; for Durham, see *Royal Commission on Markets and Tolls*, vol. 4, "Durham"; for Lancashire markets, see Manchester Corporation Market Committee, *Report on the Condition of the Sale and Supply of Fish at Ports* (1905), 3-4; "Food Committee Report," *Journal of the Society of the Arts* (10 January, 1868): 124; Burnett states that the average working-class table included fish three times a week (Burnett, *Plenty and Want*, 164). Glasgow's imports of fish increased fivefold between 1883 and 1914 (from 213,621 packages to 1,272,493 packages). See *Municipal Glasgow, Its Evolution and Enterprises* (Glasgow, 1914), 141; the number of fishing vessels at Hull, in 1868, had increased twentyfold to meet demand ("Food Committee Report," 124). It is claimed that "the invention" of fish and chips took place in Oldham in 1880: See Ambrose, *Quiet Revolution*, 20.

35. For Burnley, see *Royal Commission on Markets and Tolls*, vol. 9, "Burnley"; for Southport, see *Royal Commission on Markets and Tolls*, vol. 9, "Southport"; for Bolton, see *Royal Commission on Markets and Tolls*, vol. 9, "Bolton"; for a discussion of the use of the wholesale market for the poor, see *Royal Commission on Markets and Tolls*, vol. 8, "Brighton," and Janet Blackman, "The Food Supply of an Industrial Town: A Study of Sheffield's Public Markets, 1780-1900," *Business History* 5-6 (1962-63): 97.

36. For Pontypool see *Building News*, 31 Mar. 1893, 437; for Stalybridge, see *Royal Commission on Markets and Tolls*, vol. 9, "Stalybridge."

37. For Truro, see *West Briton and Cornwall Advertiser*, 12 Nov. 1842, 2; "selling up" the day's market goods was practiced in Accrington until at least 1910. See "Richard Looks Back on the Markets of Old," *Accrington Observer and Times*, 22 Nov. 1975; "Liverpool Life," *Liverpool Mercury*, 2d ser., no. 5 (1857): 90; on the working-class Saturday-night shopping habits see [Thomas Wright], *The Great Unwashed, by the Journeymen Engineer* (n.p., 1868, repr. London, 1970), and on the importance of cheap Saturday meat for the working classes, see M. Loame, *From Their Point of View* (n.p., 1908, repr. 1980), 159.

38. All in all it is difficult to argue, as Rule and others have (see Rule, *Laboring Classes in Early Industrial England*, 63), that markets sold unwholesome food at unfair prices.

CHAPTER 8: Patterns of Growth and Reform

1. Asa Briggs, *The Collected Essays of Asa Briggs*, vol. 1 (Urbana, Ill., 1985), 55. The only national survey of markets taken in the nineteenth century was the Parliamentary Markets and Fairs Commission survey of 1887-91. Its published reports provide information about market facilities and administration (including tolls) in several hundred English, Welsh, and Scottish towns. The investigators were less interested in the quantity and quality of the food supply than in the administration of the markets and the fairness of the rates and tolls. Although the second survey, the 1927 Ministry of Agriculture's *Report on Markets and Fairs*, was largely an investigation into facilities for the wholesale distribution of food and did not attempt to measure the relative importance of the public market as a retail center, it does provide important information about actual retail facilities. For a full citation of these sources and other sources see the note on sources at the beginning of the Gazetteer.

2. For a discussion of the era's building patterns see R. A. Church, *The Great Victorian Boom, 1850-1873* (Basingstoke, 1986), 34-36, 52.

3. B. A. Holderness, "The Victorian Farmer," in G. E. Mingay, ed., *The Victorian Countryside*, vol. 1 (London, 1981), 228.

4. J. D. Chambers and G. E. Mingay, *The Agricultural Revolution, 1750-1880* (London, 1966, repr., 1982), 110-11, 140, 182; farms in the south and east were larger than those in the west. Aside from grain production, the southeast produced

milk and orchard products, much of which went to London. See Hugh Prince, "Victorian Rural Landscapes," in Mingay, *Victorian Countryside*, vol. 1, p. 18.

5. The estimates on the regional distribution of shops are taken from Hoh-Cheung Mui and Lorna H. Mui, *Shops and Shopkeeping in Eighteenth-Century England* (London, 1989), 38-41.

6. The need to encourage town shopping for rural-based handloom weavers was the conclusion of one of the parliamentary commissioners, a Mr. Chapman: Parliamentary Papers, *Royal Commission on Market Rights and Tolls*, 14 vols. (London, 1888-91, hereafter cited as *Royal Commission on Markets and Tolls*), vol. 11, "Final Report" (1891), 58; see also Geoffrey Timmins, *The Last Shift: The Decline in Handloom Weaving in Lancashire* (Manchester, 1991), 58.

7. Friedrich Engels, *The Condition of the Working Class in England*, ed. W. O. Henderson and W. H. Chaloner (1845; Stanford, Calif., 1958), 50-51, 80-81, 86, 80.

8. Charles Feinstein, "What Really Happened to Real Wages? Trends, Prices, and Productivity in the United Kingdom, 1880-1913," *Economic History Review* 43, no. 3 (1990): 329-55.

9. See John Boyd Orr, *Poor Health and Income: Report on a Survey of Adequacy of Diet in Relation to Income* (London, 1936), 19.

10. For a discussion of the Aberystwyth case, see W. J. Lewis, *Born on a Perilous Rock* (Aberystwyth, 1980), 135-36.

11. The 1858 provisions were subsequently incorporated into the Public Health Act of 1875. Action was limited to urban sanitary authorities—namely, boroughs, Improvement Commissions Districts, and Local Government Districts. In Scotland identical powers were granted by way of the General Police and Improvement (Scotland) Act of 1862. For a discussion of these provisions, see *Royal Commission on Markets and Tolls*, vol. 11, "Final Report" (1891).

12. Between 1850 and 1875, British railway freight tonnage increased from an estimated 38 million tons to 199.9 million tons. Much of this was food. See Jeffrey Richard and John M. MacKenzie, *The Railway Station: A Social History* (Oxford, 1986), 190; for a general discussion of the coming of railway service, see G. E. Mingay, *The Transformation of Britain, 1830-1939* (London, 1986), 53-55, and Anthony Sutcliffe, "In Search of the Urban Variable: Britain in the Late Nineteenth Century," in Derek Fraser and Anthony Sutcliffe, eds., *The Pursuit of Urban History* (London, 1990), 239-40; for Worksop see *Royal Commission on Markets and Tolls*, vol. 8, "Worksop," The Hertfordshire town was Rickmansworth. See "Hertfordshire," *Victoria History of the Counties of England: Hertfordshire*, vol. 2 (London, 1908), 37.

13. *Royal Commission on Markets and Tolls*, vol. 4, "Bradford." The best single discussion of the impact of the railway on a particular town marketing system is found in Janet Blackman, "The Food Supply of an Industrial Town: A Study of Sheffield's Public Markets, 1780-1960," *Business History* 94 (1962-63): 83-97.

14. The Accrington quote is from "Laying of the Cornerstone of the New Market Hall," *Accrington Times*, 23 May 1868.

CHAPTER 9: The Grand Age of the Market Hall, 1830-90

1. See Andrew Davies, "Saturday Night Markets in Manchester and Salford, 1840-1939," *Manchester Region Historical Review* 1, no. 2 (Autumn-Winter, 1987): 4.

2. The reference to "young lovers" is from Parliamentary Papers, *Royal Commission on Market Rights and Tolls*, 14 vols. (London, 1888-91, hereafter cited as *Royal Commission on Markets and Tolls*), vol. 9, "Huddersfield"; for a description of the popularity of Liverpool's market hall see *Liverpool Echo*, 7 Apr. 1950 (Liverpool Central Library News Clipping Collection); the St. John's Market poem is by Colin Brooks, cited in *Liverpolitan* 19 (Sept. 1947) (Liverpool Central Library News Clippings Collection).

3. The reference to Newcastle is from "Icharletoni" [R. J. Charleton], *The Streets of Newcastle* (Newcastle, 1885-86), 210; the reference to Birmingham's fountain is from *Birmingham Market and Fairs Committee, Minutes and Reports*, vol. 1 (2 Jan. 1852).

4. For Bolton, see Alice Foley, *A Bolton Childhood*, cited in *A History of Bolton Markets* (n.p., n.d.); the Shudehill quote is from *The Free Lance* (May 1867), cited in Davis, "Saturday Night Markets in Manchester and Salford, 1840-1939," 4.

5. *Tweed's Guide to Glasgow* (n.p., 1874), 15.

6. "Icharletoni," *Streets of Newcastle*, 210.

7. For an example of the market hall being used for public affairs in Newcastle, see Lyall Wilkes, *John Dobson, Architect and Landscape Gardener* (Stocksfield, 1980), 2, and *Seven Hundred Years of History of Stockport Market* (n.p., n.d.), for events in Stockport.

8. For examples of the impact of new kinds of transport on markets, see *Liverpool Market Committee Minutes*, vol. 1 (9 Apr. 1842); also, for Darwen and Burnley, the Lancashire Library, *A History of Darwen's Market Hall, 1882-1982* (1982), 7; "Oldham's New Market," *Oldham Chronicle*, 7 Apr. 1906; for the Leicestershire (and Leicester) markets, see Alan Everitt, "Town and County in Victorian Leicestershire: The Rule of the Village Carrier," in Alan Everitt, ed., *Perspectives in English Urban History* (London, 1973), 235-38.

9. For Leicester, see Everitt, "Town and County in Victorian Leicestershire," 236-38; for Hull, see *Royal Commission on Markets and Tolls*, vol. 4, "Hull"; for Bideford, see Cecil Callacott, *Memories of Old Bradworthy* (n.p., 1979), 16, and *The Gazette-North Devon Directory* (1935), 153.

10. For Scarborough, see *Royal Commission on Markets and Tolls*, vol. 4, "Scarborough"; for Warrington, see Pete Williams, *Warrington in Camera* (Warrington, 1981), 27; for Blackburn, see *Royal Commission on Markets and Tolls*, vol. 9, "Blackburn"; on the discussions of how nineteenth-century women were generally excluded from public life, see Leonore Davidoff and Catherine Hall, "The Architecture of Public and Private Life," in Derek Fraser and Anthony Sutcliffe, eds., *The Pursuit of Urban History* (London, 1990).

11. The quote from Aberdeen is from Charles Wilson, *Aberdeen of Auld Lang Syne* (n.p., n.d.), 70; for St. John's Market see *Pictorial Liverpool* (n.p., ca. 1848), 235; *Ward and Lock's Guide to Liverpool*, 8th ed. (Liverpool, n.d.), 82; for Dundee, see *Dundee Advertiser*, 30 May 1877.

12. *Royal Commission on Markets and Tolls*, vol. 3, "Bristol"; ibid., "Exeter"; "Dewsbury Public Market," *The [Dewsbury] Reporter*, 25 Sept. 1925; *Royal Commission on Markets and Tolls*, vol. 4, "Sunderland"; ibid., "Windsor"; vol. 9, "Ashton-under-Lyne."

13. The reference to Glasgow is from "By-Laws for the Glasgow Bazaar" (n.p., 1883), sec. 28; Wilson, *Aberdeen*, 70; *Salisbury Journal*, 6 June 1958; in Ipswich, boys from the ragged school acted as porters at the public market; on opening day, they dressed in "red Garibaldi shirts and corduroy trousers": see R. L. Cross, "New Market, 1810-1888," *Ipswich Markets and Fairs* (n.p., 1965), n.p.

14. Arnold Bennett, *Clayhanger* (New York, 1910), 154.

15. The only reference we could find to a market (outside of London) being open on Sundays was to Leeds in 1906; see *Leeds Market Committee Minutes*, vol. 8, p. 295; for reference to Exeter's market openings see Robert Newton, *Victorian Exeter* (Leicester, 1968), 272, 309.

16. "Report on Manchester Markets," *Liverpool Market Committee Minutes*, 6 May 1872.

17. Saturday was added as a regular shopping day at the Barnstaple Market Hall in the 1980s.

18. As late as 1948 the market hall in Blackburn employed more than 1,500 persons: Blackburn Markets Committee, *Centenary Souvenir Handbook* (n.p., 1948), 49; *Liverpool Echo*, 7 Apr. 1850 (Liverpool Library News Clipping Collection).

19. Goronwy Rees, *St Michael: A History of Marks and Spencer* (London, 1969), 6-7, 14.

20. "Market Medley," *Market Trader*, 8 Oct. 1949; this is based on a count of *Kelly's Directory* (1904, 1924, and 1937).

21. This was the case in Southport: *The Southport Visiter*, 21 Oct. 1913, 12.

22. On fixed pricing see *Royal Commission on Markets and Tolls*, vol. 9, "Minutes of Evidence," 5.

23. For Rugeley, see J. A. Johnson, "The Markets and Fairs of Rugeley, 1219-1977" (dissertation, Ordinary National Diploma in Business Studies, Stafford College, 1977); for Glasgow, see *Bye-Laws for the Glasgow Bazaar*, sec. 15. In addition, article 25 outlawed hawking goods within the market.

24. For Swansea, see "Swansea Always Had Plans for the Market," *Evening Post*, 2 June 1954; for Durham, see W. Fordyce, *History and Antiquities of the County Palatinate of Durham*, vol. 1 (n.p., 1857), 362; for Blackburn, see P. A. Whittle, *Blackburn As It Was: A Topographical Statistical, and Historical Account* (Blackburn, 1852), 123; for Birmingham, see *Birmingham Market and Fairs Committee, Minutes and Reports, 1851-1878*, vol. 1 (12 Feb. 1852).

25. S. Vallings and L. Wood, *A Photographer's Dewsbury: Shops and Shopping* (n.p., n.d.), 76; *Royal Commission on Markets and Tolls*, vol. 9, "Wigan," "Stalybridge"; the Bradford market description is found in a report: City of Glasgow Improvement Trust, *Report by Special Subcommittee to Consider the Establishment of a Public Market in St. Andrew's Square* (n.p., 1883), n.p.; and for Rochdale, see *Rochdale Observer*, 10 Apr. 1982, 63.

26. The citation on aesthetic choice is from Remy Saisselin, *The Bourgeois and the Bibelot* (New Brunswick, N.J., 1984), xiii; Thomas Richards argues that the roots of "commodity culture" lay in mid-nineteenth century advertising—particularly in the kind of images set forth in the Crystal Palace Exhibition of 1851. Thomas Richards, *The Commodity Culture of Victorian England: Advertising and Spectacle, 1851-1914* (Stanford, Calif., 1990); for the Oldham citation, see *Royal Commission on Markets and Tolls*, vol. 9, "Oldham"; Bennett, *Clayhanger*, 244, 316-18; John C. Loudon, *An Encyclopedia of Cottage, Farm, and Villa Architecture* (1833; rev. ed., London, 1841), 845.

27. See Andrew Davies, "Saturday Night Markets in Manchester and Salford, 1840-1939," *Manchester Region Historical Review* 1, no. 2 (Autumn-Winter 1987): 4; see also *Hampshire Chronicle*, 3 Oct. 1857, 3.

28. *Royal Commission on Markets and Tolls*, vol. 9, "Castleford"; ibid., "Exeter"; ibid., vol. 3, "Torquay," 282-88.

29. *Royal Commission on Markets and Tolls*, vol. 9, "Burnley."

30. "Opening of Market," *Dundee Advertiser*, 10 Dec. 1881; for Burnley, see *Royal Commission on Markets and Tolls*, vol. 9, "Burnley"; for Liverpool, see "More Market Muddling," *Liverpool Review*, 6 Aug. 1887, 10; the law with

Chapter Nine
cont'd

regard to "hand-selling" in Liverpool is found in bylaw 44: City of Liverpool, *Council Proceedings* (13 Dec. 1893): 66; for Newcastle, see "Icharletoni," *Streets of Newcastle*, 35; "Conceived in Uncertainty," *Darlington Times*, 24 Feb. 1962; R. A. Barton, ed., *Life in Cornwall in the Early Nineteenth Century* (Truro, 1970), 132; *Birmingham Market and Fairs Committee, Minutes and Reports*, vol. 1 (28 Dec. 1854); Leeds Market Committee, "Minutes," vol. 5 (30 June 1878), 19; for Ashton, see *Ashton Weekly Reporter*, 9 Feb. 1856; on denial of tenancy, see Leeds Market Committee, "Minutes," vol. 7 (1899), 344.

31. The remark about strife and contention is found in *West Briton and Cornwall Advertiser*, 12 Nov. 1842, 2; for Redruth, see Frank Mitchell, *Annals of an Ancient Cornish Town* (n.p., 1978), 134; for Wolverhampton, see G. T. Rostance, *Centenary of the Opening of the Retail Market, 1853-1953* (1953), 7 (a pamphlet); see also Leeds Market Committee, "Minutes," vol. 8 (1906), 231, 295.

32. *Royal Commission on Markets and Tolls*, vol. 8, "Peterborough"; ibid., vol. 9, "Burnley"; ibid., vol. 3, "Bath."

33. T. Mckeown and R. G. Record argue that improved diet was a principal influence in the reduction of mortality of the second half of the nineteenth century. It is difficult, if not impossible, to quantify the impact improved market facilities had on this improvement, although contemporaries thought it significant: see Mckeown and Record, "Reasons for Decline of Mortality," *Population Studies* 16 (1963): 94-122.

34. The reference to Lancashire is from E. P. Thompson, *The Making of the English Working Class* (New York, 1966), 316; the reference to the stink of the streets is from Robert Renwick, *Glasgow Memorials* (Glasgow, 1908), 88.

35. John Burnett, *Plenty and Want: A Social History of Diet in England from 1815 to the Present Day* (London, 1966), 82-90; for Glasgow, see "Sale of Diseased Meat," *Glasgow Herald*, 20 Apr. 1889.

36. Arthur Redford and G. Russell, *The History of Local Government in Manchester*, vol. 3 (n.p., n.d.), 71; the London citation is found in John Hobson, *Problems of Poverty* (London, 1891), 12; the chemical analysis survey is found in "Report of the Analytical Sanitary Commission," *Lancet* (17 Apr. 1858): 398; the 1861 reference to London is from W. L. Scott, "On Food, Its Adulteration and the Methods of Detecting Them," *Journal of the Society of the Arts* 9 (1 Feb. 1861): 156-58.

37. *Royal Commission on Markets and Tolls*, vol. 4, "Hull."

38. The reference to the local boards of health is from "Conceived in Uncertainty," *Darlington Times*, 24 Feb. 1962; for Harrogate, see Harold Walker, *History of Harrogate Under the Improvement Commissioners, 1841-1884* (n.p., 1986), 338; for Liverpool, see *Ward and Lock's Illustrated Guide to Liverpool*, 8th ed. (Liverpool, n.d.), 82.

39. For Manchester market inspection, see J. T. Slugg, *Reminiscences of Manchester Fifty Years Ago* (n.p., 1881; repr. 1971), 240; for Edinburgh, see David Robertson and Marguerite Wood, *Castle and Town: Chapters in the History of the Royal Burgh of Edinburgh* (Edinburgh, 1928), 261; for Manchester's market after its sale by Lord Mosely, see *Manchester Proceedings*, vol. 4, 1849-50 (Dec. 1849), 23; for Truro, see R. M. Barton, *Life in Cornwall in the Early Nineteenth Century* (Truro, 1970), 173.

40. Arthur Redford and I. S. Russell, *The History of Local Government in Manchester*, vol. 3 (Manchester, 1940), 72-75.

41. The making and remaking of market bylaws was usually possible only through an act of Parliament. Between 1801 and 1891 some 319 English, Scottish, and Welsh towns initiated private acts of Parliament for the specific purpose of market reform—which often included strengthening and revising market bylaws. It was generally acknowledged that the transfer of ownership from private to public hands meant better sanitary conditions in the market because bylaws could be changed (see figure 8.7).

By the 1850s most large towns had placed rigid controls on the slaughtering of cattle, often by forcing all butchers to use a public slaughterhouse under municipal inspection (and, often, ownership). In the late eighteenth century, Glasgow was a pioneer among large towns in eliminating all private slaughterhouses in the city. Torquay eliminated all seventeen of its private slaughtering yards in the mid-nineteenth century, and Manchester in the 1870s; for a discussion of Dr. Carlyon see *West Briton and Cornwall Advertiser*, 12 Nov. 1847, 2, and for Dr. Middleton see "Salisbury Market House and Railway," *Salisbury and Winchester Journal*, 28 May 1859, 6; "Oldham New Market Hall" (typescript, Oldham City Library, 26 Sept. 1904).

42. Much inspection legislation simply reflected local practice. For example, section 910.15 of the Markets and Fairs Clauses Act of 1847, which prohibited the sale or exposure for sale in the market of any unwholesome meat or provisions and mandated that market officials confiscate such provisions for inspection, was merely echoing what in most markets was long-established policy; the Birmingham experience is related in *Birmingham Market and Fairs Committee Minutes and Reports*, vol. 2 (29 Oct. 1858).

43. J. R. Kaighin, *Bygone Birkenhead* (n.p., 1925), 78; a nationwide Market Authorities Association was formed in 1920 in Manchester.

CHAPTER 10: The Market and the Retail Revolution, 1890-1939

1. In only a few cities did the department store make a dent in the fortunes of the public market. Glasgow was probably the most noteworthy. As early as the mid-nineteenth century, Glasgow

was so advanced in mass retailing by way of "provision warehouses" (actually early department stores) which catered to the clothing and accessories needs of the middle and working class people, and the food chain stores, or multiple shops, such as Lipton's, that the public market suffered. The giant iron-framed "Commercial Crystal Palace" of Wylie and Lochhead in 1855 was a provision warehouse, to be followed several decades later by the department stores like Owen Owen's and Bon Marché in Liverpool—although these were much more the shopping meccas of the middle class and probably detracted only slightly from the market hall. By 1915 the department store accounted for only 3 percent of the nation's retail business. See J. B. Jefferys, *Retail Trading in Britain, 1850-1950* (Cambridge, 1954), 18-21; the Glasgow citations are from "Report by the Deputation Appointed by the Town Council of Glasgow to Visit Various Towns in England, . . . Regarding . . . Public Markets There" (Strathclyde Archives, SRA D-TC.14.8), 11-12.

2. The authors thank Mr. K. Powls and Mr. Derek Day for providing this information.

3. *Beedle Handbook of Weston-Super-Mare* (n.p., 1863), 27.

4. Lament over the decline of the public market may be found in Parliamentary Papers, *Royal Commission on Market Rights and Tolls*, 14 vols. (London, 1888-91, hereafter cited as *Royal Commission on Markets and Tolls*), vol. 8, "Cambridge"; ibid., vol. 3, "Bath." A depression in agriculture in the 1870s through much of the 1890s—the so-called Great Depression—actually helped increase the domestic food supply as many farmers diversified into fruit and vegetable cultivation, which led to increases in carrots, cabbages, peas, beans, sprouts, potatoes, berries, and fruit for national consumption. The effect of this for the local market, however, was that garden farming fell increasingly under the control of large farms and national wholesalers. By the 1920s more than half the total production of fruits and vegetables in Britain was concentrated in specialized producing areas dominated by large-scale garden farmers, all of which resulted in lower costs.

5. By the 1920s it can be said that the nation's potato supply was largely grown in Hertfordshire, Bedfordshire, Cambridgeshire, and parts of Yorkshire and Lancashire in England, and in Forfarshire, Perthshire, Fifeshire, Lanarkshire, Ayrshire, and the Lothians in Scotland. Green and root vegetables normally came from Cornwall, Kent, Essex, Hertfordshire, Bedfordshire, Lancashire, Worcestershire in England, and various points in Scotland. Strawberries were mainly obtained from South Hampshire, Kent, East Cornwall, Somerset, the Isle of Ely, the Holland division of Lincolnshire, and Norfolk in England, and the Clyde Valley and a few areas in East and West Lothian in Scotland. Plums came from Worcestershire, Cambridgeshire, Kent, and Middlesex, and raspberries from Kent and

Perthshire, while the bulk of glasshouse produce, such as tomatoes, cucumbers, and grapes, were grown in Guernsey, Worthing, and the Lea Valley. See Ministry of Agriculture and Fisheries, "Interim Report on Fruit and Vegetables," *Departmental Committee on Distribution and Prices of Agricultural Produce* (London, 1923), 20, 70-71. Two of the important dairy companies were the Cooperative Wholesale Society (known as C.W.S.) and Express Dairies. See B. A. Holderness, "Agriculture and Industrialization in the Victorian Economy," in *Victorian Countryside*, ed. G. E. Mingay (London, 1981), vol. 1, p. 185; see also Hamish Fraser, *The Coming of the Mass Market, 1850-1914* (London, 1981), 156. But in 1910 half of Liverpool's milk supply still came from city-bred cows.

6. Ministry of Agriculture and Fisheries, "Interim Report on Meat, Poultry, and Eggs," *Departmental Committee on Distribution and Prices of Agricultural Produce* (London, 1923), 31, 37.

7. For the story of the cooperative movements, see G. D. H. Cole, *A Century of Co-Operation* (n.p., 1944) and James Kinloch and John Butt, *History of the Scottish Co-Operative Wholesale Society Limited* (Glasgow, 1981). For the evolution of the chain stores, see Fraser, *Coming of the Mass Market*, 111.

8. Fraser, *Coming of the Mass Market*, 113. In Stafford in the 1880s, local butchers were able to keep out of the town a large firm of butchers specializing in the sale of "colonial" meat. *Royal Commission on Markets and Tolls*, vol. 61, "Minutes of Evidence," q. 4090.

9. Martin Purvis, "The Development of Co-Operative Retailing in England and Wales, 1851-1901: A Geographical Study," *Journal of Historical Geography* (1990): 315, 318; *Royal Commission on Markets and Tolls*, vol. 9, "Bacup." The claim that the Bolton Cooperative Society made up more than 75 percent of the town's retail trade by 1909 is no doubt an exaggeration: see F. W. Peoples, *History of the Great and Little Bolton Co-Operative Society* (Bolton, 1909), 183, 409, cited in Michael J. Winstanley, *Shopkeeper's World: 1830-1914* (Manchester, 1983), 38; Roderick Floud and Donald McCloskey, *The Economic History of Britain Since 1700* (Cambridge, 1981); the information on how the retail trades were distributed is from "Census of Distribution" as reported in *Market Trader*, 24 Jan. 1953, 13.

10. Ministry of Agriculture and Fisheries, *Departmental Committee on Distribution and Prices of Agricultural Produce, Final Report* (London, 1924), 22-25.

11. On local government discouragement of public markets, see Maggie Colwell, *West of England Market Towns* (London, 1980), 11; for the marketing boards see James R. Hammond, *Food and Agriculture in Britain, 1939-45* (Stanford, Calif., 1954), 3-6.

12. The quote is from Edward Vale, *The North Country* (London, 1937), 19.

13. *St. Austell Market House, 1842-1980* (pamphlet, n.p., 1980), 27.

14. "100 Years of S. Molton Market," *Western Evening News*, 22 Feb. 1963 (clipping file, South Molton Library); the reference to Carter's delivery system is from John Creasey and Sadie Ward, *The Countryside Between the Wars, 1918-1940* (n.p., 1984), 81; "Narberth Market," *West Wales Guardian*, 16 Dec. 1983; "Macclesfield Markets and Fairs" (typescript, Macclesfield file, Macclesfield Library), n.p.

15. On street hawking, see *Royal Commission on Markets and Tolls*, vol. 2, "Minutes of Evidence," qs. 5825-5906.

16. *Royal Commission on Markets and Tolls*, vol. 4, "Reading"; the information on both Manchester and Bolton is included in *Royal Commission on Markets and Tolls*, vol. 9, "Bolton."

17. *Cox's Liverpool Annual and Year Book, 1923* (1923), 217.

18. Cited in "Swansea Always Had Plans for the Market," *Swansea Evening Post*, 2 June 1924.

19. *Kelly's Directory, Aberdeen*, 1860, 1890; for Hull see *Royal Commission on Markets and Tolls*, vol. 2, "Minutes of Evidence" (1888) qs. 5095; *Robinson's Harrogate Directory*, 1900, 1919; for Archie Scarr, see E. P. Hennock, *Fit and Proper Persons: Ideal and Reality in Nineteenth Century Urban Government* (n.p., 1973), 218-21.

20. The quote referring to "food more cheaply" is from Ministry of Agriculture and Fisheries, *Departmental Committee on Distribution and Prices of Agricultural Produce, Final Report*, 24; on Marks and Spencer, see Goronwy Rees, *St Michael: A History of Marks and Spencer* (London, 1969), 14, 22, 27.

21. Food expenditure is still a puzzle. Although middle-income families tended to reduce the proportion of income spent on food, working-class families still spent between roughly one-half and two-thirds of their income on food—thereby gaining both a greater quantity of food and a more varied diet. Floud and McCloskey, *Economic History of Britain Since 1700*, 131-32, 134. The interwar dietary estimates are from annual consumption per person, as set out in John Boyd Orr, *Food, Health, and Income: A Report on a Survey of Adequacy of Diet* (London, 1936), 17-18; the quote from Oldham is in W. Gregory, "Markets Department," in *Oldham Centenary: A History of Local Government* (n.p., 1949), 98. Ironically, in 1888 the market hall at Oldham was described as having been in "decline" for the past year: *Royal Commission on Markets and Tolls*, vol. 9, "Oldham."

22. Glasgow market income figures are from "Report by the Deputation Appointed by the Town Council of Glasgow . . . ," 13; the "sad day" quote is from Walter Freer, *My Life and Memories* (Glasgow, 1929), 38; Liverpool market figures are from Liverpool Markets Committee, *Report of*

the Manager of the City Markets (Liverpool, 1920-21).

23. For Southport, see *Market Trader*, 19 Apr. 1952, 10.

24. The Bolton quote from 1933 is included in Borough of Bolton, *Official Re-Opening of the Market Hall* (1938), 5.

25. Ibid.

26. For Blackburn, see Borough of Blackburn, *Centenary of the Opening of Market Hall No. 1, 1848-1948* (Blackburn, 1948), 12; for renovation of St. John's Market, see City of Liverpool, Report of the Corporation Surveyor, "Improvement of the South End of St. John's Market" (Liverpool, 1882); Liverpool Markets Committee, *Report of the Superintendent of the City Markets* (Liverpool, 1900), 6; the quote about "mania for pulling down" is from "Evictions in St. John's," *Liverpool Citizen*, 20 Feb. 1889, 9; Liverpool Markets Committee, *Report of the Superintendent of the City Markets*, Reports 1920, 1921, 1927-28.

INCOME AND PROFIT, ST. JOHN'S MARKET			
	1920	1921	1927-28
Income	14,555	22,216	25,104
Surplus	1,880	9,028	11,640

Source: Report of the Manager of the City Markets (Liverpool, 1920, 1921, 1927-28).

27. Liverpool Markets Committee, *Report of the Superintendent of the City Markets*, Reports 1920, 1920-21, 1927-28, 1933-34.

28. Ibid., Reports 1925-26, 1930-31; Liverpool Markets Committee, *Report of the Manager of the City Markets for the Year 1925-1926* (Liverpool, 1926), 29-31; Liverpool Markets Committee, *Report of the Manager of the City Markets*, Reports 1920-21; 1922-23; 1925-26.

CHAPTER 11: The Public Market in the Age of the Supermarket

1. "Competitors Always," *Liverpool Daily Post*, 6 Apr. 1948, Liverpool Central Library Clippings File; *Liverpool Echo*, 4 Apr. 1950; "Long Live the Market," *Illustrated Liverpool News*, Feb. 1964; for Stockport, Ashton-under-Lyne, and Sheffield, see *Market Trader*, 2 Jan. 1954, 16; 3 July 1949, 7.

2. Arthur Marwick, *British Society Since 1945* (London, 1968), 19; Graham Maxton, *Women of Britain: Letters from England* (New York, 1941), 217; *Market Trader*, 24 Sept. 1955, 16.

3. For the postwar shortages see Marwick, *British Society Since 1945*, 71; for postwar recovery, see *Market Trader*, 2 Jan. 1954, 16.

4. See *How Britain Was Fed: Food Control, 1939-1945* (London, 1946), 31, and R. J. Hammond, *Food and Agriculture in Britain, 1939-45: Aspects of Wartime Control* (Stanford, Calif., 1954). I am indebted to Ruth Mills for providing this information.

5. For how the hygiene issue was used to shut down markets, see Cannock, *Express and Star*, 16 Nov. 1972; for Dartmouth see *Market Trader*, 21 Jan. 1967, 13.

6. The estimate on postwar housing needs is from Peter Calvocoressi, *The British Experience* (n.p., 1978), 134; for Peterborough, see *Market Trader*, 22 Mar. 1952, 9; the observations about the lack of parking are found in *Market Trader*, Nov. 1958, 27.

7. Material on the 1947 Planning Act is in J. B. Cullingworth, *Town and Country Planning in England and Wales* (London, n.d.), 269.

8. References to sociological analogs are from G. E. Cherry, *Cities and Plans* (London, 1974), 104, and Anthony Jackson, *The Politics of Architecture* (Toronto, 1970), 190-92; for the guidelines, see Ministry of Town and Country Planning, *The Redevelopment of Central Areas* (London, 1947), 27, 28, 44; for Bradford see "Market Demolition Plan Stands," *Telegraph and Argus*, 19 June 1973.

9. For Llanelli see *Market Trader*, 2 Apr. 1960, 25, and the *Telegraph and Argus*, 24 Feb. 1969; for Bradford, see "Market Demolition Plan Stands," *Telegraph and Argus*, 19 June 1973.

10. The 1945 estimate is calculated on the known date of construction for 626 markets listed in the Gazetteer; for Doncaster, see *Market Trader*, 11 Sept. 1954, 14, and 5 Mar. 1949, 8; for Sheffield, see *Market Trader*, 12 Mar. 1949, 8; for Goole, see *Market Trader*, 17 Oct. 1959, n.p.

11. The citation from Worcester is from H. W. Gwillaiam, *Old Worcester* (Worcester, 1972) vol. 1, p. 48; for Cardigan and Dartmouth, see *Market Trader*, May 1967, 15; G. T. Rostance, "Centenary of the Opening of the Retail Market Hall, 1853-1953" (Wolverhampton, 1953); for Wolverhampton and Sheffield see *Market Trader*, 6 Aug. 1955, 17; 28 May 1955; and 25 June 1955; for Newcastle, see *Market Trader*, Mar. 1955.

12. References to St. John's Market are from "This Liverpool Market," *Liverpool Daily Post*, 17 Jan. 1955 (Liverpool Central Library Clippings File); "The Other Side," *Liverpool Daily Post*, 29 Nov. 1949, see also 6 Apr. 1948, and 14 June 1947; Liverpool, *Report of Market Manager* (Liverpool, 1960-61), 7; *Market Trader*, 28 Feb. 1959, 24.

13. For Sheffield see *Market Trader*, 30 July 1949, 7; the 1947 planning advice is from Ministry of Town and Country Planning, *Redevelopment of Central Areas*, 79; the reference to arcades is found in D. Barber, "Planning for Retail Trade," in Association for Planning and Regional Reconstruction, ed., *Town and Country Planning Textbook* (London, 1950), 295.

14. For Tavistock see *Market Trader*, 22 Nov. 1958, 27; for Wolverhampton see *Market Trader*, 19 Feb. 1955, 16; for Richmond see *Market Trader*, 10 June 1967, 41; for Royton see *Market Trader*, 6 Aug. 1955, 17.

15. Vera Brittain, *England's Hour* (New York, 1941), 124; Ministry of Town and Country Planning, *Redevelopment of Central Areas*, 111. The influential architect was J. M. Richards: see Richards, *An Introduction to Modern Architecture* (Harmondsworth, Eng., 1940), 92-93; for Bridgnorth, see Nikolaus Pevsner, ed., *Shropshire* (Harmondsworth, Eng., 1958), 82; J. S. Allen and R. H. Mattocks, *Industry and Prudence: A Plan of Accrington* (n.p., 1950), 45; for Bradford see "Market Demolition Plan Stands," *Telegraph and Argus*, 19 June 1973, and H. A. N. Brockman, *The British Architect in Industry, 1841-1940* (London, 1975), 55; for Ludlow see *Six English Towns* (London, 1978), 168.

16. *Market Trader*, 20 Dec. 1958, 18; J. B. Cullingworth, *Town and Country Planning in England and Wales* (n.p., n.d.), 268; for Sheffield see *Market Trader*, 24 May 1958, 24.

17. On the movement of multiple shops into the public market, see *Market Trader*, 13 Aug. 1949, 7; for example, the Plymouth market, *Market Trader*, 3 Dec. 1949; also, *Market Trader*, 1 Oct. 1949, 10. Woolworth's offered £2,000 rent for a part of Oswestry's Marketcross market: *Market Trader*, 14 May 1960, 26.

18. For Plymouth, see *Market Trader*, 2 Feb. 1952, n.p.; for Newcastle, see *Market Trader*, 3 Sept. 1960, 25.

19. The Liverpool lament is from Hannah Reilly, "Nostalgic Christmas," *Liverpool Echo*, 28 Dec. 1963 (Liverpool Central Library Clippings File); the reference to the housewife of the future is from *Market Trader*, 9 Apr. 1949, 7.

20. The complaint about package design is in *Market Trader*, 17 July 1954, 13.

21. Material on the evolution of modern shopping patterns is from *Market Trader*, 9 Apr. 1949, 7; 26 Feb. 1966, 43; 29 Aug. 1964, 15; 19 Sept. 1959, 25; 19 Feb. 1955, 15.

22. *Market Trader*, 5 Aug. 1967, 49.

23. The reference to competition is the view of the editor of *Market Trader*, 26 Apr. 1958, 22; see also *Market Trader*, 7 May 1966, 18; the comment on generational use is from *Market Trader*, 17 July 1954, 13.

24. For example, see descriptions of the Middlesborough market, in *Market Trader*, 8 Mar. 1952, 9, and the Newport (Wales) market in *Market Trader*, 29 Apr. 1967, 22.

25. For Huddersfield see *Market Trader*, 6 Aug. 1966, 39; for Cardigan see *Market Trader*, 27 May 1967, 15; see also *Market Trader*, 22 Apr. 1967, 43.

26. For these views of market hall traders, see *Market Trader*, 16 Apr. 1949, 7; 17 July 1954, 13; 7 Sept. 1957, 16.

27. The advice to the small independent trader is found in *Market Trader*, 2 Jan. 1954, 16; 17 July 1954, 13; and 16 Apr. 1949, 7; the quote on market humor is from *Market Trader*, 25 July 1964, 37.

28. For Kidderminster see *Kidderminster Shuttle*, 6 Sept. 1972; with reference to Devon and Cornwall, see *Market Trader*, 20 Aug. 1949, 7; for Stockport, see *Market Trader*, 2 Jan. 1954, 16; for the market history series, see *Market Trader*, May 1966, 18.

29. On preservation, see *Market Trader*, 15 Nov. 1958, 22; for Newport, see "Welsh Market Notes," *Market Trader*, 13 May 1967; for Dartmouth, see *Market Trader*, 18 Feb. 1967, 15.

30. These descriptions of the Manchester and Liverpool markets are from Janice Anderson, *Markets and Fairs of Great Britain* (London, 1988), 119, 123; the reference to dead urban heartland is from Kenneth O. Morgan, *The People's Peace: British History, 1945-1989* (Oxford, 1990), 191.

31. The quote on predicting market removal is from *Market Trader*, 26 Nov. 1966, 71; the citations to Nottingham and Wolverhampton are from *Market Trader*, 19 Nov. 1966, 45, 11; Wolverhampton's town reconstruction plan was adopted in 1944. See G. T. Rostance, *Centenary of the Opening of the Retail Market Hall, 1853-1953* (County Borough of Wolverhampton, 1953), a pamphlet; for Wakefield see *Market Trader*, 18 July 1959, 8; for Huddersfield and Sheffield see *Market Trader*, 10 Jan. 1959, 24; "All in the Name of Progress," *Huddersfield Daily Examiner*, 3 Apr. 1990, 10; "Design for the Seventies," *Huddersfield Daily Examiner*, 6 Apr. 1970.

32. For Bristol see *Market Trader*, 17 Jan. 1959, 28; for Dudley and Kettering, see *Market Trader*, 21 June 1952, 12; for Sheffield, see *Market Trader*, 8 Oct. 49; see also *Market Trader*, 26 Mar. 1955; for Bradford, see letter by S. K. Llanwarne to the *Telegraph and Argus*, 14 July 1973, also *Telegraph and Argus*, 14 Oct. 1969, *Yorkshire Post*, 3 Nov. 1973.

33. County Borough of Blackburn, *Centenary of the Opening of Market Hall No. 1, 1848-1948* (souvenir handbook, 1948), and Laing Development Co., "Blackburn Central Development" (Blackburn Central Library, 1961), a pamphlet; "Tenants Still in Dark About Their Future," *Blackburn Times*, 10 Jan. 1964.

34. For Preston see *Market Trader*, 10 Nov. 1966; for Lancaster see John Catt, *History of Lancaster Markets* (Lancaster, 1984).

35. "Trading Architecture: The Bolton Market Place," *Architects' Journal* 189, no. 16 (19 Apr. 1989): 44.

36. "Survey on the Covered Market Hall" (Stockport Central Library); for views of the "modern" market see "Market Medley," *Market Trader*, 11 Sept. 1954, 14.

GAZETTEER
AND
GUIDE TO LOCAL
SOURCES

THIS GAZETTEER PROVIDES INFORMATION ON 626 KNOWN PUBLIC RETAIL markets constructed between 1750 and about 1945 in 392 cities and towns in England, Wales, and Scotland; it also lists a large number of new markets constructed after 1945 as replacements for earlier market buildings. The Gazetteer does not attempt to list all new market buildings constructed since 1945, only the replacements. Privately built shopping arcades are not included in this survey. Generally, corn markets (or corn exchanges) and other wholesale market buildings are not included unless they were open to retail trade on a regular basis. It is probable that more wholesale markets were open to retail sales than the following list suggests.

Primary Sources of Information on Local Public Markets

It was noted in 1922 by the Linlithgow Parliamentary Committee on marketing that there was little readily available information regarding the markets of the country. Since that time the Ministry of Agriculture and Fisheries survey of 1927 has made the task of the historian somewhat easier by identifying existing markets, although the survey report is largely concerned with the wholesale aspect of selling agricultural produce. Many of the sources listed below are helpful, but too often the student is faced with the task of using a variety and often spotty collection of sources in attempting to piece together the history of "public" retailing on a national or regional/local level. In many instances there is no substitute for the local library and regional archives. None of the sources listed below help the historian to determine the amount of goods entering the public market at a particular time. The authors gratefully acknowledge the generosity of many local librarians and archivists for their assistance in preparing this gazetteer.

Nineteenth- and Early Twentieth-Century Sources

(1) PP-35: Parliamentary Papers, *Report of the Royal Commission on Municipal Corporations* (London, 1835-39), "Index" (1839), vol. xviii.i. In this survey of 261 towns undertaken by parliamentary commissioners, particular attention is given to town governance and public services. Some commissioners gave specific information with regard to public market provisions of the town, including management, finance, and the physical nature of the market, for forty-four towns. Coverage is inconsistent, however, and thus only in cases where it is known that the reporting commissioners paid particular attention to market facilities is this source cited in the Gazetteer. Coverage of Scottish markets was generally inferior to coverage of English and Welsh markets. It may be noted that with regard to Scotland, Sir John Sinclair's survey of Scottish towns, the *Statistical Account of Scotland, 1791-1799* (21 vols., repr. 1983), and the second survey, *The New Statistical Account of Scotland, 1845* (15 vols.), include considerable information about the condition of town markets and the roads to them.

(2) PP-88; Parliamentary Papers, *Royal Commission on Market Rights and Tolls,* 14 vols. (London, 1888-91). This is the only nineteenth-century parliamentary survey of markets. Particular emphasis is on market tolls. It includes considerable information for many towns (including interviews with market officials), although it is inconsistent in coverage. Coverage of Scottish markets was inferior to coverage of English and Welsh markets.

(3) Ministry of Agriculture and Fisheries, *Report on Markets and Fairs in England and Wales* (London, 1927), parts 1-6. Survey of all major markets, by county and market town. Helpful in identifying public markets and providing data with regard to size, nature of use—occasionally with descriptions of use—and ownership, it concentrates on distribution of wholesale agricultural products, including cattle markets. It seldom provides dates of origin. Some illustrations are included.

(4) Lewis: *Lewis's Topographical Dictionary of England* (London, 1831, 4 vols.; 1835, 5 vols.; 1842, 4 vols.; 1848-49, 4 vols.) provides limited information on markets in hundreds of towns in England and Wales, often giving rudimentary information such as market location, when the market was built, and its general architectural character. The researcher will want to consult directories like *Kelly's Directory* for brief descriptions of the markets and a listing of market sellers. Trade directories are helpful in identifying the level of market activity, for most list the number and type of businesses in the public market. A guide to directories is Michael Keen, *A Bibliography of the Trade Directories of the British Isles, in the National Art Library* (London, 1979).

(5) Local Newspapers: The opening of a new market was often the occasion of extensive local newspaper coverage which detailed market history, building use and construction, and, often, the speeches made at opening ceremonies. When known, this Gazetteer provides the date the market was officially opened in order to allow the student to better find newspaper accounts. In addition to local newspapers, many local libraries have "news clipping" files which will often contain a collection of news items on the public marketplace and market buildings.

Official Reports and Minutes

Most public markets were owned by municipal governments or by quasi-governmental bodies such as Improvement Commissions. It was usual for such bodies to have a Markets Committee, which administered the markets and in doing so kept detailed books, issued market bylaws, and published reports. Seldom do these bodies report on the precise volume of trade within a market, but they often provide records of market rental and toll revenues, building projects, and market inspection. These records are often included in town council papers and can be found today in local libraries or district and regional archives. Many towns have published abridged and printed versions (often called "extracts," or "annals") of town council business over a long period of time, and in many cases these are helpful in identifying market building activities.

Architectural Periodicals

A large number of market building projects were given coverage by the leading architectural journals, *The Builder, The Building News, British Architect,* and *Architect,* although they accorded space for plans and illustrations only in a few cases. Many of these are cited in the Gazetteer. There is now a new index to *The Builder* illustrations: *The Builder Illustrations Index, 1843-1883,* ed. Ruth Richartson and Robert Thorne (London, 1994).

Modern Sources

There are no general histories of the public market or market buildings, and overall the public market and the marketplace have received scant attention from historians. This is true of the market as an economic and social institution as well as the market as a building type. Market buildings have generally been dismissed as architecturally insignificant (see, e.g., H. S. Goodhart-Rendel, "Victorian Public Buildings," in Peter Farriday, ed., *Victorian Architecture,* 1964). A good but brief account of the public market can be found in Thomas Markus, *Buildings and Power: Freedom and Control in the Origin of the Modern Building Type,* 1993. Nikolaus Pevsner, *A History of Building Types,* 1976, deals briefly with market halls; also helpful is the *Buildings of England* series, 1951 (52 vols.), ed. Nikolaus Pevsner et al. The buildings are listed by county, and many of the architecturally important markets are given a brief description, although this survey expresses no interest in market function or internal layout. (Note also the corresponding *Buildings of Wales,* and *Buildings of Scotland* series.) On market hall construction, only Arthur Walmisley's *Iron Roofs,* 1988, provides descriptions of the design of market buildings. Only a few regional studies devote attention to the modern public market, either from a social-typographical or an architectural viewpoint. These include Maggie Colwell, *West of England Market Towns,* 1980; Derek Linstrum, *West Yorkshire Architects and Architecture,* 1978; and Alexander Clifton-Taylor, *Six English Towns,* 1978, which deals with Chichester, Richmond, Tewkesbury, Stamford, Totnes, and Ludlow. A few towns, like Leeds, have published histories of their markets, and most towns have a written municipal history which devotes some space to the public retail market; in rare cases a special publication exists on the market and market hall. When known, these are included in the individual bibliographies in the Gazetteer. None of the few histories on food and food supply provide insights into the role of the public market in the sale and distribution of food.

(1) *The Markets Yearbook,* published annually since 1955 by World's Fair, Oldham, includes information regarding present market location and ownership, market days, and whether the market is indoor or outdoor. *The Yearbook* seldom provides historical information.

(2) *Market Trader* (a.k.a. *Market Trader's Review*) is the official journal of the National Market Traders Association (weekly, 1922-); it includes news about relations between municipal government and market traders (particularly in the post-Second World War era when town redevelopment schemes threatened many markets) and tells how public market dealers responded to the challenge of modern retailing. The *Market Trader* was (after ca. 1950) included as a supplement to the trade journal, *The World's Fair,* and published in Oldham.

(3) *VCH: The Victoria History of the Counties of England,* ed. H. A. Doubleday and W. Page (current editor is C. R. Elrington), 1901- , is a historical encyclopedia of the English counties arranged according to county. These volumes are often the best source of information on the evolution and development of the public market. Each county forms a set for which there are several volumes, some of which deal with each city, town, and village in the county.

The student of market history is also directed to a number of recent guides on building and architecture, in particular Colin Cunningham, *Town Halls,* 1981, which provides information on some of the market structures built as a part of a town hall scheme, and Julian Orbach, ed., *Victorian Architecture in Britain ("The Blue Guide"),* 1987, which cites many markets of architectural interest constructed between 1837 and 1914 which were extant in 1987; Janice Anderson's *Collins Guide to the Markets and Fairs of Great Britain,* 1988, gives information on how to locate present-day markets, some of which are in historical buildings. For information on particular architects, the student will want to begin with H. M. Covin, *A Biographical Dictionary of British Architects, 1600-1840*, 2d ed., 1978; and L. Wodehouse, ed., *British Architects, 1840-1976: A Guide to Information Sources*, 1978.

Key to the Entries and Abbreviations

The entries are arranged alphabetically by town name. Also appearing on the first line is the county. For towns in which more than one market structure was built, each of the separate buildings is designated by a number in parentheses.

The entry for each market consists of the following (when known): market name; market type; the date (year or exact day) the market was opened and the year(s) of renovation or remodeling; location in the town; cost of construction (in £ sterling) and the size (in square feet); the name of the architect and where the architect was from (if the principal designer of the building was not an architect, the person's title follows the name); other contractors or builders involved with the project; a brief description of the building; and current status of the building.

Following the basic entry, certain town markets of outstanding size or interest or importance are described.

The final section of each entry lists primary sources used in gathering data that may be consulted for more information.

GAZETTEER

ABERAVON — GLAMORGAN

(1) Town Hall and Market. 1826. Lower floor of town hall. (2) Market Hall. General market. 1850. East side of railway. Destroyed by fire in 1907. (3) Market Hall. General market. 1909. Water and Church Streets on the site of old cattle market. £6,000. Architect: James Roderick, Surveyor. Brick with stone dressing. Destroyed in 1973.

SOURCES: *The Builder,* 9 May 1908, 6 May 1909; *Building News,* 20 Jan 1899.

ABERDARE — GLAMORGAN

(1) Market House. 1853. Market Street. Destroyed by fire about 1900. (2) Market Hall. 1903. Market Street. 15,600 sq. ft. Owned by Aberdare Markets and Town Hall Company. Extant in 1992.

SOURCES: Aberdare Markets and Town Hall Company, Aberdare.

ABERDEEN — GRAMPIAN

(1) Flesh Market. 1806. Located in east quarter of town. £5,000. 86 stalls in a "commodious set of buildings." Owned by Incorporation of Fleshers. Demolished. (2) New Flesh Market. 1816. George Street. 42 stalls. Cast-iron pillars and roof. Privately owned for butchers who were not members of the Incorporation. (3) Market Hall. General market. 1842. £27,000. 33,390 sq. ft. Architect: Archibald Simpson. Owned by Market Company. Reconstructed (at cost of £14,000) after fire of 1882. Reconstruction Architects: John and William Smith. Wrought-iron roof added as part of the reconstruction. Demolished. (4) Fish Market. 1899. £5,000. 15,336 sq. ft. Architect: Wilson.

At the close of the eighteenth century Aberdeen's markets were scattered around the town but with a principal market in Luxembourg Close. Like the town's architecture, the town markets were regarded as lamentable. A doubling of population between 1801 and 1821 and a new canal brought increased pressure for a covered market. This was undertaken in the 1830s when a group of citizens, including the architect Archibald Simpson, purchased land for a market hall and procured an act of Parliament to carry out a wide-scale town re-newal scheme. The opening of the market in May 1842 was marked with a "great promenade concert" and the first purchase in the market was an eleven-pound salmon. The hall, described as "the most elegant building of its kind in the country," had an interior market which measured 315 ft. by 106 ft., with a wood roof 45 ft. in height. The floor was divided by 56 stone pillars into a wide nave and 2 side alleys which were occupied with 54 butchers' shops; the galleries above provided space for shops for linen, cotton, woolen goods, ready-made clothing, hardware, and books. There were 74 shops and a fish market on the basement level. The hall was originally lighted with 270 gas burners. The market held a near monopoly on many branches of the town's retail trade (e.g., meat, fish, and dairy products) until the last decade of the nineteenth century. The Market Street front was a majestic stone classical granite portico supported by square columns. The building was severely damaged by fire in 1883 and rebuilt, but then demolished for a new hall within a shopping center in the 1970s.

SOURCES: *Aberdeen Journal,* 24 Apr 1883, 3 May 1883, 5 May 1833; *Aberdeen Town Council, Minutes and Proceedings,* 1833; *Aberdeen Weekly Journal,* 16 Aug 1918; Sir Henry Alexander et al., *The Building Chronicle,* n.d.; *The Builder,* 22 Aug 1891, 12 Sep 1891, 14 Jan 1899; G. M. Fraser, *Antiquities of Aberdeen and Its Neighborhood,* 1913; Ronald Harrison, *Archibald Simpson and the Architecture of Aberdeen, 1790-1847,* 1978; J. B. Nicol, "The Aberdeen Market," in *The Archibald Simpson Centenary Celebrations,* 1944; W. Walker, *Reminiscences of Aberdeen,* 1901 (repr. 1904); James Wilson, *Bon Accord Repository,* 1842; Charles Wilson, *Aberdeen of Auld Lang Syne,* 1948; Robert Wilson, *An Historical Account and Delineation of Aberdeen,* 1822.

ABERGAVENNY — GWENT

(1) Enclosed general market. 1796. Architect: John Nash. Open courtyard surrounded by stalls. Altered as covered market in 1826 (Architects: J. Peene and D. Wescott). Further improvements in 1864. Destroyed in 1870. (2) Market Hall. General market. 1870. Located in Cross Street. £7,000.

18,730 sq. ft. Architects: Wilson and Wilcox, of London and Bath; Contractor: Moreland, Gloucester. Built by the Improvement Commissioners. Gothic façade with tower. Extant in 1988.

SOURCES: *The Builder*, 31 Dec 1870; Monmouth District Museum Services, *The History of the Market in Abergavenny*, (n.d.); Colin Cunningham, *Townhalls*, 1981, pp. 254, 274; drawings (in color), Royal Institute of British Architects, Library.

ABERTILLERY   GWENT

Market Hall. General market. 1893. £4,000. Architect: Alfred Swash, MSA, Newport. Builder: A. P. Williams, Abertillery. Extant in 1988.

SOURCES: *The Builder*, 19 Mar 1892; *Building News*, 15 Sep 1893; *The Market Trader*, 9 Feb 1952.

ABERYSTWYTH   DYFED

(1) Meat Market Hall. 1823. St. James Square. Extant in 1980. (2) Market Hall. General market. 1836. Located in Market Street. Known as The Palladium Market in 1920s. Destroyed by fire in 1934. (3) John James Market Hall. General market hall. 1871. Located in Terrace Road. £1,100. 8,750 sq. ft. Architects: Szlumper and Aldwinck, of London and Aberystwyth. Builder: James Evans, Aberystwyth. Owned by Aberystwyth Market and Public Hall Company.

SOURCES: *The Builder*, 3 Sep 1870, 28 Nov 1896; W. J. Lewis, *Born on a Perilous Rock*, 1980.

ACCRINGTON   LANCASHIRE

(1) Market Hall. General market. Opened 23 Oct 1869. Blackburn Road. £19,000. 21,960 sq. ft. Architect: J. F. Doyle. Owned by local Board of Health. Façade refurbished, 1986. Extant in 1992. (2) Umbrella Market Hall. General covered market. 1962. Adjacent to Market Hall. £173,677. Owned by Corporation. Extant.

The doubling of population in the twenty years after 1850, the dangerous state of the streets, and a need to enhance its image in order to acquire parliamentary representation led to the building of a large and ornate market hall in 1869. The new building, on the site of an iron foundry and old cottages, was opened with great fanfare (5,000 school children joined the opening ceremonies inside the hall) and with predictions that the market would lower the town's food prices and banish dishonesty and fraud. The stone building is of an unrestrained Renaissance style (the architect described it as "partly Grecian") with a 9-bay front, Corinthian pilasters at the ends and center, with a Triumphal Arch with round-headed doorway topped by groups of sculpted figures. It was applauded at the time as being a "living treasure of art," but a century later was deemed as "roistering vulgarity." The 3-division iron roof supported by columns and elaborate cast- and wrought-iron brackets, has a heightened center clerestory; the market floor is divided into 3 wide aisles, with shops all round the interior wall; a gallery (now offices) lay above the shops. The interior iron work was painted blue-gray, light red, and buff with green, gold, and vermilion column caps. The market became the hub for the town's tramway system.

SOURCES: *PP-88*; *The Accrington Observer*, 18 Oct 1869; *Accrington Times*, 23 May 1869, 30 Oct 1869; J. S. Allen and R. H. Mattocks, *Industry and Prudence: A Plan For Accrington*, 1950; *Blackburn Times*, 30 Oct 1869; *The Builder*, 28 Jul 1866; J. W. Singleton, ed., *The Jubilee Souvenir of the Corporation of Accrington*, Accrington, 1928.

ALDERSHOT   HAMPSHIRE

Aldershot General Market. Contracts let 1858. Architect: T. Goodchild.

SOURCES: *Building News*, 8 Oct 1858, 29 Oct 1858.

ALLENTON   DERBYSHIRE

Market Hall. 1960. Osmaston Road. Owned by Derby City Council. Extant as market.

ALRESFORD   HAMPSHIRE

Market House. General market. 1866. West Street. £1,530. 784 sq. ft. Architect: William Hunt. Owned by Alresford Market House Company. Probably built as a result of the coming of the railroad. Built as a market hall, but soon thereafter became known as the Town Hall. Town purchased market rights in 1920s. The building ceased to be used as a market in the 1920s and was sold to a private party in 1924 for £800.

SOURCES: E. R. Hedges, *Alresford Displayed*, no. 9, 1984.

ALTRINCHAM   CHESHIRE

Market Hall. 4,800 sq. ft. Owned by the Borough Council. Extant in 1990.

ALVERSTOKE   HAMPSHIRE

Market Hall. General market. 1812. Located near the beach. Not used as a market after 1850s.

SOURCES: *VCH*.

AMBLESIDE   CUMBRIA

Market Hall. General market. 1863.

ANDOVER   HAMPSHIRE

Guildhall. General market. 1825. Located in lower floor of the town hall. Architect: J. Langdon, London. Extant in 1976.

APPLEBY   CUMBRIA

(1) Market House. General market. 1811. Located near the parish church. £1,000. Architect: James Smirke. Owned by the Corporation. (2) Market House. General market. 1867. Rebuilt in 1911.

SOURCES: Lewis; F. W. Garnett, *Westmoreland Agriculture, 1800-1900*, 1912.

ARBROATH   TAYSIDE

(1) Town House. General market. 1803. Located in High Street. 2,000 guineas. Architect: Logan. Rebuilt in 1844. (2) Corn Exchange Market. General market. 1855. Included general retail market facilities.

ASHBOURNE   DERBYSHIRE

Market Hall. General market. Opened 13 Dec 1861. Located in Market Place. £1,435. 1,188 sq. ft. Architect: B. Wilson, Derby. Paid for by six men of the town. Market on lower floor with assembly rooms above. Pilasters and projecting portico to front. Described at its opening as of the "Renaissance" style and "a noble exterior of stone, not of your shabby bricks." Extant but no longer used as a market.

SOURCES: *The Derby Mercury*, 23 Oct 1861, 17 Aug 1864.

ASHBURTON   DEVONSHIRE

Market Hall. General market. 1850. Located in North Street. Owned by Lord Clinton. Extant in 1978 as town hall and offices of the Urban District Council.

SOURCES: *The Builder*, 17 Oct 1846; Francis Pilkington, *Ashburton, The Dartmour Town*, 1978.

ASHBY-DE-LA-ZOUCHE   LEICESTERSHIRE

Market Hall. 1857. Located in Market Street behind the town hall. Converted to town hall; reverted to market use in 1958. Extant in 1988.

ASHTON-UNDER-LYNE   LANCASHIRE

(1) The Shambles. General market hall. Opened 2 Jul 1830. Located between Warrington and Market Streets. £4,000. Owned by the Corporation after 1849. Expanded in 1849. Demolished in 1867. (2) Market Hall. General market. 1867. Located on site of former hall between Warrington and Market Streets. Enlarged in 1881 and 1930. Extant. (3) Fish Market Hall. 1882. £6,000. 3,420 sq. ft. Architects: John Eaton and Son; Contractor: William Neal, Ashton-under-Lyne. Owned by the Corporation. Attached to rear of Market Hall. Extant.

Despite its lack of a designated market place, early nineteenth-century Ashton was the market center for a number of nearby towns. By the 1820s Ashton's market-ground was so crowded that townsfolk and vendors coming from the outside had difficulty in finding a place to set up their stalls. Equally aggravating for rate payers was a Saturday evening market which was set up in the streets, causing much traffic and inconvenience. On demand by ratepayers, the lord of the manor established a Market Square and a Market House. A new market house was built in 1830, and then a large brick hall with stone dressing in 1867. This building has a total of 19 bays and a central clock tower with polychromatic brick decoration, a multiple division roof of cast- and wrought-iron on cast-iron columns. A 1930 addition has windows with stained glass inserts.

SOURCES: *VCH; Ashton Centenary Handbook, 1847-1947*, 1947; W. M. Bouman, *England in Ashton-Under-Lyne*, 1960; *The Builder*, 4 Mar 1882.

AYLESBURY   BUCKINGHAMSHIRE

Market Hall. Meat and corn market. Opened 11 Oct 1865. Located on the site of the old White Hart Hotel. £9,000. 4,050 sq. ft. Architect: David Brandon; Builder: E. Conder; Stonecarver: Jackson of Maidahill. Owned by Public Market Company.

SOURCES: *The Builder*, 12 Mar 1864, 30 Jul 1864, 28 Oct 1865.

AYR   AYRSHIRE

Butter Market. General market. Ca. 1873. Erected under the Ayr Burgh Act of 1873.

BACUP   LANCASHIRE

Market Hall. General market. Opened Aug 1867. Located in Queen and Bank Streets. £6,300. 9,000 sq. ft. Architect: Joseph Brierley, Civil Engineer. Owned originally by local Board of Health which had purchased market rights from manorial owner ca. 1865; ownership later taken over by Corporation; sold to private concern in 1957. Broad center nave with 2 side aisles with shops round the sides. Town had many cooperative stores which provided serious competition for the new market. Described at the time as "commodious rather than ornamental." Extant in 1988, but market moved to Temple Court in 1956.

SOURCES: *PP-88; VCH; Bacup Times*, 24 Aug 1867.

BAKEWELL · DERBYSHIRE

Market Hall. General market. Converted to public library in 1960.

SOURCES: *The Market Trader*, 29 Oct 1960.

BANFF · GRAMPIAN

New Market. General covered and walled market. 1831. North end of Low Street. Owned by Town Council. Extant in 1988.

SOURCES: *PP-88*.

BARNSTAPLE · DEVONSHIRE

(1) Meat Shambles. Covered market. 1812. High Street to Anchor Lane. 34 stalls. (2) Fish Shambles. 1846. Architect: R. D. Gould, Borough Surveyor. (3) Pannier (Vegetable) Market. General market hall. Opened 2 Nov 1855. Located between Bowtport Street and High Street. £16,000. 45,000 sq. ft. Architect: R. D. Gould, Borough Surveyor. Owned by the Corporation. Enlarged 1867. Extant in 1997. (4) Butchers' Row. 1855. Located adjacent to the Pannier Market. 33 shops. Architect: R. D. Gould, Borough Surveyor. Owned by the Corporation. Extant in 1990. (5) Fish Market. 1875. Architect: R. D. Gould, Borough Surveyor. Contractor: John Gribble.

A covered row of stalls for the sale of meat was erected in 1812 in the High Street (to Anchor Lane) for the sale of meat, and despite considerable demand for a market hall (permissive legislation had been obtained in 1811) the pannier market remained uncovered and in the streets until 1855 when the present hall was built. This hall, it was claimed, was built by "the Liberals in the Town Council." It was in the "Italian" style, and of red brick relieved with dark blue and yellow bricks for quoins and arches. The hall portion of the building (320 ft. by 68 ft.), is laid out with rows of wooden tables on which the sellers display their baskets of goods. The center roof is supported by circular ribs, painted blue, which rise from the caps of 2 rows of pillars. On its opening day the market was fully occupied by panniers containing the usual agricultural products, as well as tools, earthenware, boots and shoes, and gloves. In 1927 the market hall was described as one of the largest of its kind in the country—having about 500 market sellers, most of whom were growers from the nearby countryside.

SOURCES: *PP-88*; *PP-35*; *Building News*, 5 Nov 1895; W. F. Gardiner, *Barnstable 1837-1897*, Barnstable, 1897; Joseph B. Gribble, *Memorials of Barnstable*, 1830; Lois Lamplaugh, *Barnstable: Town on the Taw*, 1983.

BARROW-IN-FURNESS · CUMBRIA

(1) Market Hall. General market. 1864-69. Market Street to Cornwallis Street. £3,750 (partial). 33,840 sq. ft. Architects: Paley and Austin. Multiple bay with decorative brickwork and 3-division roof. Originally built as town hall and market hall with later additions. Purchased from railway company by Corporation in 1874. Demolished in 1969. (2) Fish Market. 1902. 1,092 sq. ft. Architect: Smith. (3) Market Hall. 1969. Market Street. Part of new Town Centre scheme.

SOURCES: *VCH*.

BARRY (CADOXTON) · GLAMORGAN

(1) Market Hall. Opened 11 Dec 1890. Barry Dock Road and West Street. £3,672. 2,960 sq. ft. Architects: Habershon and Fawckner, of London and Newport. (2) Market Hall. General market. 1891. Court Road and Barry Road, Cadoxton. £3,000. 7,200 sq. ft. Architects: Seward and Thomas, of Cardiff and Cadoxton. Owned by Barry Town Market Company.

SOURCES: *The Builder*, 20 Dec 1890, 14 Mar 1891; *Building News*, 20 Dec 1890, 13 Mar 1891.

BASINGSTOKE · HAMPSHIRE

Lesser Market. General market hall. 1884. Located in Upper Wote Street. Extant in 1988.

SOURCES: *PP-88*.

BATH · AVON

(1) General covered market. Ca. 1802. (2) Market Hall. General market. 1863. High Street. £6,000. Architects: Henry Hicks and Thomas Isaac, Bath. Part of Guildhall complex. Large arched entrances flanked by columns lie one to either side of Guildhall—each entrance opens into an arcade which in turn leads to the large central domed hall. Glass and iron roof on cast-iron columns. Central domed area used as fish market. Altered 1892-95. Extant.

SOURCES: *PP-88*; *The Builder*, 31 Aug 1861; Market plans can be found in the Bath City Records Office, Guild Hall, Bath.

BATLEY · WEST YORKSHIRE

Market Hall. General market. 1878. Top of Market Hill. £5,180. 6 butchers' shops and 28 stalls. Architect: Steed Ellis, Batley. Owned by the Corporation. 90-ft. high clock tower. Gothic style. Basket-shaped chandelier—with 50 lights—in the hall. Demolished.

SOURCES: *Building News*, 20 Dec 1872; M. H. Haigh, *The History of Batley 1800-1974*, 1974; *The Reporter*, 11 May 1878.

BEDFORD   BEDFORDSHIRE

Town Hall and Market. Ca. 1839. Architect: Harvy L. Elmes. Arcaded lower floor of the town hall in the "late Gothic style."

SOURCES: *PP-88;* drawing, Royal Insititute of British Architects Library.

BERKHAMSTEAD   BEDFORDSHIRE

Market Hall. General market. 1863. Architect: E. B. Lamb.

BERWICK-UPON-TWEED   NORTHUMBERLAND

Town Hall. General market under town hall. 1761. In Margate Street. 1,200 sq. ft. Architect: Joseph Dodds. Owned by freemen of the city. Eastern lower floor was a piazza for poultry, meal, butter, and eggs and was called the Exchange. Stone with Tuscan columns and 150-ft. tower with spire.

SOURCES: *PP-88.* John Fuller, *The History of Berwick-upon-Tweed,* 1794.

BEVERLEY   HUMBERSIDE

(1) Butchers' Shambles. 1752. Northeast end of the market place. Converted to Corn Exchange in 1825. (2) Fish Market. 1777. Demolished in 1982.

SOURCES: *Building News,* 25 Sep 1885, 9 Aug 1886; G. Oliver, *A History of Beverley,* 1829; M. Turner, *The Beverley Guide,* 1830.

BEWDLEY   HEREFORDSHIRE

General covered arcade market. 1818. Extending from town hall to marketplace.

SOURCES: Lewis.

BIDEFORD   DEVON

Pannier Market. General market hall. Opened 15 Apr 1884. Located in Bridge Street. £4,317. 21,000 sq. ft. Architect: J. Chudley, Newton Abbot. Contractor: J. Foaden, Ashburton. Owned by the Corporation. Extant.

Bideford's Pannier Market Hall of 1884 was built in the higher part of town and covers most of the irregularly shaped old market place which was laid out in 1675. It is of red brick with terra cotta foliage friezes, and yellow brick floor, and with a 5-division roof, 2 divisions of which have clerestory windows; a Butchers' Row on the lower front level occupies half of the market space, with the remainder used for a general market hall on the higher rear level (access to which is by an interior stair and 2 exterior entrances). A few years after its opening it was claimed that the new market resulted in a better supply of food for the town and that the coming of the railway made it pos-

sible for local farmers to send dairy products away before they spoiled. The shops in the Butchers' Row were first taken by "country" butchers because the town butchers opposed the market.

SOURCES: *Annual Report on the Health of Bideford,* 1950; *The Builder,* 6 Oct 1883; *The Building News,* 27 Oct 1882; *"Gazettes" North Devonshire Directory and Yearbook,* 1935; Grant and Peter Christie, *Book of Bideford,* 1989.

BILSTON   WEST MIDLANDS

Market Hall. General market. Opened 9 Aug 1892. Church Street. £10,000. 19,500 sq. ft. Architects: Horton and Company, of Wednesbury. 45 shops (11 butchers', 8 fish, 26 general) and 95 stalls designed by C. L. N. Wilson, Civil Engineer. Owned by the Corporation. Elaborate brick Jacobean front; 2 arched entrances with 3 windows above. Demolished in 1972. Present market hall is operated by the Borough Council.

SOURCES: *The Builder,* 20 Aug 1892; *Building News,* 7 Mar 1890, 14 Mar 1890; illustrations and plans: Wolverhampton Central Library, Wolverhampton.

BIRKENHEAD   MERSEYSIDE

(1) Old Market. General market hall. 1834. Hamilton Street. 16,650 sq. ft. Architect: Rampling, of Liverpool and Birkenhead. Originally owned by Improvement Commissioners. (2) New Market. General market hall. 1845. Adjacent to Old Market with entrances from Albion, Hamilton, Market, and Oliver Streets. £25,000. 56,330 sq. ft. 42 shops and 76 stalls. Engineers: Fox and Henderson, of Birmingham. Owned by the Corporation. Destroyed by fire in 1977. (3) Market Hall. 1977. Grange Shopping Precinct. 233 units. Owned by Wirral Borough Council.

The New Market of 1845, built by Fox and Henderson, the same firm that built the Crystal Palace, was the largest building in Britain constructed on cast-iron pillars. It was 430 ft. long with 24 bays and a 3-division iron roof with louvers and skylights. A total of 700 tons of iron was used in its construction. Its 2 interior fountains by John Seeley were eventually moved to Arrowe Park.

SOURCES: *The Civil Engineer and Architect's Journal,* Vol. viii, 1845; J. R. Kaighin, *Bygone Birkenhead,* 1925; W. W. Mortimer, *The History of the Hundred of Wirral,* 1847.

BIRMINGHAM   WEST MIDLANDS

(1) Market Hall. General market. Opened 12 Feb 1835. Located between Bull Ring and Worcester Street. £79,785. 39,785 sq. ft. Architect: Charles Edge. Erected by Birmingham Street Commis-

sioners; built by Improvement Commissioners; later (after 1851) owned by the Corporation. Largely destroyed by bombing in 1940; exterior walls existed until 1965 and used as enclosure for open market. (2) Coleshill New Market Hall. 1837. Architects: Messrs. Robins. Privately owned. Closed in the 1850s. (3) Meat Market Hall. Ca. 1851. 5,040 sq. ft. Used as a retail market on Saturdays only. Replaced by new building in 1897. (4) Fish Market. 1869. Adjoining Bull Ring Market Hall. Extended in 1883. Owned by Corporation. (5) Smithfield Vegetable Market Buildings. 1886. St. Martin's Lane from Jamaica Row to Moat Lane. Ca. £21,000 (not including frontage buildings). Covering of vegetable market and erection of shops and hotel as new frontage to market. Architects: Osborne and Reading, of Birmingham. Sculpture by John Roddis. Style described as "English Renaissance of the Stuart Period." Extended in 1892 and 1900. Largely wholesale. (6) Meat Market Hall. 1897. Bradford, Sherlock and Cheapside Streets. £48,000 (including wholesale and slaughterhouse sections). 96,000 sq. ft. Architects: Essex, Nicol, and Goodman, Birmingham. Owned by Corporation. Design of picturesque and original character in the "Spanish Renaissance" style; red brick and buff terra cotta. Wholesale hall is principal area; retail market hall includes 80 butchers' stalls. (7) Rag Market. 1907. Jamaica Row. Second-hand market. Demolished in 1957. (8) James Street Fish Market Hall. 1931; refurbished, 1988. (9) The New Bull Ring Market Hall. 1966. 250 stalls on three levels, connected by escalators.

Beginning in 1769 a board of Street Commissioners acquired five acts of Parliament (the last in 1828) to carry out numerous urban reform projects, including attempts to control the town marketing scattered in and around High Street. By 1806 the High Street markets were moved to the newly cleared Bull Ring. The reconstruction of the Birmingham Canal in 1834 resulted in increased market activity in the town and further demands for new facilities to alleviate the quarreling, rioting, and crowdedness of the existing market. An act of 1828 allowed for the building of a market hall stretching from the Bull Ring in High Street to Worcester Street—and hence the clearing of all buildings between those streets and Bell and Philip Streets. The new market, described as a "covered avenue," had entrances at each end with massive Doric columns, and was 365 ft. by 108 ft. and 60 ft. high. The interior had 600 stalls, and a large fountain stood at the center until 1880. The building suffered extensive bomb damage during World War

II. From 1940 to 1956 its walls served as the enclosure of an open-air market.

SOURCES: *Birmingham Markets and Fairs Committee, Birmingham Market Hall, 1835-1935*, 1935; *The Builder*, 30 Mar 1861, 7 Mar 1874, 2 Sep 1876, 19 Dec 1876, 24 Jul 1880, 11 Jun 1881, 16 Jul 1881, 25 Oct 1884, 5 May 1894, 12 May 1894, 3 Aug 1895, 2 Oct 1897, 6 Nov 1897; *Building News*, 8 Jul 1881, 7 Sep 1883, 20 Apr 1894, 27 Apr 1894, 26 Jun 1894, 14 Sep 1894, 9 Nov 1894, 18 Sep 1896, 8 Oct 1897, 27 Apr 1900, 19 Oct 1900; J. T. Bunce, *A History of the Corporation of Birmingham*, 1878; J. T. Bunce and C. A. Vince, *History of the Corporation of Birmingham, 1848-1902*, 3 vols., 1878; Robert K. Dent, *Old and New Birmingham, 1879-80*, 1894; Robert K. Dent, *The Making of Birmingham*, 1894; J. Doran, *Our Great Towns*, 1878; C. Gill and A. Briggs, *A History of Birmingham*, 1951; C. Gill and C. Robertson, *A Short History of Birmingham*, 1938; C. Gill, "Birmingham Under the Street Commissioners, 1769-1851," *University of Birmingham Historical Journal*, 1948; B. Little, *Birmingham Buildings: The Architectural Story of a Midland City*, 1971; W. Hutton, *History of Birmingham*, 6th ed., 1896; *Kelly's Directory of Birmingham, Staffordshire*, etc., 1896; D. McCulla, *Victorian and Edwardian Birmingham From Old Photographs*, 1973; *Notes on the City Markets and Abattoirs, City of Birmingham*, 1926; *Reports of Birmingham Markets and Fairs Committee, 1851-1870, Minutes*, 7 vols.; Z. Salzman and P. Styles, *A History of the County of Warwick*, Vol. 7, "City of Birmingham"; J. Zuckerman, ed., *Birmingham Heritage*, 1979.

BISHOP AUCKLAND   DURHAM

Town Hall and Market. 1862. £6,000 (estimated). 3,440 sq. ft. (market hall only) Architect: Johnson, of Newcastle. 100-ft. tower. Perhaps never used as a market. Extant in 1988.

SOURCES: *The Builder*, 18 Feb 1860, 7 Apr 1860, 19 May 1860.

BISHOPS CASTLE   SALOP

Market House (also known as Old Market Hall; and Powis Institute). General market. Ca. 1780. Shropshire Street. Owned by the Earl of Powis. Powis Coat of Arms in aedicule on site. Demolished in 1951.

SOURCES: Lewis; *Bishop's Castle Guide*, 1922-26; I. M. Evans, 1987.

BLACKBURN   LANCASHIRE

(1) Market Hall (a.k.a. Market Hall Number One). General market. 1848. Bounded by King William Street, Lord Street, Victoria Street, and the town

hall. £28,000. 19,874 sq. ft. Architect: Terrence Flanagan, Engineer for Bolton, Blackburn, Clitheroe, and West Yorkshire Railway. Contractor: R. Ibbotson. Owned originally by the Blackburn Improvement Commissioners; transferred to the Corporation in 1852. 72-ft. tower. Altered in 1935; demolished in 1962; replaced by New Market. (2) Market Hall Number Two. General market (originally fish market). 1872. £8,000. By the 1880s this was a retail dry-goods market. (3) Fish Market. 1874. (4) New Market Hall. 1964. 65,000 sq. ft. (280 stalls), with car park above. Part of town center redevelopment scheme.

The markets of Blackburn were originally held in the Old Market Place around the Old Cross (opposite Church Street) and with stalls extending along nearby streets—including Market Street Lane which had butchers' stalls on both sides. In 1803 the administration of the markets was passed from its ecclesiastical owner to the town Trustees, who undertook market reforms until the 1841 act of Parliament transferred market affairs to the new Improvement Commissioners. By the late nineteenth century Blackburn was known for the large quantity of fish bought and sold in its public markets, retail and wholesale.

The Market Hall of 1848 was the town's first public building of importance and was noted for its beauty. It was described as "completely unique in its appearance" and in the "early Italian palazzo" style. Built of Longridge stone, the structure was 186 ft. by 109 ft. The roof was divided into 3 spans, and the building had eight entrances, with the principal entrance beneath the campanile. One-half of the building had a cellar lighted by ranges of side windows. The interior had 34 shops, most having individual fireplaces; and there were 4 rows of stalls lengthwise and 4 rows across forming 3 passages. The gas lighting was described as providing "a very pretty and comfortable effect." By 1877 the hall was yielding an annual revenue of £4,500. The interior of the hall was reorganized and remodeled along a modern and "artistic" manner in 1935. In the post-1945 years the hall came to be considered too small to meet the needs of the town. Despite its great popularity, in 1962 it was demolished to make way for a town center redevelopment scheme which included a new market hall.

SOURCES: *VCH*; W. A. Abram, *Blackburn Times*, 1877; County Borough of Blackburn, *Centenary of the Opening of Market Hall No. 1, 1848-1948*, 1948; *County Borough of Blackburn, Wholesale and Retail Markets*, 1964; "Blackburn Market House," in *Practical Mechanics Journal*,

(1) 1848-49; P. A. Whittle, FSA, *Blackburn As It Is: A Topographical, Statistical and Historical Account*, 1852.

BLACKPOOL   LANCASHIRE

(1) St. John's Market. General market hall. 1844. Originally owned by private market company; acquired by Local Board of Health in 1853. Demolished in 1895. (2) General covered market. 1873. On the site of open market since 1853. Extended in 1888. (3) St. John's Market Hall. General market. 1938. East Topping Street. Requisitioned by the military during World War II; replaced by shopping center car park in 1955.

SOURCES: *VCH; The Builder*, 7 Sep 1872, 23 Aug 1879; *Building News*, 6 Sep 1872, 8 Jan 1897; *Market Trader*, 24 Sep 1955.

BLAINA   GWENT

Town Hall and Market. 1882. Architects: Wing and Johnson, of Abergavenny.

SOURCES: Colin, *Townhalls*, p. 282.

BODMIN   CORNWALL

(1) Assize Hall. General market house. 1815. (2) Market House. General market. 1839. Architect: W. Harris, Bristol. In 1833 it was argued that "a greater nuisance than Bodmin meat market never was induced" because of its lack of cover.

SOURCES: R. M. Barton, *Life in Cornwall in the Early Nineteenth Century*, 1970; J. S. Polsue, *Lake's Parochial History of the County of Cornwall*, Vol. 1, 1867-73 (repr. 1974).

BOGNOR REGIS   SUSSEX

General covered market. 1822. Located in The Steyne next to St. John's Chapel. Erected by Richard Clark; purchased by Local Board in 1875 for £500. Destroyed ca. 1930.

SOURCES: *VCH*; Gerard Young, *A History of Bognor Regis*, 1983.

BOLTON   GREATER MANCHESTER

(1) Market Hall. General market. Opened 19 Dec 1856. Knowsley and Corporation Streets. £72,414. 64,492 sq. ft. 600 stalls. Architect: G. T. Robinson. Contractor: William Tomkinson, Liverpool. Owned by the Corporation. Enlarged in 1865 (fish hall), 1871, and 1894. Interior rebuilt in 1935. Incorporated into Chapman Taylor Partners redevelopment scheme in 1989. (2) Covered general market (wholesale and retail). 1871. Located in Great Moor Street. Owned by Corporation. Closed in 1932. (3) Ashburner Market. General market hall. 1932. Located in Ashburner Street. Owned by Corporation. Extant in 1990.

A preeminent example of mid-Victorian architecture, the Bolton Market Hall of 1856 was proposed as a measure to improve the town's health by removing food sales from the unsanitary open market, to bring the public market in closer proximity to the town's growing population, and to provide for the sort of civic improvements and architectural display which the town fathers saw as being important to elevate the town to a more worthy rank. Improvement trustees had taken control of the local market rights from the local lord of the manor in 1826, after which the open market was reorganized and improved. The decision to build the new covered market was made by the town's first markets committee following the passage of the Bolton Improvement Act of 1850. An architectural competition, judged by George Godwin, the editor of *The Builder*, produced a short list of five plans, from which the plan of G. T. Robinson was selected. The uneven site was at the junction of Great and Little Bolton—heretofore only connected by wooden foot bridges—and held many cramped and unsanitary dwellings, the demolition of which along with the building of a viaduct across the River Crowl to connect the two Boltons, effected a "transformation of the most marvellous kind." Completion was delayed because the 66 foundation piers had to be rebuilt at a point when the roof construction was underway.

The principal entrance to the 1½-acre building is through a central Corinthian portico supported by 6 50-ft. columns. The structure was originally built with stalls and shops enough to accommodate 600 salespeople. In 1894 the blank arcades of the original classical façade were opened to accommodate shop fronts. The hall's glass roof with its turreted central peak soared 112 ft. above the market floor; a 7-division roof with 2 central transepts, it was the most complex example of the early iron-framed queen-rod truss-roof construction. The market was opened on 19 Dec 1855 to an audience of 18,000 to 20,000 including 3,000 women of Bolton seated in the galleries. In the 1920s its central avenue was used by nearby dairy people for the sale of eggs, butter, cheese, and dressed poultry. It was estimated at this same time that the adjacent fish market (both retail and wholesale) sold nearly 2,300 tons of fish annually. The interior was modernized in 1935, and in 1989 traditional market hall trading continued as the market was refurbished and incorporated into a larger new shopping scheme by Grosvenor Developments and the Metropolitan Borough of Bolton.

SOURCES: *Architects' Journal*, vol. 189, no. 16, 19 Apr 1989; *Bolton Chronicle*, 22 Dec 1855; *Bolton Journal*, 3 Nov 1849; *The Builder*, 22 Mar 1851, 8 Jan 1853; *County Borough of Bolton, Centenary Celebrations, the Market Hall, 1855-1955*, 1955. The Bolton Library has a considerable collection of drawings and plans of the Market Hall.

BOSTON   LINCOLNSHIRE

Covered fish market. 1872.

SOURCES: Lewis.

BRADFORD   WEST YORKSHIRE

(1) Market House. 1792. Market Street and Bank Street. Built by Lord Rawson. Originally built as a market in 1782 by town citizens for an improved market but the project was blocked by the lord of the manor; purchased by manorial owner and enlarged as Bank Street Market Hall in 1792-1801. (2) Market House. 1824. Kirkgate, Darley Street and Rawson Place. Built by manorial lord because of the unpopularity of Bank Street Market Hall; behind the Manor Hall. (3) Kirkgate Market Hall. General market. 1872 (extended between 1873 and 1878). Kirkgate and Darley Streets to Godwin Street on site of 1824 hall. £83,381. 75,000 sq. ft. 136 stalls and 52 shops. Architects: Lockwood and Mawson, of London. Owned by the Corporation. Demolished in 1973. (4) Rawson Place Market. Opened 13 Nov 1875. Godwin Street, Rawson Place, and James Street. £98,670 (including all additions up to 1930). 61,956 sq. ft. (in 1905). Architect: T. C. Hope, Bradford. Owned by the Corporation. Largely destroyed as a result of enemy action during World War II; rebuilt in 1956-58 and again in 1994 (at a cost of £4.8 million); parts of the original market stonework have been retained. Extant as a market, 1994. (5) Butchers' and Fish Market. Meat and fish market hall. 1874. Rawson Place, underside of Godwin Street, opening into the Rawson Square Market Hall. £10,000. 63 shops and stalls inside; 16 shops front Rawson Place. Owned by the Corporation. (6) James Street Market Hall. General market. 1905. £14,000. 14,769 sq. ft. (in 1930). Glass and iron screen frontage to James Street; part of Rawson Place market complex. First built as open market on old burial ground in 1890. Renovated in 1930 as a fish market, and refurbished in 1988 at cost of £500,000. Original roof retained. (7) John Street Market. 1920. Coppy Quarry Estate. £46,261. Former fairgrounds; long rows of glass-roofed stalls. Rebuilt in 1969, again in 1978. (8) New Kirkgate Market. 1973. (9) Shipley Market Hall. 1961. (10) Keighley Market Hall. 1971.

Prior to 1792 Bradford's market was held in a narrow street where "miserable horses trotted up and down." A group of citizens attempted to reform the market by building a market hall in 1782 but the project was blocked by the manorial lord, who then purchased the structure, added to it, and by 1801 had moved the town's market activities to it. In 1824 the market was then moved to a new hall at the rear of the Manor Hall. Over time this market became a great nuisance. The Corporation purchased the market and market rights from the Rawson family in 1867 for £200,000, and soon after constructed two large halls at very close proximity between three adjacent streets: the Kirkgate Hall between Kirkgate and Godwin Streets, and the Rawson Place Hall between Godwin and John Streets facing Rawson Place (described below). Both buildings were described in 1888 as "very much more elaborate and expensive than are necessary for market purposes" and as "handsome buildings and a credit to the town." In 1930 the Rawson Place Market was described as the chief retail market of the city for the sale of foodstuffs. When the Rawson Place market hall, with its domed interior hall with a single-span roof of glass and iron and two domed towers, was enlarged in 1905 it was extended to cover over the formerly open-air James Street Market. This new James Street Market front was of a substantial glass roof with a glass screen front; it was later converted to a fish market and continues Bradford's reputation as a major retail and wholesale fish center.

Lockwood and Mawson's Kirkgate Hall (opened in 1872 but not completed until 1878) was a large cast-iron and glass structure with considerable ornamental ironwork fit onto a highly irregular and uneven site, and with noteworthy attention to the design and arrangement of the interior space. Preliminary to designing the building Mawson visited market halls in Paris, Hamburg, and Rotterdam. The central entrance on Kirkgate Street was a lofty archway enclosed by a sliding gate produced by the Coalbrookdale Company, and with sculpture above representing Pomona and Flora, the goddesses of fruit and flowers, by Keyworth of London. The market floor was level with an entrance at Darley Street, but the Kirkgate entrance is reached by ascending 30 steps and the Godwin entrance is reached by descending 32 steps. In the interior, there were two octagonal pavilions 50 ft. in diameter, which gave access to 6 "avenues" for market goods. The interior, which was painted green and gold bronze, had 36 octagonal-shaped covered stalls and 52 open stalls, and with "roomy shops" along the inner sides lined with white glazed brick. Around the perimeter were 52 shops, some of which opened to hall. A hotel and the Central Free Library occupied a considerable portion of the exterior façade. Stall arrangement was "so managed that no stall will possess an undue advantage in point of position over another." After considerable

public controversy in the 1960s the building was demolished in 1973.

SOURCES: *PP-88; Bradford Association, Handbook to Bradford* (n.d.); *The Builder,* 31 Dec 1871, 20 Jul 1872, 3 Aug 1872, 21 Feb 1874, 1 Aug 1874, 23 Oct 1875, 29 Apr 1899, 22 Jul 1899, 8 Feb 1902, 13 Aug 1904, 29 Apr 1905; *Building News,* 17 Mar 1889, 21 Jul 1899, Sep 29, 1899; *City of Bradford Official Handbook,* 10th ed., 1948; *Bradford Corporation, Municipal Markets: A Brief Description,* revised edition, 1951; *Kelly's Directory,* 1903; Derek Linstrum, *West Yorkshire Architect and Architecture,* 1978; J. Parker, *Illustrated Ramblings From Hipperhold to Tory,* 1904; D. G. Wright and J. A. Jewitt, *Victorian Bradford.*

BRAMPTON CUMBERLAND

Butter Market (also known as Moot Hall). General market house. 1817. Small two-story octagonal building with cupola; upper portion used as town hall, lower portion open and used for market purposes. Owned originally by the Earl of Carlisle; purchased by the Parish Council in 1896. Extant, presently used as office.

BRECON POWYS

Market Hall. General market. 1841. The Struet. £4,500 (original cost). Architect: T. H. Wyatt. Owned by Brecon Market Company, then Corporation per act of 1862. Extended in 1845. Extant in 1994 as market.

SOURCES: Edwin Pool, *Illustrated History and Biography of Brecknockshire,* 1886.

BRENTFORD GREATER LONDON

(1) Town Hall and Market House. 1850. Replaced the 1635 Market House. Architect, F. Byass. Building renovated extensively since 1929. Presently used as a Magistrate's Court. (2) Bretford Covered Fruit Market (largely wholesale). 1892 (extended in 1905). Kew Bridge. £8,000. 1½ acres in size. Architect: J. H. Strachan, Surveyor. Owned by the Corporation. Closed in 1974; demolished in 1981.

SOURCES: *VCH; The Builder,* 17 Oct 1891, 23 Sep 1905; *Building News,* 22 Sep 1905.

BRIDGNORTH SALOP

New Market Hall. 1855. High Street at Postern Gate and Listley Street. Architect: Griffiths, Stafford. Impressive polychrome brick work. Built by a market company then leased by local Board of Health (1860) but never used as market because local traders won a perpetual injunction disallowing any interference of trade rights of High Street merchants. Converted to use for private shops. Extant in 1990.

SOURCES: *Bagshaw's Shropshire Directory of 1851; Kelly's Directory of Hertfordshire and Shropshire,* 1905; W. J. Macefield, *Bridgnorth As It Was,* 1978; J. Robinson, *Architecture of Northern England,* 1986.

BRIDGWATER   SOMERSET

(1) General market hall. 1826-30. Cornhill. 15,092 sq. ft. Architect: Benjamin Baker, Bridgwater. Central feature of main façade is circular Ionic portico with dome and lantern. Extant in 1991. (2) General covered market. 1873. Located in Main Street. £4,277. Owned by Corporation.

SOURCES: *PP-35;* Lewis.

BRIERLEY HILL   STAFFORDSHIRE

General market building. 8,100 sq. ft. Privately owned.

BRIGHTON   SUSSEX

(1) Market House. 1774. Market Street. Demolished ca. 1828. (2) Market Hall. General market. 1830 (rebuilt in 1921). Adjoins the Town Hall between Market Street and Black Lion Street near the East Cliff. Built on the site of the 1774 Market House. £60,000 (including cost of Town Hall). Architect: Thomas Cooper, Brighton. Owned by Improvement Commissioners under an act of 1825. Destroyed. (3) Floral Hall. General fruit, flower, and vegetable market (largely wholesale, but included some retail traders). 1900. Market Street. Owned by the Corporation. Severely damaged in 1940 (walls remained until 1976). (4) Brighton Municipal Market Hall. General market. 1937 (replaced 1900 Floral Hall, but in different location; Wholesale Fruit and Vegetable Market transferred to this location). Circus Street. 2 acres in size. Owned by the Corporation. Extant in 1992. (5) Brighton Fish Market. Pre-1825. Located near Lamprels Swimming Baths. Discontinued use in 1960 (moved to new premises adjacent to the Wholesale Fruit and Vegetable Market in Circus Street at a cost of £9,000).

SOURCES: *VCH.*

BRISTOL   AVON

(1) Fish market. 1744. Located behind Exchange, St. Nicholas Street. Owned by the Corporation. Demolished in 1844 (incorporated into the 1849 Exchange Market). (2) St. Nicholas Market. General covered market. 1744. Architect: James Foster. Impressive Palladian entry façade. Behind Exchange. Owned by the Corporation. Incorporated into the 1849 Exchange Market. Extant in 1990. (3) Flower Market. 1745. Behind Exchange. Architect: Samuel Glascodine. Owned by the Corporation. Incorporated into the 1849 Exchange Market. (4) St. Nicholas Butchers' Market, 1775. Behind the Exchange. £5,000. Additional meat market with glass roof and partially open sides added in 1808 between St. Nicholas Street and Exchange. (5) Exchange Market. General market hall. 1849. 3 arcades and hall (reconstructed in 1872 and 1883). Located behind the Exchange with principal entrance on High Street. Incoporated the 1744-45 fish, meat, flower, and general markets. £50,000. 16,280 sq. ft. Architect for the reconstructions: Mr. Pope, City Architect. Extant. (6) Union Street Market (a.k.a. St. James Market). Meat and general market hall (wholesale and retail). 1771 (built as a walled and partially covered market; rebuilt in 1858). Located in Union Street. Owned by the Corporation. Closed in 1907. (7) St. Nicholas Street Fish Market Hall. St. Nicholas and Baldwin Streets. 1872 (rebuilt in 1884) (Baldwin Street front by Gingell, 1897). Corporation owned. (8) Welsh Market House. General (for sale of goods from Wales). 1776. On the Back at Queen Square. £340.

Bristol was England's second largest city in the mid-eighteenth century when a complex of new markets was built as a result of a local government order prohibiting street marketing. These markets, with an impressive arched Palladian entrance at High Street, were known as the Exchange Markets or St. Nicholas Markets, and consisted of a series of connected arcaded halls placed to the back of Bristol's finest eighteenth-century building, The Exchange, and occupied several blocks west from High Street to St. Nicholas Street. At the time these markets were claimed to be the most commodious and beautiful markets in England. They were reconstructed in 1849 as a glass roofed avenue off of High Street leading to a series of arcades and market halls (a poultry and butter market, a butchers' market, a fruit and vegetable market, and a flower market, with an adjoining fish market). The market still functions as a public market.

SOURCES: *PP-35; PP-88; Bristol Journal,* 25 Jun 1808; Gordon Priest, *A History of Building Policy for Bristol,* 1972; H. B. Burrough, *Bristol,* Bristol, 1970; A. Gomme, M. Jenner, and B. Little, *Bristol, An Architectural History,* 1979; John Latimer, *Annals of Bristol,* 1887-1893; *Arrowsmith's Dictionary of Bristol,* 1906; Walter Ison, *The Georgian Buildings of Bristol,* 1952; G. F. Stone, *Bristol as It Was and Is,* 1908-1909; *Western Daily Press,* 10 Apr 1943; John Wood, *A Description of the Exchange of Bristol,* 1745; illustrations of the Exchange Markets and other information on the Bristol markets may be found in the Braikenridge Collection, Local History Collection, Bristol Library. Few Corporation Records of the Markets have survived, but those available can be found listed in Elizabeth Ralph, *Guide to the Bristol Archive Office,* Bristol, 1991.

BRIXHAM
DEVON

Market and Town Hall. General market, 1886. Bolton, Fore, and Church Streets. £2,500. 3,900 sq. ft. Architect: G. S. Bridgeman, Torquay. Carried out by Market Commissioners, per act of 1837.

SOURCES: *The Builder,* 22 Dec 1877, 3 Oct 1885; *Building News,* 14 Dec 1877, 8 Oct 1886.

BROMYARD
HEREFORD

Market Hall, 1843.

BRYNMAWR
GWENT

Market Hall. General market (and public hall). 1894. Alma Street. £2,500. 6,000 sq. ft. With gallery at one end and platform at the other. Architect: E. A. Johnson, Abergavenny. Owned by Borough Council. Extant as market, 1994.

SOURCES: *Building News,* 9 Mar 1894.

BUILTH WELLS
POWYS

Market House. General Market, 1875. £3,500. 2,079 sq. ft. Architects: Haddon Brothers, Hereford. Owned by Market Company. Italian Gothic, with clock tower and interior glass and iron roof. Extant in 1987.

BURNLEY
LANCASHIRE

(1) Covered Market. General market (including meat, fish). In the Market Place. 1829. £3,000. Built by Burnley Market Company. Demolished in 1866 to provide room for new market. (2) Victoria Market. Covered (shed) market for fruit and vegetables. Ca. 1840. 19,800 sq. ft. St. James Street. Owned by market trustees (Burnley Market Company), sold to Corporation in 1865. Demolished in 1873. (3) Market Hall. General market. Opened on 1 Jan 1870. New Market Place (created by demolishing Polk, Fountain, Rodney Streets). Ca. £9,000. 20,880 sq. ft. Architect: James Green, Portsmouth. Owned by the Corporation (per Burnley Market Act of 1865). 3-span wrought-iron roof, supported on cast-iron columns. Entrance portico with Roman Doric columns. Demolished in 1966 for redevelopment scheme. (4) New Market Hall. General market. 1967. Coporation owned. Modern brick and glass structure.

The first covered markets in Burnley were two shedlike structures, one called "Victoria Market" in St. James Street, and the other built in the market place in 1829 by a newly formed Market Company (with capital of £3,000). This company (and the market rights) was bought by the Corporation in 1865 for £22,569—a price which some town council members regarded to be exorbitant. The council then planned a new market hall in 1865. When this large new hall was opened in 1870 it was hailed as "an event of great importance" for the 40,000 residents of the townships of Burnley and Habergham Eaves. The building, in what was termed "Palladian Italian" style, was a large parallelogram (180 ft. by 116 ft.) with a 3-division iron roof, and an entrance portico with 4 attached Roman Doric columns and cast-iron gates. A planned clock tower was not built. The interior had 32 shops (12 ft. by 15 ft. each) and 128 lineal yards of stallage in the center of the hall. Additional shops were situated at the basement level. At the time of its opening the town's mayor expressed the hope that the new market hall "will bring about a very wholesome system of competition among the various trades." Within a decade the market had a reputation of being orderly and well regulated.

SOURCES: *PP-88; VCH;* Walter Berrett, *The History of Burnley From 1850,* 1951; *The Builder,* 7 Apr 1866; John Kreishaw, *Burnley in the Nineteenth Century,* 1897. "Newspaper Scrapbook," District Central Library, Burnley.

BURSLEM
STAFFORDSHIRE

(1) Market Hall. General market. 1836. Wedgewood St. 124 "places" for market traders. Architect: Samuel Ledward. Ownership: Market Trustees. Demolished in 1957. (2) Fish Market. 1851. Ground floor of Town Hall. Ownership: Market Trustees. (3) Market Hall. General market. 1879. Market Place and Queen St. £19,000. 16,200 sq. ft. Architect: E. M. Richards, C.E., Borough Surveyor. Included a 96-ft. tower and fine interior cast-iron Gothic Revival details.

SOURCES: *VCH; The Builder,* 12 Jul 1879; *Building News,* 22 Mar 1878, 18 Jul 1879, 22 Aug 1879.

BURTON-ON-TRENT
STAFFORDSHIRE

(1) Market Hall. General market. Opened on 24 Oct 1883. £12,000. 9,810 sq. ft. (hall only). Architects: Dixon and Moxon, of Barnsley. Sculpture by Roddis, of Birmingham. 21 interior shops along three sides, 4 shops as exterior front. (2) Fish Market. 1925.

SOURCES: *The Builder,* 3 Nov 1883; *Building News,* 18 Feb 1881, 2 Nov 1883.

BURY
GREATER MANCHESTER

(1) Market Hall. Enclosed general market. 1839 (glass roof added in 1868). £26,000. 32,625 sq. ft. Owned by the Earl of Derby, purchased by town in 1872. (2) Fish Market. Covered market. Ca. 1872. £2,160. (3) Market Hall. General market. 1901. Market Street and Moss Lane. £14,500. 30,000 sq. ft. Architect: Archibald Neill, Leeds. To replace 1839 building. Owned by the Corporation.

The Bury Market Act of May 1839 stated that the market place had become inadequate for its purpose and that the streets and market place were greatly obstructed and rendered dangerous to the inhabitants of the town. The architect was instructed "to produce such an external and internal architectural appearance as may serve to at once indicate the uses to which the buildings are to be devoted, and of a sufficiently imposing and important character." The new hall of 1901 included an octagonal domed entrance used for the sale of fruit, flowers, sweets, and toys. All told the market had 100 stalls and 24 shops, with a separate Fish Market. The structure was destroyed by fire in November 1968.

SOURCES: *PP-88; VCH; The Builder*, 14 Mar 1891, 11 Jul 1891; *Building News*, 13 Mar 1891, 11 Sep 1891, 20 Dec 1901.

CADOXTON   GLAMORGAN

[see BARRY]

CAERNARFON   GWYNEDD

Market Hall. General market. 1832. Market Street. Architect: J. Lloyd. Extant in 1987.

SOURCES: *Architecture in Wales: Plans and Projects, 1780-1914*, Welsh Arts Council, 1975.

CALLINGTON   CORNWALL

Covered Pannier Market. 1832. In 1856 a new street was built from Saltash Road along the back of the Fore Street properties to give easier access to the market. Entrance from behind Market House Inn.

SOURCES: Sheila Lightbody, *The Book of Callington*, 1982.

CAMBORNE   CORNWALL

Market Hall. General market. 1866. Church Street at Market Place. £4,000. Architect: William Bond. Owner: John F. Basset, manorial lord. Large side entrance to market. Clock tower and large assembly room over market hall. Large quadrangular building.

SOURCES: *PP-88*.

CANNOCK   STAFFORDSHIRE

Market Hall. 1869. £897. 50 stalls. Architect: Lloyd, Wolverhampton. Owned by Cannock Market Hall Company (with over 700 shareholders). Converted into movie house, 1919. Demolished in 1969.

SOURCES: *VCH; The Courier*, 27 Aug 1948.

CANTERBURY   KENT

(1) Fish Market. Covered. 1789. Entrances on High and Burgate Streets in Longmarket. Architect: Jessie White. Owned by Town Council. Converted into 2 shops in 1892. (2) Vegetable Market. 1824. Lower floor of Corn Exchange. Served as entrance to Longmarket (formerly Butchery Lane), the open market place. No longer used by 1930. Destroyed by bombing, 1942.

SOURCES: *PP-88*; A. M. Oakley, *Canterbury Markets* (pamphlet), Canterbury City Council, 2d ed., 1986.

CARDIFF   GLAMORGAN

(1) New Market. General market. Opened Dec 1835. St. Mary Street. Owned by Borough Council. Front section removed to provide site for 1884 market. (2) St. Mary Street Market Buildings. General market hall. 1884. St. Mary Street. £12,000. Architect: J. P. Jones. Owned by Borough Council and leased to Solomon Andrews who financed the building. Five-story-high front. Rebuilt after a fire in 1886, again with a five-story front, with grand archway entrance to the market. Both retained the market hall portion of the 1835 New Market. (3) St. Mary Street Market. General market hall and fish market. 1891. St. Mary Street. £16,000. 16,200 sq. ft. Architect: W. Harpur, C.E., Borough Engineer; Ironwork Contractor: A. Handyside and Co., Derby. Owned by Borough Council. Replaced (1) and (2) above. Extant in 1991. (4) Working Street Market Hall. General market. 1901. Working Street. 9,954 sq. ft. Architect: W. Harpur, C.E., Borough Engineer. Owned by Corporation.

The 1891 St. Mary Street Market Hall is notable for its construction and adaptability to site. Its roof of cast iron, wrought iron, and steel is of "simple Belgian truss" design and the main columns are 24 ft. 6 in. center to center. The butchers' shops are lined with white glazed brick to a height of 6 ft. The assymmetrical form of the site (about 200 ft. by 81 ft.) was addressed by creating butchers' shops on the ground floor of varying widths, while allowing for a symmetrical ground floor and roof quadrangle, complete with a gallery holding 53 shops (see illustration of floor plan and photo of interior). The market design is unusual in that a central double row of glass-roofed provision shops divided its 4 interior avenues, each shop facing an aisle of stationary stalls for greengrocers and butchers' shops along the side walls. The butchers' shops were given cast-iron countertops. A fish market was placed at the Trinity Street end of the hall.

SOURCES: John F. Andrews, *Keep Moving* (n.d, n.p.). *The Builder*, 23 May 1891, 15 Jul 1899, 2 Feb

1901, 2 Mar 1901; *Building News*, 4 Nov 1881, 28 Sep 1883, 15 May 1891; *The Engineer*, 13 Apr 1888; *Engineering*, 20 Jan 1893, 17 Feb 1893, 3 Mar 1893.

CARDIGAN   DYFED

Market House. General market. 1859. £2,174. Architect: R. J. Withers, London. Owned by Corporation. Extant in 1987. Connected to Gothic Revival Guildhall; when first opened it was so brightly lit by the glass roof that "yards and yards" of calico had to be hung on the roof of the market (interior) to keep the sun from the butchers' meat. Extant.

SOURCES: *Architecture in Wales: Plans and Projects, 1780-1914*, Welsh Arts Council, 1975; *Building News*, 29 Jan 1858, 12 Mar 1858; *The Market Traders Review*, 27 May 1967.

CARLISLE   CUMBERLAND

(1) Butchers' Market. Covered. 1801. (2) Market Hall. General market. Opened 2 Oct 1889. Between Scotch Street and Fisher Street. £35,000. 63,000 sq. ft. Architect: Arthur Cawston, RIBA, and Joseph Graham, Carlisle; roof design by A. T. Walmisley, C.E. Owned by Corporation. Refurbished in the 1980s and still serves as an important public market.

At the time the new market was built in 1889, numerous markets were scattered throughout Carlisle: a butter market, a market for poultry and fruit in Lowther Street, a Green Market in front of the Town Hall, a potato market in Castle Street, and a butchers' market. Most of these were unprotected and caused "exceedingly overcrowded" streets. The growing population and the coming of the Midland Railway made Carlisle a major market center for many nearby towns. An act of Parliament of 1873 allowed the Corporation to purchase the market rights from the Duke of Devonshire. Built on the site of the old Butchers' Shambles, Cawston and Graham's design was selected from among 36 entered in a competition. Designed in "the simplest form of the Renaissance style," it included a 160-ft.-high "Jubilee Tower" at the northwest corner, an arcade with shops connecting the market to the town's principal shopping street, and an advanced 3-division iron roof designed by T. Walmisley, C.E. When it opened, the market included 38 butchers' shops.

SOURCES: *PP-88; The Builder*, 13 Apr 1861, 11 Dec 1886, 1 Jan 1887, 3 Dec 1887, 12 Oct 1889; *Building News*, 10 Dec 1886, 23 Dec 1887; *Carlisle Journal*, 4 Oct 1889; *The Engineer and Architect*, 30 Mar 1888, 13 Apr 1888.

CARMARTHEN   DYFED

Market House. 1846. Architect: F. E. H. Fowler.

CASTLE CARY   SOMERSET

Market Hall. General market. 1856. On site of old market house. £2,300. 1,536 sq. ft. Architect: F. C. Penrose, London. Gothic and Jacobean exterior, with assembly room above. Included a mezzanine for the sale of cheese and a long covered gallery on the north end for butchers' stalls.

SOURCES: *The Builder*, 10 May 1856.

CASTLEFORD   WEST YORKSHIRE

(1) Castleford Market. General market hall. Opened 12 Jul 1880. Carlton and Aire Streets. £13,038. 25,029 sq. ft. Architects: Malcolm Paterson and Malcolm Wheater. Owned by the District Council. Destroyed by fire on 31 Dec 1927. (2) New Market. General market hall. 1929 (reconstructed behind remaining façade of the 1880 structure; addition made in 1934). 27,756 sq. ft. Extant in 1988; façade slated for demolition in 1992.

SOURCES: *Market Trader*, 10 Oct 1959; *Pontefract and Castleford Express*, 1 Oct 1970, 4 Mar 1971. Photographs held by Wakefield Metropolitan Library.

CHAGFORD   DEVONSHIRE

Market House. General market. 1862. Hexagonal with slate roof, Gothic entrance, topped with cupola.

SOURCES: Rosemary Ann Lander, *Views of Old Bideford*, 1983.

CHARD   SOMERSET

Town Hall and Market House. Meat market. 1834. 1,376 sq. ft. Owned by the Corporation. Two-story portico. Extensive covered shambles attached.

SOURCES: *PP-88*; Lewis.

CHELTENHAM   GLOUCESTERSHIRE

(1) Market House. General market. 1786. Located opposite North Place. Owned by the Paving Commissioners. Demolished in 1808. (2) Market House. General market. 1808. High Street. (3) The Bazaar. General covered market with arcade. 1823. 3,528 sq. ft. Architect: possibly Edward Jenkins. Originally built by Lord Sherbourne. Triple-arch Gothic entrance on Bennington Street. Removed in 1867.

SOURCES: S. Blake and R. Beacham, *The Book of Cheltenham*, 1982; S. J. Griffith, *History of Cheltenham*, 1826; Gwen Hart, *A History of Cheltenham*, 1965 (repr. 1981).

CHERTSEY SURREY

General market house. 1810. Bridge Street. Replaced 1599 market house, which was demolished in 1809.

SOURCES: *VCH.*

CHESTER CHESHIRE

(1) Covered general markets. 1828. Located on both sides of Northgate Street. Builder: Mr. Royle. Plan attributed to Major H. Bowers. (2) General market hall. Opened 10 Mar 1863. Located in Northgate Street. 41,634 sq. ft. Architects: W. and J. Hay, Liverpool; Builder: Roberts, of Chester. Included a fish market at the northwest end of the building. Owned by the Corporation. Extended 1881 at a cost of £5,958. Demolished. Flamboyant baroque with grand entrance. Interior with butchers' shops on sides and farm products in center; upper end had a crockery mart, and a fishmongers' market was within a large bay to the right side. Of the interior it was said (in 1867) that "if it were the architect's aim to provide something original, he has achieved it."

SOURCES: *The Builder,* 7 Feb 1863; *Building News,* 2 Dec 1881, 2 Jun 1882, 2 Jul 1886; *Gresty and Burghall's Chester Guide,* 1867 (revised by John Hinklin, 1867); Brian Harris, *Barthelomew City Guides,* Chester, 1979; Joseph Hemingway, *History of the City of Chester From its Foundation to the Present Time,* Vol. 2, 1831; Herbert Hughes, *Chronicle of Chester. The 200 Years 1775-1975,* 1975; Thomas Hughes, *The Stranger's Handbook to Chester,* 1856 (repr. 1972).

CHESTERFIELD DERBYSHIRE

Market Hall. General market. 1857. £5,485. 14,760 sq. ft. Located in Market Place. Architects: Davies and Tew. Builder: George Thompson. Redecorated in 1875 by Crosley of Newark under the direction of S. Rollinson, Architect, Chesterfield. Owned by the Corporation. Award winning renovation in 1981. Extant in 1988.

SOURCES: *The Builder,* 27 Feb 1875, 21 Jul 1900; *The Market Trader,* 15 Apr 1976.

CHICHESTER SUSSEX

Market Hall. General market. Opened 20 Jan 1808. 4,703 sq. ft. Located at Swan Back Gate in North Street. Architect: John Nash. Owned by the Corporation. Per act of Parliament of 1807. Simple and dignified façade of Doric columns supporting a classical entablature and balustrade.

SOURCES: *PP-35; PP-88; VCH; The Builder,* 26 May 1870; *Building News,* 12 May 1871; Francis W. Steer, "The Market House, Chichester," *Chichester Papers,* Vol. 3, No. 27, 1962; "Plans and Elevation of Market House at Chichester [with notes]," Royal Insititute of British Architects, Library.

CHIPPENHAM WILTSHIRE

New Hall (a.k.a. Neeld Hall). General market house and covered shambles. 1833. High Street. Owned by Joseph Neeld, M.P., Grittleton. Enlarged in 1851. Open ground floor loggia was used as market. Extant in 1990 (converted for use as Town Hall) but under threat of demolition.

SOURCES: *PP-88;* Lewis; Department of the Environment, *Listed Buildings,* Chippenham; George White, *Chippenham in Bygone Days,* 1965.

CHORLEY LANCASHIRE

Town Hall and Market. General market. 1802. Market on lower floor. Built by John Hollingshead, Esq. Described at the time as "a neat stone building." Replaced in the 20th century by Flat Iron Market in Clifford Street.

SOURCES: *PP-88;* Lewis; *Market Trader,* 5 Sep 1959.

CHURCH STRETTON SALOP

General market house. 1840.

CLEVEDON AVON

Market Hall. General market. 1869. Alexandra Road. £1,120. Architect: Hans Price. Owned by the Corporation. Built in the style of a Chinese pagoda. Extant in 1988.

SOURCES: *Clevedon From the Village to Town,* Clevedon Civic Society, 1981; Jennifer Clapp, "Clevedon," *Bristol and West Country Illustrated,* Aug 1980.

COCKERMOUTH CUMBERLAND

Covered general market. Ca. 1830. Located at the Kirkgate and Church Lane. 7,740 sq. ft. Ownership transferred from the Earl of Egremont to Market Company in 1837; then to Market Trustees and leased to the Local Board in 1869.

SOURCES: *PP-88.*

COLCHESTER ESSEX

(1) Dutch Bay Hall (a.k.a. The Exchange). Butter and poultry market. 1803. Northwest end of High Street. Architect: David Laing. Owned by the Corporation. Building sold in 1819 to cover litigation costs. Ground floor continued to be used as corn market. Early fine nineteenth-century neo-classical façade with projecting colonnade. Extant. (2) The Market Place. General covered market. 1813. Located near the Town Hall.

£10,000. Privately owned. Appears to have been unsuccessful: closed prior to 1848.

SOURCES: A. F. J. Brown, *Colchester 1815-1914*, 1980; Bernard Drew, *The Fire Office, Being the History of the Essex and Suffolk Equitable Insurance Society*, 1952; *White's Directory of Essex*, 1848; *Kelly's Directory of Essex*, 1899.

COLNE   LANCASHIRE

Market Hall. 1898. Located in Docicray Street. Owned by the Corporation. Destroyed by fire in 1935.

CONGLETON   CHESHIRE

(1) Assembly Room and Market Hall. General market. 1823. Owned by Sir Edmond Antrobus, Bart. Neat and commodius edifice with assembly rooms above, addition to earlier Town Hall of 1803. (2) Town Hall and Market. 1864. High Street. Covered market in arcaded ground floor. Massive tower above.

SOURCES: *PP-35*; Lewis.

COPPERHOUSE   CORNWALL

Market House. General market. Located in Copperhouse Square. Tower and clock removed in 1930. Extant in 1985.

SOURCES: Cyrill Noall, *The Book of Hayle*, 1985.

CORSHAM   WILTSHIRE

Market House. General market. 1784.

COVENTRY   WARWICKSHIRE

(1) New Market. General market house. 1845. (2) Market Hall. General market. 1867. Located between Smithford Street and West Orchard. £20,000. 16,404 sq. ft. Architect: Frederick Peck, London; Builder: Tomlinson. Red, blue, and white brick with Bath stone dressing and impressive 135-ft.-high clock tower. Included a fish arcade. Per special act of Parliament of 1863. Owned by the Corporation. Destroyed in enemy action in 1940. (3) Market Hall. General market. 1958. £385,000. 92 yards in diameter. Circular building with parking garage. 160 stalls and 40 shops. Britain's first postwar market hall. Owned by the Corporation. Remodeled, 1995.

SOURCES: *PP-35*; *PP-88*; Lewis; *VCH*; *The Builder*, 16 Aug 1845; *Building News*, 25 Dec 1908; *Market Trader Review*, 15 Mar 1952; 15 Nov 1958. Benjamin Pool, *Coventry: Its History and Antiquities*, 1970.

COWES   ISLE OF WIGHT

Market House. General market. 1816. High Street. Destroyed in the Second World War.

SOURCES: E. H. Gooch, *A History of West Cowes*, 1946.

CREWE   CHESHIRE

(1) General covered market. 1848. Owned by the London and Northwest Railway Company. A series of huge longitudinal umbrellas built on low pillars. (2) Market Hall. General market (built as wholesale cheese market, but gradually became retail general market). 1854. Located in Prince Albert Street and Earle Street. £3,000. 15,200 sq. ft. Architect: Charles Meason. Yellow and red brick; Italianate; tower added in 1871. Owned by John Hill. Extant in 1988.

SOURCES: *The Builder*, 7 Jan 1878, 20 Jul 1878; W. H. Chaloner, *The Social and Economic Development of Crewe*, 1954.

CROYDON   SURREY

General market below town hall. 1809. Moved from this site prior to 1889.

SOURCES: *VCH*.

CRYMYCH   DYFED

Market Hall. General market. 1922. Located in Central Square. £827. 3,195 sq. ft. Built by Crymmych [sic. the earlier spelling is with a double 'm'] Market Hall Company (a joint stock company formed in 1911). Of the seven original shareholders, three were local farmers and two were Crymych shopkeepers. Currently owned by Bro Preseli Rural Enterprise. Extant in 1992.

SOURCES: "Memorandum and Articles of Association of the Crymmych Market Hall Company, Ltd.," 1911.

DARLINGTON   DURHAM

(1) Market House and Town Hall. 1808. £2,000. Owned by group of "local gentlemen." (2) Shambles. Butchers' market. 1815. East of the Town Hall. (3) Market Hall and Town Hall. General market. Opened 2 May 1864. Located in High Row. £16,356. 17,380 sq. ft. Architect: Alfred Waterhouse. Built because of concern for market hygiene. Described at opening as an elegant Gothic building, it was of white brick with stone dressing; included a clocktower with 5 bells. Open arcades on the north and east sides of the market hall enclosed in 1866 at an additional cost of £2,611. Originally owned by the local Board of Health; then the Corporation. Refurbished in 1978; extant as market.

SOURCES: *PP-88; The Builder,* 19 Dec 1863; Peter Wilkes, *Our Glorious Market Heritage,* 1972; see also Darlington Library Newspaper Clippings File.

DARTMOUTH — DEVONSHIRE

Old Market. Market House in center of piazza (surrounded by covered arcaded general market). 1829. Located in Victoria Road. Built on land reclaimed from the Old Mill Pool. Owned by the Dartmouth Town Council. Refurbished in the 1980s. Extant in 1990.

SOURCES: *The Builder,* 19 Dec 1904; *Market Trader Review,* 21 Jan, 18 Feb 1967.

DARTMOUTH HARDNESS — DEVONSHIRE

Covered market. Ca. 1788.

DARWEN — LANCASHIRE

(1) Greenway Market. General market. 1847. Privately owned. (2) Market Hall. General market. Opened 24 Jun 1882. Railway Road at School Street. £20,000. 10,400 sq. ft. Architect: Charles Bell, London. Built over the River Darwen. Market was built instead of town hall; exterior of Darwen stone; *The Builder* called it a "simple, but effective," Italian style. Owned by the Corporation. Extant.

SOURCES: *VCH; The Builder,* 9 Oct 1880, 31 Jul 1882; *Building News,* 15 Aug 1879, 5 Sep 1879, 24 Oct 1879; *A History of Darwen's Market Hall, 1882-1982,* The Lancashire Library, 1982.

DAWLEY — SALOP

(1) General market house. Ca. 1836. High Street. (2) Market Hall. General market. 1867. High Street. Owned by Market Hall Company. Used as a bank in 1958.

SOURCES: *VCH.*

DENBIGH — CLWYD

Market Hall. General market. 900 sq. ft. Owned by the Corporation.

SOURCES: *Building News,* 26 Apr 1912.

DERBY — DERBYSHIRE

(1) Market House. General market. 1831. Owned by the Corporation. (2) Market Hall. General market. 1866. Town center. £29,045. 24,200 sq. ft. Architects: T. C. Thorburn and G. Thompson; interior decorative details by Mr. Cantrill and Owen Jones; roof construction by Mr. Haywood. New fish market alongside market hall in 1926. Renovated in 1938 and then extensively in 1988 at a cost of £4,300,000. Extant in 1998.

The public market system in Derby was reorganized in 1830. Prior to that the town's marketing took place in what had come to be regarded as an exceedingly unsafe, crowded, and inconvenient open market place and covered walkway (called "the piazza") which had acquired a notorious reputation as the locus for bull baiting, riot, and crime. In 1830 the Corporation erected a "new market ground" and a covered market with 100 shops for the sale of meat, butter, and vegetables. The growth of the town and the district led to the construction of a Market Hall in 1864-1866. This red-brick hall in a modest Italianate manner, had a semi-circular wrought-iron and glass roof supported by 22 decorative iron columns, with a span of 86 ft. and 2 small side roofs. 38 tall iron-framed Gothic windows were spaced along all sides. A gallery rings the interior walls, under which are housed 40 large shops. When the hall opened, the center space had 150 stalls. The hall has been carefully restored and still functions as a market.

SOURCES: *The Builder,* 19 May 1860, 26 May 1866; *Derby Market,* Derby Corporation, Markets Department, 1933; *County Borough of Derby, Markets Committee, Official Handbook,* 1955; County Borough of Derby, Markets Committee, *Derby Market Hall Centenary Handbook,* 1966; *Glover's Directory of Derby,* 1858.

DEVIZES — WILTSHIRE

(1) New Hall. Cheese market. 1752. Wine Street. Architect: Lawrence. Rebuilt in 1810. Original had open piazza. (2) Shambles. 1771-1803. Short Street. Incorporated into the Market Hall of 1835. (3) New Market House. General market. 1835. Short Street. Architect: Pollard, Frome. A two-story façade of 3 bays with clocktower; 2 interior halls. Owned by the Corporation. Extant in 1988.

SOURCES: *PP-88; VCH;* Edward Bradby, *The Book of Devizes,* 1964; *Listed Buildings, Devizes,* The Department of the Environment.

DEVONPORT — DEVONSHIRE

Market Hall. General market. 1852. Between Cumberland, Duke, Market, and Catherine Streets. £35,000. Architect: S. P. St. Aubyn. 124-ft. Italianate tower. Owned by Lord St. Levan. No longer used as market. Extant in 1991.

SOURCES: *PP-88.*

DEWSBURY — WEST YORKSHIRE

(1) Market Cross Market. General market. 1826. 2,304 sq. ft. Town Square. Architect: James Nowell. A series of flat-roofed shops with a tall open temple-like structure above, with colonnade and cupola. Demolished in the 1850s. Trading continued on this site until 1937. (2) Market

Hall. General market. 1903. Located in Crackenedge Lane. 16,569 sq. ft. (in 1927). Wholesale portion of building opened in 1886. Owned by Corporation; market rights purchased from lord of the manor in 1860s. Refurbished and held 36 shops in 1988. Extant. (3) New covered market. 1937. Foundry Street and Cloth Hall Street. A large number of covered stalls.

Although the Market Cross buildings were demolished in the 1850s, trading continued in the open market place until 1937. By this time, however, the principal retail marketing center had shifted to the market hall at Crackenedge Lane (also the site of the "Fish Row"). The hall, which included 36 shops, was built with the same glass-and-iron screen construction and with a glass-and-iron roof, as an addition to the existing (1886) wholesale market. A new market hall was proposed in 1937 but not built.

SOURCES: *Dewsbury Reporter*, 25 Feb 1899, 24 Dec 1931, 30 Jun 1978; *Dewsbury District News*, 13 Feb 1934, 8 May 1937; Derek Linstrum, *West Yorkshire Architects and Architecture*, London, 1978; *Market Traders Review*, 23 Jun 1957.

DOLGELLAU   GWYNEDD

General market hall. Opened 11 Aug 1870. £2,200. 2,340 sq. ft. Architect: W. H. Spaull, Owestry. Includes assembly room and reading room.

SOURCES: *The Builder*, 27 Aug 1870.

DONCASTER   SOUTH YORKSHIRE

(1) Butter Cross and Shambles. 1756. At Baxtergate entrance to medieval marketplace. Architect: John Platt. Classical octagonal structure, supported on Doric columns and topped with wooden lantern. (2) Market Hall. General market. 1849 (new wing added 1871; second addition 1873). Located in New Street and Goose Hill in the marketplace. £17,475. 24,201 sq. ft. Architect: John Butterfield, Corporation Steward. Owned by the Corporation.

SOURCES: *The Builder*, 5 Sep 1846, 26 May 1866, 27 Feb 1869; *Doncaster Civic Trust Newsletter*, Nov 1986; *Doncaster Yesterday*, no. 1, Doncaster Museum and Art Services, 1980; Doncaster Corporation Papers, Council and Committee Orders, and Minute Books of the Estate and Finance Committees are located in the Doncaster Borough Archives; *Market Traders Review*, 11 Sep 1954.

DORCHESTER   DORSET

Town Hall and Market House. General market. 1791.

SOURCES: Lewis; *The Architect*, 1849, vol. 1, p. 349; *The Builder*, 5 Aug 1865.

DOUGLAS   ISLE OF MAN

(1) Butchers' Hall. 1900. (Altered in 1956 to provide a general market.) Market Hill and North Quay. £5,410. 4,800 sq. ft. Owned by the Corporation. Still in use as market in 1992. (2) Fish/vegetable market. 1900. Adjacent to Butchers' Hall, opposite side of Market Hill. £3,000. 4,945 sq. ft. "Work carried out by" A. Ernest Prescott, Borough Engineer. Built entirely of iron. Went out of use as market in 1956; extant as a club in 1992.

DOVER   KENT

(1) Covered fish market. 1827. Located in Mill Lane off Town Wall Street (per 1881 map). (2) Market House. General market. 1848. Market Square. £4,003. Owned by the Corporation. Exterior with Corinthian columns. Town museum housed on upper floor. Extant in 1988.

SOURCES: *PP-88*; J. Bavington-Jones, *Dover, A Perambulation*, n.d.; *Building News*, 3 Sep 1858; *Dover Express*, 4 Oct 1983.

DUNDEE   TAYSIDE

(1) New Butchers' Shambles. Meat market. 1772. Located in and around the new Trades Hall (possibly incorporating the area known in 1835 as "Butchers' Row"; apparently new covered green market was appended ca. 1820, although Dundee map of 1878 shows an open "Green market" in the square off High Street at Crichton Street). (2) Victoria Market. General market hall. 1881. Located between Victoria Road and King Street. £40,000. 22,360 sq. ft. 10 shops fronting Victoria Road with 2 large market halls to rear. Architect: Robert Keith. Four-story building in the Scottish Baronial style. Financed by David Stewart. Demolished. (3) New Fish Market. 1890. Located at what was formerly known as Newsomes Circus. £2,600. 9,130 sq. ft. Architect: Mackison, Borough Engineer. (4) Caledonian Market Halls. General market. Located in Hawkill. Owned by the Corporation.

After a long history of marketing scattered through the streets of the town center, Dundee market authorities proposed a scheme for demolishing a large area of houses along the Nethergate Street for the erection of a market hall. When it became apparent in 1877 that this proposal would not be implemented, a local solicitor, Mr. David Stewart, stepped in "to furnish Dundee with Markets" in the form of the new and elaborate "Victoria Market Hall"— a 1½-acre structure from King Street to Victoria Road planned in consultation with the Police Commissioners who acted as the local town market authorities. The Victoria Market consisted of a small "King Street Arcade" of 5 shops under a semi-circular iron-and-glass roof; the Main Arcade of 31 shops, a glass-roofed two-story structure (160 ft. by 50 ft.); and then farther on, the Charles Street Market Hall (92 ft. by 155 ft.) for butchers; a butter market hall (32 ft. by 35 ft.); a fish market (155 ft. by 45 ft.); and a fruit and vegetable market hall (94 ft. by 155 ft.).

SOURCES: *PP-88; The Builder*, 27 Mar 1858, 20 Jun 1877, 18 Aug 1877, 30 Aug 1890; *Building News*, 15 Jun 1877, 15 Mar 1878; James Donnan, *A Brief Sketch of the History of Dundee*, 1853; *Dundee Advertiser*, 30 May 1877; *Dundee and Dundonians 70 Years Ago*, 1892; *Dundee Delineated, or a Historical Description of That Town*, 1822; C. McKean and D. Walker, *Dundee*, 1884; Plans and photographs of the Victoria Market are located at the National Monuments Records of Scotland, Edinburgh.

DURHAM   DURHAM

New Place Butter Market. Market hall. General market. 1852. Entrance from Market Place; extends to Back Lane. £12,000. 21,760 sq. ft. Architect: P. C. Hardwick. Owned by Market Trustees. Three-story interior with cast-iron roof. With Guildhall forms a Gothic façade to complement adjoining St. Nicholas Church. Still used as market in 1991.

SOURCES: *PP-88*; W. Fordyce, *History and Antiquities of the County of Palatine of Durham*, Vol. 1, 1857.

EASTBOURNE   SUSSEX

Market Hall. General market. 1888. Located in Grove Road. £6,000. 6,720 sq. ft. (plus 80-ft.-long market arcade with 9 shops). Architects: Fuller and Oakden, of Eastbourne and Lewes. Owned by a market company.

SOURCES: *Building News*, 13 Apr 1888.

EBBW VALE   GWENT

Market Hall. General market. Opened 22 Dec 1883. Located near London and Northwestern railway stations. £3,000. 6,000 sq. ft. Architect: E. A. Johnson, Abergavenny. Owned by the Ebbw Vale Market Company.

SOURCES: *The Builder*, 2 Sep 1882; *Building News*, 1 Sep 1882, 18 Jan 1884.

EDINBURGH   LOTHIAN

(1) Market Exchange and Shops. General market. 1754. Located in High Street. £31,457. Exchange Hall plus 42 shops. Owned by the Town Council. Apparently little used as a retail market. (2) Green Market. Covered vegetable market. 1823. Beneath North Bridge. (3) Fish Market. Opened 4 Nov 1876. Located adjacent to (south side) Waverly Station. (4) Waverly Market. General market hall. 1876. Adjacent to Waverly Station (north side) at Princess Street. £59,724. (Public aquarium added 1877; roof garden added 1886.) Architect: Robert Moreham, Superintendent of Works, Edinburgh. Originally known as Vegetable Market. Elegant partially glass-roofed bazaar with roof serving as public park at Princess Street level. Owned by the Corporation. Demolished in 1974. (5) Fish Market. 1895. Located in Cranston Street.

One of the most noteworthy characteristics of late-eighteenth-century Edinburgh was its want of public buildings, particularly those for markets. Every conceivable kind of merchandise could be bought along the Royal Mile (Lawnmarket, High, and Cannongate Streets) and into the side streets, the crowds rendering the town intolerable. The butchers of the town sold from the series of "closes" between High Street and the Tron Church (including "Fleshmarket Close") and at the point where the North Bridge was eventually erected. Until 1823 fruits and vegetables were sold in the High Street from sellers' carts which were usually arranged on both sides of the street. In that year fruit and vegetable selling was moved to an open and partially covered structure under the North Bridge. Here it remained (as the "Green Market") until the North British Railway Company encroached onto the space, which led to the construction of the new "Waverly" Market. This large modern iron-and-glass general market hall was built in 1866 (roofed in 1876) on the south side (and below the level of) Princess Street. The central hall is of a "U" plan with cast-iron columns supporting a flat roof. Approximately 30 large iron-framed glass skylights were protected with iron railings, allowing the remainder of the large roof to be used as a public garden at the Princess Street level. The market interior was frequently used for public functions (e.g., 20,000 people filled the market in 1879 to hear a speech by William Gladstone). A new fish market was built nearby.

SOURCES: *PP-88*; W. Ballingall, *Edinburgh, Past and Present*, 1877; *Brydone's Guide Through Edinburgh*, 1856; *Building News*, 16 Oct 1874; City of Edinburgh, *New Market and Slaughterhouses* (pamphlet), 1910; Edinburgh Markets Committee, City of Edinburgh, *New Markets and Slaughter Houses* (pamphlet), 1910; *Edinburgh Market Committee "Session" Papers*, 1873-1895; Peter Genmell, *A Short History of the Old Green Markets and of the Waverly Market, Edinburgh*, 1906; J. Gifford, C. McWilliam, and D. Walker, *Edinburgh*, 1984; J. Grant, *Old and New*

Edinburgh, 1888; W. McLaren, "Old Edinburgh Markets," in *Evening Dispatch,* 29 Jul 1942; David Robertson and Marguerette Wood, *Castle and Town,* 1928; City Library, "Press Cuttings File"; "Markets Committee Minutes and Reports" are located in the City Archive, Edinburgh.

EGREMONT   CUMBRIA

Market Hall. General market. 1883. Owned by the Corporation.

SOURCES: *Bulmer's 1901 Directory.*

ELGIN   GRAMPIAN

New Market. General market hall. 1851. High Street and South Street. 18 shops and 2 "halls." Architects: Mackenzie and Mathews. Altered and enlarged in 1884.

SOURCES: Charles McKeen, *The District of Moray. An Illustrated Architectural Guide,* 1987; *Elgin Courant and Morayshire Advertiser,* 7 Feb 1851.

ELLESMERE   SALOP

Market Hall. General market hall. 1897. Scotland Street. 6,400 sq. ft. Brick hall with large arched entranceway. Owned by Council. Extant in 1994 as market.

SOURCES: *Shropshire Magazine,* 9 Mar 1975.

ELLSMERE PORT   CHESHIRE

York Road Market. Covered general market. 1934. York Road. 14 shops and 31 stalls under a shed-type structure, open to the front and sides.

ELY   CAMBRIDGESHIRE

Market and Corn Exchange. 1846.

ENFIELD   GREATER LONDON

Covered general market. 1904. Architect: Sidney Canfield. Octagonal market building with Corinthian columns.

SOURCES: Lewis; *VCH.*

EPSOM   SURREY

Market and Town Hall. General market. 1883. 2,720 sq. ft. Architect: Traherne.

SOURCES: Lewis.

EXETER   DEVONSHIRE

(1) Lower Market. General market hall. 1837. Fore Street. Architect: Charles Fowler. Destroyed in 1942. (2) Higher Market. General market hall. 1838. Queen Street. £19,000 (Dymond's estimate). Approx. 32,200 sq. ft. Architect: George Dymond, Bristol (completed by Fowler). (3) Fish Market. Located behind the Higher Market. Demolished.

Up until 1824 the markets of Exeter had been held in the streets and in that year an act was obtained to move into a purpose-built covered space. Because of a dispute between the two wards of the town over the placement of the proposed market, a second act was passed in 1834 allowing for the construction of two market halls, one in 1834 in Fore Street known as the Lower Market, and the other in 1836 in Queen Street known as the Higher Market. By 1888 it was argued that the town had too much market accommodation, partly because of the prevalence of door-to-door street hawking, leaving the markets to "the lower class." Both new markets were expensive (the sites alone cost over £40,000) and necessitated the removal of a considerable number of medieval lanes and houses. Both markets were of architectural significance. The Higher Market, by Dymond (executed by Fowler), was in the manner of a neoclassical Grecian temple, fronted in Bath stone with pedimented central entrance with Greek Doric columns. In addition to a large general market hall, the building included a fish market with 12 shops and a central fountain for cooling and washing purposes, a grand central avenue of granite pilasters (serving as a fruit market), and in the gallery above that a "horticultural hall." The Lower Market, acclaimed for technical innovation, especially roof construction of iron and laminated timber, was destroyed in wartime bombing.

SOURCES: *PP-35; PP-88; Architectural Magazine and Journal,* Vol. 3, 1836; B. Cherry and N. Pevsner, *Buildings of England, South Devon,* 2d ed. 1989; Robert Newton, *Victorian Exeter 1837-1914,* 1968.

FALMOUTH   CORNWALL

Market Hall. General market. 1812. Located on the Moor. £2,500. Owned by Earl of Kimberley; leased by Corporation since 1875. Separate butchers' market added later.

SOURCES: *PP-88; Kelly's Directory, Cornwall,* 1883; J. S. Polsue, *Lake's Parochial History of the County of Cornwall,* Vol. 1, 1867-73 (repr. 1974).

FENTON   STAFFORDSHIRE

Market Hall. General market. Ca. 1831. Located south side of Market Street (now King Street). Architect: C. J. Mason, builder. Small single-story brick building. Proximity to Stoke-on-Trent and Longton markets diminished its importance.

SOURCES: *VCH.*

FISHGUARDS   DYFED

Market House and Town Hall. General market. Ca. 1834. 4,500 sq. ft. Originally owned by

Fishguard Market House Company; presently owned by District Council. Extant in 1992.

FLEETWOOD   LANCASHIRE

(1) Enclosed general and fish market. Opened 7 Nov 1840. Located at Adelaide and Victoria Streets. Owned by Sir Peter Fleetwood, manorial lord, then after 1889 by the Corporation. Walled and paved market space. Demolished. (2) Market Hall. General market. 1891. Adelaide and Victoria Streets. 25,794 sq. ft. Brick with central arched doorway flanked by windows. Interior market under single-span iron roof, unencumbered with supporting columns, and with movable benches. Extant in 1992. Now known as "Fleetwood Traditional Market." (3) Market Hall. 1990. £750,000 development scheme. 60,000 sq. ft. Owned by Corporation.

SOURCES: C. Rothwell, *A History of Fleetwood on Wyre, 1834-1934*, typed ms., District Central Library, Fleetwood; *The Market Trader*, 18 Mar 1933, 13 Aug 1960; the District Central Library, Fleetwood, holds a collection of photographs of the 1891 market.

FOLKSTONE   KENT

Market House. General market. 1831.

SOURCES: Lewis; *Building News*, 24 Dec 1858.

FORRES   GRAMPIAN

Agricultural Hall (a.k.a. New Market). General market hall. 1847. Located at the Toll Booth in Tyler Street. (Rebuilt 1893. Architects: A. and W. Reid, Elgin.) Owned by the Forres Town Council. Extant in 1988.

SOURCES: *The Builder*, 30 Sep 1893; A. H. Forbes, *Forres: A Royal Burgh, 1150-1975*, 1975.

FOWEY   CORNWALL

Market House. General market. Ca. 1800. Located in Trafalgar Square. Owned by the Viscount Vallefort and Philip Rashleigh. Extant in 1975.

SOURCES: *Fowey Guide*, 1975.

FROME   SOMERSET

(1) Market House. Ca. 1831. (2) Second market proposed 1873. £4,000. Architect: W. J. Stent.

SOURCES: Lewis; *Building News*, 14 Mar 1873.

GAINSBOROUGH   LINCOLNSHIRE

General market hall. Ca. 1904. 3,438 sq. ft. Owned by the District Council.

SOURCES: *The Builder*, 13 Feb 1904.

GARSTANG   LANCASHIRE

Market Hall. General market. Extant.

GLASGOW   STRATHCLYDE

(1) King Street Meat and Fish Markets. Enclosed and partially covered. 1754. Opposite sides of King Street. Beef Market, 7,616 sq. ft.; (opposite) Mutton Market, 6,048 sq. ft.; and Fish Market, 1,720 sq. ft. Fish Market was covered over in 1808. Green Market (£1,530) established nearby in Candleriggs in 1797. All were with stone façades with Ionic columns; entrances led into enclosed and partially covered spaces. (2) Covered market. 1808. Fruit. Located in Bell's Wynd, Candleriggs. (3) Bazaar. General market, covered hall. 1817. Located in Candleriggs. £60,000. 11,493 sq. ft. Architect: John Carrick, City Architect, along with Dr. Cleland. Owned by the Corporation. Rebuilt in 1840-43; added to in 1848; added to again and rebuilt in 1852; rebuilt in 1875 at a cost of £17,000; current size 16,296 sq. ft. Extant in 1992, but not for sale of food. (4) Fish Market Hall. 1873. Bridgegate. £30,377. 14,350 sq. ft. Renovated in 1988. Extant in 1992. (5) Paddy's Market. Old clothing market. 1875. Grandyke Street. £17,000. 16,296 sq. ft. 403 stalls. Demolished. (6) Bird and Dog Market. £1,433. 6,480 sq. ft.

Because of street congestion and increased market activity, by the mid-eighteenth century Glasgow market authorities adopted a policy to remove marketing from the streets (extending from the Tolbooth and Market Cross) and to organize them into separate enclosed (walled) and partially roofed markets—often distinguishing between incorporated, or city, merchants and "country," or Clydesdale, merchants—within the town center. A prohibition against selling garden produce in the streets was enacted in 1758 for the purpose of concentrating this activity in an enclosed space. This was done principally at a "Green Vegetable Market" (in 1758) at Candleriggs and Trongate Streets, for the Incorporated Gardeners and then for the country sellers at sheds in Ingram Street. The Candleriggs Green Market had an imposing entrance decorated with Ionic columns supporting a pediment. A fruit market was established in nearby Bell's Wynd in 1808. A market for country butchers was established in Bell's Wynd, and potatoes were sold only in a specially designated market in Candleriggs Street. In 1754 the three new adjacent markets in King Street brought the sale of meat in from the streets and from the Old Beef Market in the Trongate Street: a new Beef Market, roofed with slate and paved with freestone and with stalls placed between stone pillars; a Mutton Market; and a Fish Market, where sale benches were covered with lead and equipped with running water. The façade on narrow King Street had three arched entrances, each with an ornamental stone front; Ionic columns supported pediments above, flanking the three gateways into the open-air and partially roofed markets. The Incorporation of Butchers transacted business in a "hall" to the rear of the Beef Market. These King Street Markets, with their "spacious ornamental gateways," were admired at the time as being "completest of their kind in Britain." Additional meat stalls were housed at the Trongate, and butter, eggs, cheese, and milk selling was moved first to the grounds of the Ramshorn (in 1791), and then by 1813 to St. Andrew's Square.

When the 1800 Glasgow Police Act granted the City Council greater regulatory powers, market officials adopted a policy of centralizing all market activity (with the exception of meat sales) at a large new site called the Bazaar on the site of a bowling green in Candleriggs Street. Even though the push for it grew out of a need to accommodate sellers of garden produce, the new market, which opened in 1817, was in fact a general market selling everything from fruit to poultry to toys and books. The "Bazaar" portion was 2 covered "alleys" with 32 shops running the length of the market and was adjacent to a partially covered market for the sale of fruits, vegetables, eggs, butter, and poultry; there was a separate corn market. The market underwent frequent alteration. In 1840 it was expanded and rebuilt to include a "City Hall" above. By the late 1880s the market covered a space of 70,900 sq. ft.— including a flower market and a cheese market across South Albion Street. By the 1880s, however, the market had largely become a wholesale market, and the neighborhood of the Bazaar was described as a "frightful terra incognita" inhabited by "wretched and desperate classes." A Glasgow Improvement Trust report of 1883 recommended that the wholesale portion of the Bazaar market be moved to a new location and the Bazaar be improved as a retail market. This was not carried out, and within a decade the market had become almost exclusively wholesale. One Glaswegian noted that "it was indeed a sad day for the poor folk of Glasgow when [the bazaar market] ceased to exist."

SOURCES: *The Builder*, 30 Dec 1876, 25 Oct 1890; *Building News*, 2 Aug 1895, 27 Dec 1895; Corporation of City of Glasgow, *Municipal Glasgow, Its Evolution and Enterprises*, 1914; James Cleland, *The Former and Present State of Glasgow* (Glasgow and Clydeside Statistics Series), 1836; Walter Freer, *My Life and Memories*, 1929; J. Gardiner, "Markets of Glasgow," *Old Glasgow Clubs*, Vol. 4 (1922-23), 1923; The Glasgow City Archives, *Standing Orders, Byelaws and Orders in Council*, n.d.; *The Glasgow Herald*, 11 Jul 1817, 9 Aug 1872; James McCall, *Glasgow Ancient and Modern*, Vol. 2, n.d.; J. D. Marwick, *Extracts From the Records of the Burgh of Glasgow*, 12 volumes, 1573-1872, 1876-1912; Robert Reid, *Glasgow Past and Present*, Vol. 3, 1884; Robert Renwick, *Extracts From the Records of the Burgh of Glasgow of Charters and Other Documents*, n.d.; *Tweed's Guide to Glasgow and the Clyde*, 1874.

GLOSSOP   DERBYSHIRE

Market House and Town Hall. Covered market house behind the town hall. 1845. £8,500. Architects: Weightman and Hadfield, Sheffield. Owned by the Duke of Norfolk. Improved and redecorated in 1972 by High Peak District Council. Extant.

GLOUCESTER   GLOUCESTERSHIRE

(1) Eastgate Market House. General market. 1768. Also, at same time, the Southgate Market for butter and vegetables. (2) Eastgate Market Hall. General market . Opened 29 Apr 1856. Eastgate Street (opposite the Guildhall). £9,000. 17,425 sq. ft. Architect: Maberly. Replaced 1768 market. Owned by the Corporation. Only the façade is extant, fronting a new market hall built as part of new Eastgate Shopping Centre in 1968.

> The Eastgate Market Hall was called "an ornament to the city." Its Bath stone façade had a portico of 4 Corinthian columns, surmounted by bell tower and illuminated clock. The roof was a single span with an extended roof section along the side. Originally the market housed 67 butchers' stalls and shops, 4 fish stalls, and 64 poultry, butter, and egg stalls. It was claimed that in its first 100 years of operation, the market served 150 million "satisfied customers." By 1933 the lament was that "formerly the farmers' wives brought their butter and eggs, but this has now died out and the stalls are let to regular tenants."

SOURCES: *PP-88*; Lewis; *The Builder*, 19 Jul 1862; A. Kent, *History of Old Market Clock*, handwritten ms., Gloucester Library, 1973; M. D. Lobel, ed., *Historic Towns—Maps & Plans*, n.d.; *Market Trader*, 14 Apr 1957; *The Offical Handbook of the Gloucester Corporation Markets*, 1936.

GODALMING   SURREY

The Pepper Pot. Covered market. 1814. Located at Church and High Streets. Stands on the site of a larger, earlier market house. Octagonal plan with cupola. Erected by subscription; owned by the town. Extant in 1990.

SOURCES: *PP-35; VCH.*

GOOLE — HUMBERSIDE

(1) Market Hall. 1875. Originally a covered corn market at Doncaster, moved to Goole site by a Mr. Bennett. £1,445. Architect: John Butterfield, Corporation Steward, Doncaster. Owned by a market company. Destroyed by fire in 1891. (2) Market Hall and Town Hall. General market. 1896. Boothferry Road and Gladstone Terrace. Lower portion of town hall. £20,000. 7,000 sq. ft. Architect: W. J. Tennant, Pontefract. Brick. Owned by the Town Council; purchased market rights in 1893. Large extension built to rear at later date.

SOURCES: *PP-88; The Builder*, 18 Aug 1894; *Building News*, 24 Sep 1875, 9 Feb 1894, 20 Jul 1894, 14 Dec 1894; *Market Trader*, 17 Oct 1959.

GOSPORT — HAMPSHIRE

Market House. General market. Ca. 1803. High Street. A fine square building of white brick.

SOURCES: William Gates, *The Portsmouth That has Passed: A Panorama of a Thousand Years*, 1987.

GRAVESEND — KENT

Gravesend Borough Market. General market hall. 1902. Located east of town center. 10,700 sq. ft. Owned by the Corporation. Still used as a market in 1992.

SOURCES: *PP-88*.

GRANTHAM — LINCOLNSHIRE

Butter Hall. Ca. 1879. Town acquired market rights in 1879 from local lord.

SOURCES: *PP-88*.

GREAT TORRINGTON — DEVONSHIRE

Market House. General pannier market. 1842. (Central roof covered over with glass in 1892.) 2,990 sq. ft. Owned by the Corporation. Extant in 1988.

SOURCES: *"Gazette" North Devon Directory and Yearbook*, 1935.

GREAT YARMOUTH — NORFOLK

Fish Market. Covered market. 1864. Located at Fish Wharf at South Denes. £26,297 (including site). 30,000 sq. ft. Roof supported on 148 iron columns. Added to in 1903.

SOURCES: *PP-88; Yarmouth Directory, 1913-1914*.

GROSMONT — YORKSHIRE

General market. 1831. Built on the site of the old market. Owned by the Duke of Beaufort.

GUILDFORD — SURREY

Vegetable Market. 1798. Located in High Street. Built by Lords Onslow and Grantly; owned by Corporation from 1834. Removed in 1887.

SOURCES: *PP-88; PP-35;* Lewis; *VCH.*

GUISBOROUGH — CLEVELAND

Town Hall and Market Hall. General market. 1821. Market held in lower part of town hall; arches supported on pillars.

SOURCES: Lewis.

HADDINGTON — LOTHIAN

Town House (a.k.a. Assembly Block). General market. 1788 (addition to the 1748 Robert Adam building). Market below; assembly room above. Also known as Assembly Block; market probably not used as market when completed. Extant.

SOURCES: William Forbes-Grey, *A Short History of Haddington*, 1944; ELDC Planning Department, *A Walk Around Haddington*, 2d ed., 1986.

HADLEIGH — SUFFOLK

Market House. General market. 1813. Built by subscription.

SOURCES: Lewis.

HALIFAX — YORKSHIRE

(1) New Market. General market. 1810. Southgate and Market Streets. £3,736. 49,500 sq. ft. Owned and run by private company from 1810 to 1853; purchased by Corporation in 1853. (2) Lower Market. Covered general market. Ca. 1853. 49,500 sq. ft. Market Street and Southgate Street. Demolished in 1968, replaced by Westgate Market of closed stalls and conversion of historic Piece Hall to retail market purposes. (3) Borough Market Hall. General market. 1896 (arcade opened 1892). Southgate and Market Streets. £120,000+; 88,290 sq. ft.; 44 exterior shops; 98 interior shops; numerous stalls. Architects: Leeming and Leeming, Halifax and London; Contractor: George Charnock, Halifax. Owned by the Corporation. Palatial front with flemish gables, Florentine palazzo windows, and thin baroque turrets; also described as "French Renaissance." Interior and exterior refurbished in 1973.

Although fitted with numerous modern amenities in recent times, the Borough Market Hall of 1896 has changed little since its opening on 25 Jul 1896 by the Duke and Duchess of York (later King George and Queen Mary). Halifax market rights were acquired for the town by a market company in 1810 and then purchased by the town in 1853 soon after it was incorporated. The company built a large partially covered market between Southgate and Market Streets in 1810, called the old Shambles, although by the late nineteenth century these markets were considered "worse than ancient, they are ugly." The new market hall of 1896, the palatial "Borough Markets" by Leeming and Leeming, had over 200 stalls arranged in blocks of four, 43 butchers' shops around the perimeter walls, and an adjacent arcade. The central interior feature was a large ornamental clock placed under a giant octagonal dome rising 60 ft. above floor level. The ornamental ironwork was from MacFarlane's foundry, Glasgow, and other ironwork was provided by the Phoenix Company, Derby.

SOURCES: *PP-88; The Builder,* 13 Dec 1890, 13 Jun 1891, 15 Oct 1892, 8 Aug 1896; *Building News,* 12 Jun 1891, 2 Oct 1891; *Halifax Guardian,* "Supplement on Borough Market Hall," 13 Jun 1891, 18 Jul 1896; Derek Linstrum, *West Yorkshire Architect and Architecture,* London, 1978; *The Market Trader,* 2 Jan 1960; Eric Webster, *Under the Clock, The Story of the Victorian Borough Market, Halifax,* 1985; Proposed market "Contract Drawings" for 1896 market by Leeming and Leeming are located in the Royal Institute of British Architects Library.

HANLEY   STAFFORDSHIRE

(1) Lower Green Market. General market. 1776. Built by subscription. Removed in 1813. (2) Hadley's Pool Market. Poultry and butter market. 1819. Owned by the Market Trustees. (3) The Shambles. Covered meat shambles. 1831. Between Tontine Street and Parliament Row. £3,500. Owned by the Market Trustees. Covered market with classical stone façade and cupola; 5 spacious shopping avenues. (4) Swan Passage Market. £5,350. 15,120 sq. ft. Covered fish and potato market hall. 1848. (5) Market Square Market Hall. General market. 1849. North side of Market Square. Built by Market Trustees; owned by the Local Board from 1862. Demolished in 1982.

An act of Parliament of 1813 created a board of Market Trustees to regulate and improve the markets, following which an enclosed and covered market for butter and poultry was erected at what was known as Hadley's Pool, and then a "very commodious" Market House, largely for butchers, in 1831. The Market Hall of 1849 has a three-story palazzo style façade with balustrades and rows of stone urns set above shop windows. Its shops were described as "a range of shops far above the standard of everything else in the pottery district." 4 passageways, with iron gates, led to the market hall. In 1840 it was reported that the tolls of the Hanley market exceeded those of the market at Burslem.

SOURCES: *VCH;* John Ward, *A History of the Borough of Stoke Upon Trent,* 1843; City of Stoke on Trent, Historic Buildings Survey, *Hanley General Market,* 1985.

HARROWGATE   YORKSHIRE

(1) General market hall. Opened 30 Aug 1874 (rebuilt after 1914 fire). Cambridge Street, Station Square, and Market Place. £7,004. 14,440 sq. ft. More than 80 stalls. Architect: Arthur Hiscoe. Built by the Improvement Commissioners; owned by the Corporation. Interior of white glazed brick; elegant exterior tower with clock. Destroyed by fire in 1937. (2) General market hall. 1938-39. £50,753. Architect: Leonard H. Clarke, MBE, Architect and Borough Engineer. Owned by the Corporation. Demolished in 1991 for redevelopment scheme.

Harrowgate's Market Hall of 1874 was built following a decade of controversy as to whether or not the town needed a new market. Beginning in the 1840s the town's Improvement Commissioners and others proposed a new market in order to end the practice of street hawking and to provide improved public market space to provide the town with foods "at a cheaper rate than it can be sold in the shops." Popular sentiment against increasing the rates blocked the proposal; however, with a significant increase in the town population by 1874 the proponents of market reform won the day. The roof of the large new market hall was constructed almost entirely of wood supported by iron columns; the structure had two "fronts"—one to the nearby railway station and one to Cambridge Street. The exterior with its clock tower (the clock, a gift from the Baroness Burdett-Coutts) was of stone. The interior—with more than 50 stalls—had walls of white glazed brick. The structure was partially destroyed by fire in 1914, and it was rebuilt, but in January 1937 it was completely destroyed by fire. A new market hall (with 37 stalls and 20 shops) was built in 1939. Market activity was curtailed when the premises were requisitioned for war purposes throughout 1939-45, only resuming use as a market in 1947. The building was demolished in 1991 and the market was incorporated into a four-story shopping development at the same site.

SOURCES: *PP-88; Harrogate Advertiser,* 28 Feb 1874, 5 Sep 1874, 28 Mar 1914, 10 Nov 1989; "Yorkshire Markets: Harrogate" *Market Trader* supplement in *World's Fair,* 26 Mar 1960; Harold Walker, *History of Harrogate Under the Improvement Commissioners,* 1986.

HARTLEPOOL   CLEVELAND

Town Hall and Market. General market. 1866.
£5,000. Architect: C. J. Adams, Stockton.

HARWICH   ESSEX

General covered market. 1784. Kings Quay Street
and Outerpart East. A square enclosed with walls,
the roofed shambles forming the sides of the
square; administration building (with turret and
bell) at the center of the square. Central building
removed in 1866; not used as market after ca.
1900; remaining structure demolished between
1934 and 1945.

SOURCES: Leonard T. Weaver, *The Harwich
Story*, 1975.

HASLEMERE   SURREY

Market House. General market. 1814. Market
Square and High Street. Extant in 1990.

SOURCES: F. W. Slonton, ed., *Bygone Haslemere*,
1914.

HASTINGS   SUSSEX

(1) Town Hall and Market. General market below.
1823. High Street. (2) George Street Market. General market hall. 1833. George Street. £5,500.
Approximately 1,200 sq. ft. (retail only). Three-
story building; retail market above, wholesale
market below. Market activities discontinued in
1932-33; extant 1988. (3) Round Fishmarket.
1870. Bottom of High Street. £1,000. 12 stalls (10
retail, 2 wholesale). Octagonal brick structure
with cast iron porch around all sides. Demolished
in 1928.

SOURCES: *PP-88*; Lewis; *VCH*.

HAVANT   HAMPSHIRE

Market House. General market. 1800. In the town
center. Demolished in 1828.

SOURCES: Havant Local History Group, *The
Making of Havant*, Publication No. 1, 1977.

HAVERFORDWEST   DYFED

Market Hall. General market. 1827. Roofed and
remodeled in 1833 at cost of £5,500; refurbished
1931. £5,000. Owned by the Town Council. Described in 1835 as one of the greatest improvements ever made in the town. Redeveloped as The
Forum in 1984.

SOURCES: *PP-35*; *Western Telegraph*, 30 Dec
1982; *West Wales Guardian*, 7 Sep 1984, 5 Oct
1984.

HEDNESFORD   STAFFORDSHIRE

Market Hall. General market. 1872. (A 3,600 sq.
ft. hall was in existence in 1927, operated by the
Hednesford Market Hall Company, largely for the
sale of retail produce.)

SOURCES: *VCH*; *Ministry of Agriculture and
Fisheries, Report on Markets and Fairs*, Part II, p.
138.

HELSTON   CORNWALL

Butter and Meat Market buildings. 1838. Church
Street near Guildhall. Ca. £6,800. Ca. 2,250 sq. ft.
Consisted of 40 stalls in 1888. Architect: W. Harris, Bristol. Extant as museum, 1988. A suite of
covered markets, one for butter, eggs, fish, and
poultry (later a "pork market"), and one for meat.
Timber and slated roof, granite floors, windows
on one side. By 1927 is "practically disused."
Owned by Corporation. The opening of a branch
of the Great Western Railway encouraged growth
of Helston markets in the mid-nineteenth century. Now used as Town Museum.

SOURCES: *PP-88*; J. S. Polsue, *Lake's Parochial
History of the County of Cornwall*, Vol. 2, 1868.

HEMEL HAMPSTEAD   HERTFORDSHIRE

Market House. General market. 1868. Adjacent
to Town Hall of 1851, on site of old market house.
£2,140. 1,250 sq. ft. Architect: George Low, of
London. Enclosed on two sides with glass; includes turret with market and fire bell. Of brick
and stone and in the style "prevalent in the reign
of James I."

SOURCES: *The Builder*, 10 Jul 1869.

HEREFORD   HEREFORDSHIRE

(1) Old Butter Market House. General market.
1810-30. Located in High Town. Ca. £3,000. Cupola on west end of building. Replaced timber-
framed Butcher Row. An act of 1816 enabled the
City Council to purchase land for and to erect a
new market. Survey of 1835 notes "considerable
debt incurred for building the market and slaughterhouse which are commodious and of great benefit to the town." Removed ca. 1861. (2) Butter
Market. General market hall. 1860. Located in
High Town. 13,788 sq. ft. (in 1927). Architect:
John Clayton. Owned by City Council. Constructed per Hereford Improvement Act of 1854.
Interior reconstructed in 1925. Replaced Old
Market House of ca. 1576. Extant in 1988 and still
used as a market.

SOURCES: *PP-35*; *The Builder*, 24 Sep 1910.

HERTFORD   HERTFORDSHIRE

(1) Covered/enclosed butchers' market. Ca. 1831.
North side of Fore Street. Paid for by Alderman
Kirby. Formed three sides of a quadrangle. (2) Enclosed General Market. Ca. 1888. Estimated cost,
£2,500. To replace market in streets around the

Town Hall. Market rights owned by Town Council. (Hertford covered general market in 1927 consisted of 4,986 sq. ft.)

SOURCES: Lewis; *Building News*, 30 Apr 1858, 28 May 1858; *Ministry of Agriculture and Fisheries, Report on Markets and Fairs*, Part IV, p. 176.

HEYWOOD GREATER MANCHESTER

Town Hall and Market. Proposed in 1874. Church Street. £10,000. 13,500 sq. ft. Architects: Maxwell and Tuke, of Bury. (Heywood had a covered market of 12,000 sq. ft. in 1927.)

SOURCES: *The Builder*, 26 Sep 1874; *Ministry of Agriculture and Fisheries, Report on Markets and Fairs*, Part II, p. 138.

HIGHBRIDGE SOMERSET

Market House. General market. Ca. 1856. £2,000. Owned by Market House Company (about 100 shareholders). Per 1856 act. (Highbridge had a covered market of 1,800 sq. ft. in 1927, owned by District Council.)

HOLSWORTHY DEVON

Pannier Market. Covered general market. 1857. The Square, Fore Street. 1,800 sq. ft. (1927 report lists market size as 16,893 sq. ft.) Owned by District Council. Extant and still in use as a market, 1992.

HOLYHEAD GWYNEDD

Market Hall. General market. 12,600 sq. ft. (in 1927). Owned by Lord Stanley of Alderly in 1927. Existed as market in 1967.

SOURCES: *Ministry of Agriculture and Fisheries, Report on Markets and Fairs*, Part V, p. 86.

HORSHAM SUSSEX

Market House. 1812 (reconstruction and enlargement of earlier building). South Street. 8,100 sq. ft. in lower floor. The coming of the railway in 1848 discouraged local trading. In 1927 this market was apparently still in use as a market, owned by the Horwich Urban District Council. Extant.

HOUGHTON-LE-SPRING DURHAM

Market and Town Hall. General market. 1874. Newbottle Street. £2,600. Brick glass-roofed market at rear with shops in front. Interior had ornamental fountain in center. A number of shops on the ground floor plus extension to rear for additional 17 shops. Architect: Henry Leighton and Son, of Newcastle. Demolished ca. 1965. A photograph of about 1910 shows tram car passing market entrance.

SOURCES: *The Builder*, 10 Jan 1874.

HOWDEN HUMBERSIDE

Shire Hall. General market hall. 1872. East side of Market Place. £2000. 2,516 sq. ft. Market area and 2 shops on the ground floor. Architect: M. E. Hadfield and Son, of Sheffield. Owner was a Market Hall Company formed to purchase market rights from manorial owner and to construct new market. Impressive red brick "Low Countries Gothic" building with tower, double-arched entrance, and tile roof. Upper floor periodically used as courtrooms as well as a cinema. Ceased to be used as a market in the 1920s. Extant and used as public hall.

SOURCES: Mr. K. Powls, Historian, Goole; David Neave, *Howden Explored*, 1979.

HUDDERSFIELD WEST YORKSHIRE

(1) Market Hall. General market. 1880. King Street to Victoria Street. £31,325. 27,270 sq. ft. Architect: Edward Hughes, MRIBA. Stone carving by S. Auty, Lindley. Three-story stone Gothic Revival frontage to King Street. Roof span of 71 ft. 6 in. Butchers' shops run entire length of side streets. Internal gallery. Popularity of market led to expansion of market into basement space. Described in 1959 as "a very popular shopping centre." Clock tower of 106 ft. Demolished in 1970. (2) Queensgate Market Hall. General market. 1970. "Ultra-modern" hall located on the Piazza at bottom of Ramsden Street. Replaced the 1880 hall.

SOURCES: *PP-88*; *The Builder*, 21 Sep 1878, 8 Mar 1879, 3 Apr 1879; *Building News*, 9 Mar 1877; *Market Trader*, 21 Nov 1959, p. 28; *Huddersfield Weekly News*, 3 Apr 1880; Derek Linstrum, *West Yorkshire Architects and Architecture*, London, 1978.

HULL HUMBERSIDE

(1) New Butchers' Shambles. Covered market for meat, butter, and eggs. 1806 site covered in 1834. Fetter Lane on north and Blackfriargate on south. Demolished and site used for new Queen Street Market in 1887. Owned by Corporation. (2) Queen Street Market Hall ("The Shambles"). General market. 1887. Queen Street. £23,640. 20,767 sq. ft. Architect: W. Gelder. Owned by Corporation. Multi-turreted and gabled pastiche of historical styles. Replaced old butchers' shambles. 15 shop fronts. Criticized as being too far from town center. Destroyed in 1941. (3) Sparrow Hall. Covered vegetable market. 1888. Dixon's Square. £500. 3,600 sq. ft. Owned by Corporation. Next to Queen Street Market Hall. Built for sellers of Lincolnshire farm produce. (4) North Church Side Market Hall. General market (largely fruit, vegetables, flowers). 1904. North

Church Side Street. £10,700. 10,557 sq. ft. in 1917. 74 stalls. Architect: Joseph Hirst, City Architect. Extant as Grade II listed building (used as market but use under discussion) in 1989.

SOURCES: *PP-88; The Builder,* 24 Jul 1880; *The Market Trader,* 7 Aug 1967.

HUNGERFORD   BERKSHIRE

Market House. General market. 1787. "Neat structure of brick" which contains a room for transaction of public business.

SOURCES: Lewis.

HYDE   GREATER MANCHESTER

(1) Market Hall. General market. 1927. Old market square. Demolished ca. 1967. (2) New Market Hall. General market. 1967. Market square shopping precinct. 10,750 sq. ft. with 76 stalls on three floors. Owned by Tameside Metropolitan Borough and built as part of private development scheme.

ILFRACOMBE   DEVON

Market and Public Hall. Ca. 1861. £2,500.

SOURCES: *The Builder,* 9 Mar 1861.

INVERNESS   HIGHLANDS

Market Arcade. General market hall. 1870 (site purchased in 1842). Academy Street. £3,000. 12,690 sq. ft. Architects: Matthews and Laurie. Owned by Corporation. Triple-arch entrance with iron gates into long arcade with a colonnade running down each side. Fifty cast-iron ventilation ducts placed on interior side walls. It was first feared that the glass roof would cause overheating in summer months. Rebuilt after 1890 fire. 15 shops and 28 open stalls. Prior to 1870 the town's marketing was done in numerous congested open-air markets in vicinity of High Street. Recently refurbished.

SOURCES: *Inverness Courier,* 26 May 1870; *Inverness Town Council Minutes,* 6 Apr 1870; *The Market Trader,* 3 Jul 1954; A. Gerald Pollitt, *Historic Inverness,* 1981.

INVERURIE   GRAMPIAN

Covered general market. Ca. 1844. Wood building behind Town Hall. Owned by Borough Council. Town Council outlawed the use of tents for market trading by non-residents.

SOURCES: Sidney Wood, *The Shaping of Nineteenth Century Aberdeenshire,* 1985.

IPSWICH   SUFFOLK

Provisions Market. Covered general market. 1810. Entrance at Falcon and Silent Streets. £10,000. Two spacious quadrangular ranges of buildings, about 1 acre in size—and with an obelisk fountain at the center. Stone columns create roofed piazza encircling market. Architects: William Brown, Ipswich, and B. B. Catt. Owned by the Magistrates and Body Corporate of Ipswich. Long a popular market, it was renovated in 1867. The letters "Q.C.E.," indicating "Quality, Civility, Excellence," appear on the main gate. The market declined because of competition from street hawking and deterioration of its buildings. Market moved to New Corn Exchange building in 1888, and the structures were demolished in 1897.

SOURCES: Lewis; R. L. Cross, *Ipswich Markets and Fairs,* 1965; photographs by Robert Burrows of the market can be found in the County Record Office, Ipswich Branch.

IRONBRIDGE   SALOP

Market House. General market. Ca. 1790. Nos. 2-6 Market Square. Two-story with lower floor open as 5-bay arcade for marketing; Palladian windows above. Architect possibly Samuel Wright, Kidderminster. Owned by Corporation. Extant, but arcade has been filled in with shop fronts.

SOURCES: *VCH.*

KENDAL   CUMBRIA

Market Hall. General market. 1882. Between Finkle Street and Market Place. £16,000 (including site). Ca. 9,100 sq. ft. Architect: Eli Cox, Kendal. "Renaissance" façade with towers. Interior divided into separate areas for fish, poultry, vegetables, and butchers' meat. Recently refurbished as part of Westmoreland Centre. A second market was proposed in 1887.

SOURCES: *The Builder,* 17 Jun 1871, 14 May 1881, 7 Jan 1882; *Building News,* 24 Jun 1881, 18 Nov 1881, 13 May 1887.

KESWICK   CUMBRIA

Moot Hall. General market house. 1812 (rebuilding of ca. 1695 hall). Located in center of Fancet Square. Owned by Lord of the Manor of Derwent, and at present Allerdale District Council. In 1852 its lower floor still used for weekly sale for "butter, eggs, poultry, bread-stuffs." Extant in 1990.

SOURCES: Lewis.

KETTERING   NORTHAMPTONSHIRE

Butter House. 1877. Old house refitted for use as market in Market Place. Lower floor. Owned by Local Board, although town market rights were owned by Lord of the Manor until 1881. (No covered market facilities existed in 1888; a 3,600 sq. ft. general covered market was in use in 1927, and an 11,600 sq. ft. "General Retail" covered market was in use in 1967, owned by the Kettering Corporation.)

SOURCES: *PP-88; The Builder,* 18 Aug 1877; *Markets Yearbook,* 10th ed., 1967; *Ministry of Agriculture and Fisheries, Report on Markets and Fairs,* Part V, p. 86.

KIDDERMINSTER   HEREFORD

(1) Market House. General market. 1822. (2) Market Hall. General market. 1869 (enlarged in 1884 and in 1932). Located in Oxford Street between Vicar and Worcester Streets to High Street—with several old buildings removed to provide new approach to the market. Original cost £3,000. 120 stalls. Owned by Corporation. In 1884 the Oxford Street entrance had large pediment above arched entrance (with stairs), and interior with cast-iron columns supporting glazed roof. Demolished in 1978 as part of redevelopment scheme after considerable public controversy; market removed to former carpet factory in Worcester Street. "The old retail market had a very real place in the affections of Kidderminster people and its passing was deeply regretted."

SOURCES: *PP-35; VCH; The Builder,* 11 Nov 1871. *Borough of Kidderminster, Kidderminster Borough Markets, 1952-53;* Kidderminster Library, "Press Clippings Collection."

KILMARNOCK   STRATHCLYDE

Corn Exchange and Market. General market. 1863. Located in London Road and Green Street. £6,000. 5,184 sq. ft. market area at south end. Architect: James Ingram. Corn Exchange area owned by Corn Exchange Company while market and 2 shops owned by Town Council; current owner is Kilmarnock and Loudoun District Council. Italianate, 2 stories with rusticated lower story and large windows above; 110 ft. "Albert Tower." Sculpted busts of Lord Clyde and Prince Albert. Extant in 1990 as Grand Halls and Palace Theatre.

SOURCES: A. McKay, *The History of Kilmarnock,* 5th ed., 1909; *Buildings Index,* Kilmarnock Library, Dick Institute.

KING'S LYNN   NORFOLK

(1) Saturday Market House. General market. 1802. High Street near St. Margaret's Church. "Plain brick building." News room and billiards room above. Demolished. (2) New Market House. General market. 1832. Located west side of Tuesday Market Place and extending backwards to Common Staith. £3,800. Paid by shareholders but ownership rested with Corporation. "A handsome cemented front with an upper and lower portico." A Corn Exchange was built next to this site in 1854 and had been periodically used as the site of the public indoor retail market. Demolished.

SOURCES: *PP-88; PP-35;* H. J. Hillen, *History of the Borough of Kings Lynn,* 1907 (repr. 1978).

KINGSTON UPON THAMES   SURREY

Market House/Town Hall. General market. 1840. Located in Market Place. £4,000. Architect: Charles Henman, Sr. Owned by Corporation. Now called Market House. 41 market shops on ground floor in 1992. Currently being considered for alternative use and redevelopment.

SOURCES: Kingston Heritage Service, Royal Kingston; the Kingston Library has a collection of photographs of selling in Kingston.

KINGTON   HEREFORDSHIRE

Market Hall. General market. 1887. Town Center. £769. 1,500 sq. ft. Architect: F. Kempson, Hereford. Owned by Corporation. Red brick. Clock tower added in 1897. Extant in 1987.

KIRKBY LONSDALE   CUMBRIA

Market House. Largely for dairy products and butter. 1854. Hall above. Erected by a "public company." Cinema in upper hall in 1920s. Sold in 1972 to private interests.

SOURCES: Frank Garnett, *Westmoreland Agriculture, 1800-1900.* 1912; Alexander Pearson, *Annals of Kirkby Lonsdale,* 1930; *Westmoreland Gazette,* 1 Sep 1972.

KIRKBY STEPHEN   CUMBRIA

Market House. General Market. 1810. With piazza, called the Cloister; upper part is supported on 8 stone pillars. Used for town business.

SOURCES: Lewis.

KNUTSFORD   CHESHIRE

New Market Hall. General market. 2,475 sq. ft. Owned by Knutsford Urban District Council.

LANCASTER   LANCASHIRE

(1) Butchers' Shambles. 1774. Long narrow site between Market Street and Common Ground Street—with slaughtering sheds on one side and butchers' shops on the other. Owned by Town Burgesses. (2) Covered Market. Meat and general market. 1846. £1,600 (including land). Built on site of Shambles of 1774 plus additional land for slaughtering and an open market ("Back Market"). Owned by Corporation. (3) New Market. General market hall. 1880 (refurbished following 1909 fire). Common Garden Street (two entrances), James Street, and Corn Market Street (a

new street)—with additional entrances from Market Street and Market Gate. £8,000. 23,100 sq. ft. Architects: Messrs. Handysides, Derby. Owned by Corporation. Interior had 33 shops and 65 stalls, 28 of which were for butchers when the market opened. Fish market included. Unusual 5-bay roof. Refurbished at cost of £330,000 between 1961 and 1975. Destroyed by fire in 1984.

SOURCES: *PP-88*; *VCH*; P. Brown, *A Pictorial History of Lancaster Market*, 1985; John Catt, *A History of Lancaster's Markets*, (Local Studies No. 7), 1988; *The Builder*, 7 Jul 1894; *Building News*, 2 May 1879, 6 Jul 1894; F. Shaw, "Chief Sanitary Inspector's Report on the Covered Market, Feb 1954," ms., District Central Library; *Lancaster Guardian*, 20 Sep 1879; 29 May 1880. Plans of the 1880 market are located with the District Central Library, Lancaster.

LAUNCETON   CORNWALL

(1) Butter Market (a.k.a. Corn Market). Covered butter and poultry market. 1842. Broad Street. £8,000. Owned by Corporation. Oval structure surmounted with a bell turret. "Italian Style." Demolished in 1921. (2) Meat Market. Covered. 1840. "Near the Church." (3) Pannier Market. Covered general market. Ca. 1926. Market Street in Race Hill. 4,869 sq. ft. Extant in 1997.

SOURCES: *PP-88*; *Kelly's Directory, Cornwall*, 1883, p. 922.

LEEDS   WEST YORKSHIRE

(1) Bazaar and Shambles. Meat and general market. 1824. £15,000-20,000. A portion being the Old Moot Hall. 60 shops arranged in 2 rows; additional market space upstairs known as the "Bazaar" for fancy goods, millinery, and clothes. Private owners. Converted to other use in 1858. Demolished in 1898. (2) South Market. Covered general market. 1824. Between Hunslet Lane and Meadow Lane. £22,000. Open market with considerable covered space. Large colonnaded circular pavilion surrounded by roofed stall area. 88 stalls and 49 shops. Private owners. Robert Chantrell, architect. Failed by 1830s and became center for wholesale leather trade. (3) Central Market Hall. General market. 1827. Duncan Street. £30,000. 234 ft. long; 67 shops, 56 stalls. Architect: Francis Godwin. Owned by private company which went bankrupt in 1831. Two-story front with Tuscan columns. Interior balcony used as a "bazaar" for fancy goods. One-third of market occupied by butter merchants. By 1841 Borough officials prohibited establishment of private markets. (4) Meat Market. Covered market. 1856. Located in Briggate. Built per Leeds Improvement Act of 1856 which prohibited out-door stalls in Briggate. Corporation owned. (5) Kirkgate Market Hall. General market. 1857. Located in Vicar's Croft in Kirkgate (open-air market since 1826). £26,630. 36,360 sq. ft. Architects: C. Tinley and J. Paxton; contractor was Nelson and Sons. Owned by Corporation. Influenced by design of 1851 Crystal Palace, being almost entirely of glass and iron—including a glass screen wall with a "Tudor" motif, and 3 longitudinal roofs. Ten entrances. By 1888 market tenants complained that exterior needed shops in front to attract customers. (6) New Market ("Block Shops"). 1876. Behind Kirkgate Market. £110,598. Approximately 18,000 sq. ft. addition by the Corporation. 90 shops. By 1888 the market had a restaurant for 200 persons. (7) Fish Market. 1896. Kirkgate. £8,469. 11,277 sq. ft. Addition to Kirkgate Market Hall. Brick with patent tubular iron roof. Architect: Morant, Borough Surveyor. (8) New Meat Market Hall. Retail and wholesale. Opened 24 Jul 1899. New York Street. £25,319. 28,000 sq. ft. Architects: Walter Hanstock and Son, of Leeds and Batley. Owned by Corporation. 25 shops in 2 rows with 12-ft.-wide avenue in between. Also included slaughterhouses, clod storage. 70-ft. clock tower over main entrance. (9) New Kirkgate Market Hall. General market to replace the 1857 structure. 1904. Vicar Lane, Kirkgate. £116,750. 24,000 sq. ft. (with 1876 additions, the 1904 market bringing total areas of market to 4 1/2 acres, including some older market structures and a hotel). A new central entrance was added in 1912, at which time the central clock was removed. In 1975 fire destroyed the rear two-thirds of the market (the 1876 addition). The 1904 structure was refurbished in 1992, and is one of the largest markets in Europe. Architect: Leeming and Leeming, Halifax and London. Owned by Corporation. Extant.

> The Kirkgate Market Hall of 1904 exists as one of the finest examples of market hall architecture, although in its day the market was criticized as being too elaborate and a submission to "modern commercialism." Initial impetus for replacing the hall of 1857 with a new structure was the intended widening of Vicar Lane and a desire for a "more picturesque" building than the existing market. Its flamboyant eclectic façade, described by its architects as "Renaissance," is surmounted by domes and turrets. Corner entrances increase the market's prominence. The interior is dominated by a grand clock and complex glass-and-iron roof; 23 shops face the exterior onto Kirkgate, Vicar Lane, and Ludgate Hill. 83 shops line the interior, 20 of which were butchers' shops in 1908; there were 84 stalls. The covered retail marketing space of the Kirkgate markets in 1967 was 198,000 sq. ft.

SOURCES: *PP-88; The Builder,* 13 Jan 1900; *Building News,* 26 Apr 1901, 21 Jun 1901, 25 Nov 1904, 2 Dec 1904, 9 Dec 1904; *City of Leeds, Opening of the New Market Hall,* Jul 1904 (pamphlet); K. Grady, "Profit, Property Interests and Public Spirit: The Provision of Markets and Commercial Amenities in Leeds, 1822-29," The Thoresby Society, Vol. 44, 1976; E. P. Hennock, *Fit and Proper Persons: Ideal and Reality in Nineteenth Century Urban Government,* 1973; Derek Linstrum, *West Yorkshire Architects and Architecture,* 1978; G. Rees, *St. Michael: A History of Marks and Spencer,* 1969; "Herbert Yorke" [Archie Scarr], *Mayor of the Masses: History and Anecdotes of Archibald William Scarr,* 1904; Steven Burt and Kevin Grady, *Kirkgate Market: An Illustrated History* (1992). Many publications relating to the markets, including *City Council Proceedings, the Annual Reports of the General Manager of the Markets, the Market Committee Reports, Market Bylaws and Orders,* are held by the Local History Library, Central Library, Leeds; the library also holds a large collection of photographs and some plans; *Markets Committee Minutes* are held in the City Hall Archive.

LEEK   STAFFORDSHIRE

(1) Old Town Hall. General market. 1806. At foot of Market Place. Lower floor for market stalls. Erected on site of old market cross of stone. Market area was dark and inconvenient and was abandoned by market people. Demolished in 1872. (2) Butter Market. General market hall. 1897. In the Market Place. Originally for butter/poultry but later a general market, including wholesale. Extended in 1936 at a cost of £2,500. Architect: Thomas Brealey, Leek. Owned by Town Council, current owner is Staffordshire Moorlands District Council. Builders: Heath and Lowe, Leek. Hall used for sports events in interwar years. Extant in 1988.

SOURCES: *Leek Post,* May 1836; *Staffordshire Weekly Sentinel,* 16 Jan 1937.

LEICESTER   LEICESTERSHIRE

(1) Fish Market. Fish and poultry. 1881. Unusual iron-frame construction. Architect: William Millican, Leicestershire. Now used as shops. (2) Leicester had several noteworthy wholesale markets. The Corn Exchange, 1856, with its impressive "Rialto Bridge" exterior staircase, was located in the Market Place. Though it was originally planned as a "market hall," it was used as a corn market. Victoria Market Hall, 1889, by architect Walter Brand, was also a wholesale market. Despite its architectural noteworthiness, it was demolished in 1972. With seemingly little concern for market improvement, Leicester had one of Britain's largest open-air markets.

SOURCES: *The Builder,* 15 Sep 1900, 22 Feb 1902; *Building News,* 12 May 1871, 28 Apr 1899, 21 Feb 1902; *Leicester Mercury,* 29 Dec 1972, 28 Nov 1983, 7 Oct 1985; Jack Simmons, *Leicester Past and Present,* Vols. 1 and 2, 1974.

LEWES   SUSSEX

(1) Market Hall. General market. 1793. Built by Improvement Commissioners to replace market of 1564; sold to the Corporation in 1886. Leased to Women's Institute for market in 1929. Also known as Market House. (2) Town Hall and Market House. 1873. Architect: W. E. Baxter.

SOURCES: Lewis; *VCH.*

LICHFIELD   STAFFORDSHIRE

(1) Market House. 1785. (2) Market Hall and Corn Exchange. General market. 1848. Conduit Street (formerly known as Butchers' Row). £2,300. Architects: Thomas Johnson and Son. Leased and in 1900 purchased by the Corporation. Tudor or "Elizabethan" style. Market held on bottom story behind an arcade of 4 arches. Described in 1888 as being small and unsatisfactory. Refurbished in 1990s.

SOURCES: *PP-88;* Howard Clayton, *Cathedral City,* 1977.

LINCOLN   LINCOLNSHIRE

(1) Shambles. Covered meat market. 1774. Adjoining Butchery Lane. Used until at least mid-nineteenth century. (2) New Corn Exchange and Market House. Fruit and vegetable market (ground floor). Opened Jan 1880. Corner of Cornhill and Sincil Streets. £9,000. Approximately 7,280 sq. ft. Architects: Bellamy and Hardy, Lincoln. Owned by Lincoln Corn Exchange and Market Company; current owner is Lincoln City Council. Replaced Corn Exchange of 1847. Extensive restoration between 1976 and 1983 at cost of £1,800,000. Reopened 11 Jul 1983. Extant as a market. (3) New Butter Market. General market (particularly butter, eggs, poultry). 1938. Sincil Street (adjoining Corn Market of 1880). £35,877. Architect: Robert Atkinson; Builder: William Wright, Lincoln. Incorporated entrance from old butter market of 1736 which was located in High Street.

SOURCES: *Building News,* 12 Dec 1879, 7 Apr 1899; "Lincoln's Fairs and Markets, 1700-1900" typed ms., Lincoln Central Reference Library.

LISKEARD   CORNWALL

(1) Market House. General market. 1822. Well Lane. £800. Architect: J. Foulston. General market, including fish, on lower floor, poultry on upper floor. Operated as a market for more than

one hundred years. Two-story bay front with triple-arch entrance. Expanded in 1865. Demolished in 1954. Present site of Boots chemist. (2) Town Hall/Market. Meat market. 1859. Opposite the Market House. 1,484 sq. ft. Architects: H. Rice and Mr. Reeves, Surveyor. Italianate in Cheeswring granite; bell tower with clock.

SOURCES: *The Builder*, 22 Jul 1905; *The History of the Borough of Liskeard*, revised by W. H. Paynter, n.d.; *Kelly's Directory, Cornwall*, 1883; an illustration of both markets is included in John Allen, *The History of the Borough of Liskeard*, edited and revised by W. H. Paynter, n.d.

LIVERPOOL   MERSEYSIDE

(1) St. John's Market Hall. General market. Opened 7 March 1822. Great Charlotte Street and Market Street. £36,813. 74,115 sq. ft. Architect: John Foster, City Architect. Owned by Corporation. Brick one-story parallelogram with 8 stone-trimmed entrances and 136 windows; 5-section roof; 5 interior shopping "avenues" consisting of 58 shops and 404 stalls. Originally "brightly illuminated every night by 144 gas lights." Flagged floor. General marketing space enlarged when fish market was removed in 1835. New shop fronts added to Elliot Street end in 1883. Proposal for demolition defeated in 1925. Estimated 25,000 people shopped in the market on a typical Saturday in the 1950s. Demolished in 1963. (2) Old Fish Market. Covered market. Ca. 1826. James Street. Corporation built in effort to break private monopoly of fish trade. (3) St. James's Market Hall. General market. 1827. Great George Street. £13,662. 27,738 sq. ft. Architect: John Foster, City Architect. Owned by Corporation. Exterior shops added later. Served the south part of town and Harrington. Closed in 1893. (4) St. Martin's Market Hall. General market. 1829. Scotland Road and Bevingtonbush. £25,743. Architect: John Foster. Originated as alternative to the ancient market at White Cross. Built to serve the residents in Everton and Kirkdale. Two fronts, each with Doric portico of 4 columns. Five-avenue interior. By 1889 described as "the dirtiest, the dreariest, and the dingiest" of Liverpool's markets. Increased to 36,600 sq. ft. by 1926 with 7 shops, 135 stalls, 407 "spaces" and 6 refreshment stalls. By 1920 used mostly as a secondhand clothing market, sometimes known as "Paddy's Market." Partially destroyed during Second World War but continued as important market for old clothing. Market transferred to Juvenal Street in 1957, then to Great Homer Street in 1967. (5) Retail Fish and Game Market Hall. 1835. Great Charlotte Street (opposite the St. John's Market Hall). £30,389. 19,800 sq. ft. in 1921. Square building with plain stone front; new front and market enlarged in 1873. In 1921 had 24 shops, 72 "slabs,"

and 20 cellars. Owned by Corporation. Gutted by bombs in December 1940 and used with temporary repairs until 1957. (6) Islington Market. Partially covered general market. 1822. Doric entrance at one end. Closed in 1842. (7) Gill Street Covered Market. 1843. Gill Street. 24,104 sq. ft. Described as a "failure from the beginning." Closed in 1862. (8) North Market. Covered market. 1922. Approximately £13,000. 63,000 sq. ft. Owned by Corporation. (9) Garston Market. Covered general market. 1956. Island Road. To serve new housing estates, first (in 1923) as an open market. Owned by Corporation. (10) New St. John's Market. General market. 1965. New market hall part of larger shopping development and a multistory car park, replacing the St. John's Market of 1822.

When Liverpool Town Council erected a large covered market on vacant land in Great Charlotte Street in 1819, it established a policy of intensive municipal support of public marketing which was to last for a century and a half. St. John's Market Hall, opened in 1822, was the first of Britain's giant market halls and ushered in an era of "modern" marketing for Liverpool residents. One hundred years later the market was still being described as one of the finest in the country—largely because of its size, but also because it still preserved market space for farmers who attended the market on Saturdays with farm produce—"thus bringing the producer into direct touch with the consumer." Well into the twentieth century Liverpool market authorities believed that the public market was necessary for stimulating competition, lowering food prices, and improving food supplies for the town's population. But while St. John's Hall and the nearby Retail Fish Market were successes and enjoyed great popularity, the attempt on the part of the town's Markets Committee to establish covered markets for outlying districts of the town (e.g., St. James's, St. Martin's, North Market) was for the most part a failure.

The popular enthusiasm for St. John's Market was not shared by the market authorities who failed to keep the market hall in an up-to-date condition. Market income accruing to the town—in 1922 alone it amounted to over £50,000—was mostly diverted to rate relief and not for market improvements, and hence by the late 1950s the market was regarded as old fashioned, unsanitary, and out of step with new developments in retailing. In 1963 the 1822 structure was demolished in favor of a new market of about the same size but situated within a modern shopping center.

SOURCES: Lewis; "Herbert Yorke" [Archie Scarr], *A Mayor for the Masses*, 1904; *Architec-*

tural Magazine and Journal, Vol. 2, 1835; *The Builder*, 18 Mar 1861, 10 Mar 1866, 1 Mar 1873, 9 Sep 1876, 21 Jul 1877, 28 Jun 1879, 23 Aug 1879, 17 Jul 1880, 27 Aug 1881, 3 Jul 1909; *Building News*, 31 Mar 1876, 30 Mar 1888, 14 Oct 1898, 13 May 1904; *Cox's Liverpool Annual and Year Book*, 1923; City of Liverpool, *Official Industrial Handbook*, 1956; *The Liverpool Echo*, 17 Aug 1964; *Liverpool Markets, Official Handbook*, 1935; *Market Trader*, 28 Feb 1959; *Stranger in Liverpool, or History and Descriptive View, Liverpool*, 1832 (10th ed); Liverpool Central Library has a "News Clippings" file on Liverpool markets, as well as the Reports of the Superintendent of Markets, various Market Committee Minutes and Reports; the library's photo collection includes many photos of the markets; other views of the St. John's Market are in Thomas Allen, *Lancashire*, Vol. 2, and William Henry Pyne, *Lancashire Illustrated in a Series of Views*, 1831.

LLANDOVERY   DYFED

Market Hall. Ca. 1800.

LLANELLI   DYFED

(1) Market Hall. General market. Ca. 1828. Hall Street. Architect: Thomas Lewis. (2) Pavilion Market Hall. General market. 1894. Town Center. £4,650. 30,900 sq. ft. Architect: George Walkeys; Roof contractor: John Lysaght, Bristol. Owned by Local Board of Health, then Corporation. Used to house the Welsh National Eisteddfod. Demolished in 1967. (3) New Market Hall. 1972. Part of £325,000 redevelopment scheme. 29,000 sq. ft. market with parking garage overhead and adjoining supermarket. Extant.

SOURCES: *Market Trader*, 1 Oct 1960; W. W. Brodie, *The Opening of the New Market Hall, Llanelly*, 1895.

LLANIDLOES   POWYS

Town Hall. General market on lower floor. 1908. Great Oak Street. Architect: Frank Shayler and Ridge, Shrewsbury. Site provided by Llanidloes Corporation, construction paid for by Mr. David Davies. English Renaissance style with Art Nouveau influence. 5-bay Cefn stone-arcaded front as entrance to Market Hall. Openwell stone stair with ornamental ironwork. Apparently replaced the 1839 town hall. Presently used as market.

SOURCES: CADW (Welsh Historic Monuments), *Buildings of Special Architectural or Historic Interest, Llanidloes.*

LONGNOR   STAFFORDSHIRE

Market Hall. General market. 1873. Reconstruction of old market hall, paid for by Sir John Harpur Crew. Picturesque structure of 4 double doors as entrance; vaulted and arched interior.

LONGTON   STAFFORDSHIRE

(1) Market Hall. General market. 1789. Lane End. Built by subscription. (2) Union Market Hall (a.k.a. Old Town Hall or Court House). General market. 1814. Commerce Street and Market Street. Owned by a company of shareholders. Five-bay brick structure, with lower piazza and a central Venetian window. Demolished in 1950. (3) New Market and Town Hall. General market. 1844. Times Square extending back to Market Lane (Transport Lane). Built by Improvement Commissioners. (4) Town Hall and Market. General market. Opened 5 May 1863. In Times Square, with market fronting on Stafford Street. £10,250 (market only). 45,630 sq. ft. (including Town Hall portion). Architect: John Burrell, Longton. 17 shops front both street and market interior; 230 market stalls. Italianate, with Minton tiles and stone on market frontage. Extant 1998.

SOURCES: *VCH*; *The Builder*, 23 Mar 1861; *Keates's Gazetteer and Directory of the Potteries*, 1873-74; *Property News*, 24 Mar 1988.

LOSTWITHIEL   CORNWALL

Market House. 1781.

LOUTH   LINCOLNSHIRE

Market Hall. General market. 1866. £5,967 (estimated). 13,050 sq. ft. Architects: Rogers and Marsden. Various colors of red brick; Venetian Gothic with tall clock tower above entrance inset between identical projecting wings; large rear wall of glass above wood doors. Stone above door inscribed, "1866 Samuel Throught, Mayor." Present owner is East Lindsey District Council. Extant in 1997, occupied by Yorkshire Clothing Company.

SOURCES: Lewis; *The Builder*, 13 Aug 1893; *Louth Standard*, 18 Jul 1969.

LUDLOW   SALOP

Market Hall and Town Hall. General market on lower floor. Opened 17 Oct 1889. Center of Castle Square. £5,800. 6,750 sq. ft. Replaced a brick market house of 1706 which was criticized for its lack of architectural attractiveness. Architect: Henry A. Cheers, Twickenham; Contractor: Richard Price, Shrewsbury. Paid for with public funds and subscription in commemoration of Queen

Victoria's Jubilee. Owned by Corporation, then South Shropshire District Council. Two stories; red brick with white stone facing in neo-Elizabethan manner. Controversial design. Later described as "Ludlow's bad luck," and as an architectural "monster." Popular market with 34 stallholders in 1975. Demolished in 1986.

SOURCES: Lewis; *Building News*, 18 Nov 1887, 25 Nov 1887, 1 Nov 1889; Shropshire Libraries, *Ludlow Album*, 1981; *Ludlow Heritage News*, May 1986; David Lloyd and Peter Klein, *Ludlow: A Historic Town in Words and Pictures*, 1984; John Robertson, *Architecture of Northern England*, 1986; *The Shrewsbury Chronicle*, 18 Oct 1889; *Shropshire Magazine*, Apr 1975.

LUTON   BEDFORDSHIRE

(1) Corn Exchange and Market House. Meat and provisions market on ground floor. Opened 18 Jan 1867. £6,000 (including Exchange portion). Adjacent to Town Hall. Local Board of Health leased market rights in 1850 from private owner, with provision that a new market would be constructed. Gas lit but claimed to be too dark to detect quality of goods. Demolished in 1952. (2) Market Hall. General market. 1925. Cheapside and Walter Streets (site of the old Plait Hall of 1870). 26,000 sq. ft. Corporation purchased market rights in 1911. Demolished in 1972. (3) New Market Hall. General market. 1972. Arndale Centre; Church Street. 39,000 sq. ft. Upper floor with entrance by escalator or ramp. Car park above.

SOURCES: *PP-88*; Luton Corporation, *Luton Market, A Shopping Revolution*, 1972.

LUTTERWORTH   LEICESTERSHIRE

Town Hall and Market House. 1836. Approximately 3,050 sq. ft. Architect: Joseph Hansom, Hinckley. Lutterworth Town Estates Trust purchased market in 1923 from Earl of Denbigh. Pedimented portico of Ionic columns above the rusticated lower (market) story. Triangular in shape. Extant (but not as a market), 1992.

SOURCES: *Architects Magazine and Journal*, Vol. 3, 1836; *The Market Trader*, 25 Sep 1954.

LYNTON   DEVON

Market Hall. General market. 1901. Market hall with shop, lavatories, and waiting room. Architect: W. H. Chowins, Surveyor to Council; Builder: Woolway and Sons, Barnstaple. Local stone with Bath dressing.

SOURCES: *The Builder*, 29 Jun 1901.

LYTHAM   LANCASHIRE

Market Hall. General market. 1848. £1,000. 3,600 sq. ft. Architect: Charles Reed, Liverpool. Built by Lytham Improvement Commissioners. Red brick with stone details with center archway flanked by Tuscan columns; with 17-ft.-square bell-and-clock tower. The arrival of the railway to Lytham in 1846 brought outlying villagers to the town, hence creating the need for a new market. Market flourished until 1880s. Extant in 1977.

SOURCES: *VCH*; *The Builder*, 25 Mar 1848; Kathleen Eyre, *Sand Grown*, 1980.

MACCLESFIELD   CHESHIRE

Butter Market House. General pannier market. 1823. Built as part of Town Hall. Architect: F. Goodwin. Market closed in 1939. A large covered market called The Shambles existed in 1811; date of construction unknown. Leased to Corporation in 1811. Proposal to build a new covered market not carried out.

SOURCES: "Markets and Fairs," typescript, Macclesfield Library, n.d.

MADELEY   SALOP

(1) Madeley-Wood Market House. General market. 1763. (2) Market Hall and Arcade. General market. 1870. West end of High Street. Built by Lord of the Manor. Not held after 1903. Building demolished ca. 1961.

SOURCES: Lewis; *VCH*.

MAIDENHEAD   BERKSHIRE

Market House. General market. Ca. 1877. £1,330. Architect: A. Keen. Market in 1831 was held under "handsome and commodious" town hall. Demolished in the 1960s.

SOURCES: Lewis.

MAIDSTONE   KENT

(1) Covered market. Vegetable and fish market. 1780. High Street at the site of the old market cross. Paid for by subscription, including Corporation contribution of £30. Demolished in 1805. (2) Covered Market. 1805. High Street (replaced 1780 structure). Long arcaded building with pitched roof. (3) Butter Market. Covered market. 1806. Lower end of Middle Row, below the meat shambles. Octagonal, supported by 8 wooden columns. (4) Corn Exchange and Market. Covered market below. 1825. High Street to Earl Street. Ca. £13,000 (included land). Owned by Corporation. Replaced 1805 market. Unsatisfactory as a corn exchange and underused as a retail market. (5) Corn Exchange and Market. General market. 1835. High Street to Earl Street. 3,600 sq. ft. Architect: John Wichcord. Owned by Corporation. Seven arched bays on west side open to ground floor market. New arcading and colonnades short-

ened; further altered in 1869 as Kent Hall above. Converted to shops by 1880s and general market discontinued. Recently redeveloped. Current market in Lockmeadow.

SOURCES: *PP-88; PP-35;* Raymond V. Hewitt, ed., "Maidstone 1549-1949" *The Official Charter Brochure,* 1949; J. M. Russell, *The History of Maidstone,* 1881 (repr. 1978); Wichcord's drawings of the Market and Corn Exchange are held by the Maidstone Museums and Art Gallery.

MALMESBURY   WILTSHIRE

Town Hall and Market. 1845. Located in Cross Hayes. Two-story Tudor-style building, with arched openings for ground floor market. Extended, with arched openings, in 1921. Extant.

MANCHESTER   GREATER MANCHESTER

(1) Brown Street Market. General covered market. 1822. (2) London Road Market. Covered. 1824. London Road and Fairfield Street. Sold in 1874. (3) Mulberry Market. Covered market. 1833. Mulberry Street. (4) Victoria Fish Market (a.k.a. the Old Shambles). 1831. Market Place. On site of former butchers' shambles. 8,900 sq. ft. Stone building. In 1927 sold fruit and poultry as well. Destroyed in 1940. (5) Meat Market Hall. 1846. Retail and wholesale (included fish). Extended in 1877. "Handsome building but seldom used." (6) Shudehill Market and Market Hall (a.k.a. Smithfield Market). Vegetable and general market. 1854. At Shudehill. 107,360 sq. ft. Included shops and Eagle Street fruit market, old clothes, and fish and meat nearby. Began in 1822 as open-air market. 4-span slate roof. Originally open to two sides but later glazed. Extended in 1885 to provide covered facilities for local farmers and gardeners whose marketing activities were blocking the street in front of hall. By 1927 chiefly for wholesale trading, with the general retail market moved to Campfield Market. Demolished in the 1970s. (7) Fish and Poultry Market Hall. 1873. At Shudehill Market complex. £48,000 (entire). 9,000 sq. ft. (for retail sales). Architects: Speakman and Hickson. Extended in 1879 at cost of £15,200. Four entrances, each with carved panels above, inspired by the Bible. Grade II listed building, probably the best of the Shudehill complex. Demolished in 1975. (8) Knots Mill Market. Partially covered. 1877. Knots Mill. £18,000. 64,000 sq. ft. Architects: Mangnall and Littlewood, of Manchester. (9) Higher and Lower Campfield Markets. Two covered general markets, one wholesale and one retail. 1877. Deansgate, Tonman Street, and Liverpool Road. £20,390. 60,000 sq. ft. Architects: Mangnall and Littlewood. Large iron-framed structure; sides enclosed in 1882. (10) Old Clothes Market Hall.

1885. Oak Street and Swan Street. Opposite Smithfield Market. Earlier "hall" adjacent to Smithfield Market in area known as "The Cribs." Until about 1894, when it was moved to a site on Oak Street. (11) High Street Market Hall. General. 1970s. In Arndale Centre, Market Street. 180 stalls on 2 levels.

By the late eighteenth and early nineteenth centuries the practices of forestalling and regrating in the market place along with unsanitary conditions and poor transportation and storage facilities had increased the price of food for Manchester's growing population. The town was described as filthy and noisome and the market place as crowded and dangerous, and in general a hindrance to trade. The inadequate supply of food in 1792 and again in 1812 led to food riots in the market place, and in 1817 a riot in the potato market led to the reduction of prices in that market. For the sixty years after about 1760 the town's manorial Court Leet purposely scattered the markets throughout the town. Upon purchase of the markets (for £200,000 per the Manchester Markets Act of 1846), the Corporation began the process of centralization of market activity at Shudehill while gradually eliminating many of the old street and other markets. The centerpiece of this policy was a new covered market (originally open on two sides, then glazed soon after) at Shudehill in 1854. It was expanded in 1867, a fish and poultry market added in 1873, and further expanded in 1885. By 1900 it was the largest covered market in Britain.

Manchester's Markets Committee was often more concerned with profits than with assuring a quality local food supply for a low price. By 1927 the total amount contributed to the relief of the rates was over £900,000. Under manorial ownership of market rights, all meat and fish were required to be sold in the public markets and not in private shops; but when the Corporation purchased the markets and market rights, butchers were allowed to set up shops for retail sale of meat or fish in any part of Manchester upon the payment of an annual license fee—thus the new meat market of 1846 was little used because butchers preferred to pay the license fee than to enter the public market. To keep the apparent widespread sale of unwholesome cheap meat in check, the Markets Committee, in the 1870s, built new wholesale meat and fish markets so that the town would gain a supply of good cheap meat and fish. In the same year the Corporation, in order to attract a more plentiful supply of fruit coming into the city, established a new wholesale fruit market.

SOURCES: *The Builder,* 18 Aug 1885, 17 Oct 1885; *Building News,* 19 Sep 1873, 7 Dec 1877, 28

Feb 1902; W. E. Axon, *Annals of Manchester to 1885*, 1886 (repr. 1987); Borough of Manchester, *Proceedings of the Council*, 1844-96; Bradshaw's *Manchester Journal*, vol. 1, no. 25, 16 Oct 1841; City of Manchester, Markets Department, *Markets Handbook*, 1953; Nicholas Joseph Frangopulo, *Rich Inheritance: A Guide to the History of Manchester*, 1962 (repr. 1969); Manchester Markets Department, Manchester Corporation, *Facts Without Figures Concerning the Manchester Markets* (pamphlet), 1936; James Ogden, *Manchester: A Hundred Years Ago*, 1783 (repr. 1887); A. Redford and I. Russell, *A History of Local Government in Manchester*, 3 vols., 1939-40; Roger Scola, *Feeding the Victorian City: the Food Supply of Manchester 1770-1870*, 1994.

MANSFIELD   NOTTINGHAMSHIRE

Food Hall. General market. Ca. 1967. 2,880 sq. ft. Owned by the Corporation.

MARGATE   KENT

(1) Market Hall. General market. 1821. Adjoining Town Hall in Market Place. £4,000. Architect: Edward White. One story "in the Tuscan order" with interior supports of iron pillars. Corporation acquired rights in 1851. Demolished ca. 1897. (2) New Market Hall. 1897. Small arcaded iron structure at front façade of Town Hall. Altered in 1925. Extant in 1990.

SOURCES: G. W. Bonner, *The Picturesque Pocket Companion to Margate*, 1831; photographs, Central Library, Margate.

MARKET DRAYTON   SALOP

Butter Cross. 1824. Cheshire Street. 120 stalls (in 1994). Built by manorial lord; currently owned by District Council. Market rights acquired by local government ca. 1914. Extant as a market in 1994.

SOURCES: *Shropshire Magazine*, Aug 1975.

MARTOCK   SOMERSET

Market House. 1753 or 1791. Butchers' shambles on ground floor. Owned by lords of manor until 1954, but market rights purchased by Parish Council in 1883. Restored in 1961.

SOURCES: *VCH*.

MATLOCK   DERBY

Market Hall. 1868.

SOURCES: *Derby Mercury*, 20 May 1868, p. 8. There was only an open market in 1927.

MELKSHAM   WILTSHIRE

Market House. 1847. £6,236. Extant as Town Hall. Classical façade; stone.

MERTHYR TYDFIL   GLAMORGAN

(1) Market Hall. General market. 1835. High Street. Architect: R. T. Jones. Owned by Corporation per Market Act of 1835. Described in 1967 as "famous old Market Hall." Demolished in 1967. (2) New Market Hall. General market. Ca. 1969. Victoria Street. Part of new shopping development.

SOURCES: *The Market Trader*, 11 Mar 1967.

MEXBOROUGH   YORKSHIRE

Market Hall. General market. 1879. £4,000. 5,300 sq. ft. Architects: Tacon and Rawson, Rotherham. Brick and stone. Three entrances. Public rooms above. Built by Local Board which had established an open air market in 1872.

SOURCES: *PP-88*; *The Builder*, 9 Sep 1876, 18 Aug 1877; *Building News*, 26 Sep 1879; "Yorkshire Markets: Mexborough," *The Market Trader*, 12 Mar 1960.

MIDDLESBOROUGH   CLEVELAND

(1) Town Hall and Market Hall. General market. 1846. Behind the Town Hall in Market Square. £2,000 (entire). 150 stalls. Architect: William L. Moffat, Doncaster. Octagonal market with cupola. Owned originally by Improvement Commissioners, then by Corporation after 1853. By 1888 the market had declined because town growth was elsewhere. Extant in 1981. (2) South Bank Market. Covered general market. 1875. Normandy Road, Ash, Oak, and Jackson Streets. £5,000. 8,640 sq. ft. (market only). Included a "spacious town hall." Privately owned.

SOURCES: *PP-88*.

MIDDLETON   LANCASHIRE

Market House and Shambles. General market. 1791. Architect: George Steuart, London. Owned by Lord Suffield (market rights leased to market commissioners in 1861). Semi-circular front of 102 ft., with a range of warehouses for general merchandise. At time of construction there was no market within 5 miles of town. Commemorative jugs were made bearing an illustration of the market, with an inscription and date: "Septr. 30th. 1791." Demolished in 1851, with open-air market thereafter. Present indoor market is of recent construction and owned by Rochdale Metropolitan Borough Council.

SOURCES: Lewis; *VCH*; Middleton Public Health Department, "Market Inspector Report of 12 Feb 1970," Rochdale Metropolitan Borough Council, Market Office, Rochdale.

MILLOM   CUMBRIA

Market House. Ca. 1890. In Market Square. Of "free Tudor style." Extant in 1988.

MINEHEAD   SOMERSET

Market House. 1902. In the Parade. Architect: W. J. Tamlyn, of Minehead. "Baroque."

SOURCES: *The Builder*, 15 Feb 1902.

MOLD   CLWYD

Town Hall. General market. 1833. Chester Street. 2,682 sq. ft. Architect: T. Jones. Market on ground floor.

MONK CONISTON   LANCASHIRE

Market Hall and Town Hall. 1790. On site of old butchers' shambles. Later enlarged.

SOURCES: *VCH*.

MONMOUTH   GWENT

(1) Market House. 1837 or 1839. Priory Street. Architect: G. V. Maddox. In "Greek Revival" style with market within lower piazza. Upper story removed following 1963 fire. Extant as part of museum.

SOURCES: Lewis; *The Market Trader*, 18 Feb 1967; Welsh Arts Council, *Plans and Projects, Architecture in Wales, 1780-1914*, 1975.

MONTGOMERY   POWYS

Town Hall and Market. Ca. 1790. Located in Town Square. 2,100 sq. ft. Georgian with upper floor rebuilt in 1828; market in open arches below. Extant.

SOURCES: *The Market Trader*, 20 Sep 1958.

MORETON-IN-MARSH   GLOUCESTERSHIRE

Market Hall. 1887. High Street along Fosse Way. Architect: Ernest George. Fine Tudor style, with turret above arched lower floor for market. Erected by Algernon Mitford. Acquired by North Cotswold Rural District Council, 1951. Extant in 1997.

SOURCES: Julian Orbach, *Blue Guide, Victorian Architecture in Britain*, 1987; Peter Davey, *Arts and Crafts Architects*, 1980.

MOUNTSORREL   LEICESTERSHIRE

Market House. 1793. Erected at expense of Sir John Danvers. Disused by 1831.

SOURCES: Lewis.

NANTWICH   CHESHIRE

Market Hall. General market. 1868. Market Street. £3000-4,000. 10,725 sq. ft. Architect: Thomas Bower. Town acquired market rights from Marquis of Cholmondeley. Elizabethan style. 3-division iron roof with clerestory. Extant as market, 1988.

SOURCES: *The Builder*, 23 Sep 1865.

NARBERTH   DYFED

Victoria Hall. General market. Market Street. 4,500 sq. ft. (in 1927). Owned by Narberth Market and Public Hall Company, Ltd. In 1832 a "new and commodious" market place was provided by the De Rutzen family who prohibited the use of private dwellings and streets for the sale of market goods.

SOURCES: *West Wales Guardian*, 16 Dec 1983.

NEATH   GLAMORGAN

(1) Town Hall and Market. 1820. Market within open arched lower floor; an "elegant" building. (2) Covered Market. 1837. Green Street. £1,650. 22,040 sq. ft. Undertaken per Neath Market Act of 1835. Covered portions around three sides; greatly altered and fully roofed in 1877 to form a hall; altered in 1879, 1883. Described in 1850 as "a prominent feature in modern improvements." Demolished in 1903. (3) Market Hall. General market. 1904. Green Street (same site as 1837 market). £8,000. 20,646 sq. ft. Owned by Corporation. Iron and glass roof. Extant as market.

SOURCES: *Transactions of the Neath Antiquarian Society*, vol. 5, 1934-36.

NELSON   LANCASHIRE

(1) Market Hall. General market. 1889. Market Square. £11,000. 19,620 sq. ft. (in 1927). Tower with clock added in 1894. Owned by Corporation. Demolished. Library now on site. (2) Market Hall. General market. 1967. In Arndale Center. 13,824 sq. ft. (3) Fish Market. Covered market. Extant in 1990.

NETHER STOWEY   SOMERSET

Market House. Ca. 1810. South of Market Place. Ownership under lord of manor. With a colonnade of 7 bays; facing older octagonal market house of ca. 1750. Discontinued by 1839. Demolished by 1900.

SOURCES: *VCH*.

NEW MILLS   DERBYSHIRE

Market Hall. General market. Ca. 1850. Market Street. 2,304 sq. ft. Originated as an extension of the Crown Hotel. Extended in early 1880s with a "Victorian" façade. Privately owned and parts of the building were used for a variety of purposes, including a cinema. Extant as a market, 1994.

SOURCES: New Mills Heritage and Information Centre and New Mills Library.

NEWARK-ON-TRENT   NOTTINGHAMSHIRE

Market Hall. General market. 1884. Middlegate at Market Place, addition to Town Hall. £2,500. 5,832 sq. ft. Red brick exterior and white brick interior; floor of asphalt ("Eureka concrete"). Includes 24 shops and stalls down center aisle; central iron roof with glass on north side. Architect: Charles Bell, London. Described as "badly built" and little used in 1888. Owned by manorial lord, later by Corporation. Extant in 1987.

SOURCES: *PP-88; The Builder,* 19 May 1883; *Building News,* 1 Sep 1883; Lewis; John Robinson, *The Architecture of Northern England,* 1986.

NEWBURY   BERKSHIRE

Town Hall and Market. 1881. In Market Place. Ca. £4,000. Architect: J. Money, Newbury. Gothic Revival structure of red and blue brick. Lower floor known as the Shambles. In 1888 it was largely for butter and poultry, with large open market nearby.

SOURCES: *PP-88; PP-35; The Builder,* 6 Mar 1861, 30 Mar 1861, 7 Mar 1874; *Building News,* 27 Feb 1885; Lewis.

NEWCASTLE-UNDER-LYME   STAFFORDSHIRE

Covered Market. General market. 1854. West side of Market Place. 7,200 sq. ft. Later owned by Corporation. Originally divided into 3 market areas; proposal for a new market in 1953.

SOURCES: *VCH.*

NEWCASTLE-UPON-TYNE   TYNE AND WEAR

(1) Fish market. 1829. Sandhill, east end of the Exchange. Architect: John Dobson, Newcastle. Handsome building supported on circular range of Doric columns. Opened with great fanfare but thereafter faced problem of unruly fishwives. (2) Grainger ("New") Markets. Opened Oct 1835. Grainger Street to Clayton Street. £36,290. 127,920 sq. ft. Architect: John Dobson, Newcastle. Owned by Corporation. (3) New Green Market Hall. Vegetable and general market. 1883. Grainger markets. Replaced portion of 1835 hall; two-story frontage with shops; single-span arched roof with partial glazing. Now linked to Elton Square shopping and leisure complex. (4) Fish Market. 1880. Exterior of red brick and stone, elaborate interior walls of white and colored brick with bands of terra-cotta. Located on the Quay between Swing and High bridges. £7,000. 5,600 sq. ft. Architect: A. Fowler, Borough Surveyor; sculpture by George Burn. Originally open every day for retail and wholesale trading. "A great expense has been incurred in . . . bringing fish within the reach of the poorest of the population."

By the late eighteenth century Newcastle's selling activity centered in 3 areas: an open general and fish market at the Sandhill; a cluster of markets, including a butchers' market (regarded as "the greatest meat market in England") in what was known as the Biggs Market; and vegetable sales in Pilgrim Street. In the years after about 1806 and into the 1820s these markets were increasingly regarded as a nuisance and insufficient and thenceforth were reformed on a piecemeal basis. A new meat market was built in 1808; a new vegetable market in 1812; and fish selling was reorganized at Sandhill with a new market in 1826. Then in the early 1830s Richard Grainger, the city architect and author of a new city plan, made a sweep of the old markets and centralized most of them inside two vast halls (1835). Located between the new Grainger Street and Clayton Street (the old Nun's Field), the buildings were designed by John Dobson for the Corporation. The two large gas-lighted halls, one for meat and poultry, the other for vegetables, were of different design. The butchers' market (338 ft. fronting Grainger Street), a *tour de force* in bold neoclassic public market design, had 196 interior shops along 4 "avenues," each 19 ft. wide, with plastered walls, ceilings, and intersecting beams. It received daytime lighting from 360 windows and 50 skylights and had a large fountain which held 1,000 gallons of water. The vegetable or "Green" market along Clayton Street was 134 ft. by 57 ft., with an impressive wood hammer-beamed ceiling and clerestory, provided space for interior shops on both sides facing into areas of market benches. It gradually became a general market, including shops for secondhand books and "six penny pot pies." When they opened in 1835, the new markets were regarded as "the most spacious and magnificent" markets in Europe. The opening was commemorated with a sit-down dinner for 2,000 men, with 300 women looking on from the gallery. The nearby Biggs Market remained as a miscellaneous and general open-air market (although by 1927 a portion had been covered) and already by the late nineteenth century was regarded as a nuisance and presented unfair competition to local shopkeepers. The Grainger Market butchers' hall of 1835, although considerably altered, still exists as a daily market, as does the replacement vegetable market of 1883.

SOURCES: *PP-88; PP-35; The Builder,* 20 Jul 1878, 22 May 1880; T. Fordyce, *Local Record and Historical Register of Remarkable Events . . . Newcastle, 1833-1866,* 1867; Icarletoni (R. J. Charleton), *The Streets of Newcastle,* 1885-86; *First Report, Newcastle-Upon-Tyne,* 1835, vol. 2; John Sykes, *Local Records, or Historical Records of Northumberland,* 1833, vol 2. (1866 edition); L. Wilkes and G. Dodds, *Tyneside Classical: The Newcastle of Grainger,* 1964; the original Grainger plans no longer exist, but the Newcastle Central Library holds facsimile copies as well as photographs of the market; the bound Library Newsclippings file has material on the markets as well.

NEWPORT   GWENT

Market Hall. 1887. High Street district. 36,700 sq. ft. Architects: Linton and Kirby. Owned by Corporation. Extant in 1988.

SOURCES: *Market Trader,* 29 Apr 1967.

NEWPORT   ISLE OF WIGHT

Market House and Town Hall. 1816. High Street. £10,000 (includes town hall). Architect: John Nash. Two-sided market piazza with 3-bay entrance beneath a giant classical portico with pediment. Tower added in 1887. Butchers' shops added at rear in 1888. Extant in 1992. Current market is in nearby Corn Exchange.

SOURCES: *PP-88; VCH; Barzee's Picturesque Illustrations of the Isle of Wight,* 1834; Nikolaus Pevsner, *The Buildings of Hampshire and the Isle of Wight,* 1967; Bill Sheppard, *Newport Isle of Wight Remembered,* 1984.

NEWPORT   SALOP

Market Hall. General market. 1858. Town Center. 9,000 sq. ft. Owned by Newport Market Trading Company, per act of 1858; rights purchased from Earl of Sutherland. Upper gallery. "Completely modernized" by 1967. Extant as market in 1990.

SOURCES: *The Builder,* 9 Apr 1870, 31 Dec 1870; *Shropshire Magazine,* Jul 1975.

NEWTON ABBOT   DEVON

(1) Covered Market. 1826. Wolborough Street. £3,000. Built by Reverend Richard Lane, manorial lord. Two detached buildings, one with a corn storage chamber above. Demolished in 1871. (2) Pannier, Butter, and Market Halls. 1871. Market Walk and Courtenay Street. Ca. £5,730 for market portion. 18,172 sq. ft. Architect: John Chudleigh, Jr.; Contractor: Jacob Harvey, Torquay. Owned by Wolborough Local Board which had purchased market rights in 1867.

Italianate, with tower at theater end. Two connecting halls, one a pannier or butter market; the other served as a fish and vegetable market. Alexandra Hall, a large public hall, stood to the front (later used as a cinema). Altered and enlarged in 1981-82. Extant as a market, 1990.

SOURCES: *The Builder,* 25 Nov 1871, 1 Sep 1906; Derek Beavis, *The Story of the Town's Past,* 1985; *The Herald Express,* 1 May 1978; Roger Jones, *A Book of Newton Abbot,* 1979; Naomi Murrin-Pyne, "The History and Development of Newton Abbot Market," *O.N.D. Business Studies, South Devon College,* 1972.

NEWTOWN   POWYS

Market Hall. 1870. High Street and Horsemarket Street. 9,000 sq. ft. Architect: David Walker, Liverpool. Ironwork by Haworth, Rochdale. Owned by Corporation. Yellow brick and terracotta in the "Lombardic" style; clock pediment on High Street façade. Included refreshment room and living space for superintendent, with shops on two sides.

SOURCES: *The Builder,* 31 Dec 1870.

NORTHAMPTON   NORTHAMPTONSHIRE

Covered Market. Corporation-owned retail market of 50 stalls.

NORTHWICH   CHESHIRE

Market Hall. General market. Ca. 1967. Vale Royal Borough Council. Extant.

NOTTINGHAM   NOTTINGHAMSHIRE

(1) Central Market Hall. 1928. £45,000. 54,000 sq. ft. Owned by Corporation. Over 350 "units" for 200 traders. Closed 1972. (2) Victoria Centre. Market hall. Ca. 1972. Multi-level market.

SOURCES: *PP-88; PP-35; Building News,* 25 Jan 1878; Lewis; *The Market Trader,* 26 Nov 1949, 23 Jul 1960, 19 Nov 1966, 23 Dec 1967; *Records of the Borough of Nottingham, Extracts From the Archives of the Corporation,* vol. 9, 1836-1900.

OAKENGATES   SALOP

Market Hall. 1896 (rebuilding of earlier hall.) In 1975 market given partially covered quarters adjacent to Town Hall.

SOURCES: *Shropshire Magazine,* vol. 28, no. 4, Oct 1975; *VCH.*

OKEHAMPTON   DEVON

(1) Market Building. 1826. Built to remove the shambles from the street. (2) Town Hall and Markets. General market. 1876. Market Street. Architects: E. Harbottle and J. Crocker, Exeter. "An extensive range of spacious buildings." Owned by

Corporation. Extant in 1992. (3) Pannier Market Hall. Butter and poultry. 1880. £1,000. 4,500 sq. ft. (in 1927). Owned by Corporation. Extant in 1997. (4) Butchers' and General Market Hall. 1900. Located between the Pannier Market and Technical School. £1,600. 6,401 sq. ft. Architect: J. Archibald Lucas, Exeter. Owned by Corporation. Local dressed stone and white brick; glass roof to north. Cafe added by 1927. Extant.

SOURCES: *Building News*, 24 Aug 1900; *Whites History, Gazetteer and Directory of the County of Devon*, 1890.

OLDHAM LANCASHIRE

(1) Victoria Market Hall. 1856. Curzon Street. £18,000 (includes land and later improvements). Built by private company, but unsuccessful because of street market competition; purchased by Corporation in 1866 (per Oldham Borough Improvement Act of 1866) for £10,654. (2) Fish Market. Hall. 1873. Adjoins hall of 1856. £3,000. 3,200 sq. ft. (20 stalls). Architects: Mangnall and Littlewood, Manchester. Renovated in 1909 at cost of £1,400. Demolished in 1938 and replaced with modern fish shop with frontage to Albion Street. (3) New Victoria Market Hall. General market. 1906. On site of old hall, Albion and Henshaw Streets. £30,000. 18,471 sq. ft. (enlarged by 1927 to 37,710 sq. ft.). Architects: Leeming and Leeming, Halifax and London; Contractor: E. Stephenson, Oldham. Built in two phases to allow use of old market during building. Described as "Renaissance" in style, of brick with stone dressing. Interior of glazed brick, with iron and glass shops facing interior. Destroyed by fire in 1974. (4) New Market Hall. 1975. Located on site of 1906 building. 127 stalls. Adjacent to well-known "Tommyfield" open market.

SOURCES: *PP-88*; Lewis; *VCH*; *The Builder*, 7 Jun 1873, 16 Apr 1902, 22 Oct 1904; *The Market Trader*, 29 Aug 1959; *Oldham Centenary—A History of Local Government*, 1949; *The Oldham Chronicle*, 7 Apr 1906.

OSWESTRY SALOP

(1) Cross Market Hall. General market. Opened 6 Jun 1849. Bailey Head and Willow Street. £3,202. 20,430 sq. ft. Architect: Thomas Penson. Owned by Market Trust per Oswestry Markets and Fairs Act of 1848. Butchers' market at Willow Street entrance. Central arched entrance with side arches; iron gates; clock added in 1854. Site was cleared of shops and dwellings. Enlarged in 1880, 1900, 1903, and street made at rear (New Street). Requisitioned for war use, 1939-45. Demolished in 1963 for site of new multiple shop premises. (2) Powis Market Hall. Largely butter, cheese, and poultry. Opened 6 Jun 1849. Bailey Square. 7,380 sq. ft. Built onto old guildhall, with partial glass roof, by Earl of Powis for the town. Plain front edifice with clock tower added in 1869. Reconstructed in part in 1951. Demolished in 1964 and replaced with a "new building of modern design."

SOURCES: William Cathrall, *The History of Oswestry*, 1855; *The Market Trader*, 8 Oct 1955; *Oswestry Corporation Markets Handbook*, 1959; *Shropshire Magazine*, vol. 27, No. 8, Feb 1975; Isaac Watkin, *Oswestry*, 1920.

OXFORD OXFORDSHIRE

Covered Market. 1774. Between High Street and Jesus College Lane (Market Street). 55,260 sq. ft. (in 1927). A block of 40 butchers' shops with smaller block of poultry shops; each block surrounded by a colonnade and divided by a north-south avenue, each quarter of shops being separately roofed. Separate covered fish market and a market house. Extended in 1830s with shops to Market Street side. Architect: John Gwynn. Built per Improvement Act of 1771 and managed by an improvement commission, including university representatives, until 1889, then Corporation. Extant as a market.

SOURCES: *PP-88*; *VCH*; *The Builder*, 30 Mar 1861, 13 Apr 1861, 3 Nov 1883; *The New York Times*, 28 May 1989.

PADIHAM LANCASHIRE

General market. 1912. £30,000. Architects: Pollard and Pollard.

SOURCES: *Building News*, Oct 1912.

PEMBROKE DYFED

General market. 1819. Main Street, attached to Town Hall. Paid for by public subscription with Corporation providing site; Corporation purchased rights from Sir John Owen for £800. Demolished.

SOURCES: *PP-88*.

PEMBROKE DOCK DYFED

Market House. General market. 1826. Pembroke and Melville Streets. £4,630. Owned by the Admirality. South half not roofed until 1886. Contractor: Fox and Henderson, of Birmingham. Bought by Corporation, 1881. In the past this market was the place where dockyarders handed over their pay to their wives. Refurbished, 1981.

SOURCES: *The Market Trader's Review*, 24 Jul 1955; *Pembrokeshire Magazine*, vol. 31, Feb 1985.

PENRITH CUMBRIA

(1) Meat market. Ca. 1807. (2) General covered market. Ca. 1855. £3,800. 10,000 sq. ft. Owned by

the Duke of Portland, then the Corporation after 1875. In 1880s it was claimed that the market was in decline because of a better market in Carlisle. Used for storage in 1960s.

SOURCES: *PP-88.*

PENRYN   CORNWALL

Market House and Town Hall. 1839. Main Street. Extant.

PENZANCE   CORNWALL

(1) Market and Guildhall. General market. 1837. Market Jew Street. Architect: H. J. Whiting. Replaced the 1614 Market House. Ionic order with portico and central dome. Owned by the Corporation. Extant in 1997. (2) Fish Market. 1845. Prince's Street. Also for poultry and butter.

SOURCES: *PP-88; PP-35*; R. M. Barton, ed., *Life in Cornwall in the Early 19th Century,* 1970; Cyril Noall, *The Book of Penzance,* 1983.

PERSHORE   WORCESTERSHIRE

Co-Operative Fruit Market. Covered fruit and vegetable market. 1910. 41,040 sq. ft. Owned by the Corporation.

SOURCES: *The Builder,* 7 May 1910.

PETERBOROUGH   WORCESTERSHIRE

(1) General covered market. Located at Market Place. 13,275+ sq. ft. Owned by the Corporation. (2) Covered fish and meat market. Adjacent to general market. 1,602 sq. ft.

SOURCES: *The Market Trader's Review,* 22 Mar 1952.

PETWORTH   SUSSEX

Market House. General market, 1793. £184. Weekly market in lower open arcaded ground floor. Owned by the Lord of the Manor. Altered and discontinued use as market in 1860s.

SOURCES: J. R. Armstrong, *A History of Sussex,* 1961 (repr. 1974); P. Jerome, *Tread Lightly Here,* 1991; *Sussex County Magazine,* Nov 1930; *West Sussex Gazette,* 9 Mar 1967.

PLYMOUTH   DEVONSHIRE

(1) Pannier Market. General partial covered market. 1807. 3 acres. Located between Cornwall and Drake Streets. £10,000. 33,600 sq. ft. (2) General market, 1888-89. £22,000. Ca. 36,705 sq. ft. Architect: C. King and Lister, Plymouth; Contractor: A. R. Lethbridge & Son and (1889) W. Trevena. The 1899 addition: Entrances from Drake Street, Market Avenue and Cornwall Street. Destroyed in 1941 during the Blitz. (3) New Pannier Market Hall. 1952. New George Street and Cornwall

Street. £269,548. Ca. 33,000 sq. ft.

The inadequacy of the old markets in Plymouth rendered necessary the building of a vast walled and partially enclosed market in 1807. Within the first two years market revenues had doubled. 3 acres in size but with only 3 entrances, the market had covered pavilions (constructed of granite columns) for vegetable, butter, fish, and poultry sales, and with butchers' stalls, a "pot market" and (later) shops. By mid-century this market was regarded to be inconvenient and unsightly. Plans for a modern market hall (on the same site) were initiated in 1853 but construction was not begun until 1888. This large hall was replaced in 1952 by a new hall with a roof of 7 concrete arched bays and glass walls.

SOURCES: Lewis; *The Market Trader's Review,* 22 Aug 1959; Llewellyn Jewitt, *History of Plymouth,* 1873; R. W. Worth, *History of Plymouth,* 1890.

PONTEFRACT   YORKSHIRE

(1) Butter Cross. 1763. Reconstruction of 1734 building. Hipped roof, stone balustrade. Extant. (2) Market Hall. General market. 1860. Located in Market Place. £5,100. Façade severely truncated and hall replaced with new hall in 1957 at cost of £23,061. Architect: James Wilson, Bath. Owned by the Corporation. Original hall façade had elaborate pediment (with carving of two bulls, poultry, game, and town coat of arms) and balustrade. Market opened in 1860 by Prime Minister Palmerston.

SOURCES: *PP-88*; Lewis; *The Market Trader's Review,* 9 Dec 1959; Derek Linstrum, *West Yorkshire Architects and Architecture,* 1978; Wilson's market drawings are located in the Royal Institute of British Architects Library, London.

PONTYPOOL   GWENT

(1) General market hall. Pre-1846. (2) Vegetable Market. Covered market. 1875. (3) Market Hall. General market. 1893. £29,205. 21,972 sq. ft. Architects: Robert Williams and O. J. Lougher, of Pontypool. Owned by the Corporation. Extant in 1988.

SOURCES: *The Builder,* 28 Jan, 9 Apr 1898; *Building News,* 27 Jan 1893, 31 May 1893.

PONTYPRIDD   GLAMORGAN

General market. 1893. £6,000. Architect: T. Rowlands.

PORTSMOUTH   HAMPSHIRE

Fuller's Hall and Market. General market 1886. Located between Charlotte Street and Pye Street.

Architect: Charles Bevis, Southsea. Contractor: Light Brothers, Landsport. With concert hall above. Demolished.

SOURCES: *PP-88; PP-35; Building News*, 8 Oct 1886.

PRESTON   LANCASHIRE

(1) General covered market. 1875. 36,000 sq. ft. Owned by the Corporation. 4 rows of stalls under single roof supported by iron columns and open on all sides; a second covered market was erected in Liverpool Street in the 1950s. (2) New Market Hall. 1972. 92 stalls and shops. Owned by Corporation.

SOURCES: *PP-35; The Builder*, 13 Aug 1872, 6 Apr 1872, 20 Apr 1872; *Building News*, 6 Apr 1872.

PWLLHELI   CAERNARVON

General market hall. 3,348 sq. ft. Owned by the Corporation.

RADCLIFFE   LANCASHIRE

General market. 1851. Erected by the Earl of Wilton.

SOURCES: *VCH.*

RADSTOCK   GLOUCESTERSHIRE

General market hall. 1897. £2,500. 3 avenues of stalls. Clerestory roof of steel girder work. Enlarged and improved in 1925.

SOURCES: S. Lloyd Harvey, *Radstock Market*, 1950 (pamphlet); Chris Howell, *Round Here in Them Days*, 1980; *Some Old Pictures of Midsomer Norton and Radstock*, 1979.

RAMSGATE   KENT

General market house. Ca. 1838. Located under the town hall. £1,409. Owned by the Corporation.

RAWTENSTALL   LANCASHIRE

Central Market Hall. General market. 1855. Tup Bridge. 11,088 sq. ft. Owned by the Corporation. Expanded 1912, 1924. Partially destroyed by fire in 1946. Extant.

READING   BERKSHIRE

(1) General covered market. 1800. Market Place to Fischer-Row. Owned by the Corporation. Half the building was two ranges of butchers' shops with covered passage between them; the other half was a "covered portico" furnished with seats for market women. (2) Market Hall. General market. 1854. Broad Street. Built onto the Corn Exchange. Owned by the Corporation. Partially covered, including 5 shops. Described as too small and inconvenient in 1888. Demolished in 1936.

SOURCES: *PP-88; PP-35; Building News*, 30 Sep 1889; Daphne Phillips, *The Story of Reading*, n.d.; *Reading Chronicle*, 16 Feb 1979.

REDHILL   SURREY

Market Hall. General market. 1860. Station Road and London and Brighton Road. £3,400. Architects: Francis and Francis, of Redhill. Owned by the Corporation. Enlarged in 1891 at a cost of £6,000, and again in 1903 at a cost of £7,000. Assembly Room above. Demolished in 1982.

SOURCES: *VCH.*

REDRUTH   CORNWALL

(1) Meat market. Ca. 1829. (2) Market House. General market. 1834. Built by Lord de Dunstanville. Sold by the Redruth Market Company in 1958. (3) Butchers' Market. Rebuilt in 1878. £2,500. Built by Gustave Lamart Basset. Contractor: Kinsman, of St. Day. Owned by Market Company until 1958. Destroyed by fire, ca. 1986.

SOURCES: *PP-88*; Frank Michell, *Annals of An Ancient Cornish Town*, 1978; *Notes on the History of Redruth*, 1948.

RETFORD   NOTTINGHAMSHIRE

(1) Market Hall. General market. 3,204 sq. ft. Owned by the Corporation. (2) Covered meat shambles. 2,160 sq. ft.

RICHMOND   YORKSHIRE

Market hall. General market. 1854. Toen Center. £915. Owned by the Corporation. Stone. 3-span roof with 3-bay façade; center bay as entrance. Refurbished in 1990 by Town Council, design by Patricia Brown of Weightman & Brown, York. Reopened 11 Aug 1990. Extant.

SOURCES: *PP-35*; Julia Ghert and H. Blades, *Remembering Richmond*, 1985; Nikolaus Pevsner, *Yorkshire, The North Riding*, 1966.

RIPLEY   DERBYSHIRE

General market. 1882. On the site of the Old White House, Market Place. Architects: Tait and Langham. Extant, but not as market.

SOURCES: *Building News*, 8 Mar 1878.

ROCHDALE   LANCASHIRE

(1) Market Hall. General market. 1824. Yorkshire Street, Toad Lane, and Lord Street. £30,000. 16,650 sq. ft. Market rights purchased by Rochdale Market Company from Lord Byron in 1822 for £500. Destroyed in 1843. (2) General market hall. 1844-45. 16,650 sq. ft. Architect: Robinson. Owned by Rochdale Market Company. Electric lighting installed in 1896. Destroyed by

fire in 1937. (3) Market Hall. 1939. Yorkshire Street. £80,000 (original estimate). Architect: S. H. Morgan, Borough Surveyor. Market rights purchased by the Corporation in 1936 for £112,000. Demolished in 1975. (4) Market Hall and covered market. 1976. Town center.

An act of Parliament in 1822 allowed the new Rochdale Market Company to purchase town market rights, and then to construct a covered market in 1824. In 1842 the Company purchased and removed the existing buildings from Exchange Street to Blackwater Street, fronting Toad Lane, and erected a new market hall. In the late nineteenth century this market was described as both too small and one which "leaves nothing to be desired," including 29 butchers' shops and stalls for numerous goods including fruit, china and glassware, books, and drapery goods. The building extended from Toad Lane to the back of a row of shops on Yorkshire Street with an arcade entrance from Yorkshire Street. The interior was laid out with 25 shops facing into a market floor with three avenues. A fish and game and potato market existed in the "top market," a partially covered area outside the hall. A fire in 1937 destroyed the hall, and a new hall was opened in 1939.

SOURCES: *PP-88; VCH;* Rochdale Market Company, "Minute Book," 1844. *Rochdale Observer,* 10 Apr 1982.

ROTHERHAM   YORKSHIRE

(1) The Shambles. Ca. 1801. Market Place to Church Street. Built by Company of Proprietors of the Market, per act of Parliament. A nearby Butter Market and Corn Exchange was constructed at about the same time. (2) General market hall. 1879. Market Place to Church Street. £10,315. 17,190 sq. ft. Architects: Hill and Swann, Sheffield. Owned by the Board of Health until 1871 and then by the Corporation. Destroyed by fire in 1888. (3) Market Hall. General market. 1889. £4,000. Architect: Archibald Neill, Leeds; Contractor: Mr. Wortley, Doncaster. Demolished in 1971. (4) Centenary Market Hall. 1971. To replace the hall of 1889.

The Market Hall of 1879 consisted of a 3-division slate roof supported by cast-iron columns, originally open on all but the front which had a "striking" iron-and-glass arcade entrance with circular dome surmounted by an ornamental clock turret. The sides were soon closed with wood and glass. While the 1879 market was criticized for being too utilitarian in design and "hardly worthy of our Corporation," the hall of 1889 was of brick and in the "Tudor style" with brick piers into which were fit double 3-light windows. Above the entrance was a 45-ft.

"quaint" turreted and embattled tower finished with pinnacles, described as a "credit to our town." It was surrounded by shops, some of which open to both street and market. The 3-division roof was made of wrought- and cast-iron and glass, and was supported by iron pillars. The interior had 4 "shopping" avenues, and a cast-iron drinking fountain in the center. The site is now a car park.

SOURCES: The Rotherham Markets Committee Minutes and Reports are held in Rotherham Central Library, Archives and Local Studies Section. *PP-88; The Builder,* 12 Aug 1871, 9 Sep 1876, 18 Aug 1877; *Building News,* 11 Aug 1871, 14 Sep 1888; John Guest, *Historic Notices of Rotherham,* 1879; "Yorkshire Markets: Rotherham" in *The Market Traders Review,* 5 Mar 1960; *Rotherham Advertiser,* 28 Jan 1888, 14 Dec 1889, 21 Dec 1889.

ROYSTON   HERTFORDSHIRE

Market House. General market. Ca. 1836.

SOURCES: *VCH.*

ROYTON   GREATER MANCHESTER

Market Hall. General market. Opened 16 Sep 1880. £2,500. 6,480 sq. ft. Erected by the Local Board which had been formed in 1863; later owned by District Council. Part of larger scheme which included a Town Hall and Library. Demolished ca. 1955.

SOURCES: *VCH; The Market Trader's Review,* 27 Sep 1952, 6 Aug 1955.

RUGELEY   STAFFORDSHIRE

(1) Market House. 1778-90. £317. 1,000 sq. ft. Destroyed in 1878. Brick structure with open market below. (2) Market Hall. General market. Opened 25 Jun 1879. £7,000. 27,270 sq. ft. Architect: N. T. Foulkes, Birmingham. Owned first by the local Board of Health, then Corporation. Demolished in 1978. (3) Market Hall. Ca. 1980. 45 indoor stalls plus outdoor market. Owned by Cannock Chase District Council.

The red brick hall of 1878 was in the "middle-pointed" Gothic style, with stone detailing and tracery, stained glass windows, and a green slate roof. A clock tower with steeple, which rose 90 ft. above the ground, stood over an 8-ft.-square entrance lobby. The interior had ornate cast-iron columns and roof supports. Although the structure also included a reading room, public assembly room, and fire engine station, the nave portion was used as the market hall. Only the clock tower remains.

SOURCES: *Architect,* 26 Mar 1870; *Rugeley Times,* 11 Mar 1972, 22 Apr 1978, 17 Jun 1978; J.

A. Johnson, "The Markets and Fairs of Rugeley, 1259-1977," Thesis, Ordinary National Diploma, Stafford College, May 1977; *Kelly's Directory of Staffordshire*, 1880; E. C. Toye, "Down Your Way," *Rugeley Post*, 11 Feb 1976.

RUNCORN   CHESHIRE

General market hall. 6,921 sq. ft. Owned by Runcorn U. D. C.

RYDE   ISLE OF WIGHT

Market House and Town Hall. General market. 1830. High Street and Union Street. £500. 3,200 sq. ft. Architect: James Sanderson. Extended in 1860s. Owned by the Corporation. Rusticated lower floor, with projecting colonnaded entrance supported on Ionic pilasters. Clock tower with open turret. Market activity ended in 1914. Extant in 1988 as Borough Council Offices.

SOURCES: *Kelly's Directory*, 1839; Nikolaus Pevsner, *The Buildings of Hampshire*, 1967.

SALFORD   LANCASHIRE

Market and Town Hall. General market. 1825. Browning Street to Church Street. 24,336 sq. ft. Architect: Richard Lane, Manchester. Owned first by Market Company, then Commissioners of Police, now Corporation. Extant.

Originally known as Salford New Market Building, it was acquired by the Commissioners of Police in 1834, and then became property of the new Corporation in 1844. The stone portico consists of 2 Doric pilasters and 2 Doric columns supporting a pediment; an entrance hall has 4 Doric columns. An assembly hall was above and market space below, with additional market space to the rear. Frequent enlargement (1847, 1848, 1853, 1862, 1875, and 1908) extended the market to the rear. By 1890 the entire town hall-market structure was 312 ft.long.

SOURCES: *Manchester Evening News*, 17 Jul 1904; *Manchester City News*, 17 Jul 1930.

SALISBURY   WILTSHIRE

General market hall. 1859. £2,887. 16,000 sq. ft. Architect: John Strapp, engineer; ironwork by W. Mahon, of Manchester. Built by Salisbury Railway and Market House Company; now owned by the Corporation. Extant as central library.

The new market house at the west side of the Market Place opened on 24 May 1859, thus ending centuries of the sale of food and other commodities (including hemp and cheese) in the open air . Led by the town's sanitary reformer, Dr. A. B. Middleton, the project was undertaken by public subscription in the form of a joint-stock company, the Salisbury Railway and Market House Company, per an act of Parliament, after the Salisbury Town Council abandoned plans for a new market due to lack of funds. The new market was intended for general retail as well as wholesale purposes—particularly the sale of cheese and grain—and to encourage sellers from long distances to come to the town, thereby generating lower food prices. The 77 ft. by 174 ft. oblong building was constructed of Bath stone and has 3 glassed-in arches divided by rusticated Tuscan piers which support a pediment over the central doorway. The interior of glass and iron was described at the time as being "after the style adopted in the Crystal Palace [of 1851]." A special railway entered the building in the left side, under a gallery for corn storage, thereby connecting the town center with a distant railway junction. The market declined in the 1870s and fell into disuse by 1914. It was demolished in 1975 but the façade was incorporated into the structure for the public library.

SOURCES: *PP-88*; *VCH*; *Building News*, 19 Mar 1858; Dennis Cobbold, "A Survey of Salisbury Railway and Market House," undergraduate dissertation, Department of Archeology, Southhampton, 1980; W. S. Oglethorpe, *Salisbury Railroad and Market House Company*, 1859; *Royal Commission on Historical Monuments of England, Ancient and Historical Monuments in the City of Salisbury*, vol. 1; *Salisbury Journal*, 6 Jun 1958; *The Salisbury and Winchester Journal and General Advertiser*, 28 May 1859, 4 Jun 1859; Wiltshire Library and Museum Service, *Salisbury Library: A Brief Historical Account of the Public Library With a Note on the Market House*, n.d.

SANDBACH   CHESHIRE

Town Hall and Market House. General market hall. 1890. £4,500. Architect: Thomas Bower, Natwich. Donated by Lord Crewe.

SOURCES: *The Builder*, 27 Sep 1890; John Robinson, *Architecture of North England*, 1986.

SCARBOROUGH   YORKSHIRE

General market hall. 1854. St. Sepulchre Street, Post Street, Dumple Street, and St. Helen's Square. £12,100 (estimate). 16,761 sq. ft. Architects: J. Irvine (died before completion), of Scarborough, and George Townsend Andrews. Built by the Market Company, per act of Parliament in 1852, later owned by the Borough Council. Extant in 1988.

A plaque on the market hall states that the structure "replaced the congested street market held in the old town since the middle ages." With Whitby stone front and brick sides and rear, the structure is of an imposing "Tuscan style" 5-bay front with entrances on the side bays and with columns between. The market has a single-span roof of iron and glass. Additional light is given by 13 semi-circular windows high on each side. When opened the market had 36 shops and numerous stalls.

SOURCES: *PP-88; Scarborough Gazette*, 11 Aug 1853.

SCUNTHORPE   SOUTH HUMBERSIDE

General covered market. 1906. £2,437. 5,700 sq. ft. Architect: A. M. Cobban, Engineer.

SOURCES: *The Builder*, 10 Mar 1906.

SHEFFIELD   YORKSHIRE

(1) Norfolk Market Hall. Ca. 1784. Owned first by the manorial lord, then Corporation. (2) Norfolk Market. General market hall. 1851. 45,000 sq. ft. Architects: Weightman and Hadfield. Owned by the Duke of Norfolk. Altered in 1903. Demolished in 1959. (3) Fitzalan Meat and Fish Market Hall. 1856. Located between King Street and Fitzalan Square. 26,280 sq. ft. Architects: Weightman, Hadfield, and Goldie. Replaced in 1930. (4) Castlefolds Market. Covered vegetable market. 1877. 44,640 sq. ft. Architect: Charles Hadfield. Owned by the manorial lord. Demolished in 1971. (5) Castle Hill Fish and Meat Market Hall. 1930. Owned by the Corporation. Extant in 1997. (6) New Castle Market. 1962. (7) Sheaf Market Hall. General market. 1971.

Sheffield's markets were highly concentrated in the center of the town and it was noted in the late nineteenth century as an exceptional instance in which the public markets were well managed in the hands of a private owner. The Duke of Norfolk expended large sums on improving Sheffield's markets—first by way of separating retail marketing from the killing of cattle and wholesale marketing, and then the development of three contiguous large market halls: a meat and fish market (Fitzalan), a vegetable market (Castlefolds), and general market (Norfolk). Railway access and close connection to wholesale markets allowed these markets to become known for their low prices. By the 1880s Sheffield had more public retail market space (80,000 sq. ft.) in the city center than most larger cities, and it was said that half the population of Sheffield shopped in the public markets. The Corporation purchased the market property and market rights from the Duke of Norfolk in 1876. The largest of the halls, known for its "human interest," was the Norfolk general market hall which was built in 1851 and included clothing, boot and shoe sales, household wares, food, and miscella-

neous goods and as late as 1949 brought a revenue of £14,397 to the city. None of the nineteenth-century buildings survive. A new market, the Sheaf Hall, was built in 1971.

SOURCES: *PP-88*; Lewis; Janet Blackman, "The Food Supply of an Industrial Town: A Study of Sheffield's Public Markets, 1780-1900," *Business History*, 1962-63, vol. 94; Ed Bramley, *A Record of the Burgery of Sheffield Commonly Called the Town Trust, From 1898 to 1955*, 1957; *The Builder*, 18 Aug 1877, 9 Oct 1880, 24 Aug 1901, 15 Aug 1903; *Building News*, 3 Aug 1877, 14 May 1880, 18 Jul 1902; *Market Traders Review*, 17 Sep 1949, 8 Oct 1949, 26 Nov 1955, 21 Jun 1958, 28 Feb 1959; Sheffield City Library, *Basic Books on Sheffield History* (bibliography), 1950.

SHIPLEY   YORKSHIRE

Market Hall. Owned by City of Bradford Metropolitan Council.

SHOREHAM   SUSSEX

Market House. General market. 1823. Described as "a mean building of brick." Removed in 1845.

SOURCES: *VCH*; Henry Cheal, *The Story of Shoreham*, 1921 (repr. 1978).

SHREWSBURY   SALOP

(1) Market House. General market. 1819. (2) Market House. General market. 1888. 36,000 sq. ft. Architect: H. A. Cheers. Owned by the Corporation. (3) Market Hall. 1927. 36,000 sq. ft. (4) Market Hall. 1967. 21,357 sq. ft.

SOURCES: *The Builder*, 29 Jan 1898; *Building News*, 12 Oct 1888, 2 Jan 1903.

SOUTH CAVE   YORKSHIRE

General market house. 1796.

SOUTH ELMSALL   YORKSHIRE

General covered market. 45,000 sq. ft.

SOUTHHAMPTON   HAMPSHIRE

(1) Audit House. General market. 1771. £7,000. Architect: John Crunden, Piccadilly. Stone building "in the Doric style," and with market in open lower floor. Owned by Corporation and originally used as council chamber above. Later enlarged. (2) St. George's Market. Butchers' and vegetable market. 1821-22. Bridge Street. Erected in order to clear the High Street of market activity. Privately owned.

SOURCES: *PP-35; The Builder*, 7 Mar 1868; *Building News*, 14 Aug 1903; Reverend Sylvester Davies, *A History of Southampton*, 1883.

SOUTH MOLTON DEVONSHIRE

(1) New Market House. General market. 1809. £1,350. Builder: John Morris. (2) Pannier Market Hall. General market. 1863. £10,200. 23,680 sq. ft. Architect: W. F. Cross, Exeter; Builder: John Cock. Owned by the Corporation. Extant in 1982.

Prior to the opening of the Pannier Market Hall in 1863 the town's marketplace was full of wooden sheds which were erected every Saturday morning and disassembled every Saturday night; there were where the market sellers sat at their panniers in all weathers. The new market, which was adjacent to the Guildhall, consists of a long and open central hall with clerestory above and an aisle on one side, and with an elegant arched entrance surmounted by sculpted rams' heads. The building was repaired and renovated in the early 1980s.

SOURCES: John Code, *Records of South Molton,* 1893; *South Molton and District Official Guide,* 1982; South Molton Town Council, *A Short History of South Molton Guildhall and Museum,* 1987.

SOUTH PETHERTON SOMERSET

General market. 1843. Architect: Morris Davis, Langport. Upper story added in 1889.

SOURCES: *VCH.*

SOUTHPORT LANCASHIRE

(1) London Street Market. General covered market. 1848. £480. 7,052 sq. ft. Architect: Thomas Withnell. (2) Chapel Street Market. General market. 1857. (3) Eastbank Market. General market hall. 1879. Located at Eastbank Street, Upper King Steet, and Market Street. £23,800. 40,000 sq. ft. Architects: Mellor and Sutton, Southport and John Dence, London. Contractor: T. Bridge, Burscough. Owned by the Corporation. Later additions. Destroyed by fire in 1913. (4) General Covered Market. 1931. Located at King Street and Market Street. Extant.

The growth of Southport's markets corresponds to the growth of its population from 4,766 in 1851 to 32,206 in 1881. The first covered market, the Victoria Market, was built in 1848, followed by a second market in Chapel Street in 1857 which was enlarged in 1863 and again in 1873. A wholesale market and a fish market were added, and then the large Eastbank Market Hall was built in 1879. At this time the longtime markets committee chairman, Alderman Sutton, became the mayor of the town. The Eastbank Hall, with its thirteen entrances to the market, had a flamboyant "classical" façade with a central entrance topped by a pediment and crowned with a group of sculpted figures. The entrance was flanked by pilasters and columns supporting figures of Flora and Ceres. Behind this was an octagonal dome clad with zinc of fish-plate pattern. The 5-division roof was supported by iron columns. The market was divided into 3 areas: general market at the front with 3 broad avenues; a fish market behind; and a wholesale market (which also sold retail). The town sought to attract greater food supplies by providing free space in the wholesale market for one year. The interior walls were of white and colored glazed brick. The market was destroyed by fire on the night of 18 Oct 1913. An open-air market took its place until 1931, when a very simple one-story structure was erected but without frontage on Eastbank Street.

SOURCES: *PP-88; VCH;* Francis Bailey, *A History of Southport,* 1955; *The Builder,* 13 Oct 1877, 3 Nov 1877, 15 Dec 1877, 20 Sep 1879; *Building News,* 5 Jun 1872, 7 Sep 1877, 26 Sep 1879; *The Illustrated London News,* 17 Sep 1881; *The Market Traders Review,* 23 Apr 1949, 19 Apr 1952; *The Southport Guardian,* 25 Mar 1903; *The Southport Visiter,* 19 Sep 1879, 21 Oct 1913.

SPENNYMOOR DURHAM

(1) Tudhoe Grange Market Hall. General market hall. 1870. Located at the end of High Street, in Salvin Estate. Built by David Syme for the Salvin Estate; ownership passed to Local Board in 1894. Stone with triple-arched front. Largely a butchers' market. Very much deserted by late 1880s; used as a cinema in 1919; later demolished. (2) Market Hall. 1870. High Street and Silver Street. £1,157. 5,402 sq. ft. Rival market to above. Single story with shops on both sides, with clock tower. Owned by local Board of Health. Demolished in 1912. (3) Market Hall. 1916. High Street. 5,600 sq. ft. Architect: George T. Wellburn, Middleborough. Replaced the 1870 hall. Incorporated into new town hall. Adapted to other use in 1950s.

SOURCES: *PP-88; Building News,* 8 Mar 1912.

ST. AUBIN JERSEY

(1) General covered market. 1772. £193. 560 sq. ft. (2) General covered market. 1826. £900. Architect: William Thompson. Paid for by public lotteries. One-story stone piazza structure with Jersey granite pillars; shops behind. Reconstructed in 1982, but not as market.

ST. AUSTELL CORNWALL

Market House. 1844. £6,000. 10,890 sq. ft. Architects: Cope, Eales, and Elmslie, London. Building of local granite, with vaulted ceiling and massive granite pillars in entrance hall. Market on ground floor, first floors, and gallery. Owned by the Market Commissioners per act of Parliament of 1842 for removing old market house and erecting "a convenient" market house. The new market made it possible for the town to ban street trading. Extant in 1988.

SOURCES: *The Builder*, 20 Nov 1847; Harold Warren, ed., *St. Austell Market House, 1842-1980*, 1980.

ST. HELENS   MERSEYSIDE

(1) General covered market. 1843. (2) Market Hall. General market. 1851. Church Street to Tontine Street. £2,000. 19,800 sq. ft. Extended in 1871; "new shed" added in 1888. Owned by the Corporation.

SOURCES: *PP-88; VCH.*

ST. HELIER   JERSEY

(1) General market. 1803. Located in Halkett Place and Beresford Street. Owned by the Corporation. Destroyed in 1881. (2) Old Market (a.k.a. Beresford Market). Fish market. 1841. Altered in 1873, 1936, and 1972. Located in Beresford and Minden Place. Owned by the Corporation. (3) Central Market. General market hall. 1882. £12,000. 33,600 sq. ft. Architects: Helliwell and Bellamy, of Brighouse. Owned by the Corporation. Extant in 1988.

St. Helier's public markets were first held in the Royal Square, and then in various covered buildings to shelter the stalls. Because of congestion, in 1800-1803 the market was transferred to land which is now Halkett Place, and here a new picturesque piazza market—a roofed colonnade around three sides of a square—was built based on the market at Bath, a model of which is in the museum in St. Helier. This was replaced with a giant new Central Market hall in 1882, with a 13-bay exterior façade of granite and numerous elaborately ornamented iron gates, grilles, lamp brackets, and railings designed by Philippe Le Suer, States Architect. The interior is dominated by a large octagonal central glass dome with a circular pool and 4-tier ornamental fountain below. The market was fully renovated in 1972.

SOURCES: G. R. Balleine, *The Baliwick of Jersey*, 1951 (rev. ed. by Joan Stevens, 1970); C. E. B. Brett, *Buildings in the Town and Parish of St. Helier*, 1984; *The Builder*, 6 Nov 1880; *Building News*, 27 Feb 1880; Beth Lloyd, *Explore Jersey*, 1984.

ST. PETER PORT   GUERNSEY

Market Hall. General market. 1832. Between Market Street and Market Square. Series of stone buildings, begun in 1780 and the "halls" completed in 1832. Extant.

STAFFORD   STAFFORDSHIRE

(1) Shirehall Market. General Market. 1790. 3-sided arcade at rear of Shirehall. Transferred to new market in 1854. (2) St. John's Market Hall (originally called the Butter Cross). General market. 1854. 14,000 sq. ft. Architect: Charles Trubshaw, County Surveyor. Extended in 1867 and renamed St. John's Hall with new entrance from Crabbery Street; enlarged again in 1880, an addition of 4,880 sq. ft. at a cost of £3,840; and again in 1882, and in 1927 to area of 20,000 sq. ft. (3) Butchers' Market. Opened 17 Dec 1880. Owned by the Corporation; built alongside St. John's Hall. Included the fish market. (4) St. John's Market. General market hall. 1989. Broad Street and Earl Street. Part of shopping complex.

The original 1853 market hall had 126 stalls when all extensions were completed. It was requisitioned for war use during the 1939-45 war; postwar rationing made it impossible for the 20 butchers and fishsellers to return to the hall when it was returned to civilian use. The market charter was revoked in 1983, and the market was moved to a shopping complex in 1989.

SOURCES: *PP-88; VCH; The Builder*, 3 Nov 1877, 4 Sep 1880, 1 Jan 1881; *Building News*, 3 Nov 1877.

STALYBRIDGE   LANCASHIRE

(1) Market and Town Hall. 1831. Market Street. £4,800. Architects: Fairbairn and Lillie. Built by Improvement Commissioners, per act of 1828. Altered in 1843, and later fully converted for municipal business. Extant in 1988. (2) Victoria Market. General market hall. Opened 18 Jul 1868. Trinity Street. £8,127 (1868 cost only). 23,553 sq. ft. (with additions). Architect: Amos Lee, Borough Surveyor. West wing with fish market added in 1881. Owned by Corporation. Extant in 1997. (3) Fish Market. 1881. 12 shops opposite the entrance to Victoria Market.

The Stalybridge Improvement Commissioners established a market in 1831 in order to alleviate the town's dependency upon Ashton-upon-Lyne for its marketing needs. When the town outgrew the 1831 structure, the new Corporation built the Victoria Market Hall, a large building of red brick with stone dressings, with a central bay with grand pilasters and polychromatic brick tower above. The interior structure was of wrought-iron tie-bar roof trusses supported on cast-iron columns. The project included construction of a new bridge across River Tame for market access.

SOURCES: *PP-88; Stalybridge Centenary Handbook 1857-1957.*

STAMFORD   LINCOLNSHIRE

(1) Butchers' Shambles. Covered meat market. 1808. North side of High Street to Broad Street. £1,500. Stone portico with side wings and entrance leading into open market. In the Tuscan manner. Architect: W. D. Legg. Owned by the Corporation. Extant as part of the library and museum. (2) Butter Market. 1861. At Red Lion Square adjoining Horseshoe Lane. 1,400 sq. ft. Architect: Edward Browning, Stamford. Two stories with 3-bay arcade at ground floor. Covered by the iron-and-glass roof removed from the old corn market of 1838. Owned by the Marquis of Exeter. Extant in 1988. (3) Meat market. 1896. Located on the site of the George Hotel Paddock adjoining Midland Railway Station. £6,000. 7,000 sq. ft. Architect: John Woolston with James Richardson, Borough Surveyor.

SOURCES: *Building News,* 7 May 1858, 28 May 1858, 30 Jul 1858, 18 Sep 1896; Alexander Clifton-Taylor, *Six English Towns,* 1978.

STAVELEY   DERBYSHIRE

Markham Hall. General market. 1893. Erected by Charles Markham. Used as market hall in 1920s by Miners' Welfare Committee. Extant.

STOCKPORT   CHESHIRE

(1) Produce Hall. 1851. £4,000. Architect: J. Stevens and Park, Macclesfield. Extant in 1992. (2) Market Hall. General market. 1861. £4,990. Architects/Builders: H. Lloyd, Bristol, J. Haywood, Phoenix Foundry, Derby. Owned by the Corporation. Extant.

> The Stockport marketplace and the Parish Church of St. Mary's sit adjacent to each other on the summit of a hill in the center of Stockport. To meet the needs of a population which by the mid-nineteenth century was burgeoning, shops and the old Market House were demolished in order to enlarge the size of the open marketplace. In 1851 the Borough purchased the market rights from the manorial owner, and in that year opened a new produce hall. In 1860 it was decided to cover the marketplace, and hence appeared the new covered market of 1861. This new hall, described as an "umbrella on stilts," was of glass-and-iron screening with an 8-division roof of slate and glass, making for an interesting modern gothic complement to the nearby St. Mary's Church. In 1868 a bridge was built to connect St. Petersgate to the market. The Stockport market has been recently refurbished.

SOURCES: Lewis; *The Builder,* 15 Sep 1860; *The Guardian,* 3 Sep 1960; *700 Years History of Stockport's Market Place, 1260-1960,* 1960; *Survey of the Market Place* (typed ms., Central Library, Stockport).

STOCKTON-ON-TEES   CLEVELAND

(1) Cross Market House. 1768. 5,310 sq. ft. Owned by the Corporation. (2) Shambles market. 1825. Tontine Street. Ca. £3,000.

STOGUMBER   SOMERSET

General market house. Ca. 1800. Located north of the church. Abandoned as a market by the 1860s.

SOURCES: *VCH.*

STOKE-UPON-TRENT   STAFFORDSHIRE

(1) Cross Street Market. General market hall. 1835. Located at the southwest corner of Market Place, extending through to Epworth Street. Used as a shambles by 1859, as a hide and skin market by 1872, and formed part of Haley and Stoke Hide Market by 1960. Extant in 1960. (2) Glebe Street Market. General market house. 1845. (3) General market hall. 1883. Located on the south side of Church Street. 10,200 sq. ft. Architect: Charles Lyman, of Stoke-upon-Trent. Owned by the Corporation. Destroyed by fire in 1982. Rebuilt in 1994.

SOURCES: *VCH; Building News,* 29 Sep 1882; John Ward, *A History of the Borough of Stoke-upon-Trent,* 1843.

STONEHAVEN   GRAMPIAN

General market. 1827. Located in Allardice Street at Market Square. Architect: Alexander Fraser. Classical two-story with arcaded shops on ground floor. Spire completed in 1856. Extant in 1997.

STOURBRIDGE   WORCESTERSHIRE

Market and Town Hall. Ca. 1826. £15,000. Owned by Commissioners. Built per act of Parliament, 1825.

SOURCES: *VCH.*

STRATFORD   ESSEX

Vegetable Market. Opened 1 Sep 1879. Adjoining Stratford Bridge Station. 24,000 sq. ft. Architect: Langtry. Contractor: W. Bangs. Owned by the Great Eastern Railway Company. Largely a wholesale market to serve London dealers.

SOURCES: *The Builder,* 23 Aug 1879, 13 Sep 1879, 21 Aug 1880.

SUNDERLAND   DURHAM

(1) General covered market. 1830. Located between High Street and Coronation Street. 62,415

sq. ft. Owned by the Corporation. Glass roof added in 1883 at a cost of £5,836. (2) Jacky White's Market. General market hall. 1967. 21,500 sq. ft. Owned by Corporation. Part of Bridges Shopping Center.

SOURCES: *PP-88.*

SWADLINGCOTE   DERBY

Market Hall. General market. Opened 29 Oct 1861. Established by Rev. J. R. Stevens as a Saturday evening market for working class people; paid for by subscription. Brick with stone dressing; 2 large windows flank a stone tablet with clock. Cupola.

SOURCES: J. Williams, *Historical Buildings of South Derbyshire and District,* n.d.

SWANSEA   GLAMORGAN

(1) Meat market. 1774. (2) Oxford New Market. General market (enclosed, but not fully covered). 1830. £20,000. 73,272 sq. ft. Architect: Roderick, Surveyor. Owned by the Corporation. Partially removed, replaced by 1897 market; remaining structure extant 1954. (3) New Market. General market hall. 1897. Located in Portland Street, Oxford Street, and Union Street. £27,000+. 81,120 sq. ft. Architect: Buckley Wilson and Glendenning Moxham, Swansea. Contractors: Bennett Brothers, Swansea. Owned by the Corporation. Destroyed in 1941 by enemy action. (4) Market Hall, 1976.

Crowded streets and public dissatisfaction with the manner in which food was handled in the Swansea open market, located in the streets surrounding the old stone Market House in Castle Street, led to an act of Parliament in 1774 which provided for the fixing of a Butchers' Shambles in the Castle Garden, the site being obtained from the Duke of Beaufort. This market failed because of a legal impediment which allowed the butchers to remain in the streets, and it was not until 1828 that another act of Parliament enabled the Corporation to borrow money to sweep away the street shambles and erect a new enclosed general market, walled but not uniformly covered, at Oxford, Union, and Orange Streets (the Ropework Fields). This large "utilitarian" market, known as the Oxford or New Market, was a gift from Richard Calvert Jones, and opened in 1830. It had a slate-roofed butchers' shambles and stalls for other trades, and cattle and corn markets. The market was highly successful and popular (it provided "porteresses" to carry the market baskets of genteel female shoppers), but in 1895, due to public demand for better enclosure, the Corporation built a new market,

which opened 22 Jun 1897, on the old market site. The new red Ruabon brick building with Bath stone dressing, and 2 60-ft. towers, had a 416-ft. frontage to Oxford Street of red Ruabon brick. The interior of this glass-roofed structure, the largest market in Wales, had a floor of patent granolythic paving. A roadway ran into the market center, and separate divisions were provided for stalls selling sweets, toys, china, books, vegetables, cheese, and other goods; there was a fish market, fifty butchers' stalls, and a wholesale meat market. Soon after its opening it was equipped with electric lighting. After turning down an offer from a private business group to purchase the building in 1938, the Corporation modernized the structure. The market was destroyed by enemy action on 21 Feb 1941.

SOURCES: *PP-35; The Builder,* 7 Sep 1889, 17 Oct 1891, 16 Nov 1895; *Building News,* Jul-Nov 1889, 9 Oct 1891; *South Wales Evening Post,* 21 Feb 1941; 6 Feb 1954; D. Ivan Savnbins, *A Brief History of Swansea Markets,* 1942; Norman Thomas, *The Story of Swansea's Market,* 1965.

SWINDON   WILTSHIRE

(1) Vegetable market house. 1852. South side of the Market Square. Architect: Sampson Sage. Owned by the Swindon Market Company. (2) Market Hall. 1854. £37,501. Architect: Edward Roberts. Privately owned; built by the Great Western Railway Company. Described as Gothic. Hexagonal roof, 40 ft. in diameter, with fountain in center of interior. Attached to Mechanical Institute. (3) Market Hall. General market. 1892. Front to Commercial Road. Privately owned. Brick with stone dressing; flamboyant Georgian style. Demolished in 1970s for car park. (3) New Market Hall. 1976. Brunel Centre. (4) Swindon Market Hall. 1995. General Market. Commercial Road (site of 1892 market). 16,000 sq. ft. Glass and brick with white cloth roof. Harrison Patience, Architect. Owner: Swindon Space Management.

SOURCES: *VCH; The Builder,* 11 Mar 1865, 21 Apr 1866.

TAIBACH   GLAMORGAN

General market. 1840. Ceased trading ca. 1900. Destroyed in 1936.

TARRING   SUSSEX

Market House. General market. Ca. 1778. Located in Market Place. Replaced old market house on same site. Extant.

SOURCES: Roger Davies, *Tarring: A Walk Through Its History,* n.d.

TAUNTON
SOMERSET

(1) Market House. General market. 1772. Ca. 1,500 sq. ft. Architect: Coplestone Warre Bampfylde, Hestercombe. Owned by the Market Trustees. By 1880s was large butchers' market, attracting many "country" butchers. Trustees held virtual monopoly on meat sales. Arcades demolished in 1930; central building extant. (2) Victoria Rooms Market. General market. 1821. Fore Street. Fish market added in 1836. Owned by Trustees. "Fine classical façade." Town Hall since 1934. Demolished ca. 1965.

SOURCES: *PP-88;* Lewis; George H. Kite, *Taunton: Its History and Market Trust,* 1926.

TAVISTOCK
DEVONSHIRE

Pannier Market. General market. 1822. 27,000 sq. ft. Architect: John Foulston. Owned by the Tavistock Parish Council. In the 1920s the central hall had stalls for general merchandise, for 50 dairy and poultry retailers, and 15 stalls for Plymouth merchants to buy up dairy and poultry products from local growers. Extant in 1997.

SOURCES: H. Tapley-Soper, *Devonshire Past and Present Historical Pictorial and Description Guide,* 1913; *Report on Markets and Fairs, Part IV: Eastern and Southern Counties,* 1927.

TENBY
PEMBROKESHIRE

(1) Market House. 1828. Between High Street and Frog Street. £1,700. Built by the Common Council. (2) Market Hall. General market. 1892. On the Promenade. Market described as one of the smallest in Wales. To mark the opening of the market, the mayor and mayoress gave a dinner to 700 working men and their wives. Extant and recently renovated.

SOURCES: *PP-35; The Market Traders Review,* 7 Aug 1967; *The Tenby Observer,* 1 Jan 1988.

TETBURY
GLOUCESTERSHIRE

Market House and Town Hall. 1817. Town center. Extensive remodeling of massive 1655 stone building, resting on stone pillars; Tudor hood-molding above windows; large cupola. Builder: William Killigrew, Chippenham. Extant as market.

SOURCES: *VCH;* Maggie Colwell, *West of England Market Towns,* 1980; *Gloucester Countryside,* Apr-May 1962; A. T. Lee, *A History of Tetbury,* 1842.

TEWKESBURY
GLOUCESTERSHIRE

General piazza market. 1789. £1,400. Located at the cross on the south side of Barton Street. Architect: Edward Edgcumbe. Portico entrance with pilasters and Ionic columns, pediment, and with side bays. Demolished in 1878.

SOURCES: Lewis; *VCH;* James Bennett, *A History of Tewkesbury,* 1830 (repr. 1976); H. Colvin, *A Biographical Dictionary of British Architects 1600-1840,* 1978; Kathleen Ross, *The Book of Tewkesbury,* 1986.

THETFORD
NORFOLK

(1) Market Shambles. 1787. King Street. Timber-walled semi-circular iron building, with new iron "market cross" nearby. (2) Market Shambles. Covered market (largely for butchers). 1837. Piazza type semi-enclosed structure attached to the Guildhall.

SOURCES: Lewis; Alan Crosby, *A History of Thetford,* 1986.

THURSO
HIGHLANDS

General covered market. 1800.

TIVERTON
DEVONSHIRE

Pannier Market Hall. General market. 1831. In center of pedestrian precinct. £8,392. 7,276 sq. ft. Remodeled in 1876 at cost of £2,000. Owned by the Market Trustees. Rectangular building with timber roof and cast-iron supports. Octagonal cupola with clock. Built to address problem of inconvenient and dangerous market in streets. Complaints in 1888 that market was "going down" and that Trustees neglected the market. Extant in 1992.

SOURCES: *PP-88;* Lewis; Frederich John Shell, *A History of the Town of Tiverton,* 1892.

TODMORDEN
YORKSHIRE

Market Hall. General market. 1879. Butterworth Street. £3,500. 9,963 sq. ft. Architect: Rodley, Borough Surveyor. 4-division roof over market hall. Owned by the Corporation. Extant in 1990.

SOURCES: *The Builder,* 26 Apr 1879.

TORQUAY
DEVONSHIRE

(1) Rotunda Market. General market. 1820. Torwood Street. Architect: John Foulston, Plymouth. Built by Sir L. V. Palk. Circular piazza market (with columns of red granite) forming a complete circle and facing into open-air market at center. Extant in part as shops. (2) Market Hall. General market. 1853. Market Street at Union Street. £3,600. 20,250 sq. ft. Architect: John Foulston. Owned by the Torquay Market Company. Large single-arched entrance between giant pilasters and with pediment above. Built on a hill, the market towered above the surrounding buildings. One of the banners carried in the town procession on the opening day of the market read

"The Hall of Economy for the Poor." The opening was celebrated with a dinner for 1,400. Refurbished in 1985. Extant as market.

SOURCES: *PP-88*; Arthur C. Ellis, *An Historical Survey of Torquay*, n.d.; *South Devon Journal*, 13 Sep 1950; *Torquay Chronicle*, 4 Oct 1853; Torquay Civic Society, *Torquay Market* (pamphlet), 1988; *Torquay Herald Examiner*, 2 Dec 1985; *Torquay Herald Express*, 24 Mar 1983.

TOTNES   DEVONSHIRE

(1) Pannier Market. General market hall. 1848. 2,394 sq. ft. Located in High Street. Owned by the Corporation. Destroyed by fire in 1955. (2) Pannier Market. Ca. 1960. 2,412 sq. ft.

SOURCES: *The Market Traders Review*, 27 Sep 1958.

TREDEGAR   GWENT

Market Hall. 1892. Built on the old market site. 6,600 sq. ft. Architect: Hitchcox, Newport. Contractor: David Davies, Cardiff. Privately owned.

SOURCES: *The Builder*, 31 Dec 1892.

TREGARON   DYFED

General market house. 1875. Architect: R. Williams.

TROWBRIDGE   WILTSHIRE

Market Hall. General market. Opened 30 Sep 1862. Located in Silver and Fore Streets next to town hall. £7,830. Architect: C. E. Davis, Bath. Built by the manorial lord; purchased by the local Board of Health from the lord, William Stancomb, for £4,400 in 1892. Local Board had to use a special town election to force local fishsellers off the streets and into the Market Hall. Owned by the Corporation. Italianate. Arcaded lower floor, with heavy columns. Façade extant.

SOURCES: *VCH*; Kenneth H. Rogers, *The Book of Trowbridge*, 1966; *Trowbridge Advertiser*, Aug 1860, 30 Sep 1862; *The Wiltshire Times*, 10 Mar 1862.

TRURO   CORNWALL

City Hall and Market Hall. 1847. Boscawen Street. £11,000. 27,000 sq. ft. Architect: Christopoher Eales, London. Builder: Joseph Pryor, Helston. Owned by the Corporation. Front entrance leads to market hall in rear. Granite palazzo frontage with campanile turret. In late 1880s it had 72 butcher stalls, 9 greengrocers, 8 fish stalls, and 3 refreshment stalls. Extant.

SOURCES: *PP-88*; *The Builder*, 20 Nov 1847; *Building News*, 3 Sep 1878, 9 Aug 1901; David Mudd, *About the City*, 1979; J. S. Polsue, *Lake's*

History of the County of Cornwall, Vol. 3, 1870; *West Briton and Cornwall Advertiser*, 12 Nov 1847.

TUNSTALL   STAFFORDSHIRE

General market. Ca. 1818. Tunstall Court. Privately owned. (2) Shambles. General covered market. 1858. East of Market Square at Boulevard and Butterfield Place. £6,000. Architect: G. T. Robinson. Single-story arcade front noted for its imposing archway and rusticated masonary. Built as attempt by town to exert itself as market center for region. It was reduced by one-third in size when town hall built in front in 1885. Built by Improvement Commissioners. Extant in 1988.

SOURCES: Lewis; *VCH*; *Building News*, 1 Jan 1858, 22 Jan 1858; *Harper's Bygone Tunstall*, 1913.

ULVERSTON   CUMBRIA

(1) Market Hall. 1878. New Market Street and Brogden Street, adjoining the British Legion Institute. £6,769. Destroyed by fire in 1935. (2) Market Hall. 9,297 sq. ft. (in 1967). Extant in 1990.

SOURCES: *The News*, 5 Oct 1935, 9 Nov 1935.

UPTON-UPON-SEVERN   WORCESTERSHIRE

Town Hall and Market House (a.k.a. Memorial Hall). 1832. Old Street. Built per act of Parliament. Ground floor served as a market for only a few years. Owned by Parish Council. Refurbished in 1921. Extant in 1997.

SOURCES: Lewis; *The Builder*, 20 Jul 1878; Pamela Hurle, *Upton: Portrait of a Severnside Town*, 1979; Emily Lawson, *The Nation in the Parish*, 1891; papers of the Memorial Hall Committee are located in the Upton Library, Old Stree.

UXBRIDGE   MIDDLESEX

Market house. 1789. High Street. £3,000. 6,860 sq. ft. Owned by the manorial lord. Loggia with colonnade, pediment, and cupola fronting High Street.

SOURCES: Lewis; *VCH*; *The Architect*, 1 Oct 1920.

WAKEFIELD   YORKSHIRE

(1) General covered market. 1847. 14,400 sq. ft. Owned by the Corporation. Destroyed in 1962. (2) Market Hall. General market. 1853. Teall Street. Built by Market Company (stock company) which had purchased the market from the Duke of Leeds; sold to the Corporation in 1902. Demolished in 1962. (3) Market Hall. 1876. Located between Teall Street, Brook Street, Westmoreland Street, and the Old Market House. 14,400 sq. ft. Architect: W. Watson. Owned first by Market

Company, then after complaints that market was dirty and ill-managed by Market Company, market purchased by Corporation in 1902. Demolished in 1962. (4) Fish market. 1937. Borough Square. (5) New Market Hall. 1964.

SOURCES: *PP-88; The Builder*, 22 Jul 1876, 20 Feb 1904; *The Market Traders Review*, 6 Feb 1960; *Pontefract and Castleford Express*, 3 Apr 1971.

WALSALL   STAFFORDSHIRE

Market House. 1809. Below St. Matthew's Church and facing square; stone structure in classical manner with 4 columns and pediment above. For butter and eggs. Corporation owned. Destroyed in 1853.

SOURCES: *PP-35; VCH.*

WARRINGTON   CHESHIRE

(1) Market Hall. General market. Opened 18 Oct 1856. Faced the Cloth Hall, Cheapside, Golden Square; principal entrance was from Sankey Street. £14,256. 47,916 sq. ft. Architects: James Stevens and Park, Manchester. Contractor: F. Bann, Stockport. Built by Corporation per Improvement Act of 1854. Market rights purchased from manorial owner in 1851. Two halls, one for butchers and general sales, the other for fish. Enlarged in 1878-84. Owned by the Corporation. Grand stone entrance with engaged column with square rusticated cinctures. Glass roof, originally partially open on sides. New street (Corporation Street) created for access to principal entrance. Demolished in 1974, although entrance façade remains. Described as first major modernization of Warrington. (2) Vegetable and General Market Hall. Ca. 1880. Market Street and Peter Street (site of old fairground). 2,800 sq. ft. Glass and iron structure. Retail and wholesale. (3) New Market Hall. 1974. Bank Street and Academy Way. £1,500,000. 67,700 sq. ft. Architect: E. H. Wood, ARIBA. Designation of Warrington as a New Town led to relocation of market to new Golden Square Shopping Precinct. The 3-level market has a roofline of 36 pyramids.

SOURCES: *PP-88;* Lewis; J. P. Aspden, ed., *Warrington Loo,* 1947; The Warrington Market Tenants Association, *The Market: Warrington Centenary 1847-1947;* Pete Williams, *Warrington in Camera, Warrington Museum,* 1981. County Borough of Warrington, *New Retail Market,* 1974.

WATCHET   SOMERSET

Market House. 1820. Extant in 1988.

SOURCES: *VCH.*

WELLINGTON   SOMERSET

(1) Meat market. Located at the side of the Public Hall. Owned by the Market and Town Hall Company. (2) General market hall. Ca. 1842. On site of old market. Owned by Wellington Market Hall Company. Extant in 1997. (3) Butter Market. 1848. Owned by the Wellington Market Hall Company. (4) Pannier Market. General covered market. 1866. Located at the side of the Public Hall. Owned by the Market and Town Hall Company.

SOURCES: *PP-88; VCH.*

WELLINGTON   SALOP

Market Hall. 1842. Ca. £5,000. 20,520 sq. ft. Built by Wellington (Shropshire) Market Company (a stock company) which had purchased the markets from Lord Forester for £700. One of largest market halls in county.

SOURCES: *Shropshire Magazine,* Vol. 27, No. 11, May 1975.

WELLS   SOMERSET

Market House. General market. 1835. East side of Market Place. £1,800. Architect: R. Carver. Owned by the Corporation. Stone, Tuscan columns and pilasters; windows added to ground floor arcade. Extant as the Post Office.

SOURCES: L. S. Colchester, *The City of Wells,* 1971.

WELSHPOOLE   POWYS

Town Hall and Market. General market. 1874. High Street. 7,758 sq. ft. Owned by the Corporation. Replaced a previous hall on the same site. Extant as a market in 1994.

WEM   SALOP

Market Hall. General market. 1904. £5,000 (includes public offices). 1,908 sq. ft. Architect: J. Brown, Shrewsbury. Contractor: G. Phillips, of Wem. Built by the District Council following purchase of market rights from Lord Barnard. In the "English Renaissance" style.

SOURCES: Lewis; *VCH; Building News,* 12 Feb 1904.

WEST BROMWICH   STAFFORDSHIRE

Market Hall. General market. 1874. Between High Street and Paradise Street. £4,952. 12,789 sq. ft. Architects: Weller and Proud, Wolverhampton. Unsuccessful, possibly because of steps up to market. Demolished ca. 1905 and now site of present library.

SOURCES: *VCH;* F. M. Hackwood, *A History of West Bromwich,* 1895.

WESTBURY — WILTSHIRE

Market Hall (a.k.a. Town Hall). General market house. 1815. Presented to the town by Sir M. Lopes. Owned by the Corporation. Stone two-story, with 3-bay colonnade on ground floor with rusticated piers and Doric columns. Extant, but market area now enclosed with shops.

SOURCES: *VCH.*

WESTON-SUPER-MARE — SOMERSET

(1) Covered general market. 1827. High Street. Probably originally partially covered but enclosed. Rebuilt in 1858; soon thereafter described as "scantily supplied" market because of the town's many shops. (2) New Market Hall. 1899. Located in High Street. Ca. £4,000 (estimate at time of competition). Architect: Hans Price and Wooler, Weston-Super-Mare. Owned by the Corporation. Used as a cinema until destroyed by fire in 1985.

SOURCES: Lewis; *The Builder,* 20 Oct 1894; *Building News,* 7 Sep 1894, 10 Sep 1897; *Handbook of Weston-Super-Mare,* 1863; *Weston Mercury,* 28 Aug 1964.

WEYMOUTH — DORSET

General market. 1854. £400. 7,200 sq. ft. (in 1927). Used as fish market, 1855. Custom House Quay. Extant in 1988.

WHITBY — YORKSHIRE

(1) General market house. 1788. Architect: Jonathan Pickernell. Erected by Nathaniel Cholmeley. (2) General covered market. 1871. 4,275 sq. ft. Owned by Sir Charles Strickland. Two stories with butchers below and greengrocers, butter and eggs, and general market above.

SOURCES: *PP-88.*

WHITCHURCH — SALOP

(1) Market Hall. Ca. 1840. High Street. 4,419 sq. ft. Extant and still used as a market in 1967. (2) Town Hall and Market House. High Street. Opened 25 Oct 1872. 12,318 sq. ft. Architect: T. M. Lockwood, Chester. Owned by the Corporation. Gothic. Extant and still used as a market in 1967.

SOURCES: *The Builder,* 9 Nov 1872; *Building News,* 10 Feb 1871, 3 Mar 1871.

WHITEHAVEN — CUMBRIA

(1) Fish market. 1819. In Market Place. Architect: Sir Robert Smirke. Owned by the manorial lord. Destroyed in 1852. (2) Market Hall. Butter market. 1819. £1,705. Architect: Sir Robert Smirke. Erected by the Earl of Lonsdale. One story with Italianate tower. Demolished in 1881. (3) Market Hall. 1881. Architect: T. L. Banks, Whitehaven. Owned by the Corporation. Lower hall for market. Extant in 1988 but no longer used as a market.

SOURCES: Lewis.

WIDNES — LANCASHIRE

Market Hall. 35,640 sq. ft. General market of 36 shops and stalls; "covered market" of 125 shops and stalls; and a fish market hall of 8 stalls. Owned by the Corporation.

WIGAN — LANCASHIRE

(1) Commercial Hall. 1816. Market Place. 7,650 sq. ft. Three floors, with shops on first two and a cloth hall on the third. (2) Market Hall. 1877. £17,000. 36,000 sq. ft. Architect: Hunter, Borough Engineer. Contractor: C. B. Holmes, Wigan. Owned by the Corporation. Demolished in 1988.

The growth of Wigan in the early and middle of the nineteenth century resulted in demands for new and larger market facilities, but it was not until 1873 that the Corporation purchased market rights from the manorial owner and acquired an improvement act (1874) to carry out market reform. The hall of 1877 was of brick and with a 3-span (partially glass) roof over one hall (200 ft. by 150 ft.) and a single-span roof over a second hall (50 ft. by 120 ft.) originally for fish. At a later date a covered exterior portico was added around two sides. The interior, which had a wood block floor and 12-ft.-square shops all round the walls, eventually had central heating. By the 1880s the hall offered a variety of goods, from bacon, wine, and cheese to sewing machines and books, and 9 stalls selling oysters.

SOURCES: *PP-88; The Builder,* 18 Aug 1877, 2 Apr 1892; *Building News,* 25 May 1877; *The Wigan Observer and District Advertiser,* 18 May 1877, 25 May 1877; *Times,* 11 Jul 1984.

WIGTON — CUMBRIA

Market Hall. Owned by the Corporation. Extant.

WINCHESTER — HAMPSHIRE

(1) Market House (a.k.a. the Old Green Market). General market. 1772. Owned by the Corporation. (2) Market Hall (1772 market house rebuilt and enlarged). 1857. High Street at Market Street. £1,200. Architect: William Coles, Town Surveyor. Builder: G. T. Fielder. Owned by the Corporation. 3-bay front with open arches between 4 columns, and extending to Market Street side with pilasters. At its opening the market was described as "a specimen of a Doric temple." Its presence was expected to increase the town's food

supply, although it is probable that the public market was already in a state of decline at the time the new market was opened. Glass roof. Continued to be used as a market for sale of local poultry, butter, eggs, fruit, vegetables, and meat; provided porters to carry customers' purchases to their homes. Used as a restaurant between 1896 and the mid-1950s. Reconstructed, 1958. Extant, but filled in with shops.

SOURCES: *PP-88*; Lewis; Thomas Stopher, *A History of Winchester Streets*, 1895 (with later additions), typescript, Hampshire County Library; *The Hampshire Chronicle, Southampton and Isle of Wight Courier*, 8 Feb 1856, 3 May 1856, 12 Sep 1857, 3 Oct 1857.

WIVELISCOMBE   SOMERSET

Town Hall and Market. 1840. £2,000. Small space below town hall. Purchased by Lord Ashburton from the Bishop of Bath in 1843. It was noted in 1888 that the coming of the railway had shifted much of the town's market activity to Taunton. Destroyed in 1961.

SOURCES: *PP-88*.

WOKINGHAM   BERKSHIRE

Town Hall and Market. General market. 1860. Market Place. £3,500. Architects: Poulton and Woodman, Reading. Owned by the Corporation. Extant in 1989.

The 1860 town hall and market is of red and blue brick with stone dressing and partly of cast-iron construction. Called a "Victorian curiosity" unsurpassed in the county, it is a heavily gabled Gothic structure of triangular shape with buttresses and a tower. The market, held on the lower floor, was famous in the first half of the nineteenth century for its supply of poultry, but by the time the new market was built it appears to have fallen into decline, possibly due to the coming of the railway.

SOURCES: *VCH*; John Betjeman and John Piper, eds., *Murray's Berkshire Architectural Guide*, 1st ed., 1949; Arthur Mee, *King's England, Berkshire*, 1964; Nikolaus Pevsner, *The Buildings of Berkshire*; *Wokingham Chronology: Appendix H, The Market*.

WOLVERHAMPTON   STAFFORDSHIRE

(1) Market Hall. General market. 1853. St. Peter's Square. £30,776. 48,870 sq. ft. Architect: G. T. Robinson. Exterior and interior renovated in 1901. Originally erected jointly by "market proprietors" (a private corporation) and the Corporation; full Corporation ownership in 1859. Demolished in 1961. (2) New Market Hall. Opened 22 Jun 1960. Shropshire Street and School Street.

£690,000. 33,246 sq. ft. Architect: A. Chapman. Includes separate food hall. Extant as market in 1994.

Despite marketplace reform carried out by newly appointed improvement commissioners in 1777 (per act of Parliament), plans for a market building were not undertaken until the town received incorporation in 1848. Soon thereafter the town markets committee collaborated with the manorial owner of the market to erect the new hall of 1853, with brick and stone bays around all sides and an imposing main entrance of 6 Doric columns on raised plinths supporting a pediment above. The hall was at first only partially covered. The covered portion formed a quadrangle which surrounded an open market, at the center of which was featured the fountain "Swan with Boy," manufactured by the Coalbrookdale Company for display at the Great Exhibition in Hyde Park, London, in 1851. The market was fully roofed in 1859, and in 1901 was renovated. In 1955 it was described as "palatial."

SOURCES: *The Builder*, 30 Mar 1861, 31 Oct 1903; *Building News*, 9 Oct 1903; G. T. Rostance, *Centenary of the Opening of the Retail Market Hall, 1853-1953* (pamphlet), 1953; *The Market Traders Review*, 19 Feb 1955, 17 Dec 1955; *The Wolverhampton Chronicle*, 12 May 1851, 9 Mar 1853.

WOLVERTON   BUCKINGHAMSHIRE

Market Hall. 10,800 sq. ft.

WORCESTER   WORCESTERSHIRE

(1) High Street Market Hall. General market. 1804. High Street. £5,034. Designed by Mayor Richard Morton. Frontage incorporated into new market in 1857. (2) Market Hall. 1857. High Street. Ca. £2,020. 233 ft. long. Architect: Armstrong. Extended in 1881; demolished in 1955. (4) Vegetable market. 1874. Located between Dolday Street and Newport Street near the Old Market on North Quay. £6,470. Architect: Rowe. Contractor: Kendrick, of Lowesmoor. Owned by the Corporation.

The need to clear the streets of trading and concentrate all market trading in a central location led to the erection in 1804 of Worcester's first market hall, built facing the Guildhall in the High Street. The hall was of stone. A principal archway was supported by Tuscan columns, over which was an ornamented pediment. It was remarked in 1819 that the quantity of fruit sold in this market was "astonishing." The new hall of 1857 retained the 1804 stone frontage, but behind was a new market hall described as "almost a copy of the transept of the Crystal Palace." The market prospered until after the Second World War. Despite a campaign by *The Market Traders Review* to save the structure, all but a small portion of it was demolished in 1955.

SOURCES: Markets Committee Books and Records are located with the Worcester Corporation Records, Hereford and Worcester County Records Office; the plans of the hall are located with Worcester City Archives, St. Helen's Branch, and photographs are located at the County Hall Branch; John Chambers, "A General History of Worcester," 1819 (written ms., Hereford and Worcester County Record Office); *PP-88*; Lewis; *VCH*; *The Builder*, 14 Nov 1874; *Building News*, 23 Jul 1858; H. W. Gwilliam, *Old Worcester*, vol. 1 (n.d., typed ms., Worcester City Library); John Chamber, *A General History of Worcester*, 1819; *The Market Traders Review*, 18 Apr 1953, 21 May 1955, 4 Jun 1955.

WORTHING   SUSSEX

Market. 1810. Located between Ann and Market Streets. Not used as market after 1859; demolished in 1969.

SOURCES: *VCH*.

WREXHAM   CLWYD

(1) Butchers' Market. 1848. High Street. 13,875 sq. ft. Architect: Thomas Penson. Refurbished in 1991. Extant. Jacobean front with prominent curved gables and arched ground floor. Interior of iron and glass, with large rear entrance in Bank Street facing Butter Market. (2) Butter (general) Market. 1879. Henblas Street. 6,325 sq. ft. Red brick with stone and tile dressing. Extant and used as a market. (3) Vegetable Market. 1927. Queen Street. 21,177 sq. ft. Demolished in 1990.

SOURCES: Welsh Arts Council, Plans and Projects, *Architecture in Wales, 1780-1914*, 1975; photographs with the Planning Department of the Wrexham Borough Council.

YARMOUTH   ISLE OF WIGHT

Market house. 1763.

YEOVIL   SOMERSET

Market Hall and Town Hall. General market. 1849. High Street. £3,500. 15,750 sq. ft. Architect: Thomas Stent. Owned first by the Special Commissioners, then by the Corporation. Destroyed by fire in 1935.

Yeovil's new market house (later called the Town Hall) of 1849 was built by the town's Special Commissioners who were empowered per an act of 1846 to purchase the market rights and to provide a new market to replace the old market house and shambles which had fallen into disrepair. A rusticated

lower story with pillars and arches supported cornice and balustrade, with an Ionic façade above. The ground floor was used for the sale of corn, fish, and meat. Some of the market stalls were moved out in 1868 to make way for shops, with the market remaining in the rear and in a covered space behind the building into the late nineteenth century.

SOURCES: *PP-88*; Lewis; *The Builder*, 27 Nov 1847, 4 Dec 1847, 8 Jan 1848; L. C. Hayward, *From Portreeve to Mayor: Yeovil 1750-1854*, 1987; *Hunt's Directory of Yeovil*, 1850.

CREDITS

Intro.1   From *The Builder* 10, no. 465 (1852): 9.

1.1   Reproduced by permission of the Greater Manchester County Record Office (ref. E7/28/2).

1.2   Courtesy East Lothian Tourist Board.

1.3   Reproduced by permission of the Heritage Library, Stockport Metropolitan Borough Council.

1.4   Drawing courtesy of Leslie Brooke.

1.5   Courtesy of Central Library, Berwick-upon-Tweed.

1.6   From *The Architect*, September 24, 1920, 193.

1.7   Author's photograph.

1.8   From *The Architect*, September 24, 1920, 194.

1.9   Author's photograph.

1.10   Reproduced by permission of Coventry City Libraries.

1.11   From *The Architect*, October 1, 1920, 208.

1.12   Print by Thomas Rowlandson, in author's collection.

1.13   From W. F. Gardner, *Barnstaple, 1857-97* (Barnstaple, 1897), 49. Courtesy of North Devon Library.

1.14   From *The Architect*, September 24, 1920, 193.

1.15   Reproduced by courtesy of the City and County of Swansea Libraries Department.

1.16   Courtesy of Berkshire Library and Information Service. Located by Marion Ogden of Wokingham.

1.17   Courtesy of the Mitchell Library, Glasgow City Libraries.

1.18   From Dorothy Whitaker, *Auld Hawkie and Other Glasgow Characters* (Glasgow: Glasgow District Libraries, 1988).

1.19   Courtesy of Boston Public Library, Print Department, Albert H. Wiggin Collection.

1.20   Courtesy of Central Library, Newcastle-upon-Tyne City Libraries and Arts.

2.1   *Ministry of Agriculture and Fisheries Report on Markets and Fairs in England and Wales*, part 1: *General Review* (London, 1927), frontispiece.

2.2   Courtesy of Manchester Central Library, Local Studies Unit.

2.3   Courtesy of Manchester Central Library, Local Studies Unit.

2.4   Courtesy of the Mitchell Library, Glasgow City Libraries.

2.5   From "Luton Market: A Shopping Revolution," a pamphlet published in 1972. Courtesy of Luton Museum Service.

2.6   Courtesy of North Devon Library and Record Office, Barnstaple.

2.7   Author's drawing, from a drawing by Edward Dore.

2.8   From David Daiches et al., *A Hotbed of Genius: The Scottish Enlightenment, 1730-1790* (Edinburgh, 1986).

2.9   From "A History of the Development of the Jersey Markets, 1882-1982," a pamphlet published for the Central Market Centenary. Compiled by Tony Tagg, States Public Buildings and Works Committee. Courtesy of Société Jersiaise Photograph Archive.

2.10   Author's photograph.

2.11   From a painting by S. Northcote. Courtesy of West Devon Area Central Library.

2.12   Author's drawing.

2.13   Author's drawing.

2.14   Drawing by William Kemperman. From a drawing of 1789.

2.15   Courtesy of Liverpool Libraries and Information Services, Liverpool Central Library.

2.16   Courtesy of Liverpool Libraries and Information Services, Liverpool Central Library.

2.17   Courtesy of Liverpool Libraries and Information Services, Liverpool Central Library.

3.1   From J. W. Singleton, ed., *The Jubilee Souvenir of the Corporation of Accrington* (Accrington, 1928), 53. Courtesy of Lancashire County Library, Accrington.

3.2   Reproduced by permission of Stockport Metropolitan Borough Council, Central Library.

3.3   Courtesy of Cornwall County Library.

4.1   Courtesy of Newcastle Library photo collection, Newcastle-upon-Tyne City Libraries and Arts.

4.2   Printed by W. A. Delamott in 1832. Reproduced with permission of the Wokingham Society.

4.3   From *The Architect*, September 24, 1920.

4.4   Courtesy of Hereford and Worcester County Libraries.

4.5   From Gerald W. Barker, *Days in Devonport* (Part IV). By kind permission of the author.

4.6   Courtesy of Shropshire Records and Research.

4.7   From *Illustrated London News*, October 13, 1883.

4.8　From *Illustrated London News*, September 17, 1881.

4.9　Courtesy of Harrogate Library.

4.10　From *Building News* 67 (December 14, 1894): 826.

4.11　Reproduced by permission of the Metropolitan Borough of Rochdale Community Services Department, Middleton Library.

4.12　Courtesy of Derby Local Studies Library.

5.1　Reproduced from *The Crystal Palace Exhibition Illustrated Catalogue* (London, 1851; Dover Edition, 1970).

5.2　From *The Architect*, September 3, 1920, p. 145.

5.3　Author's drawing.

5.4　Drawing by Leslie Brooke.

5.5　Drawing by William Kemperman.

5.6　Drawing by William Kemperman.

5.7　Courtesy of Newcastle-upon-Tyne City Libraries and Arts.

5.8　From D. Robert Elleray, *Hastings, A Pictorial History* (Chicester, 1979). Courtesy of Hastings Library Local Studies Collection.

5.9　From *Building News*, February 17, 1893.

5.10　From *The Architect*, September 24, 1920.

5.11　Courtesy of Kirklees Cultural Services.

5.12　Author's photograph.

5.13　From Arthur C. Ellis, *An Historical Survey of Torquay* (Torquay, n.d.), 289. Courtesy of Devon County Council (Torquay Library).

5.14　Author's photograph.

5.15　Author's drawing.

5.16　Author's drawing.

5.17　Suffolk Record Office, Ipswich (Ref. K485/356).

5.18　Original drawing by W. Sidney Causer, reproduced with kind permission of Wolverhampton Art Gallery.

5.19　Illustration by S. J. Loxton, *Bristol Evening News*, September 14, 1908.

5.20　S. Blake and R. Beecham, *Book of Cheltenham* (Cheltenham, 1982). Courtesy of Cheltenham Art Gallery and Museums.

5.21　From William Henry Pyne, *Lancashire Illustrated in a Series of Views* (n.p., 1831). Courtesy of Liverpool Libraries and Information Services.

5.22　Courtesy of Liverpool Libraries and Information Services, Liverpool Central Library Collection.

5.23　Courtesy of Newcastle-upon-Tyne City Libraries and Arts.

5.24　Courtesy of Newcastle-upon-Tyne City Libraries and Arts.

5.25　Courtesy of Newcastle-upon-Tyne City Libraries and Arts.

5.26　Reproduced by permission of Birmingham Library Services.

5.27　*Fashionable Guide and Directory* (Brighton, 1843). Courtesy of Local History Library, Brighton Central Library.

5.28　Courtesy of National Monuments Record of Scotland, Edinburgh.

5.29　Courtesy of Wirral Library Service, Central Library, Birkenhead.

5.30　Façade and roof scheme: author's drawings. Plan: from *Architectural Magazine and Journal* 3 (1836): 13.

5.31　Courtesy of the Local Studies Centre, Darlington Library, County Durham.

5.32　Reproduced by Permission of Coventry City Libraries.

5.33　From *Building News*, October 2, 1891.

5.34　From *The Builder*, January 5, 1853, 24.

5.35　From *The Builder*, January 5, 1891.

5.36　From *The Architect*, October 18, 1872.

5.37　Author's photograph.

5.38　By permission of Leeds Central Library.

5.39　From *Illustrated London News*, September 17, 1881, 281.

5.40　Drawing by Misses F. and C. A. Greene. Courtesy of Towneley Hall Art Gallery and Museums, Burnley Borough Council.

5.41　Drawing by Arthur Hiscoe. Courtesy of North Yorkshire County Library.

5.42　From *Building News*, November 8, 1889, 634.

5.43　Leeds Library photo collection. By permission of Leeds Central Library.

5.44　Courtesy of City of Bradford Metropolitan Council, Markets Unit.

5.45　From *Building News*, November 8, 1889.

5.46　Courtesy of Local Studies Library, Sheffield Libraries and Information Services.

5.47　From *The Architect*, October 19, 1872.

5.48　From a program published by City of Leeds, "Opening of the New Market Hall by the Rt. Hon. G. Balfour, M.P., Friday, July 1, 1904."

5.49　Reproduced by permission from the Heritage Library Stockport Metropolitan Borough Council.

5.50　Photograph from the collection of Wolverhampton Libraries.

5.51　Reproduced by kind permission of Wigan Heritage Service.

5.52　Author's drawing.

5.53　From *The Builder*, May 19, 1883.

5.54　From *The Builder*, May 1, 1869.

5.55 From John Tomlinson, *Victorian and Edwardian Chester* (Chester, 1976). Courtesy of Chester Library, Cheshire County Council.

5.56 From *Building News*, October 24, 1879.

5.57 From *Building News*, October 2, 1891.

6.1 Reproduced by permission from the Heritage Library Stockport Metropolitan Borough Council. Photo collection, Stockport Library.

6.2 Reproduced by permission from the Heritage Library Stockport Metropolitan Borough Council. Stockport Library.

6.3 Photo from collection of Michael Federspiel.

6.4 Author's drawing.

6.5 From *Building News*, March 31, 1893.

6.6 Author's drawing.

6.7 Town plans, 1851 and 1891. Courtesy of District Central Library, Burnley.

6.8 Author's drawing.

6.9 Reproduced by courtesy of the City Museum and Art Gallery, Stoke-on-Trent (Historic Buildings Survey).

6.10 Photograph from the collection of Wolverhampton Libraries (ref.: L1/BILS/I/3).

6.11 From the collections of the Bolton Museums and Art Gallery.

6.12 From *A History of Lancashire Markets*, Local Studies No. 7 (Lancashire City Museums, 1988). By kind permission of P. W. Brown.

6.13 Author's drawing.

6.14 "Official Re-Opening of the Market Hall," a pamphlet, 1938, Borough of Bolton.

6.15 From *The Builder*, October 4, 1877.

6.16 From *The Builder*, October 4, 1873.

6.17 Courtesy of Bibliothéque Nationale, Paris.

6.18 From *Practical Mechanics Journal* 1 (1848-49).

6.19 Courtesy of Newcastle-upon-Tyne City Libraries and Arts.

6.20 From *Building News*, March 31, 1893.

6.21 From *The Builder* 5, no. 40 (September 10, 1853), 578.

6.22 By permission of Leeds Central Library.

6.23 From A. T. Walmisley, *Iron Roofs* (n.p., 1900).

6.24 Courtesy of Derby Local Studies Library.

6.25 Courtesy of Derby Local Studies Library.

6.26 From *The Engineer and Architect*, "Supplement," May 13, 1888.

6.27 Drawing by William Kemperman.

7.1 Courtesy of North Devon Library and Record Office.

7.2 From Jon Catt, *A History of Lancaster Markets* (Lancaster, 1968). By permission of Lancaster Library.

7.3 Courtesy of City of Bradford, Metropolitan Council, Markets Unit.

7.4 From *Building News*, October 24, 1879, 94.

7.5 Courtesy of Liverpool Libraries and Information Services, Illustrations Collection.

7.6 From *Centenary of the Opening of Market Hall No. 1: A Souvenir Handbook* (Markets Committee, County Borough of Blackburn, 1948), 6. Courtesy of Lancashire County Library, Blackburn Library.

7.7 Reproduced by permission of Birmingham Library Services.

7.8 Courtesy of Liverpool Libraries and Information Services, Illustrations Collection.

7.9 Courtesy of Local Studies Library, Sheffield, Libraries and Information Services.

7.10 Courtesy of Lancashire County Library, Blackburn Library.

8.1 Photograph by Chris Oliver.

8.2 Author's survey of 464 markets of known date built between 1751 and 1950. See Gazetteer.

8.3 Author's survey of 591 markets constructed between 1751 and 1950. See Gazetteer.

8.4 Calculated from Parliamentary Papers, *Royal Commission on Market Rights and Tolls*, 14 vols. (London, 1888-91), vol. 1, Appendix B: "Local Acts, Local and Personal Acts, and Provisional Order Acts (Passed Since the Year 1800)," 225-30, and from author's survey of 626 markets built between 1751 and 1940. See Gazetteer.

8.5 Author's survey of 396 markets of known date, between 1751 and 1940. See Gazetteer.

8.6 Author's survey of 464 markets identified by type between 1751 and 1945. See Gazetteer.

8.7 Calculated from 319 local acts of Parliament, in *Royal Commission on Market Rights and Tolls*, vol. 1, Appendix B.

8.8 Calculated from 319 local acts of Parliament, in *Royal Commission on Market Rights and Tolls*, vol. 1, Appendix B, and from author's survey of 626 markets built between 1751 and 1940. See Gazetteer.

Map 8.1 Map prepared by Susan Pyecroft with assistance from Department of Geography, Central Michigan University.

9.1 Reproduced by permission of Birmingham Library Services.

9.2 Photograph by A. D. Moore.

9.3 Kirklees Cultural Services.

9.4 From Alan Everitt, ed., *Perspectives in English Urban History* (London, 1973), 236. Reprinted with permission of Macmillan Press, Ltd.

9.5 Courtesy of National Monuments Record of Scotland, Edinburgh.

9.6 Courtesy of North Devon Local Studies Centre.

9.7 Courtesy of Arts and Recreation Division, Aberdeen District Council, Central Library photo collection.

9.8 Reproduced by permission of Birmingham Library Services.

9.9 Courtesy of Lancashire County Library, Accrington.

9.10 Courtesy of Lancashire County Library, Accrington.

9.11 Courtesy of Local Studies Library, Sheffield Libraries and Information Services.

9.12 Courtesy of Liverpool Libraries and Information Services.

10.1 From *Building News* 84 (March 6, 1903): 338.

10.2 From *The Builder*, May 27, 1871, 405.

10.3 Adapted from *Ministry of Agriculture and Fisheries Interim Report on Fruit and Vegetables* (London, 1923).

10.4 Courtesy of Lancashire County Library, Accrington Library.

10.5 Courtesy of Kirklees Cultural Services, Huddersfield Library Collection.

10.6 From Southport Library Collection, Sefton Leisure Services.

10.7 Author's photograph.

10.8 From *Centenary Opening of Market Hall N. 1, 1848-1948* (1848). Courtesy of Lancashire County Library, Blackburn.

11.1 Courtesy of Local Studies Library, Sheffield, Libraries and Information Services.

11.2 Author's drawing.

11.3 Author's drawing, adapted from *Luton Market: A Shopping Revolution* (Borough Planning Division, Luton Corporation, 1972). Courtesy of Luton Corporation.

11.4 From G. T. Rostance, *Centenary Opening of the Retail Market, 1853-1953* (County Borough of Wolverhampton, 1953). Copyright Wolverhampton Borough Council.

11.5 From the collection of Wolverhampton Libraries.

11.6 Courtesy of Local Studies Library, Sheffield, Libraries and Information Services.

11.7 Courtesy of Kirklees Cultural Services, Huddersfield Library.

11.8 Author's drawing.

11.9 Courtesy, Blackburn Library photographic collection.

11.10 Photo courtesy of D. Wardle.

11.11 From *Architects' Journal*, April 19, 1989.

INDEX